Shared Histories

The Publications of the Southern Texts Society

THE UNIVERSITY OF GEORGIA PRESS  ATHENS AND LONDON

To Sylvia

Shared Histories

TRANSATLANTIC

LETTERS BETWEEN

VIRGINIA DICKINSON REYNOLDS

AND HER DAUGHTER,

VIRGINIA POTTER,

1929–1966

Much love
Angie-

Edited by Angela Potter

Publication of this book was made possible in part by a grant from the Watson-Brown Foundation.

Published by the University of Georgia Press
Athens, Georgia 30602
© 2006 by Angela Potter
All rights reserved
Designed by Erin Kirk New
Set in 11.5 on 15 Walbaum by Bookcomp, Inc.
Printed and bound by Maple-Vail

The paper in this book meets the guidelines for
permanence and durability of the Committee on
Production Guidelines for Book Longevity of the
Council on Library Resources.

Printed in the United States of America
10 09 08 07 06 C 5 4 3 2 1
10 09 08 07 06 P 5 4 3 2 1

Library of Congress Cataloging-in-Publication Data

Reynolds, Virginia Dickinson, 1883–1966.
Shared histories : transatlantic letters between Virginia
Dickinson Reynolds and her daughter, Virginia Potter, 1929–1966 /
edited by Angela Potter.
p. cm. – (The publications of the Southern Texts Society)
Includes bibliographical references and index.
ISBN-13: 978-0-8203-2793-8 (cloth : alk. paper)
ISBN-10: 0-8203-2793-X (cloth : alk. paper)
ISBN-13: 978-0-8203-2802-7 (pbk. : alk. paper)
ISBN-10: 0-8203-2802-2 (pbk. : alk. paper)
1. Mothers and daughters—United States—Correspondence. 2. Mothers and daughters—Europe—Correspondence. 3. Reynolds, Virginia Dickinson, 1883–1966—Correspondence. 4. Potter, Virginia, 1908– —Correspondence. I. Potter, Virginia, 1908– II. Potter, Angela, 1945–
III. Title. IV. Series.
HQ755.85.R485 2006
973.91092'2—dc22   2005032419

British Library Cataloging-in-Publication Data available

FOR *Jenny*

"I keep all your letters. Someday you might want to do

something with them."

VIRGINIA DICKINSON REYNOLDS

1 FEBRUARY 1942

"Your letters are really wonderful and like a breath of fresh air to me! —

I can't bear to part with any of them."

VIRGINIA STUART POTTER

7 NOVEMBER 1960

CONTENTS

ACKNOWLEDGMENTS

Following Virginia Potter's death, the discovery of the extensive two-way correspondence on which this book is based offered the opportunity for her and her mother's story to be examined and shared. This book would not have been possible were it not for the sequestration of the letters by Virginia Potter, and I am enormously grateful to her for not disposing of them and for thoughtfully squirreling them away at the back of a cupboard.

Numerous people have helped to bring this book about. I would like to thank Peter Bardaglio for pointing me in the right direction. The following have provided information both general and personal, and I am grateful to them all: Philippa Barder, Jeremy Burge, Ann Clayton Martin, Sylvia Coote, Lady Louisa Cosgrave, Marigold Curling, Margo Doucet, Camilla Dunne, Maxine Eugster, Hugh Fell, Tony Gould, Loveday Llewellyn, David Lockwood, Penny Parmigiani, the late George Plum, Dorothy Rainey, Sir Patrick Sinclair, and Anthony Verey. I would like to thank Jenny Potter, who has provided support, memories, and photographs and helped to recapture the personal.

Assistance from the readers and staff at the University of Georgia Press has been much appreciated, and I would particularly like to thank the series editor of the Southern Texts Society, Michael O'Brien, for his unflagging guidance and constructive criticism over the years. His suggestions and recommendations have helped to steer the book toward its final form, and I am most grateful to him.

Finally, I am particularly indebted to Paul Brassley, whose encouragement has been constant throughout the years of transforming a jumble of disorganized letters into a book. When my stamina wavered, his enthusiasm and inspiration kept me focused. I would like to offer him special thanks, and also Charlie and Caroline for their support and patience.

INTRODUCTION

The correspondence in this volume records the dialogue between a Virginian mother and daughter from 1929 until 1966; the mother, Virginia Dickinson Reynolds, lived in Richmond, and the daughter, Virginia Stuart Reynolds (later Potter), in 1935 moved to England. Their letters paint a portrait of life in a particular era and within a particular socioeconomic class in a time of tremendous political and cultural change. Those written immediately before, during, and after World War II are rich with insights into American and British social and political life, and this collection forms one of the first publications of letters between civilian family members experiencing life in the war in both the United States and Europe. The letters offer a commentary on the mid-twentieth century and give the reader an idea of what it was like to live in those years and the variety of daily events that occurred. The letters chronicle how the women felt at the time, rather than through the distorted lens of memoir, and offer a contemporaneous study of class, gender, and racial attitudes, in words written by women of a social standing not usually given to literary accomplishment, who were writing *en famille* and so unguardedly.

Their transatlantic exchange carried on in peace and war for nearly forty years. When it began, Herbert Hoover was serving as president, George V reigned as King of Great Britain, and Ramsay MacDonald was prime minister. Both countries were struggling to emerge from the depths of economic depression, young people listened on the wireless to the bands of the swing era, and the fastest form of transport traveled at a little over three hundred miles per hour. The correspondence ended in 1966 with Lyndon Baines Johnson as president, Queen Elizabeth II on the throne, and Harold Wilson as prime minister. Both countries were flourishing in an economic boom, their young people were watching the Beatles on television, and the fastest form of transport could reach out into space. Living through these momentous times, the women reveal in their letters attitudes toward and involvement in national and international affairs, from presidential and prime ministerial elections to civil rights, desegregation, coronations, politics, the Second World War, and the demise of the British Empire. Both women moved in high society. Each was conservative, alert to fashion, interested in culture and good works, extremely sociable, and vexed by the inadequacies of her man. In short, they were fairly typical as women of their class and moment. But, as representatives of two generations, the mother and daughter differed. The mother was reared in a late Victorian world, in a postbellum South where women were obliged to be tough, even relentless. The daughter became a Bright Young Thing and was shy of toughness, though circumstances forced it on her, especially the experience of living through the Second World War in and near London.

On her father's side, Virginia Dickinson Reynolds came from a migrant New England family. She was first cousin once removed to the poet Emily Dickinson, although their paths did not cross, as their lives overlapped by only three years. Reynolds did, however, become good friends with Emily's niece and literary heir, Martha Dickinson Bianchi. Reynolds's great-grandfather Samuel Fowler Dickinson (1775–1838, Emily's grandfather) was a lawyer who cofounded Amherst College in 1821, a project that dissipated his wealth, so that his sons had no hope of living as gentlemen of leisure.[1] His eldest son, Edward, who was to become Emily's father, remained in Amherst to become a prominent lawyer and treasurer of the college. But a younger son, Reynolds's grandfather, Samuel Fowler Jr., moved to Georgia as a young man, although he continued to visit Amherst occasionally; in 1852 Emily wrote to her brother Austin of a visit by "Uncle Samuel's family."[2] Samuel's youngest son, Loren, married a Virginian heiress who had been orphaned during the Civil War.[3] The youngest of their three children, Virginia Cole Dickinson (later Reynolds, the mother in this book), was born in Richmond in 1883. So the Dickinsons, in common with many families, included in their ranks men who fought on both sides in the Civil War. Samuel Fowler Dickinson Jr. and Loren Dickinson were both vigorous secessionists. The latter fought for three years for the Confederacy. His daughter, Virginia Reynolds, in an anthology of tributes to Martha Dickinson Bianchi, summed up her father's fervent beliefs and wrote that "the passionate strain in the Dickinsons which produced the white heat of Puritanical virtues in New England" made of her father, Loren, "an enthusiastic and unreconstructed 'rebel' in the Confederate States."[4]

Loren Dickinson died in 1909 a disillusioned man who drank to soften the long-nursed blow of defeat. As an unpublished family memoir puts it, he was "the sort of Southerner who thought 'Damned-Yankee' was one word." His belief in the Lost Cause mirrored that of many white southerners for whom, in Sara M. Evans's words, "Southern domestic ideology continued to be framed by the needs and anxieties of the planter class and permeated with racist assumptions."[5] His wife, Virginia Fendley Dickinson, was of that same class, for her father had owned a substantial plantation near Petersburg, a local coal mine, and around one hundred slaves. Their family home had been destroyed in 1864, when the troops of General Benjamin Butler — the infamous "Beast" of New Orleans — mistakenly took the house for a Confederate signal corps base and burned it to the ground. This act and its memory fixed the brutality of the war firmly in the Dickinson family mind for generations and led the members to the conventional southern belief that the war had been unnecessary because slavery was coming to an end, anyway, and that the war's destruction confirmed the misguided and hasty philosophies of the Yankees, but also occasioned the poverty of the planter class. In fact, neither the Dickinsons nor the Fendleys did badly, certainly not before the war. The 1850s had been a boom time for cotton and slaves. From Virginia alone, sixty-eight thousand slaves were exported to the lower South and Southwest during that decade.[6] In 1860 the Richmond City Directory listed sixty-nine businesses dealing with "Negro traders . . . agents . . . [and] auctioneers." Notices appeared in the local press almost daily to advertise the sale of between "twenty-five to fifty Negroes."[7] Slavery was not an industry in decline. But the postbellum era was not an economic disaster either, though then prosperity required more effort, and it was prudent to embrace northern economic ways. This transition was easier for a family that already had one foot in New England.

In January 1908 Virginia Cole Dickinson married James Stuart Reynolds (1872–1956), one of four children born and raised in West Haven, Connecticut, of a family descended from early-seventeenth-century English settlers in Wethersfield. Two of his three sisters, Alice and Madeleine, remained in Connecticut all their lives, and a third, May, married a wealthy financier from Montreal, Huntly Drummond. Around the turn of the century, Stuart Reynolds was working as the chief clerk of the New York, New Haven, and Hartford Rail Road. His reasons for moving to Virginia are not known, but he came to settle in Richmond, where he prospered.

Stuart and Virginia Reynolds inhabited a world of economic and racial privilege. The two, eventually with their only child, came to live in the Chesterfield, an expensive downtown service apartment block, staffed (except for white managers) entirely by African Americans who came from their segregated neighborhoods to clean and cook. Like the public realm, this domestic world was governed by strict rules and divided by sharp boundaries, apparent to both servant and employer. Later those boundaries would shift and break down, and in 1964 Virginia Reynolds was horrified to find a "negro in the Chesterfield dining room twice lately having dinner!" But earlier she had luxuriated in a sense of comfort and racial stratification. In 1942 she hurt her knee and many servants were summoned to care for her. "Here I am living as if I were on a plantation in ante-bellum days 'befo' de War,'" she wrote. "I have an old coloured nurse who tells me every day that I am *beautiful*. . . . Erma comes every day to clean silver and polish furniture etc., and Carrie [Reynolds's maid]. . . . I am giving orders every moment from the sofa where the afflicted knee reposes, bound up, and only slightly swollen now. The gardenia bush gives me the slight illusion of the deep south, and when Martha says, 'Chile, ain't you too cool in that thin covering?' I am absolutely in the feudal age once more." But even then, Reynolds did not see race as unproblematic and was aware that miscegenation, at least, meant an uncertainty in boundaries. In 1944 she observed of her maid and her maid's fiancé: "Mr. James Gregory (Carrie Washington's fiancé) . . . is very nice looking with a lofty look, which savages so often have. In fact, I thought he was quite distinguished looking. He and Carrie are pure negro, which I like so much more than the very disconcerting mulatto type — I always find myself wondering whose ancestors have strayed from the straight and narrow way — One girl was almost as white as I am with long pale hands — I can't take that! It implies too much — There is so much pathos in the implications that it disturbs me — and too much reproach."

A woman like Virginia Reynolds was expected to undertake civic obligations. In her case, the pursuit of culture had personal roots. She had never had a formal college education, and this omission often made her uneasy. In 1941 she wrote, "The 'Woman's Who's Who in America' keep writing for my life history, and I am so discouraged when I read the questionnaire and so ashamed to admit how little I have done and how really *un*educated I am (as to degrees, etc.) I don't answer." But someone of her class needed, if respectability was to be maintained, to contribute, and Richmond provided many opportunities. It contained as many as thirty-four theaters in 1913 and was a leading center for music and theater in the first half of the twentieth century. Both Reynolds and her daughter acted in and directed many productions for the city's Little Theatre League. The mother served as executive board member of the Edgar Allen Poe Society, was a founding member of the Richmond Symphony Orchestra, and belonged to the English Speaking Union and the Poetry Society of Virginia. Through her husband's membership, she enjoyed the facilities of the Country Club of Virginia and the Commonwealth Club, and in her own right belonged to the Woman's Club, founded in 1894. This last provided a regular focus, particularly (much later) its reading group formed in 1952 under the chairmanship of Reynolds's friend Helen DeWitt Adams, where writers from Sophocles to Arthur Koestler were studied. The women's club movement, founded in 1868, provided for cultural and intellectual stimulation and gave opportunities for white women to test their skills at public speaking, much as the church provided an organizing infrastructure for African Americans. The interests of the Richmond's Woman's Club included welfare, community action, international relations, politics, and social activities. Notables were invited to speak, and performers to perform. Martha Graham, who in 1931 taught dance to Reynolds's daughter in New York, visited the club in 1932, though she was not received enthusiastically. As the revolutionary founder of modern dance, her radical choreography was not appreciated by club members, who found her style too avant-garde for their tastes.[8]

However, Reynolds could break the mold of this conservatism and was capable of quirky independence. She was, for example, not as hostile to Franklin Roosevelt as most in her class. When he died in 1945, she observed, "Some people disliked him, of course, especially the rich ones, because his politics for twelve years have somewhat reduced their incomes. But that might have happened anyhow, and personally, in these last years, I have been one of his ardent admirers."

Earlier she had been in favor of women's suffrage, though in Virginia (as elsewhere in the South) the issue was complicated because of race, and suffragism did not necessarily imply liberalism. Radical Reconstruction had enfranchised African American men, but not white or black women. When the prominent abolitionist Wendell Phillips said at the time, "I hope in time to be as bold as John Stuart Mill and add to that last clause 'sex'!! But this hour belongs to the negro. As Abraham Lincoln said, 'One War at a Time': so I say, One question at a time. This hour belongs to the negro," in formal politics this meant men.[9] In this context, prosuffragists argued that granting the vote to white women would satisfy white supremacists keen to hold on to power, and also outnumber the mass of immigrants eligible to vote. Tactics could be employed to prevent black women from voting, much as black men who, hedged about by state tax or literacy laws, or as victims of violent intimidation, rarely succeeded in casting their ballots. As late as 1940 less than 2 percent of the southern black population voted.[10] By 1910 women could vote in Wyoming, Idaho, Utah, and Colorado, but nowhere in the South. Gradually suffragism, inspired in part by the activities of the British suffragettes, became a more fashionable cause, and in 1914 the mainstream organization of the General Federation of Women's Clubs endorsed the campaign, thereby bringing greater credibility and respectability to the movement. But the South remained tardy, and most of its states, including Virginia, ratified the federal Nineteenth Amendment only in 1920.[11] Virginia Dickinson Reynolds would have been able to cast her first vote in Richmond at the age of thirty-seven years.

If she was representative of her generation and milieu, her daughter Virginia Stuart Reynolds was representative of hers. The elder Reynolds's

involvement in suffragism, autodidacticism, strong political beliefs, and assiduous pursuit of matters civic and cultural contrasted sharply with the
younger's less serious lifestyle, which extended to liking the theater and
dance but stopped short of serious reading. (In Montreal in 1933, the latter
was invited to a dinner to meet Vita Sackville-West, "but of course refused,"
preferring to spend the weekend skiing.) Born in 1908, she was educated
in Richmond, New Haven, and France and, when young, traveled extensively to Britain, Europe, and North Africa with her parents. She would not
have labeled herself a flapper, but her life in the 1920s was hedonistic. With
hemline up, makeup on, and cigarette in hand, the flapper rejected politics and enjoyed the lighthearted pursuits of dancing and partying. Zelda
Fitzgerald asserted, "I think a woman gets more happiness out of being gay,
light-hearted, unconventional, mistress of her own fate, than out of a career
that calls for hard work," and Fitzgerald wanted her daughter to be a flapper "because flappers are brave and beautiful." [12] Virginia Stuart Reynolds
did not need to be encouraged to dance. Indeed, when she was at school in
southwest France in 1926, the local doctor diagnosed poor circulation and
suggested that she drink red wine and take up dancing. As a result, she was
always given red wine with dinner, much to the envy of her fellow students,
and was escorted by a chaperone to Biarritz Casino, where the local gigolos
taught her to tango.

In 1931 her base shifted to New York, where she studied acting and dance
for a year under Martha Graham, Louis Horst, and others at the Neighborhood Playhouse. She frequently stayed with her wealthy uncle, Huntly
Drummond, in Montreal. In 1935 she moved to England, where she intended only a sojourn. But she met and married an Englishman named
Gerald Potter, who proposed to her on the very evening they met. She did
not accept his offer as swiftly as it had been delivered, but they married in
1936 and settled in London. The lives she and her new husband led were
glamorous. They dined at the Berkeley and the Savoy Grill, ate caviar and
drank champagne, and motored down to Hampshire in a "high-powered
Lagonda" for yachting weekends. This was an era of conspicuous consumption for the upper classes, but high unemployment for many. The highly
stratified class system, which led George Orwell to describe England as the
most class-ridden country under the sun, was not entirely dissimilar from

that to be found in the American South, though class could not be equated with race. In England the three layers of working, middle, and upper class were subdivided so that the nuances of social status were infinite and fairly inflexible, although some social mobility did occur between the wars. Gerald Potter, as an ex-Etonian Grenadier Guards officer, but not an aristocrat, was somewhere between the lower end of the upper class and the upper end of the middle class.

As Ross McKibbin observes, in attempting to define the English upper class, "More perhaps than for any other class, formal criteria of membership are lacking." [13] It was not just a matter of income. Although he sets the required minimum income level at ten thousand pounds per year in 1919 purchasing-power terms (the equivalent in 1939 would have been about eight thousand pounds), McKibbin admits that many of the peerage and gentry would have had less. He also argues that interwar society was not exactly the same as the upper class, although many members of either would also have been recognized as belonging to the other. In both, membership was defined by mutual recognition, based not only on money but also on acceptable breeding, education, cultural assumptions, and social affiliations. The number of people involved, he calculates, was no more than forty thousand and perhaps as few as twenty thousand, or between 0.1 and 0.05 percent of the population, and they would have had annual incomes in excess of one thousand pounds. Many of these would have been recognized as part of the upper-middle class, which at the beginning of the twentieth century would have included the traditional professions: the church, law, medicine, and officers of the armed forces. By the middle of the century, this upper-middle class would have been expanded by an influx of those from the technical, scientific, and commercial occupations on their way up, and also, according to G. D. H. Cole (writing in 1955), by many of those on the way down, who before the war would have thought of themselves as upper class. [14]

Gerald and Virginia Potter probably fit quite neatly into this last group. There is no available information on their prewar annual income, although it seems likely that it was less than eight thousand pounds and more than one thousand pounds. Gerald had several of the attributes that McKibbin associates with membership of the upper class. He had been to Eton, one of the few schools that McKibbin identifies as "indubitably upper class"; before the war he enjoyed the "vestigial gentry life-style" that went with a commission in the Brigade of Guards (comprised of the Grenadier, Coldstream, Scots, Irish, and Welsh foot guards); and he had numerous titled friends. Her American origins were no barrier to Virginia's social position – as McKibbin points out, many society hostesses were American – and she was presented at court, the upper class's "most characteristic rite of passage." Their wedding was considered sufficiently distinguished to feature on a Gaumont British newsreel in 1936. After the war Gerald went into the fishing business in Devon for some years, before becoming a market gardener, although much of the couple's income continued to be derived from their private resources. On the one hand, economically, it would have been difficult to sustain a view of them as part of the diminishing postwar upper class. On the other hand, they continued to associate with the same group of friends they had known before the war, many of their new postwar friends were wealthy or titled or both, and Gerald had the time and resources to establish himself as a leading competitive yachtsman. In many ways, therefore, Gerald and Virginia may be seen as typical representatives of the elite whose socioeconomic position was extensively affected by the war.

The 1930s was a decade of enormous contrast in Britain. Between 1936 and 1938, 55 percent of the country's wealth was owned by 1 percent of the population.[15] The expansion of some commodities (electronics and light engineering) and the demise of heavy industry (steel and shipbuilding) led to marked regional variations in prosperity and poverty. The National Government, a coalition of the three major political parties, was formed in 1931 in an attempt to rescue the country's ailing economy. Mass unemployment, precipitated by the Wall Street crash and aggravated by the slump in world trade, was widespread in many areas, particularly the northeast, from where unemployed workers marched to London from Jarrow in 1936. That same year Edward VIII abdicated in order to marry the American divorcée Wallis Simpson and thereby created a constitutional crisis.[16]

Virginia Potter entered this world with more awareness of the wealth than of the poverty. Fashionable 1930s London, as described by Sir Henry "Chips" Channon, member of Parliament, was a "dazzlingly expensive and luxurious 'high society' made up of royalty, politicians, the Anglo-American wealthy set and show-business celebrities."[17] Certainly there was an attempt to promote an integration between the English and American elite, a phenomenon that went back to the late nineteenth century. It worked both ways. English hostesses were keen to include wealthy and entrepreneurial Americans, partly for their style, but also to bring riches to a world somewhat diminished by inflation and increased taxes. Americans were keen to break into the English elite, or, as Ross McKibbin puts it, "Conquering the English social system was a task several American women set themselves."[18] Those who had succeeded included Lady Cunard, Lady Astor, the Duchess of Roxburghe, and, of course, Wallis Simpson, who failed to become queen but at least achieved the status of an exiled duchess.

Recently married women in London society would have been introduced at court, and in 1937 Virginia Potter was presented to George VI and Queen Elizabeth, the only American to be presented at that particular court. Her relief at not having to be presented to Queen Wallis was clear, her disapproval of the late king's "bad taste" profound. But she went far in her Anglophilia. In 1938 she renounced her American citizenship, having not anticipated the horrified response of her American friends and family, and only then realized, but too late, the significance of her action. To her dismay, she even merited a mention in the *New York Herald Tribune*. So, by 1939, as Britain was drawn into war, Virginia Potter had become Anglicized. By 1937 she was speaking of "us poor Londoners" and spoke with horror of "swarms of *Australians*, etc."

To that war, her mother responded with a fervent enthusiasm, by way of defending what both a Virginian and an English person would designate as Anglo-Saxon culture, which was thought to need defense from many enemies. These opponents included African Americans and trade unions at home, as well as Nazis abroad, with Germans especially eliciting tremendous denunciations. "My hatred of that race has gone to such fever heat that I don't know how I shall sustain it if the war lasts any time," Virginia Reynolds wrote in September 1939. "But my hatred of them is *not* because they are at war — It is a profound distaste for their very being — their language, looks, fat, attitude of mind, thick headedness, sadism, coarseness — *even* their literature. I cannot stand *anything* Teutonic, and the sooner they are swept from the earth the happier I will be." Both women were anti-

Semitic too. "The papers here continue to be very gravely excited about the jews in Germany and their plight," the mother wrote in 1938, "but someone tonight told me after having had a family of Semites next to him all summer at Virginia Beach, he felt that Hitler was doing the only thing you could do with a jew. I hope they won't all come over here." In 1940 the daughter lamented the wartime death of English gentlemen and contrasted it with the spectacle of "fat jews going to their businesses." They inclined, indeed, to a fairly indiscriminate xenophobia. "This boat has almost every nationality on earth aboard her. Most of them *dreadful*," is the elder's shipboard comment from the summer of 1939. And both reserved their greatest contempt for the middle class. The mother, on a transatlantic liner in 1936, wrote, "Some middle class English from the Midlands asked me to play Bridge last night. He wasn't bad but she was *the* most impossible woman I have ever seen so I will remain caché tonight." The daughter, in the same year, met her husband's new employer and observed, "A very nice little man and 'gentlemanly', though not exactly a gent. He rather murders the King's english, but doesn't try to be what he's not." Similarly, when her brother Fendley married beneath him, Virginia Reynolds could visit his home only with grave reluctance: "I actually went inside Fendley's house the other day. I was delivering a Christmas present and Marian came to the door, so I had to go in. She was rather flustered. The house is very *neat* – and hopelessly middle-class – I shall never understand how he could do it." Such denunciations strike a harsh chord in the twenty-first century, but they typified many of the views held by the white middle and upper classes at the time.

America's general reluctance to enter the Second World War prior to Pearl Harbor is well documented, so that the mother's enthusiasm for joining was, even in Virginia, at first suspect. In 1940 only 7.7 percent of Americans were ready to participate.[19] But anxiety for her daughter's predicament, coupled with a dislike for anything German, spurred Reynolds into raising funds for the war effort. In June 1940 she became one of three million American women who volunteered for the Red Cross, and took a course in the preparation of surgical dressings. After December 1941 her commitment ceased to be so odd. Richmonders dug victory gardens, arranged collections of scarce material needed for munitions, held blackout and air raid practices, and organized ration boards. Stuart Reynolds, Virginia's husband, ran Richmond's British War Relief program. Between them, they cajoled many into giving funds; became involved in Civilian Defense; sold war bonds; entertained visiting British troops; worked for the Ration Board, Fight for Freedom, and the Free French Relief Committee; and knitted nearly sixty sweaters. By the end of the war, most civilians had become involved in the war effort, and 725 Richmonders had paid with their lives.

The Second World War forms a significant part of the story of mother and daughter. Letters written between 1939 and 1945 form the largest section of this collection and provide a portrayal of wartime conditions in the United States and England. As one of the first publications of letters between civilians in America and Europe, this correspondence adds a new dimension to the available literature. With no prospect of reunion for some years, the women used the letters as a lifeline and set out their thoughts and activities in greater detail. Virginia Potter, as the mother of a child under fourteen, was exempted from call up. However, she supported the families of soldiers in her husband's regiment by writing to them and sending clothes and presents, and signed on as a volunteer with the Women's Voluntary Service, founded in 1938 by Eleanor Roosevelt's close friend the Dowager Marchioness of Reading, who urged members to "forget your home, leave beds unmade, leave the house dirty, don't look after your husband's meals," and become involved in war work. By the end of the war, one million women had signed up.[20] The organization arranged evacuations, clothing exchanges, transport, and distribution of ration books and ran British Restaurants. These last, introduced in 1940, were subsidized by the government to provide basic square meals at low cost. By 1944 two thousand had been set up around the country.[21] From 1941 Virginia Potter worked in the British Restaurant in Windsor twice a week and helped to serve more than three hundred meals a day.

She did, that is, what many upper-middle-class women did. Those farther down the social scale joined the wartime work force, which, according to Penny Summerfield, reached 7,750,000 workers at its height in 1943, or 51 percent of all adult women, of whom more than eighty thousand joined the Women's Land Army to boost the drive to produce food.[22] Between 1942 and 1944 a land girl was taken on by the Potter family at their wartime house rented from Eton College, to assist with growing fruit and vegetables and with raising chickens, geese, ducks, and rabbits for meat and egg production, until the Land Army requested her transfer for work of more national importance. In 1943 a government survey revealed that married women were split on their attitudes toward working after the war: 39 percent were in favor of continuing working, and 36 percent were not. After the war, as in the States, the trend to revert to the domestic sphere was apparent, and by 1951 only 35 percent of adult women were employed. Summerfield concludes that "World War II did not overturn the identification of women."[23]

The conditions of wartime England were challenging, and accounts of rationing, endless lines ("queues"), and food shortages are familiar. On a national level, America's Lend-Lease program introduced in 1941 was of enormous benefit to Britain's beleaguered population. Around half the goods transferred from the States to the Allies were munitions, but more than five billion dollars was spent on food shipments up to the end of the war.[24] On a personal level, food parcels were a godsend. Virginia Reynolds sent the Potter family, and other friends and relations, parcels containing all types of food unavailable in Britain throughout the war, from Richmond and from Montreal. As rationing continued until the 1950s, these cornucopias were received with gratitude and delight, even though the contents did not always arrive intact.

American military personnel based in Britain were well supplied with goods through the U.S. Army supply system. On arriving in the country, troops were advised not to criticize either the content or the paucity of Britain's diet and were exhorted not to eat too much if invited to eat with a family, "otherwise you may eat up their weekly rations." They were urged not to find fault with the "food, beer or cigarettes" and to "remember they have been at war since 1939."[25] David Reynolds writes that "about three million American servicemen and women passed through the United Kingdom in 1942–45," so the potential for causing offense through differences in etiquette were considerable.[26] Virginia Potter invited many such Americans and Canadians to dine and was driven to offer comments on the generosity of some visitors and the overindulgence of others, so the above instructions were variously observed. Many visiting American troops did find the English diet unpalatable and often preferred to remain in camp, where they were guaranteed familiar food.

Virginia Potter's letters were written from the home front, but accounts of her husband's direct involvement in hostilities are often relayed from his letters. As an officer in the Grenadier Guards, he was posted to Belgium and France prior to the evacuation of the British Expeditionary Force at Dunkirk in 1940, when around 340,000 men were rescued from the coast by a flotilla of craft from destroyers to fishing boats.[27] He "fought for 56 hours on end," was wounded, managed to get to the beaches, was "shelled twice walking onto the destroyer" and "twice bombed on the way to England." After his recovery, and appointment to staff posts in Britain, he took part in the Italian campaigns of 1943–44. On more than one occasion, Virginia Potter was to refer, not unreasonably, to her husband's guardian angel.

Mother and daughter, of course, experienced the war differently. Virginia Reynolds was only a little inconvenienced: prices and taxes rose, there was rationing on gas and some foods, travel was restricted, and Richmond was flooded with noisy soldiers. It was different for Virginia Potter, who saw her prewar world begin to explode. This contrast mirrored the wider fate of the two countries. According to David Reynolds, by the end of the war, Britain had lost a quarter of its national wealth, whereas the United States had gained 50 percent in real terms.[28] Richard Overy writes that it was fashionable to consider that Churchill had sold out to "his richer cousins, leaving the future of the British Empire hostage to American wishes." It is well understood that Britain would not have defeated the Nazis without American intervention, and by 1945 the "special relationship" that Churchill had assiduously cultivated with Roosevelt had paid off in terms of hegemony.[29] Certainly the Reynolds and Potter families believed in that relationship, but it is doubtful whether they were representative, at least of American opinion. David Reynolds asserts that the concept was "always much more a British idea than an American."[30]

Conditions in postwar Britain did not improve until the 1950s. Lend-lease was terminated in 1945 and a loan from the United States of $3.75 billion was negotiated by John Maynard Keynes to prop up Britain's ailing economy.[31] Between 1946 and 1948 bread rationing was enforced, and, according to Ina Zweiniger-Bargielowska, many other rations, "especially of popular items such as meat, bacon, and ham, as well as fats, now fell to their lowest level (that is, below wartime)."[32] Virginia Potter wrote to her mother, "*What* I would have done without your parcels from home, I simply *can't imagine*!!" and relates the story of a radio comedian who had proposed to a girl, not because she was pretty, but because "she has some friends in the States who send her parcels." Although a spending boom eventually ushered in the consumer society of the 1950s, rationing did not finally end until 1954.

Britain's political role changed considerably after the war. India's independence in 1947 marked the beginning of the decline of the British Empire, which was to be replaced by the Commonwealth. The West's suspicion of the Soviet Union's intentions led to the Cold War and the formation of NATO in 1949, of which Britain was a founding member. In November 1956 the Suez crisis erupted, when Britain and France, together with Israel, invaded Egypt in response to the Egyptian government's nationalization of the Suez Canal. This issue, which Arthur Marwick refers to as the "watershed," made many Britons realize that their country was no longer a major world power.[33] Public opinion was sharply divided over the advisability of the invasion, and these divisions are reflected in Virginia Potter's letters.

Postwar American women were split between those who embraced the new opportunities that wartime work had offered – in 1944 more married women were employed than single women for the first time – and those who reverted to the traditional women's world of domesticity. Fanny Christina Hill, a working-class black woman, asserted that "the war made me live better" and that her sister "always said that Hitler was the one that got us out of the white folks' kitchen."[34] But a woman such as Virginia Reynolds, over sixty years of age by the end of the war, was happy to revert to the prewar status quo and was anxious later to preserve it. Caught up in the nation's mood of anxiety over the Cold War and the perceived threat of Communism, she supported the anti-Communist investigations of Joseph McCarthy's House Un-American Activities Committee. She did not support the increasing call for desegregation and considered it "unspeakable" that the National Guard had to be called in to escort African American students into a white school in Little Rock, Arkansas, in 1957.[35] When more liberal attitudes prevailed, HUAC became discredited, and integration was mandated, Reynolds held on to her original philosophies while recognizing with regret that change was inevitable. On the whole, however, her economic status changed little.

This was not the case with the Potters, who began gently to slide down the economic scale, and might have slipped farther but for subsidies from Richmond. In 1946 they moved to Devon, in southwest England, where Gerald Potter invested in a Brixham fishing business. Many trawlers had been taken over by the Admiralty during the war, and those that remained had often been attacked by submarines and aircraft, so that catches fell to a third of their prewar level by 1941. In 1945, therefore, fish stocks were plentiful and the country was short of food, so fish prices were high and catches were good. The fishing business did not appeal greatly to Virginia Potter, but she went along with it and made much play of calling herself a "fishwife." By 1949, however, food production generally had increased, and so had landings of fish; fish prices collapsed.[36] In that same year the Potters purchased their family home near Brixham, where they were to stay for the remainder of their married lives. Unusually for an English house, it had shutters, a balcony, and a veranda, and so had qualities reminiscent of a southern home.

In the 1950s Gerald Potter turned away from the trawling business to try his hand at market gardening. The croquet lawn was dug up, the orchard trees grubbed out, and both were converted into an acre of horticultural land, where produce was planted, grown, picked, and carted to local markets. A gardener was employed and the paraphernalia of market gardening was purchased: tools, seed boxes, cloches to speed growth and protect against the vagaries of the British weather, crates for deliveries. In the house worked a cook, a housekeeper, and two maids; a nanny looked after two daughters, born in 1940 and 1945. In time the number of staff gradually diminished.

So these letters narrate a world that was changing and marked by innovation. Virginia Reynolds saw this coming, more discerningly than her daughter. "The world which we must live in after this awful war will, of necessity, be a very different one from even the one you came into," she wrote in 1943. "There will be new ideals, and new opportunities. Many places will be opened up and exploited, I think, and a great shifting of populations."

Some changes were fairly trivial, and usually disdained: chewing gum, instant coffee, ballpoint pens, and zip codes. Such things helped to occasion a sense that a more civilized world was in decline. "Like you, I find almost no one has good manners now," the mother observed in 1945. "Certainly, most Americans have very bad ones — only the older generation is thoughtful — These young things over here have been completely ruined in that way, by an inept idea that young people must be allowed to 'follow their bent', to 'express themselves'. It is called 'Progressive Education' — Those who have been subjected to its vicious influences can't read properly, nor write, nor *spell anything*, nor speak the language, and they have no conception of the niceties of life. You expect to have them put their feet on your best furniture, slap you on the back, and say 'Hello' to everyone."

Travel altered from those prewar years when mother and daughter had moved around North America, crossed and recrossed the Atlantic. Once there had been the leisurely grandeur of private carriages on the weekend skiing train from Montreal to the Laurentians, and on the New York–Montreal sleeper (the "Montrealer"), and the walnut comfort of first-class cabins on transatlantic passenger liners. Then travel was not only a means to an end, but a social, cultural, and gastronomic experience. In these movements, the family was not unusual. When the depression lessened, Americans began to travel increasingly, and by 1938 the tourist industry was the third largest in the United States.[37] Later, however, travel became more functional, with crowded trains and cramped flights, if initially flights that tried to mimic the older amenities. Virginia Reynolds continued to travel to England by sea up to the early 1960s, but she also began experimenting with flying. In a letter of 1954, she vividly describes her first journey by air from London, when she had to "land at Shannon for dinner in the restaurant complete with champagne."

Similarly, means of communication changed. At first telephones were used only to herald bad news and were regarded with mixed feelings, especially by those (as was the case with these women) who were inveterate worriers. Calls were very expensive and therefore brief, they had to be booked in advance, and they tended to come through at inconvenient times to anxious recipients anticipating unpleasant information. Cables, marconigrams, and telegrams conveyed urgent messages, but letters were the main means of imparting the stories, thoughts, gossip, and details that made up the stuff of everyday existence. But gradually the telephone calls became cheaper and more frequent. References to telephone conversations began to infiltrate the letters and by the 1950s and 1960s play a more frequent role.

These letters trace not only the events taking place on the world stage but also a remarkable and intense personal relationship, moving through decades of family life, with all its thoughts, anxieties, and foibles. One dimension of the personal was the business of men. But, so absorbed were the women in each other, that in the letters their men tended to be side-lined. Virginia Reynolds was conscious of a value in keeping this distance. When her own mother died in 1941, she wrote to her daughter, "There is a terrific pathos in the *maternal succession* in our family. . . . I don't feel that way about the men. I suppose because I am a woman and don't understand them. . . . Maybe the whole thing hinges on the fact that *you* are a woman and you are the person I have always loved the most." In principle, both women accepted the rule of men while considering women to be superior as a gender. They reluctantly accepted the idea of a man's world because that was the order of things, and it would not have occurred to them to change it. But this acceptance was mixed with much hostility, especially from Virginia Reynolds, who, as she herself put it, "was born *furious.*" She wrote that "men are incurable" and "women should strike as in Lysistrata," while counseling women to give in to men, "for that is the only way they can get a chance." Elsewhere she said, "Especially men, are so often just the victim of *glands* — If they recover from that, they might be all right as husbands — I am beginning to be almost a man hater — They seem so utterly stupid to me, and they have made such a mess of this world, which could be quite enchanting if they had any sense — However, they have *proved* they haven't, so that's that." Nevertheless, four men recur in the narrative of the letters and merit discussion.

Virginia Reynolds's husband, Stuart, had worked as secretary and treasurer of the Richmond Foundry and Manufacturing Company until his retirement in 1932, when he was appointed its vice president. In 1920 he had helped to found the Richmond Manufacturers' Association and was its first president from 1921 to 1923. He lived the life of a sociable businessman, a man fond of golf and card games, particularly poker, which he would play regularly at the Richmond Country Club. He also belonged to the Commonwealth Club and served as treasurer and secretary of the Virginia branch of the English Speaking Union. During the war Reynolds threw his energies into Richmond's British War Relief, first as secretary and then as chair. In 1946 he was awarded the King's Medal for his services, although such was the shortage of metal in postwar Britain that the actual medal could not be struck until 1948, when it was formally presented to him. In appearance, he was a tall and handsome man, possessed of a dry sense of humor and a gentle relaxed demeanor. Virginia Reynolds talks in her letters of his "careless" sartorial sense and "cheerful disposition," but also of an inclination toward "negativity." As such, he greatly differed from his wife and they tended to live parallel lives. For one thing, Stuart Reynolds was not an enthusiastic traveler. After several excursions to Europe with his wife and daughter in the 1920s and 1930s, he preferred to limit his trips to Connecticut and Montreal, where he would visit his sisters and their families. Or he would stay in Richmond and socialize with his contemporaries. Virginia Potter was very fond of her father but did not see him as a forceful character. In choosing her husband, it could be said that she overcompensated.

Almost more important was her mother's brother-in-law, Huntly Redpath Drummond, the second son of Sir George Drummond, an industrial chemist and businessman who had emigrated from Scotland in 1854 and settled in Montreal. Huntly was educated in Montreal and at Rugby School in England, where he was the school captain in 1882. He married May Reynolds, Stuart's sister, in 1899, though she died in 1931, leaving him a widower for twenty-five years. He owned a large house in Montreal's prominent Square Mile district, a skiing lodge and estate in the Laurentian Mountains, and a summer house in Beaconsfield to the west of the city. As he had no children of his own, his niece from Virginia became a surrogate daughter. She and her parents spent many months of each year in Canada, where they had a wide circle of friends. Virginia Potter admitted more than once that her carefree sojourns in Canada during the 1920s and early 1930s were the happiest in her life. Taking the place of the home-loving Stuart Reynolds, Huntly Drummond often accompanied mother and daughter on trips abroad, a role Huntly particularly welcomed, as his love for Virginia Reynolds was obvious. Virginia Potter described Drummond as much more "bubbly" when his sister-in-law was present.

Drummond succeeded his father as president of Redpath Sugar Company in 1910, became a director of the Bank of Montreal in 1912, its chair from 1943, and its honorary president from 1946. Between 1920 and 1949 he was a senior member of the Board of Governors of McGill University, from which he received an honorary doctorate in 1943. (Much to his annoyance, William Beveridge, founder of Britain's welfare state, of which Drummond heartily disapproved, was honored at the same ceremony.) Drummond also served as governor of Alexandra Hospital, honorary president of the Royal Trust Company, vice president of Canadian Red Cross, and president of the Montreal Board of Trade. As importantly, he collected art enthusiastically and served as a council member of the Art Association of Montreal, later the Montreal Museum of Fine Art. Among his extensive collection were works by Renoir, Bracques, Pisarro, and Monet. His sister-in-law, Virginia Reynolds, did not grasp the shrewdness of such acquisitions. In 1938 she wrote with a puzzled shudder, "I was really astonished when he told me he had bought another Pisarro and was thinking of a *Bracques* − He has gone modern up to the neck." Drummond was extremely generous to the Reynolds and Potters during his lifetime and, among many other gifts, in 1937 paid for Gerald Potter's yacht, *Carmela*. He also donated much of his wealth to local, national, and international philanthropic causes. During the war he covered the cost of two Spitfires for the Royal Air Force, one of which was named *Jennifer* after his great niece, Jennifer Potter, and the other *Bougie*, the nickname of Virginia Reynolds.[38] (She was delighted by the thought of the "Bougie swooping over Germany and blowing up a few Nasties.") Philanthropy aside, Huntly Drummond was an enthusiastic yachtsman, rider, and athlete, and in 1905 was among those who pioneered skiing and ski jumping in Canada. He believed strongly in the beneficial properties of sport and did not himself give up skiing until shortly before he died in his ninety-third year.

An enjoyment of sailing, instilled into the younger Virginia Reynolds by Drummond at an early age, may well have been a factor in her decision to marry Gerald Edward Winter Potter. Their first weekend together in 1935 was spent sailing in the Solent off the Hampshire coast. Later, in 1947, he was "bitten by ocean racing" and went on to become a world-class yachtsman. In 1959 he led the British team to victory in the Admiral's Cup. An exacting skipper, Potter won many ocean races during his sailing career either for other yacht owners (including the Royal Ocean Racing Club) or in his own boats, the last of which he sold in 1964. Virginia Potter always maintained that she was never worried about her husband when he was at sea; he was much more trouble when he was on land.

Gerald Potter was born in London in 1907 to an English father and an American mother. He was brought up at Castle Priory, Wallingford, in Berkshire. His family's circumstances were comfortable, as a result of a nineteenth-century involvement in the cotton industry of northwest England, to which the American South had once sent its bales. However, Gerald's father took his own life in 1917, when suffering from manic depression. This loss affected his son deeply, though he did become close to his uncle and guardian, Cyril Potter, and he was fond of his two sisters, Aline (known as Lallie, later Burge, still later Butler) and Joan (later Verey). Nonetheless, Gerald craved masculine affection and guidance. The guidance, if not the affection, he first found by being educated at Eton College and the Sandhurst Military Academy, after which he joined the Grenadier Guards. In 1936 he resigned his commission after an argument with his commanding officer, but rejoined the regiment in 1939 at the start of the Second World War. He served throughout the war in Britain and Europe and won the Military Cross for his part in the Italian campaigns of 1943.

Enormously energetic, Gerald was a good shot, walked miles every day, and worked hard at any venture he undertook. He held a flying license but never pursued flying once the RAF had turned him down for his extreme shortsightedness. He inherited his mother's artistic talent but rarely used it, turning instead to home movies, by which he recorded many events public and private, from military life in Egypt in the 1920s to Cowes Regatta, the Fastnet ocean race, transatlantic crossings on the Queen Mary, and Lincolnshire shooting parties in the 1950s. What attracted the young Virginia to him was his ability to "make any party go," the genial hospitality that often left him and his guests in an alcoholic "daze." She writes, too, of his "terrific energy" and how he always "got things done." But she also says that he had a "difficult disposition." With toughness, wit, and loyalty to friends went unpredictability and a tendency to oscillate between charm and intimidation. In 1958 the Potters visited an old friend of Gerald's family in Wallingford, who recalled a "terribly naughty little boy." Inside the tough exterior, this little boy lived on, personified not least by the extensive train set he enjoyed in his attic. But his later years were not happy. In the 1960s he developed the first signs of the arthritis that was to cripple him. His last fifteen years were painful and frustrating, for he was trapped inside an uncooperative body that would not allow him the physical activity he craved.

The marriage did not always run smoothly. During the war the Potters lived in Windsor close to their good friends Viscount and Viscountess Anson, with whom they shared chickens and raised a pig. (Bill Anson was a fellow officer in the Grenadier Guards.) Virginia Potter was to write effusively of their times together and how they enjoyed a social life in spite of, or more probably because of, the war, by deliberately making the best of it, as they "all knew that eventually most of [them] would be killed." Gerald Potter and Anne Anson made the best of it by having a brief fling in 1945, during a difficult time in the Potter marriage. In retaliation soon after, Virginia Potter spent four months in Virginia and Canada, when she, too, had an affair. She had known the French Canadian Pothier Doucet since 1929, and he had been in love with Virginia ever since they met. He had stayed in touch with her in the vain hope that one day they would get together. Pothier was the antithesis of Gerald in both character and physique and was insufficiently forceful to attract Virginia on a permanent basis. Nevertheless, he had many charms and was described by those who knew him as "kind," "caring," and possessed of a great sense of humor.

Herbert Emile Theodore (Pothier) Doucet (1907–89) was the eldest of three children born in Montreal to Rene Pothier Doucet and Elizabeth Mazzuchi. He was educated at Montreal High School and the Royal Military College, Kingston, Ontario, where he specialized in engineering. From 1929 he worked for a general engineering contractor in Montreal while serving with a territorial regiment, the Canadian Black Watch, which was mobilized in 1939. He went on active service in Europe and was awarded the Legion d'Honneur and the Croix de Guerre. From 1943 he was second in command of the Perth regiment and by the end of the war had been promoted to colonel. He was active in the hostilities in Italy at the same time as Gerald Potter. He remained in the military throughout his working life and retired in 1963 as deputy adjutant general at the army headquarters in Ottawa.

During the war Pothier and Virginia spent a good deal of time together, both with and without Gerald. Pothier visited the family home frequently when he was based nearby, and Virginia often traveled up to London to see him. At the end of the war, he volunteered for the Canadian Occupation Forces in Europe so as to be near her. Of the wide coterie of friends Virginia had had in Montreal in the late 1920s and early 1930s, Pothier was by far the most significant. In 1946 he sent her a gold chain and heart to commemorate the exact day of their meeting in 1929. According to letters from him, he waited seventeen and a half years before finally acknowledging that her acceptance was never going to be forthcoming. After their affair in Montreal in 1946, and after many deliberations with her mother and uncle, Huntly Drummond, Virginia decided that she would remain in England with her husband and family. So in 1948 Pothier married Lilias Margaret Savage in Montreal; they later adopted a son and a daughter. That Virginia Potter kept his love letters until she died, however, bears testimony to her strong feelings for him.

Most relationships are formed out of a previous experience and involve duplication or rejection, or a mixture of the two. Ginnie (the nickname for Virginia Potter) chose to marry a man who was very different from her father. Did Bougie do the same? Unfortunately, little is known about the character of Loren Dickinson, Bougie's father, so comparison between him and Stuart Reynolds is not possible. But it was well known in the family that Reynolds was dominated by his wife's strong personality and even by her money. Stuart's unsuccessful financial sense both provoked his wife's censure and led her into playing the stock market. "Stocks went up a trifle today and Saturday but everyone has the jitters about what those idiots in Washington may do" is a typical comment of hers, in this case in 1938. So she became the provider after her husband retired. Much of Bougie's life was spent away from Stuart in the company of female friends and acquaintances in pursuit of cultural interests, unshared with her husband.

Nonetheless, her vigor and determination were offset by his gentleness and easygoing temperament, which led to a general contentment within their marriage, punctuated by irritations rather than serious adversity. She voiced complaints about her husband in the letters. "Stuart seems fairly well," she noted in 1947. "He can't do anything, and I don't see how he stands it, as he has very few resources and isn't interested in many things or many people, but outside of occasional sarcasm in my direction, and others as well, he is usually in a good temper — He has never thanked me for anything I have *ever* done for him, but I am used to that, so I can laugh."

Such confessions created a collusion between mother and daughter, allowing them to cope with the unpleasant fact that men were necessary, but often trying. There developed a mutual allegiance of mother and daughter, which was certainly stronger than the marital bond of either. Bougie, especially, lived through her daughter. "Of course no one can, or could, or would, ever take your place with me," she wrote soon after Ginnie's wedding. "That is final, and there is even a little grim satisfaction in the thought that in the matter of daughters I have had 100% satisfaction. Perhaps sometimes .05% off for crying when people spoke to you and, lately, lying in bed beyond the decent hour for arising. But the rest is par excellence. I expected and demanded a charming and lovely daughter full of understanding and I got it."

Ginnie, drawn into a close relationship with her forceful mother, viewed her father's forbearance more as a weakness than a strength, and was attracted to the polar opposite in her husband. Gerald was a volatile character who demanded plenty of attention and often became aggressive. Ginnie learned to avoid conflict, which in any event she despised, by submitting to his whims. She herself had personality and presence yet was dominated by her husband and would admit to taking the "line of least resistance," rather than indulge in vitriolic argument. Her stoicism and sense of duty carried her through. Humor, too, acted as a cohesive force. Gerald's wit and Ginnie's natural aptitude for entertaining storytelling produced a complementary vitality and strength that was capable of trouncing many marital transgressions. What was missing at the center of the marriage was filled, and compensated for, by their wide circle of friends, with whom they socialized and had fun. Their dinner parties were meticulously planned with the

best of food and drink, and invariably the carpet was rolled back for dancing into the early hours to recordings of Fats Waller and Ella Fitzgerald,
and later Bill Hailey and the Comets. Their marriage was fortified, too, by
physical activity — much of their life revolved around sailing. Summer was
dominated by local outings, ocean races, and regattas. Yacht crew members, disheveled and unshaven, predominated around the house and were
offered generous hospitality to welcome them ashore. Ginnie viewed these
visits partly as onslaughts, partly as opportunities to have a good time, and
always with a determination to do the best for her husband. In winter they
traveled north for shooting parties, mostly to Lincolnshire and occasionally
to Scotland. In spite of Ginnie's urban upbringing, she enjoyed the latter
very much, to her surprise. Her year was punctuated by frequent visits to
London, the world she really enjoyed, where she socialized with visiting
Americans, Canadians, and her metropolitan friends and went to the theater to revel in a good play.

The exceptional closeness between my grandmother and mother resulted in a mutual dependence. Bougie had high social and ethical aspi-
rations for her daughter, which were fulfilled by Ginnie's marriage to an
English Guards officer with the right social credentials, by their similar
philosophical outlooks, by Ginnie's willingness to comply with her mother's
wishes and desire to gain approval — "I hope you are proud of your off-
spring" is in the first line of an early letter — and by the raising of two
daughters in whom she tried to instill the same values. This in turn created
a dependency on her mother for guidance. Throughout the correspondence
she sought opinions and advice from Bougie, who conducted a running
seminar on what to think and how to behave. So, from New York in 1932,
Ginnie asked, "How late can one wear *velvet* and not be déclassée? 'cause I
wondered if I could wear my black velvet evening dress while there?" This
habit reveals an uncertainty on my mother's part and a benign autocracy
on my grandmother's. Arguably this could be interpreted as an unhealthy
basis for a relationship. But it seemed to work. The psychological bases
for relationships are varied, and this one was born, I believe, of a mutual
respect that flourished despite the authoritarian overtones.

Still, their differences were many. Bougie was politically engaged and
keen to express her opinions on world events and philosophies, whereas

Ginnie was apolitical and approached her letters as a way to express personal experiences. This asymmetry was occasioned mostly by temperament, but also by the fact of different readerships. My mother's letters to her parents were intended to be circulated among American family and friends, particularly to her aunt Florence Dickinson Stearns (who lived in Richmond) and her uncle Huntly Drummond. With the raconteuse's gift of turning even the most pedestrian events into entertaining stories, Ginnie was keen to keep her distant family amused with her exploits. However, I do not think that Bougie's letters to Ginnie were shared with Gerald to the same extent, certainly not as a matter of course. I suspect that Ginnie's reluctance to do so was a way of retaining the intimate relationship she held with her mother. Some letters were, however, private and marked as such. Financial matters, for example, were addressed to Bougie alone. As for intimate matters, both came from generations that resisted bluntness on matters concerning sexuality. They each preferred obliqueness. Bougie talked of the death of her first grandchild only as Ginnie's "troubles," and Ginnie referred to Gerald's affair only as a "débâcle." It was seen as sentimental and pointless to dwell on problems, and such understatements deliberately reflected their determination to move on and look to the future.

Although the tone of some of the letters in this collection may come over as condescending and elitist (and it must be admitted that they were snobs), in practice both Bougie and Ginnie enjoyed the company of people from all backgrounds. They were generous to many and often helped to resolve their problems. In particular they supported those who worked for them, and observers have noted the real affection with which they were regarded by members of their staff. Sometimes they made snap dismissive judgments, but they were not too proud to change their minds and embrace those to whom they were not at first attracted.

I anticipated the visits to England from my grandmother with great pleasure, as she added another dimension to our family for the summer months. In appearance Bougie was not traditionally beautiful, although she had penetratingly dark eyes and great charisma. Her appeal to members of the opposite sex was well known, and even as an older woman she drew people to her through her strength of character and sense of fun. Never overtly interested in fashion, her taste in clothes was classical. In the early 1960s she talks of clothes making "no impression" on her "whatsoever," yet she was elegant and well dressed.

Bougie provided stimulating company. She was knowledgeable in fields in which I was ignorant, and had a great sense of the absurd, a combination that made our outings highly entertaining. I shall always be grateful to her for nurturing in particular my love for twentieth-century classical music. She may have held traditional tastes in literature and art, but she was an enthusiastic admirer of Stravinsky and Shostakovich and often took me to concerts in London to hear their works. To me she seemed worldly and capable, an image dented only by her fear of anything with wings. Many was the time a butterfly, unwise enough to fly into the house, had to be rescued from the flailings of her panic.

Ginnie was less sure of herself than her mother. Behind her confident facade was a rather timid person. Being a trained actor, she never appeared unconfident; she had great presence and was always cheerful and vivacious in company. Her insecurity nevertheless led to an overarching concern with appearance and a desire to do the right thing. She was much teased by the family when, in the mid-1970s, I told her I had been involved in a television program the previous evening. Her response, rather than inquiring as to the nature of the program, was "Oh good, dear. What did you wear?"

Physically Ginnie was very beautiful. She was tall, dark, and slim and always elegantly dressed. Her interest in fashion was more assiduous than her mother's and her bearing more striking. My soignée mother, who was horrified when I took to "black leather boots and a black leather coat" in the 1960s, had a definite idea of how people should dress (and not dress).

Ginnie had a wide circle of friends composed of all age groups. She made a point of drawing younger people into her circle, both for their different perspectives on life and as an insurance against being left friendless once she found herself in what she referred to as the "funeral bracket." On the occasion of her magnificent and glamorous eightieth birthday party in London, the guests ranged from their twenties to their nineties. She moved easily between the age groups, making unlikely introductions and producing first-rate food and drink in generous quantities. Like her husband, she had the ability to make any party go. Moreover, her social stamina was legendary, and on that eightieth birthday she was still knocking back drinks at two o'clock the following morning.

My mother's southern roots never left her. Outwardly she may have become Anglicized, but powerful feelings evoked by the American Civil War certainly lived on in our family well into the 1960s. In 1961, while practicing the piano, I embarked, somewhat unadvisedly, on "John Brown's Body Lies A'mouldering in the Grave." Ginnie, normally averse to displays of anger, stormed into my room and reproached me soundly, saying, "I will not have that tune played in my house." This outburst at my amateur rendition of the Unionist Battle Hymn took place over one hundred years after John Brown's raid on the federal arsenal at Harper's Ferry, but alerted me instantly to the strength of feeling that still linked my mother to the Confederacy, and to attitudes founded in another time and place.

The correspondence, from which this volume makes a selection, is now housed in my home in Devon, since I and my sister inherited the letters when my mother, Virginia Potter, died. Their initial discovery in 1991 was a revelation, as none of our family had any idea of their existence. Suitcases and boxes at the back of a cupboard in her London flat, to which she had moved in 1984, revealed an abundant archive of family memories, stories, and records. As she had very carefully drawn up her will and specified exactly which possessions were to be bequeathed to which friends and relations, it seems as though the letters were left as a deliberate surprise for us. I suspect she did not want to inform my sister and me of their existence in case we felt duty bound to publish them. She gave us the choice of using them or throwing them away. As it proved, there was much pleasure in discovering this unheralded bounty and having the privilege of unraveling the stories of Bougie and Ginnie (to use now their familiar nicknames), and to learn of their lives during an era otherwise lost to memory. Ginnie had moved this bulky secret from house to house and even, in the case of Bougie's letters, from continent to continent. I helped Ginnie clear up Bougie's apartment in Virginia after her death in 1966 and yet had no inkling that these letters had been sequestered and shipped to England. The correspondence no doubt provided Ginnie with a tangible link to her late and much-loved mother, on whom she doted and whose death she mourned greatly. It is easy to imagine her taking Bougie's letters out to read from time to time to relive past moments and indulge in the memory of their close relationship.

There are thousands of letters, written on blue, white, buff, and (occasionally) pink writing paper. Almost all have their originating address die-stamped on the first page. Some were written on flimsy airmail paper that rustles as they are unfolded, others on substantial crackly vellum that presses solidly against the constraints of their envelopes. Many letters were tied by jute or rubber bands in chronological bundles; others were scattered randomly in suitcases along with photographs and letters from other sources. This collection is now arranged strictly in order by year. The letters' tangibility is a constant reminder of my mother and grandmother, and of the lives both remembered and gleaned of these two Anglophile American women, whose bond was exceptionally close, and whose unanticipated epistolary bequest has enabled their story to be told.

When I untied the string of each bundle of letters and the shards of long-perished rubber bands broke away, the strands of my family story gradually unfolded, and I began to view these two women from a middle-aged perspective, rather than from that of a child or young relative. I felt keenly that I was trespassing on the intimacies of a powerful bond, but as I repeatedly came across passages from my grandmother urging her daughter to "do something" with the letters, I realized it was a deliberate legacy and that they were happy for their story to be told.

1. On Samuel Fowler Dickinson, see Richard B. Sewall, *The Life of Emily Dickinson* (London: Faber and Faber, 1976). On Amherst College, see William S. Tyler, *A History of Amherst College during the Administrations of Its First Five Presidents: From 1821 to 1891* (New York: F. H. Hitchcock, 1895).

2. Millicent Todd Bingham, ed., *Emily Dickinson's Home: Letters of Edward Dickinson and His Family* (New York: Harper Brothers, 1955), 247.

3. For her memoir, see Angela Potter, ed., "Confederate Money: A Memoir of the 1850s and 1860s," *Southern Cultures* 9 (Winter 2003): 88–98.

4. Virginia Dickinson Reynolds, "Clad in Victory," in Winnifred Brown and Alma W. Watson, eds., *Guests in Eden: Emily Dickinson, Martha Dickinson Bianchi* (New York: Zeta chapter, Phi Delta Gamma, Columbia University, 1946), 13.

5. Sara M. Evans, *Born for Liberty: A History of Women in America* (London: Collier MacMillan, 1989), 108.

6. "Appendix Table 4: Net Importation (+) or (−) of Slaves, by Age, Sex, and State, 1850–1860," in Richard Sutch, "The Breeding of Slaves for Sale and the Westward Expansion of Slavery, 1850–1960," in *Race and Slavery in the Western Hemisphere: Quantitative Studies*, ed. Stanley L. Engerman and Eugene D. Genovese (Princeton, N.J.: Princeton University Press, 1975), 207.

7. Virginius Dabney, *Richmond: The Story of a City* (Charlottesville: University Press of Virginia, 1990), 111.

8. For an account of Richmond's Woman's Club, see Sandra Gioia Treadway, *Women of Mark: A History of the Woman's Club of Richmond, Virginia, 1894–1994* (Richmond: Library of Virginia, 1995).

9. Wendell Phillips, "American Anti-Slavery Anniversary," *Standard* (May 13, 1865): 2, quoted in Ellen Carol DuBois, *Feminism and Suffrage: The Emergence of an Independent Women's Movement in America, 1848–1869* (Ithaca, N.Y.: Cornell University Press, 1978), 59.

10. Susan M. Hartmann, *The Home Front and Beyond: American Women in the 1940s* (Boston: Twayne, 1982), 124.

11. For literature on women's rights and suffragism, see Nancy F. Cott, ed., *No Small Courage: A History of Women in the United States* (Oxford: Oxford University Press, 2000); Evans, *Born for Liberty*; Rosalind Rosenberg, *Divided Lives: American Women in the Twentieth Century* (London: Penguin, 1993); and Marjorie Spruill Wheeler, *New Women of the New South: The Leaders of the Woman Suffrage Movement in the Southern States* (New York: Oxford University Press, 1993).

12. Clipping of unattributed newspaper interview in 1924 with Zelda Fitzgerald, Zelda Fitzgerald scrapbook, quoted in Nancy Milford, *Zelda* (New York: Harper and Row, 1970), 160.

13. Ross McKibbin, *Classes and Cultures: England 1918–1951* (Oxford: Oxford University Press, 1998), 1. McKibbin gives a detailed account of the British class system; I adapted much of the remainder of this paragraph from his work.

14. Ibid., 35.

15. John Stevenson, *British Society, 1914–45* (London: Penguin Books, 1984), 330.

16. For sources on Britain in the 1930s, see Piers Brendon, *The Dark Valley: A Panorama of the 1930s* (London: Pimlico, 2000); Malcolm Muggeridge, *The Thirties* (London: Fontana Books, 1967); and Stevenson, *British Society*.

17. Stevenson, *British Society*, 133.

18. McKibbin, *Classes and Cultures*, 27.

19. Hugh Brogan, *The Pelican History of the United States of America* (London: Penguin Books, 1985), 574.

20. Penny Summerfield, "Woman, War and Social Change: Women in Britain in World War II," in Arthur Marwick, *Total War and Social Change* (London: Macmillan, 1988), 95–118.

21. For information on British Restaurants, see Raynes Minns, *Bombers and Mash: The Domestic Front, 1939–45* (London: Virago Press, 1980), 23 and 73; and R. J. Hammond, *History of the Second World War: Food, Vol. II* (London: HMSO, 1956), 352–421.

22. The Women's Land Army, whose members were known colloquially as "land girls," was originally formed in the First World War to recruit female farm workers to increase homegrown agricultural production. The army was re-formed in 1939.

23. Summerfield, "Woman, War and Social Change," 95–118.

24. I. C. B. Dear, ed., *The Oxford Companion to the Second World War* (Oxford: Oxford University Press, 1995), 682.

25. *Over There: Instructions for American Servicemen in Britain* (1942; repr. Oxford: Bodleian Library, 1994), 15.

26. David Reynolds, *Rich Relations: The American Occupation of Britain, 1942–1945* (London: HarperCollins, 1995), 433.

27. Dear, *Oxford Companion*, 312–13.

28. Reynolds, *Rich Relations*, 53.

29. Richard Overy, *Why the Allies Won* (London: Jonathan Cape, 1995), 249.

30. Reynolds, *Rich Relations*, 439.

31. Peter Hennessy, *Never Again: Britain, 1945–1951* (London: Vintage, 1993), 97.

32. Ina Zweiniger-Bargielowska, *Austerity in Britain: Rationing, Controls, and Consumption, 1939–1955* (Oxford: Oxford University Press, 2000), 218.

33. Arthur Marwick, *British Society since 1945* (London: Penguin Books, 1892), 106.

34. Sherna Berger Gluck, *Rosie the Riveter Revisited: Women, the War and Social Change* (Boston: Twayne, 1987), 23.

35. For Virginia's response to the *Brown v. Board of Education* decision, see Matthew D. Lassiter and Andrew B. Lews, eds., *The Moderates' Dilemma: Massive Resistance to School Desegregation in Virginia* (Charlottesville: University Press of Virginia, 1998).

36. For further information, see R. Robinson, *The Rise and Fall of the British Trawl Fishery* (Exeter, Eng.: Exeter University Press, 1996), 176–187.

37. Gary B. Nash and Julie Roy Jeffrey, *The American People: Creating a Nation and a Society* (New York: Longman, 1998), 864.

38. In the 1920s the cartoon character Barney Google owned a horse named Sparkplug, which often protested at its weariness. The day after Virginia Reynolds had complained of feeling "as weary as Sparkplug," her daughter happened to learn at school that the French word for sparkplug is *bougie*. Thereafter the nickname Bougie, always pronounced with a soft *g*, stuck and was used by virtually everyone. It was sometimes spelled *Boogie*, which is how Ginnie generally wrote it.

EDITORIAL NOTE

Spelling that is incorrect is indicated by [*sic*]; erratic spelling mistakes in words normally spelled correctly have been silently corrected. Illegible words are indicated by a question mark within square brackets. Differences appear where American and English spelling vary — for example, *color* and *colour* — and these are unchanged. Similarly, there are many instances of proper nouns beginning with lowercase letters (*english*, *riviera*), and improperly hyphenated words (*left-overs*, *de-mobbed*, *un-aristocratic*); these, too, have been left as in the original.

Words inserted to improve sense are enclosed within square brackets. Where lengthy passages have been edited out, the omission has not been indicated. Punctuation was frequently written in the form of dashes, and these have been replaced by em dashes. Information given in footnotes includes brief biographical summaries of characters referred to, sources of further reading, and/or relevant background details. Footnotes are not given for well-known people, or for those for whom information was unobtainable.

As opening and closing salutations have been omitted to save space and allow inclusion of a greater number of letters, the letters from Virginia Dickinson Reynolds (Bougie) have been italicized and those from Virginia Stuart Potter (Ginnie) left in roman to distinguish them from one another. Mailing instructions ("via S.S. Aquitania sailing Jan. 14 Southampton" or "via S.S. Washington sailing Jan. 18 New York") have been omitted. Many of the letters written during the war had been opened, read by a censor, and resealed with a label marked "opened by examiner no. [−]." These too have been omitted. Both correspondents numbered each letter in wartime in order to keep a check on their arrival; these numbers have been left out. Following the first appearance of a new address, subsequent letters sent from that place have been truncated to a shortened form.

To provide continuity and to give the reader a sense of the whole, I have selected passages of a general interest and from each year, rather than offering letters with specific slants, interests, or from a limited era. Letters written during the Second World War have been awarded greater space because of the extraordinary circumstances of the time. I have tried not to give too many examples of each type of event but have included a wide range of social, cultural, and sporting activities that typify the kind of lives they were leading.

The extant letters total 1.6 million words. They have been edited down to less than 10 percent of that length. In some years correspondence from Bougie is missing; there are no letters from her prior to 1936, excepting one written in 1918, and none for the years 1948–50. Occasionally other large gaps occur in this collection, which are due either to paucity of letters or to deliberate excisions.

Shared Histories

Prewar Letters

11th February 1929   3418 Drummond Street
                                                 Montreal[1]

My adorable Boogie and Papa-Daddy —

    The trial is over and successfully so — I think —[2] I hope you are proud of your offspring for going up to Ottawa alone because I think I was very brave — went up with Brown, the maid on the 1.05 arriving there at 4 p.m. — went straight to my rooms at the Château. Mrs. Barry German came in to see me, bringing a little cheer to the situation, also my feather and tulle — She took me to Mrs. Phillips and left me there — I walked into a room full of people, none of whom I had ever laid eyes on before — chose someone I thought was Mrs. Phillips and was introduced to her husband and their secretary, a rather stern male who handed me a large envelope full of instructions and commanded that I read them — I read all about arriving at the left door on the right wing and going to Room 260 on the 2nd floor of the third wing on the left side — etc — but no mention of who I was to go with or how, so I walked up to a girl named Winterbotham, asked her if I might go with her to the presentation as she was staying at the Château along with one Miss Carpenter. She acquiesced, and I was much relieved — had a talk with Mrs. Phillips who is charming though very dignified, and a trifle cold —

    After we practised curtseying, I came home with Winterbotham-Carpenter in their taxi, and I ordered one for the evening — Had dinner ordered upstairs, of which I ate practically nothing, and then dressed in silver lamé plus silver lamé train, feathers, silver kid shoes with brides-maid buckles, silver stockings, and a large bouquet of rose red roses tied with wide silver lamé ribbon (sent from Hunt).[3]

Went off with the two American girls to Parliament Hill — the wind blew off my feathers and nearly ruined my roses, but they came to — got fixed up in the dressing-rooms, where Miss Choate (one of the girls who was being presented, and who was staying with Mrs. Phillips) was strutting about the place — she is Mrs. Phillips' god-daughter and grand-daughter of Rufus Choate and can hardly stand the strain — a *poisonous* female — [4] I cannot stand superior people who say mean things about fat girls in glasses from Kansas City — (there was one in our presentation party — very nice, though).

There were lots of soldiers in red coats and much braid about the corridors and an enormous band playing somewhere — we got in line a few minutes after nine, and were presented not much later, thank heaven — The standing in line must be awful — I was next to last in line in our crowd, following Miss Prather (Kansas City!) — gave my pink card to the Aide — it passed along the line of Aides in *braid* but I never heard my name being mentioned — just have a vague recollection of trying to smile sweetly to their Ex's — and trying to make a graceful bow — and it was all over —

Went upstairs in the balcony and was able to sit down and watch the others — I have never seen so many funny sights as some of the people that were being presented — They did look awful — But there were some who looked splendid — Mrs. Phillips especially — How the Willingdons stood there and bowed for two hours I *don't know* — [5] But they did —

At eleven o'clock it was over, I found my friends and we came home — I tore off feathers and train and in a few minutes Mrs. German came for me and took me to the Country Club to a supper party she was giving — and there was a dance going on — I sat between Mr. Mayer, in the consulate or something, and Major Todd (or Stanley as I called him) in lots of uniform and braid — Mrs. Phillips was in the party, also Rat Poison (Miss Choate). We had good champagne and Stan and I got along very well, he is charming — tall, though not good-looking, about 30 I imagine, anyway perfectly sweet — and Mr. Mayer a small insignificant little man in glasses but very nice, and we had a grand conversation all about Paris —

The workmen outside woke me about 7 – but I stayed in bed 'til 12 – and believe me, I felt awful – lost my breakfast – Finally managed to get up and dress and then felt all right – went to Government House to lunch at 1 with the 2 same girls and enjoyed it. Sat between Col. O'Connor and Mr. Mieville, the secretary to the Gov. General – both very nice – the Willingdons were delightful – the French Minister was there, and of course all the aides, I didn't adore any of them – though one is *six foot seven*. They showed us all over the house, and we left about two-thirty – I had an hour to send flowers to Mrs. Phillips, undress and dress in traveling clothes, pack, pay my bill and catch the 3.30 train back. I got there seven minutes before the thing pulled out – and it was a relief, but my *"friend"* had arrived, and I didn't feel so hot in the train – Anyway it was lucky!

Arrived home at 6.30 and was so glad to come home – I felt as if I had been away for several months – Had dinner alone with Aunt May and told her all about my trip.[6] I forgot to say that Mr. Mayer said I made the best curtsey! One man I met said he admired my bravery by coming up all alone, I said I would probably be presented with several medals in the next war, if my courage doesn't waver – As a matter of fact I wasn't nervous at all except for that awful tea – and I wouldn't give anything for having gone to Ottawa.

1. The Montreal home of Huntly Drummond.

2. The event was Ginnie's formal presentation into Canadian society, where she was received by the governor-general of Canada in Ottawa at what was known as the Canadian Drawing-Room. She attended this "trial" on her own, accompanied only by a Drummond household maid as her aunt, May Drummond, was not only temporarily indisposed but, as a Canadian citizen, not permitted to present her American niece.

3. "Hunt" was a nickname for Huntly Drummond.

4. Rufus Choate, 1799–1859, lawyer, state senator 1841–45, attorney general of Massachusetts 1853.

5. George Freeman-Thomas, 1866–1941, was from 1924 first Viscount Willingdon, and governor-general of Canada from 1926 to 1931. Marie Adelaide Willingdon née Lady Brassey, 1875–1960, was the first Viscountess Willingdon.

6. May Drummond née Reynolds, d. 1931, Ginnie's aunt.

4th March 1929   The New Colonial Hotel
                                                    Nassau – Bahamas[1]

I hope you are both cooler than I am – here I sit at 5 p.m. – trying to write to you and the sweat is pouring from every pore – O God! O Montreal – how I miss the frozen North – I just *pine* for it.

We arrived this morning after a rather tiresome voyage, and I was glad to put my foot on terra firma. The first night out I slept under four blankets – and last night entirely nude –

Saturday passing Cape Hatteras was quite fun – for a while – I sat way up on the top deck with the wind moaning, and the waves foaming and fretting and thought it was grand until about 6 o'clock, when I began feeling *green* so I piled off to bed where I stayed 'til the next morning at 10.30 – Sunday wasn't quite as bad except I was chased all over the boat by a twin of *Alfred Fuchs*, a Mr. Griswold, *travelling salesman*, who took pictures of me on the bow, stern, aft, etc.

The boat docked at 8.30 this morning – a lovely island – white beach and waving palms set in an emerald sea – dotted with pink and white houses – gay-colored dresses and coal black niggers – incidentally it is perfectly *flat* and damned hot – The *enormous* hotel is bright pink with pale-green window sashes and royal blue iron grill balconies! – a big terrace where one sits in the cool of the evening, a small aquarium where blue and yellow fish swim – several tennis courts – palm trees and *very* few flowers – and last but not least – a *bar* from where the Americans never emerge –

1. Ginnie accompanied her aunt, May Drummond, "instead of a lady's maid – all the work and no pay," on a trip to the Bahamas for three weeks.

19th March 1929   Nassau – Bahamas

Yesterday was a red letter day – Ethel Olive and her ma hired a boat for the day, and asked me, also Sheila and Honor and three other girls.[1]

The sea was rather rough as we were in the *open*, and the boat rocked horribly – I lay down and vowed I would never be roped into going on another fishing-party. Nearly everyone in the party did the same thing. But when I heard Mrs. Joseph say we were going to Sandy Cay for lunch, I sat up and took notice, as to go to Sandy Cay has been my one ambition since I came — It is an adorable island sitting out in the middle of the sea — a beautiful sand beach nearly all around the island, and a grove of coconut palms — It is divine!!

We got ashore in the little rowboat, and immediately undressed, and went swimming. As it was a hen-party except for the Captain whom we *hoped* wasn't looking, we took off our suits and went in au naturel — think of that greenyblue water, white coral sand, an island of coconut palms, and *beautiful* nymphs sporting in the water — Doesn't it sound marvellous — I won't vouchsafe for all of them being nymphs, but Sheila and Honor certainly pass — Sounds like a dime novel, this description of mine! I took one snap of three of them when they were looking, and one when they *weren't*. Then we put our suits back on, and had a picnic lunch on the sands — and lay about deliciously lazy — Mrs. Joseph went off fishing for an hour and a half — and when she came back we had to leave the enchanted island. Sheila and I hung on outside of the boat, and sang all the way home, and in this way I escaped feeling grim, although the Gloris II was tossing mightily —

1. Sheila Mathewson, d. 1964, married Major Sir John Child in 1933.

12th June 1929   "The Gables"[1]
                                                   Beaconsfield
                                                   Quebec

I am so excited I can hardly stand it now for Lawson has just telephoned me: I had a date for dinner with him to-night and he has just called up to ask if I wanted to go up in his *sea-plane* with him! —[2] Annie and Lesley are the only ones that know — here he is now!![3] Good-bye —

— — —

Last night was certainly a *red star* one for me — I never enjoyed anything as much. Lawson came for me about 6.30 — I said good-night to Aunt May and calmly went off as if I were just going out to dinner — We drove down in the car to Dorval, then took a put-put to Dorval Island where the plane is moored — It is a beautiful little sea-plane, silver with bright blue trimmings. There is a base there where six planes are moored, with a joint cottage on the island, and two men look after the "Baby II". When the plane was ready and warmed up, they rowed me out to it, I jumped into the front cockpit, donned aviator cap and goggles, adjusted the speaking tube and we were off! We passed over Pointe Claire and circled round the "old Homestead" and I saw Lesley standing on the porch at the Arthur's – then L. announced that he was taking me to see some cousins of his – the Fred Johnsons who have an island at Senneville – (the one where Flora Guest used to live). We landed on the water, taxied up to the island and paid a call – Then flew back at sunset time to Dorval – the Lake of Two Mountains was red with the reflecting sunset, and there was a lovely crescent moon – we went to the Dixie afterwards and to the "White House", a roadhouse for dinner – then I sprung the news to Aunt May who stood it pretty well –

1. The Gables was Huntly Drummond's summer house in Beaconsfield to the west of Montreal.

2. Lawson Williams, b. ca. 1907.

3. Jean Lesley (Les) Drummond, later Ross, d. 1980, Ginnie's cousin.

6th March 1931   Montreal

Monday night I went with Potty to hear the child violinist Yehudi Menuhin, and he was *wonderful* – [1] He played something from the New World Symphony – it was a lovely programme and very diversified.

1. "Potty" was a nickname for Pothier Doucet. Yehudi Menuhin, 1916–99, was a virtuoso violinist.

5th June 1931   5 St. Ronan's Terrace

                                                     New Haven, Conn. [1]

I love you so much – and miss you so much – but it's so much worse here when I haven't anything to do. You will have to stay with me lots in New York next year, or I *refuse* to go –

1. Ginnie was staying with her aunt, Alice Eliza Reynolds (Arlee), 1866–1954, head teacher of the Gateway School in New Haven, which Ginnie attended from 1921 to 1925.

14th October 1931   The A W A Club House
                                               353 West 57 Street
                                               New York City

Nothing very eventful happened in school —[1] Tamara's and my pantomime was pronounced as rotten, but I felt so punk I didn't care how rotten it was — The 'picnic' in Gellendré's class went off quite well — then some of us (not me, thank Heaven) had to tell about our fantasies — Barbara's was very good, and we are doing it for Monday.[2] The scene is laid in a deserted automat, early one morning, and I am to be the macaroni! It's like a "Silly Symphony" cartoon, and is lots of fun to do — I quite fancy myself as spaghetti — I went to my first Automat for lunch to-day with Miriam and Tamara — a filthy hole on 6th Ave. at 44th, but had a sandwich and cup of coffee for fifteen cents —

We had the violent Miss Graham this morning —[3]

1. Neighborhood Playhouse School of the Theatre, then in the Lower East Side of New York, where Ginnie studied acting and dance for a year.

2. Mr. Gellendré, drama teacher.

3. Martha Graham, 1894–1991, was a dancer, choreographer, and the founder of modern dance. For her involvement in the Neighborhood Playhouse, see Don McDonagh, *Martha Graham: A Biography* (New York: Praeger, 1973).

20th October 1931   New York City

Friday night Gertrude and Barbara and I had dinner together in the dining-room here, then I went to their room and Gert. fitted my *"costume"* —[1] For Miss Graham's we were given a small piece of drab woolen and out of that to make a pr. of tights — They are not only so tight that we can hardly move, and utterly revealing but *transparent* — this would not be so bad if there weren't several men in the class — but that's what we are to wear, so I'll wear them — *I* don't mind if no-one else does — over this goes a mud-colored crepe dress which we wear for Horst and Ballet.[2]

I went for my bracelet at Cartier's Saturday morning — paid them $4.00 for it and it broke again that afternoon — so I am going to wait and have it made flexible all over — It is a flexible bracelet, but doesn't flex!

1. Barbara Lee, later Harding, a.k.a. "Muffin."
2. Louis Horst, 1883–1964, composer, musical director of Graham's company.

22nd October 1931   New York City
We had practice for Martha Graham w. Gertrude Shurr in the afternoon,
and I got along much better which surprised both Shurr and me! especially
as I am *stiff* all over again – they say you stay stiff for months working
with Martha – This morning we began with Martha's class – the first
exercises we ever did I still do badly, but am apparently good in some as
Martha (Her Nibs) herself came over and complimented me!! After class
Miss Shurr said "Aren't you HAPPY Virginia – It isn't very often Martha
compliments anyone" – Later Mrs. Morganthau said she was talking to
Martha and M. said I was good (!) and *murmured* something about if I
improved a bit more she might have me take classes in the 2nd yr. group as
well!![1] Can you beat it? Of course I was too thrilled – Don't tell anybody
about the 2nd class business because it was only a vague murmur.

I came back to Earth in practice class for Louis as I hadn't prepared
anything for my rhythmics, in singing class because my voice cracked, and
in Diction class, when I read with a frog in my throat – ! –

1. Rita Morganthau, founder and director of Neighborhood Playhouse, 1928–63.

26th October 1931   N.Y.C.
We didn't reach New Haven until five minutes to one, and at one I was
supposed to leave for the game! I greeted Arlee, combed my hair, snatched
up a ham sandwich and dashed off with Maybelle Kennedy and a friend of
hers to the game – It was a grand game, but you know how I *love* football!
One of the Army men broke his neck – I haven't heard of his death yet,
but it was certain! Isn't that horrible?

That evening went on a party. . . . We got home about 3.30 a.m. and I
was glad to hit the hay – It was quite a gay evening, a little too collegiate for
me – but only one drunk on our party, and not nearly as much drunkenness
that night as at the game – I have never seen such a display as *that* was –

several hundred drunks, several dozen passed out cold! And this at 3 in the afternoon — were games like that before prohibition?

2nd November 1931   N.Y.C.

We had Martha this morning — I *love* her work, but have given up any idea of being in the advanced group, though it was encouraging that they let me try. We had an *awful* pantomime to do, and I was rotten! Then practice for Horst — I had to do a lyric to a Gavotte, but seem to be totally incapable of doing *anything* for that class — To-morrow Gertrude and I are doing a skit for Veazie that I thought of, and we worked out together — It's in the gay nineties sort of bicycle built for two business — hope she'll like it! We are supposed to hand in our fantasies to-morrow — I still haven't written mine! I have a lot of research to do for Miss Irene, we had our first lecture last Thursday — [1]

The homework is becoming more stupendous each day — I will have to stop going out altogether soon —

1. Irene Lewisohn, cofounder of Neighborhood Playhouse.

8th November 1931   N.Y.C.

To-night I have to make my tights, learn some verses from the Bible, prac-tise the emotions of a brakeman, and read a book on 18th Century Archi-tecture and Decoration for Miss Irene's lecture on Tuesday — The Junior Group is giving "The Masque of the Apple" for the Christmas Festival, and we have to do research for it.[1] The play is 18th Century english, and we are now singing folk-songs. How I *loathe* folk-songs, like "Derry down, derry — Ho, down, hay down" etc.

I think it is a good idea to cut Horst's class and concentrate more on Graham, because I would like more time to practise the exercises! and for Horst's class I do more worrying, and work less than you can imagine! How-ever I will give it a chance before I make up my mind.

1. James Rendel Harris, *The Masque of the Apple* (London: Longmans, 1920).

6th December 1931   N.Y.C.

Potty sent me *six orchids*, three mauve and three yellow – the most gorgeous array you have ever seen – !! I wore *one* to lunch with Djignite at the "Park Avenue" – quite the smartest place I've ever been – like a glorified "Boeuf sur le Toit" – thousands of mink coats and diamonds (talk about the depression) but of course you can always tell "kept women" these days – they are the only people left that can afford mink – We went shopping afterwards and I bought a much-needed girdle.

Got up this morning at 10, and had brunch with Bar – and the Gertrude – read, etc., and at 3 went to Martha Graham's dance recital – It was jammed and crowded, standing room only – most exciting! I am sorry to say the first 2 or 3 numbers, though interesting from my *student* point of view, didn't thrill me much, but the "Primitive Mysteries" with Martha and the group was *too wonderful* – how I wish you could have seen it! I have rarely *ever* heard such an enthusiastic audience – they cheered and yelled and stamped their feet!

10th December 1931   New York City

This morning we had a ghastly class with Martha – an exercise like running where you stay in the same place, just slide your feet back and forth back and forth – I rubbed a piece of skin off my foot – lord, it was agony! Then Martha came along and gave me a good slap on the stomach because I was sticking it out. Peggy, to improve matters said, "What's the matter Ginnie? You look as if you were going to cry!" I didn't mean to make all this sound *pathetic*, but just to show you how tactless these creatures are –

Barbara and I have been going to so many apartments, our heads are swimming – but the only suitable one is at the Beaux Arts at 307 E. 44th St – a service apt. – one biggish room, with a couple of *murphys* [single beds] (I can hear Boogie saying, "Stuart, what is a murphy?") that fold into the wall, a studio divan, a radio, 2 cupboards, a bathroom, a tiny kitchenette with frigidaire, stove and china – a good inexpensive restaurant across the street that will send up meals for .25 extra. The apt. is $80 a month – we get 2 weeks concession and the only bills would be electricity and laundry.

I think we are going to take this. 8 blocks from school — don't you think this is a good offer? I certainly do hate to pay out $66 a month here.

17th December 1931   Apt. 914
                                                                          307 E. 44th St. !
Here we are, all settled — It's perfectly grand! I am dying for you to see it — of course at the moment it's *slightly* messy, with bags in the middle of the floor, but we are all unpacked anyway —

Tuesday, the Demonstration went off very well — I sang in the chorus — was in *one* of the Ballet dances and in three things of Louis' — all *large* groups of course — the 2nd year girls were marvellous —

O it's such fun being out of the American Wench Club, and having our own apartment —

19th December 1931   New York
We have had the most marvellous time in our new apt. I am dying to tell you all about it — We have a very comfortable studio bed that you could stay in when you are here — that is if you could put your clothes under the bed — there is no space left for toilet things or underclothes but lots of hangers and room in the cupboards —

Louis Horst is playing for *something* (God knows what) at His Majesty's Theatre in Montreal all next week! The other day M. Graham told me that my movement was good, but I needed *ten* times more strength and whosis behind it — yesterday she picked on me in every exercise, but I tell myself it is because she is anxious that I improve the whosis!

I was considering losing my breakfast yesterday, during class (I had a decidedly punk feeling in my interior) when Martha came along and slapped me in the middle — She didn't know how near she came to having my breakfast —

I am so thrilled at the thought of being with you in four days!!! The train (Montrealer) leaves the Penn. Station at 9.05, so I will be there at 8.45 when it gets in.

26th January 1932   New York

We had Louis and Veazie to-day. Afterwards there was a meeting of the Neighbourhood Playhouse Associates Inc. and Miss McCoy asked Muffin and me to attend. It was too ghastly. Judge Crane, the District Attorney, gave a little speech — You *should* have heard it! He said that they should — apart from every cultural requirement which a student should fill on entering the Playhouse — that they should be required to sign a pledge to the effect that they would never under any circumstances appear in a degrading, demoralising, or lascivious play — after they left the Playhouse!!!!! — Mary Tarcai (who had stayed on account of the tea) murmured to me "What has this got to do with sandwiches?". Then a *foul* woman spoke on the suffragist movement and women's rights — The third speech was going to be on prohibition, so I grabbed my sandwiches and fled —

31st January 1932   Montavis[1]
                                                               70 Chestnut Street
                                                               West Haven
                                                               Connecticut

Thursday did my emotional scene for Mrs. Veazie, where I was supposed to let *myself go* and break down — I got through all-right as far as memorizing and Mrs. V. said my voice and my intelligent reading of the play were about best in class, but I showed *absolutely no emotion* — "I am afraid you are inhibited, Ginnie" — I am so *sick* of being told that — what the *Hell* do they want me to do about it — When I was younger my emotion usually got the better of me in a part — now all these ye-ahs I have endeavoured to use control and restraint — and now I have to begin all over again!

1. The home of Madeleine Nason née Reynolds, 1876–1978, Ginnie's aunt.

11th March 1932   New York

I had to do an eccentric characterization for class the other day — a dumb mannequin with no palate and a peculiar facial tic, and they tell me I had

Gellendré roaring — so I felt quite proud — I feel have done quite a lot this week, n'est-ce pas? Thursday Martha had us to hip-swings for ages and I was the only one that stuck to it —

21st March 1932   New York

Thanks so much for your letter, Daddy — I ordered a berth for the midnight train Friday — lower 7 — in car K35 — "good old car K-35" — Only four more days and I'll be boarding the train. I have two week's work in that four days, hope I get it done somehow —

How late can one wear *velvet* and not be declassée? 'cause I wondered if I could wear my black velvet evening dress while there? Anyway, I'll bring the brown velvet suit and fur coat home for keeps — I may have to bring trunk — but I hope not —

13th April 1932   New York

Leslie Banks lectured to us yesterday and chatted with us, and made us feel how far away we were from Broadway and the actual theatre —[1] To-morrow we are to have Robert Edmond-Jones and there is a sign on the board that we should have some intelligent questions prepared, to ask him![2]

Monday afternoon [the students] repeated the Nursery Maid for the unemployed — not for the *benefit* of the unemployed, but they *actually invited* the unemployed!!! Can you imagine a lot of hungry mokes coming in to see a play about *nuns* — of course hardly anyone came! — I think this was about — well — I am speechless.

1. Leslie J. Banks, 1890–1952, English actor.

2. Robert Edmond Jones, 1887–1954, American writer, lecturer, director, and set designer.

21st April 1932   New York

The Demonstration comes off the 18, 19 and 20th I think — Then I'll have *ten whole* days before my leave is up!! Martha Graham wants to give a one-hour-a-day class those ten days at about a dollar per — Do you think that would be a good idea? I mean, for me to join the class?

26th April 1932   New York

Last night worked 'til six — we are now getting our teeth into "From Morn to Midnight" —[1] I am an *elderly, drunken prostitute* — what do you think of your little daughter doing that? Unfortunately I have to *cry* in the scene, so far I haven't been able to shed a tear — I can see by the look in Gellendré's eye, that if I don't get the old mood soon, he'll begin to get annoyed — but he likes my characterization.

There are three men in the scene — two of them are *nuts* (one 6 ft.4, the other about 6 ft.2), the third (Herbie) is quite nice — the Gertrude just beams at him, and hangs around all the time. It's a scream! Last night Bonnie, Teddy, Tamara, Gertrude, Muffin, Herbie and I went to the *Bowery* in search of ideas and atmosphere for our Salvation Army scene — We went to a mission where a toothless man tried to induce the poor devils there to confess their sins. Afterwards we walked into a get-together and some tough asked me if I was from the South! and I had to shake hands with him!

1. George Kaiser, *From Morn to Midnight*, trans. Ashley Dukes (New York: Brentano's, ca. 1922).

8th March 1933   Montreal

I was asked to a dinner to meet V. Sackville-West, but of course refused —[1]
I think it sounds fun, but naturally would rather go to Ivry —[2]

1. Vita Sackville-West, 1892–1962, English poet and novelist.
2. Ivry: Huntly Drummond's estate in the Laurentian Mountains north of Montreal.

25th May 1934   R.M.S. Duchess of York

                                 Canadian Pacific Steamship Lines

Arose at seven-fifteen this morning, breakfast w. Hunt at 8, and left w. Hunt in the Linc[oln] at 1/4 to 9 – felt rather grand rolling up to the gang-plank, donned in good clothes, complete with corsage of 3 orchids (gift of Mr. Drummond – he also sent some lovely pink roses). Received *six* gardenias from Potty, who was terrified they didn't arrive so I have written to him that they *did*.

Potty saw me off, also Haden Wallis, Eric, and Robin (who looked like he had lost his last friend, so he didn't stay very long).[1] Pot and Robin met for the first time, and looked each other over.

When the boat tooted and the see-ers off had to go on the dock, Huntly and Eric stood around and waited. I felt pretty grim – everyone was throwing confetti and streamers and screaming cheery nothings, and an awful band played. I felt like Yoshe Kalb in the midst of it all, only I didn't even have my Bible with me to read – [2] We finally got under way and I paid 3 calls on the head steward in order to get a snappy table, but he was never there – so I got my deck-chair and unpacked my clothes and got my flowers fixed.

Thank you ever so much for the beautiful roses, Boogie darling – it was adorable of you. Besides the flowers from you, Hunt and Pot, I had some lovely sweet peas from Mary Gordon, a box from *Brian* (!) and a large box of American beauties [roses] with no card enclosed (!?) – have you any *idea*??

I went down to lunch at 1 and the dumb cluck had put me at a table by myself – so I sat among my Amer. Beauties with the orchids (alone in my glory) but the head steward says he will put me with some people that get on at Quebec –

Will mail you a letter when the boat reaches England –

1. Eric Millar, d. 1962, Ginnie's Canadian cousin by marriage.

2. Yoshe Kalb is the eponymous hero of Israel in Joshua Singer's Yiddish novel, on which the 1937 Broadway play by Fritz Block was based.

1st June 1934   R.M.S. Duchess of York

We are going up the Clyde now — beautiful mountains and green fields in the hazy mist of a glorious afternoon — It's warm and sunny and there are several hundred gulls following our ship (so they must have found out it isn't a Scotch ship!). I have decided to stay on until Liverpool for several reasons —

a) everyone seems to be doing it

b) as things have turned out, it wouldn't be convenient. We would have to get off on a tender, go into Greenock — then take a short train ride into Glasgow and wait around for hours — and we will be in Liverpool to-morrow morning and London in the early afternoon. I'll send B.J. a telegram that I am arriving to-morrow afternoon.[1] It's kinda mouldy to turn up in London on Saturday, but can't be helped!

I have had quite a good trip on the whole — Friday and Saturday (the first 2 days) were glorious as far as the weather was concerned — I sat in a deck-chair and read most of the time — read the April and May Theatre Arts from cover to cover, and "Princess by Proxy" (given to me by Bill McGregor), and have started "Ancient Art" —[2]

I sat at the table with the doctor (Mellin's baby food, scotch, rather sweet), Mr. A.I. Eastwood (Bertie) — english, fat, fifty, jovial, and a Mr. and Mrs. Kiernan from Australia. The Australian was a bit *tough* but amusing — My beautiful American beauties from unknown admirer lasted for days and adorned our table.

By Sunday it was cold — bitter in fact — fog and raining and too cold to stay long outside. Monday we stayed *still* most of the day — there was a *heavy* fog and we were in the iceberg region (glad you didn't know this!!) — so we *crawled* along, if at all. Played bridge most of the day — I slept until twelve nearly every morning, the stewardess would come and waken me — then after dressing I would do a spot of walking, and go down to lunch. Read or talk or play teck dennis (I mean deck tennis) and shuffleboard in the afternoon — another walk — bath and dressing at 6.30 — would meet in the bar at 7.15 for the first cocktail of the day — then to dinner — movies nearly every night, also dancing (and *what* dancing — no-one on a boat can *ever* dance).

Do you know, I haven't been seasick at all — isn't that marvellous?? I haven't felt quite my gay self, a bit groggy and a trifled bored and depressed, but never felt a qualm once — thank heaven for that. I didn't miss going to a single meal — except breakfast, I missed that entirely.

Last night at 9 o'clock it was still broad day-light. We sat in the back of the boat for a while and watched the sunset. They had the ship's concert at 9 but we decided not to go. I went (with my 4 buddies) down to Tourist 3rd where we had a few drinks, watched a female tap-dancing, did a little Community Singing, etc., then returned to 1st class to dance. When the dancing stopped at 1, we pulled a piano into the smoke-room, and a woman played on the piano. She had a darn good voice too. I did an *imitation* of the terrible tap-dancer, and later a rumba — then people came oozing in and we sang and hopped about and had quite a grand time — got to bed at 3 —

Up at 11 — landing cards, tickets, etc. Am going up to London with Mr. Burrows — ³ It will be nice not having to muck about alone. I think we get in at 8 and leave for London at 10.

1. Mrs. Bulkeley-Johnson, Ginnie's London chaperone.
2. Roland Pertwee, *Princess by Proxy* (Boston: Houghton Mifflin, 1934).
3. Leslie Burrows, from Ottawa, a fellow passenger on the *Duchess of York*.

5th June 1934   7 Chesham Place
                                                London S.W.1.
                                                Sloane 4200

I thought I would wait two or three days before writing to you, in order to know a little more where I was at and be able to tell you. As I said before the Duchess was delayed on account of hanging about in the fog, so it was 12 o'clock Saturday before we reached Liverpool.

I was greeted by Claire, the maid, who said B.J. was quite ill — went in to see her and she looked like death — she has had terrible arthritis and had an operation on her knee a week ago — she said something to the effect that she would have told me not to come, but I was already on my way! I felt *very* bedraggled, hot, and a little lonely at this point — however I know B.J. now, and those things don't affect me in the least —

After I had unpacked all my things and bathed and dressed I felt worlds better. The maid ran my bath, and asked me where my sponges were, so I said I had left them on the boat!

There is another girl staying here – Jane Maitland – she's about medium height, dark, not pretty but nice-looking, *very* nice – gets her clothes at Mainbocher's –[1] Her mother and father live in Paris, and she has lived in France nearly all her life – doesn't know much about England – went to an American girls' school in Lausanne and liked them very much – adores France and doesn't like games. I think we're soul-mates. She is a deb. – is having a dance, being presented – the whole works –

Claire, the old faithful maid, is still here – she's perfectly grand. Elizabeth seems to be Jane's and my maid. Anyway she might as well be – she's Scotch, grand sense of humor, perfectly *sweet*, so I almost feel as if Janet were along! – there are 3 or 4 others but I don't know who's who –

I am going to leave my cards at the Embassy this afternoon – if I can get Jane to go with me – and then will go about this lunch doings – also will write to Mrs. Kerr – have sent letter to Ann's cousin. B.J. says I can have people whenever I like – and to tea, without notice.

1. Mainbocher was an American couturier living in Paris, among whose clients was to be the Duchess of Windsor.

10th June 1934   London S.W.1.

After I wrote to you on Wed. Jane went with me to the Embassy, where I left cards (after first going to the wrong place) – then went with her to buy some gramophone records – In the evening went out with Leslie – we had a snack at the "Blue Train" (where I *think* I saw Mary Bingham, but couldn't swear to it). Then on to see Yvonne Printemps in Noel Coward's "Conversation Piece" – just loved it, although it was a bit "Bitter-sweet-y" at times – it was marvellous to watch Printemps acting – she has more charm and personality than ten other actresses put together.[1] We went to the Savoy Grill for dinner afterwards, then danced in the big room. It being Derby night, we couldn't get a table in the main room. It was jammed –

very gay and very smart. English (rather, London, women) are *so* much smarter than they used to be —

1. Yvonne Printemps, 1895–1977, French actor and singer.

6th June 1935   St. James's Palace Chambers
                                                        22 Ryder Street
                                                        St. James's
                                                        London S.W.1.

Thursday morning Lois and I went to the Dress Rehearsal of the "Trooping of the Colour" at the Horse Guards' Parade —[1] Sheila gave us two seats — so we three flipped coins, and Margie lost.[2] It was a marvellous sight, as you can well imagine — and we had splendid seats right in the middle.

Lady Kindersley gave Lois 3 seats for a charity Matinée Thursday afternoon — she barged off with Nan McGowan to Ranelagh so Billy, Margie and I went.[3] Several good artists performed, and I enjoyed it a lot. The Duchess of York was sitting in a box and as we were in the dress circle, we could see her very well.[4]

After the theatre, I dashed back here as I had asked Jock and Betty Pearson to come in for a drink.[5] Then Ronnie Greville came to see Margie, Lois returned with Nan and some friends, Hazim Sise blew in (I ran into him at the Trooping) also Bill McGowan, etc. etc. — we could hardly move in this little room —[6] The Pearsons insisted I come and dine with them, I was feeling a bit tired, but they insisted so, that I decided *not* to be sensible and went. Got all dolled up in the sequins and dashed to their house for dinner at eight. There were just the four of us — the fourth being Gerald Potter, a cousin of Betty's — We had a delicious dinner complete with caviar and champagne — and then went to the Hungaria, which was heaps of fun — Who should be sitting at the next table to us but *Carol* who was with his brother and some female.[7] It was rather funny, considering I was with his best friends, he looked a bit surprised — At the next table H.R.H. "Hank" was sitting with a large party — behind us a party including Prince Youssoupoff so we had lots of royalty all around us.[8] The Kitzbühel singers were grand and yodelled *beautifully*, and sang and danced – and everyone entered into the spirit and had a grand time. We went on to the Florida later and were joined for a while by Carol –

I went off for a short week-end on Saturday – Gerald Potter asked me to go down to Warsash, and go sailing. I was so thrilled to be going to the country. Jock and Betty Pearson drove me down Saturday morning in their high-powered speedy, noisy, Invicta. It's *low* and *sporty* – so sporty that the person sitting on the back seat, has the most comfortable position of sitting *higher* than the windshield – so that I spent most of the time all tied up in knots, trying not to get my head blown off. It was a trifle uncomfortable, but I was so thrilled to be dashing to the country I didn't mind, and it certainly blew the cobwebs away!

We arrived at Warsash about 2.30 and found a very *hungry* Gerald, so were we all, so we dashed in and had a gin and tonic and a good cold lunch – lobster, steak and kidney pie, and gooseberries – P'raps I better do a little explaining here – Warsash is opposite Cowes, about 12 miles from Southampton – and we stayed at the Household Brigade Yacht Club, where Gerald spends all his spare time, as he is a very keen skipper and has a nice boat by name "Carmela" – I don't know what class, as I only saw her in the distance, but I should say she was about mid-way between the "Britannia" and the "Guppy"! or a sort of glorified Altair would p'raps be a better description – G. himself is in the Grenadier Guards – is about *28 or 30 – BIG* – (six ft.) *blonde* with GLASSES – and SMOKES CIGARS (all the time – can you *bear* it?) He is very nice and very amusing and doesn't seem "waffle-waffle" after you get over the shock of cigar plus glasses – really quite good-looking –

Well after we had our lunch we went sailing. Gerald had hired a dinghy for the afternoon, as the Carmela was having something done to the rudder – It was a glorious sunny afternoon, I wanted to shout for joy at the thought of sailing – There was quite a stiff breeze, and rather a choppy sea – and we *bounced* gaily along in the funny tug-like boat with such a pretentious cabin – and only a mainsail and small jib. Betty was the skipper, and Jock was part of a most difficult crew that would never obey orders – Gerald went "below" to take a snooze, and said – "Sail her over to Cowes, and we'll go in and have a drink at the Squadron" –9 We were going along beautifully when all of a sudden bump-bumpety-bump and we were aground on the "Brambles" – the Brambles being a sand-bar in the middle of the bay – and apparently the joke of the Solent, as so many *nuts* have run aground (including the Aquitania last week) Gerald roused himself from his slumbers, and slowly took off his shoes – I thought "O lordy, I hope we don't have another Huntly-Altair episode!" – But he then went into the briny wearing grey flannel trousers, yachting blazer, and skipper's natty hatting. He pushed and pushed but the fat, stubborn little boat wouldn't budge – so Jock had to go in and help – He had on a grey flannel suiting, all he had for the whole week-end, so he obviously couldn't get it wet – so he jumped in the briny in the most pansy-looking white knitted silk underwear, with little short sleeves! I wish you could have seen Gerald wandering around up to his waist (he looked like the animal that came up out of the sea, and ate all the provisions) – and large liners going by quite close to us! After more heaving and hauling we were finally off, and got back to the Club about 6.30 – Jock and Betty went off to the Inn, where they were staying; I had a room in a separate bldg. of the Guards Yacht Club, a sort of segregated female place, and eminently respectable. Some poor woman couldn't find her room so let her dress in mine. It took me 20 minutes to comb my hair as it was a mass of corkscrews – then a good hot bath and dressed –

About 7.15 we all went over to have cocktails at "The Pink Cottage" where some friends of Gerald's and the Pearsons live, Mr. and Mrs. Perry-Knox-Gore, also Mr. and Mrs. Robin Sinclair and some other man.[10] Later the nine of us dined with G. at the H.B.Y.C. – then tore over to Portsmouth where we sat in boxes at the "Coliseum", and saw a rather tough vaudeville – then to an amusement park at Southsea, where we rode in little cars that bump, etc. and also danced for a while.[11] Back about one, Gerald cooked some sausages and bacon for me, as all the servants had gone to bed – Then to bed, where I slept soundly until 9.30 –

Breakfasted alone in the Clubhouse, as Gerald was up early to get the Carmela out of the yards and anchor her off the Clubhouse – Left Warsash by eleven, and drove in his high-powered Lagonda back to London, where we lunched at the Guards Club – then he brought me back here, as he had to go on parade, and then drive back to Warsash to take the boat to Burnham-on-Crouch, as he is racing her from there to Heligoland (Germany). I wrote letters all Sunday afternoon. . . . and to see Noel Coward in "Scoundrel", the new movie.

Monday morning Lois and Margie went to the Trooping of the Colour (I lost when we flipped coins – we only had 2 tickets). I wandered down to the Mall about twelve – just as the Queen and Royal Family all passed by – so pushed my way along, and had a front line view of the Procession which passed down the Mall after "Trooping" – First the Band of the Life Guards, on horseback – then the Life Guards – all in their glorious shining armor, on black horses – then regiments of Coldstream and Grenadier soldiers, behind them the bands of the Irish Guards and Scots Guards playing lustily on the bagpipes. Even this would have been thrilling enough for me, but behind the bands rode the King, and at this point I felt I wanted to *sob*![12] He looked so old, but somehow perfectly thrilling to see the old man riding. Behind the King rode all the sons in their different uniforms – I could see their faces plainly as I was so near to them – and then more soldiers, and foreign officers in uniform – It was the most *glorious* parade I have ever seen in my life, I kept thinking of you Boogie darling – because it was all so *dramatic*, and thought how we would probably have clung to each other and sobbed if you had been there with me!

Wednesday was Derby Day – we originally planned to go with Ronnie Gaunt (beau of Margie's) who was taking all 3 of us, then the Leslie Hasletts joined the party and George Drew – Malcolm was to have come, but had to have a board meeting. We went out by train – at first it poured (it always does when I go to the races) but cleared off after a while. It is quite worth seeing as it is so *amazing* – the gypsies, the beggars, the royal family, the choc-bars, the stands, the people in top-hats, the Costermongers – and the biggest crowd you can possibly imagine. I lost on every race, but fortunately didn't put up much money!

We were back in town by 6 and had some hot tea and toast to revive us. I went out with Gerald Potter that evening, having received a telegram from him the day before that he would come up from Burnham-on-Crouch if I would dine with him Wed. night. We had quick dinner, and then to "Hervey House" with Fay Compton and Gertrude Lawrence – most disappointing, and as I had *chosen* it, I felt rather apologetic.[13] We both decided it was well-acted, but uninteresting and all about nothing. On to the Berkeley [Hotel] which was jammed owing to Derby night, but we managed to get a good table. Everybody in the world was there, and it was lots of fun — I just happened to run into masses of people I knew and G. asked if there was anyone I *didn't* know, as he would try to arrange an introduction. We had a good supper, and danced, and cracked a couple (!) of champagne bottles. Went to the Florida later which was even more crowded — all the people I hadn't already seen — and there we stayed until five having a perfectly *grand* time.

The "Trio" lunched with Aunt Bessie [today] at the Carlton, plus Aunt Esther and Mrs. Wilson.[14] When I returned the room was full of masses of people as usual — the telephone rings incessantly, and people are always popping in and out. The porter told Malcolm that he had never known people to have so many visitors! All the people in this bldg. down to the page (age 10) seem to be very amused — and when any young man turns up they say something like "Miss Rawlings is out, but Miss O'Brien and Miss Reynolds are there"! I don't think I have ever had so much fun in my whole life. Lois and Margie are *so* easy to get along with, and Margie is one of the sweetest people I have *ever known.*

About plans: the two gad-abouts are rather vague but we shall certainly be here until July 1st at least — Why don't you come over sometime the first part of July — I do hope Gerald remembers he asked me to see the Naval Review at Spithead aboard his boat — and I will get you an invitation too — I am *sure* he would love to have you, and Hunt too, if he has any room — It's going to be a marvellous sight, I should think; so it would be fun to go — and I shall do a little hinting to make sure of the invitation, when he returns from Germany — We might stay on here a week or so — and then go on that August Cruise to Northern Capitals and Russia — or a little motoring in the Tyrol with the Bentley. Do you think my suggestions are any good?

1. Lois O'Brien, later Gillespie, contemporary from Montreal.

2. Margaret Rawlings, later Hart, contemporary from Montreal.

3. Lady Kindersley née Nancy Farnsworth Boyd, d. 1977, was from Toronto. Nan Mc-

Gowan, later Daly, daughter of the first Baron McGowan, was found murdered at her home in Witney, Oxfordshire, in 1976. William Johnstone McGowan, b. 1909, was the second son of the first Baron McGowan.

4. Lady Elizabeth Bowes-Lyon, 1900–2001, the Duchess of York from 1923, later queen (1937–52) and Queen Mother (1952–2001).

5. Jock Pearson, b. 1894, was a financier and Royal Air Force officer. Bettine (Betty) Mary Pearson née Potter, 1905–84, Gerald's cousin, married 1) Jock Pearson, 2) Baron William Quarles van Ufford, and 3) Count Leopold van Limburg Stirum.

6. Ronald Greville, 1912–87, was from 1959 the fourth Baron Greville. In spite of his personal impecuniosity, he was a friend of Edward VII and was married to the heiress of a brewing fortune.

7. Carol Arthur Fellowes, 1896–1988, was the fourth Baron Ailwyn from 1976. From 1930 to 1952 he was a land agent for the Earl and Countess of Stafford.

8. H.R.H.: Prince Henry, 1900–1974, Duke of Gloucester from 1928.

9. The Royal Yacht Squadron is a yachting club founded in 1815 and based in Cowes on the Isle of Wight, where a major yachting regatta takes place annually.

10. Alexander Robert (Robin) Sinclair, 1901–72, was a businessman and yachtsman. Vera Mabel Sinclair née Baxendale, 1907–81, was a staff member at the Ministry of Agriculture from 1941 to 1945.

11. H.B.Y.C.: the Household Brigade Yacht Club.

12. George V, 1865–1936, reigned from 1910 to 1936.

13. *Hervey House*: unpublished play by the American actor and playwright Jane Cowl, alias C. R. Avery. This performance was directed by Tyrone Guthrie. Fay Compton, 1894–1978, was an English actor. Gertrude Lawrence, 1898–1952, was an English actor and dancer.

14. Elizabeth (Bessie) Drummond née Dowling, Ginnie's aunt, d. 1951.

7th March 1936[1]   *Chesterfield Court*
                                                          Curzon Street
                                                          London

Darling Ginnie,

Under separate cover I have sent you several pictures and press clippings which I hope will arrive by Monday or Tuesday and amuse you and Gerald.

Of course no one can, or could, or would, ever take your place with me. That is final, and there is even a little grim satisfaction in the thought that in the matter of daughters I have had 100% satisfaction. Perhaps sometimes .05% off for crying when people spoke to you and, lately, lying in bed beyond the decent hour for arising. But the rest is par excellence. I expected and demanded a charming and lovely daughter full of understanding and I got it. I also think I have attained excellent results in a son-in-law. Somehow I can't think of Gerald as a "son-in-law" – but just a very nice person who has chosen you as comrade. God knows I don't blame him. I am not jealous – not yet and God forbid that I lose my sense of humour to that extent, ever – so all is well.

The Times, Daily Mirror, Daily Telegraph, Daily Express, Daily Chronicle all had something. I bought several of each. I have <u>dozens,</u> literally, of photographs and much to his horror Moky discovered he had, under the influence of champagne ordered nearly £2 worth of photographs.[2] As he has to be careful, I think he's regretted it. I bought half of them from him. The Kensington and Portman Press Agencies will be able to live some time on my expenditures.

1. Written following Ginnie and Gerald's wedding at the Guards Chapel, London, on 5 March 1936.

2. Maurice (Moky) Bisdom van Cattenbroek, b. ca. 1880, a Dutchman resident in France.

7th March 1936   Elysée Park Hotel
                             2 Rond Point-des Champs-Elysées
                             Paris

Many thanks for your telegram which was handed to me when we arrived last night. The address:

Reisch Hotel
Kitzbühel-Tirol
Austria

(in case it might have been wrong in the telegram). I am not sure how Reisch is spelt. I do hope that's right – We will be there ten days or so, and then come back to this hotel (as we are leaving our extra bags here) so please write here too!

Well, to begin from the beginning, *we* thought it was a lovely wedding – and hope you did too – Actually we both *even* enjoyed it immensely, and had fun discussing it afterwards – You and Daddy looked simply GRAND, and I felt so proud of you – you were both so sweet too, and it must have been very difficult when there were so many people that you didn't know – Please give my love to darling Buncle, I will write him from Austria.[1]

I meant to telephone you in the morning, but I got up so late I didn't have time – Gerald got up early to put "Bollicky Bill" on the cargo steamer, and came back bringing me masses of papers.[2] Did you see the pictures in the "Daily Express", "Daily Sketch" and "Daily Mirror" – adorable of Roona weren't they?[3] I do hope you saw them all. We bought a Times on the way to the boat – and G. got a cabin – Everybody murmured "bride and groom" whenever they saw us – all rather fun really –

Arrived here about 6.30 – I was very proud of finding the way from St. Denis to this hotel. We have a lovely bed-sitting-room and bath (w. yellow tub!) overlooking Rond-Point and les Champs-Elysées. We had a rest – and bath – and went to Cheval Pil for dinner about 9 – then wandered up and down the Champs –

Slept late this morning, how marvellous it was not to have anything to do – The Paris Daily Mail had some headlines about us – U.S. Bride marries Guards officer, etc. I will cut it out, and keep it to show you – on second thoughts I'll send it on, but do keep it for me, please – (I love the part about the franc – and the dollar!)

1. Buncle: a nickname for Huntly Drummond.

2. Bollicky Bill: Gerald's Lagonda car.

3. Roona Fidelity Sinclair, 1932–89, later Ernle Money-Kyrle, was the honorary secretary of the Anglo-Catholic Charismatic Society of Great Britain and a member of the General Synod of the Church of England. Roona had been a bridesmaid at Ginnie and Gerald's wedding.

10th March 1936   *Bank of Montreal*
                                                      9 Waterloo Place
                                                      London

Have hired Hilda Lovejoy to be a parlour housemaid – no work below stairs, all cleaning above stairs and silver and to clean her own room. She will take Hettie in her room until she can become Mrs. Fisher.[1] Hettie will do all work except cooking below stairs, clean the stairs and the front steps and the cook's room! Hilda will help wait on the table when necessary and when Fisher has his day out.[2] Now for a cook!

I called Mrs. Arbuthnot where Hilda lives and she said she was very good and brought excellent references with her when she came. She has to come on the 17th so she will have to be paid from that time with something for living out. That is only two weeks. I will pay her. It won't be serious — wages £1 a week. I can put her to work in the house. Hilda's family lives on the Harpsden Road at Henley-on-Thames on the way to the Cokes.[3] Isn't that absurd?

Everyone in London seems excited about the Rhine business and the French are in a jitter as always.

1. Hettie Baxter, the kitchen maid.

2. Kenneth Fisher, Gerald's soldier-servant in the Grenadier Guards.

3. Dorothea Coke, author of *The Last Elizabethan: Sir John Coke, 1563–1644* (London: John Murray, 1937).

11th March 1936   *Bank of Montreal*
                                                        London

News bulletin: —

The wedding is "all over town" in the News reels. Ronnie Gaunt saw it in the Plaza. The Potters in the Curzon. I'm in the news one in Piccadilly Circus.

We went to the Nicholsons to lunch in Portland Place, marvellous flat, huge rooms, 12 people — most interesting. I sat beside a Mr. Brenton, friend of Gerald's mother and Lady McGrigor and said they were very charming![1] I told him that Gerald was the same. On the other side of me was the Archbishop of London.[2] It was amusing because the Duke of Atholl was there telling naughty stories.[3] "His Reverence" went early and the D. of Atholl said I hope I didn't drive him away. One of the stories was about <u>mother's milk</u>. "It was the best for three reasons. It's cheapest, it lasted over the week-end and the cat couldn't get at it."

I don't think the much vaunted hospitality of the Americans is any more to evidence than in England. No one could be nicer than people have been here, I must say.

1. Lady McGrigor née Amabel Somers Cocks, d. 1946.

2. Bougie probably met the Venerable Ernest Sharpe, 1867–1949, archdeacon of London 1930–47. The post of archbishop of London does not exist.

3. John George Stewart-Murray, 1871–1942, the eighth Duke of Atholl, honorary colonel Third Battalion Black Watch, and member of Parliament for West Perthshire 1910–17.

16th March 1936

Chesterfield Court
1 Chesterfield Gardens
Mayfair
London W.1.

Have sorted the linen with McNamara and copied it in the linen book purchased by McN. and locked it up.[1] Have hired a cook housekeeper, settled, Irish, good references, named <u>Flood</u>, so that the staff is now complete. She can also get us sweepstake tickets whenever we want them! Her nephew is in the know. I have always wanted a cook who could buy sweepstake tickets. Seriously, I interviewed four and chose this one on the strong recommendation of the Regina Agency. As they sent me others and said this one was the best, and as she was supposed to be capable of cooking almost anything and was less a toothless hag than the others and struck a pleasanter chord in me, I took her. I hope I haven't made a mistake. I submitted the accumulated evidence to the others, and we all agreed that this one seemed the best. She asked £75 but I got her down to £70. That is about $30.00 a month for a good cook. I don't think you can get one for less. They ask £90 and £100 at Jacksons. She was in one place five years and says she hates to change. I will pay her from the 23rd. She is free now.

You two have been in all the Gaumont-British News reels.[2] Very amusing. Have ordered the wedding pictures — only two were good and they will revamp the group.

1. McNamara (who was always referred to by a surname only), domestic factotum, previously Gerald Potter's housekeeper.

2. Footage of the Potter wedding on Gaumont British Newsreel still exists and is replicated on video, a copy of which is in the editor's possession; the original belongs to Reuters Television Library.

20th March 1936   *London W.1.*

I am now completely in the hands of your future staff. They were all there – and all exceedingly shy of each other, and being introduced and whipped into shape by McNamara and Mrs. Wallace. They went into a huddle when they saw Mrs. Flood. I said "Is there anything the matter with her?" and they said no, and then after a pause – "Well, it is better for a young couple to have someone like her". By that I gathered that in one swift glance they had decided that she knows her own mind, and no mistakes. She looked all over the kitchen flat, and announced that she was satisfied.

Fisher was also very lordly and spoke of Hettie as "My young lady". He wants to sleep on the top floor. They all want to go in Monday and get everything cleaned up and I am going to try to accommodate them. Hilda was scrubbing floors – for the time being. Fisher will sleep in the servants hall to look after the things which are now down on that floor (presents, etc.). I think, also, that I had better keep the cook away until everything is ready. I will pay her board – her pay begins on Monday anyhow. I will manage somehow. To-morrow morning, at 10.30, I am going out with Flood to buy kitchen utensils. Then this afternoon someone from Vancouver at Mrs. B.J.'s, where I was bidden to tea, said that several doctors had said that aluminium cooking things gave you <u>rheumatism</u> and that the said aluminium was very dangerous! Good God, I feel perfectly helpless with all these conflicting culinary emotions.

Tuesday, we went out in a Daimler to Hartwell.[1] Aunt Mobs treated us to lunch and then we went out to her house to tea. It looks charming and she has made a good job of it, though where she is going to put Gerald's pictures, heaven only knows.

---

1. Hartwell House in Aylesbury, Buckinghamshire, was a sixteenth- and eighteenth-century home owned by the Lee family for 350 years and sold in 1938. Hartwell had been the seat of Louis XVIII's court-in-exile from 1809 to 1814. Both Gerald Potter and Betty Pearson claimed to have seen the king's ghost, which reputedly haunts the house. Gerald was most unnerved when he found himself billeted at Hartwell in the blackout during the war. Mabel (Mobs) Lee, d. 1948, Gerald's aunt, lived in the house as a widow for twenty-five years but by 1936 had moved out to the neighboring village of Whitchurch.

25th March 1936   *London W.1.*

Your staff is all in. McNamara has been in the seventh heaven. As soon as the Wallaces got out, she reigned supreme, anyhow for a day – Mrs. Flood and I spent 2 1/2 hours – I was about to write years! – in Selfridge's buying kitchen furniture and utensils. They all came today and she is now happy. It certainly seems a happy household as the young ones were singing as I went in today. I have made one faux pas! I bought servants' blankets and then found some in a box, but I will change them for some other things which will be needed. They were all clamouring for blankets and I rushed off to satisfy them.

Mrs. Flood is very nice so far – clean and quite good looking with white hair (bobbed), positively classic features, a little like Julia, only blue eyes and smaller.[1] I have an awful feeling that they think I am "funny". But I am perfectly at home in the servants' halls, having been your maid for many years!

The servants' rooms had to have linoleum for cleanliness and looks. The floors were impossible. If these things are not approved I shall be glad to contribute them to the house. But I couldn't <u>wait</u> so took the responsibility.

1. Lady Drummond née Julia Parker Hamilton, d. 1942.

1st May 1936   32 Onslow Square
                                                  London S.W.7.
                                                  KEN. 8527

It was *perfectly horrible* having to say good-bye to you. I had dreaded it for so long, that I thought I would behave better when the moment came – however as usual, I was quite unable to check the *overflow* inside me. You, as usual, behaved marvellously, but then you always stand up to any occasion. Gerald and I both walked solemnly off and didn't speak until we were on the dock and saw you – He told me afterwards that he hadn't wanted to cry in years, but he did at that moment. It is so grand to have a husband that has sense enough to realize what a 'wonderful woman' you are (those were his words). We could see you waving until the boat turned and you were out of sight – o lordy, lordy, how I hated to see you go away – We drove practically in silence most of the way home –

We arrived home, rather weary, about 10.30 to find the Honorable Kenneth Fisher still not in, and all the servants waiting up for him! So Gerald sent them to bed — I told him about Hettie, etc. (what I had told you) but he said he couldn't sack his soldier because he had thrown over the kitchen-maid — however later something happened to enable him to do it — the jist [*sic*] of this is that the reign of the Great Fisher is *OVER*. Je me hâte de te le dire —[1] It happened Thursday about 11.15 just as we were going to bed, a faint tap was heard on the door and Lily said "Here is the key to the wine-cellar sir, Fisher left it in the door" —[2] Gerald went down to see if anything had been taken and at 1/4 to 12 when "His Nibs" returned in very sporty suiting, whistling etc. was very surprised to find Gerald clad only in bright red pajamas stalking the floor in the servants hall — When questioned as to said key, he lied about it — so there was G's chance and he said "Report for duty in the morning" — Gerald was absolutely *livid* and I was secretly tickled to death!!

The following morning I heard raucous singing coming from the serving room — "Ken" was lustily singing "I kiss and say good-bye" — Now he's back in Barracks, sleeping on a hard bed — and getting lots of discipline (I hope). I talked to Hettie and told her never to see him again if she had any sense —

The others seem to be getting along very well, and I like them all (knock on wood). Hilda returned a ten shilling note that I threw away by mistake in an envelope, and Lily stayed in yesterday on her afternoon off "because I was having guests for tea" — Whew! Can it last?? McNamara says they all like me — I am highly honoured (!).

The new soldier-servant seems very nice — is about 36 and has had experience in a house before (thank God) — by name, Bennett.

Boogie darling, I am hoping that you are having a smooth crossing — (the weather is lovely here) — I am going to miss you *horribly* but shall look forward to seeing you *SOON*.

1. *Je me hâte de te le dire:* I hasten to tell you.
2. Lily Norton, the parlor maid.

1st May 1936   *On Board Cunard White Star*
                                                      "Berengaria"

I saw Gerald's friend today en passant. He seems very nice. Also please tell
Gerald that the Purser changed my cabin and it is a great improvement. I
spent the first night in the inside one and found it stuffy and noisy. I feel that
it was Gerald's asking for it that did the trick. It is in the middle of the ship and
so far you would not know you were on a ship as far as movement is concerned.

I am not much of a public mixer and always feel rather hopeless on a ship,
especially alone.

Some middle class English from the Midlands asked me to play Bridge last
night. He wasn't bad but she was <u>the</u> most impossible woman I have ever seen
so I will remain caché tonight. Being alone, for a woman, is pretty awful. But
the accommodations are excellent and the food the best I have ever had on a
ship. Bad for me.

Last night I was sitting alone and an old man came along and practically
shouted in my ear "Are there any nail brushes on this boat?" I was startled
but realized he wasn't speaking to me — and felt relieved.

The Gala dinner was as gala as usual last night and especially dull for me
being alone. I was dragged on the floor by an awful man from <u>Lancashire</u> who
was lit and practically assaulted me on the floor, so I retired to the reading
room. I have some very good books. Esther Waters is really a masterpiece
but rather drab.[1] All about the servant class and book making. I thought of
"Bloodworthy" —[2] I must say there is an uninspiring looking lot of people on
board.

1. George Moore, *Esther Waters: A Novel* (New York: Liveright, ca. 1932).
2. Gerald's nickname for Mrs. Flood, the Onslow Square cook.

25th May 1936   London S.W.7.

On Thursday morning I went to Wellington Barracks as the King and the
Duke of Connaught were inspecting the 1st Battalion of Grenadier Guards.[1]
G. gave me 3 tickets, so I took Mum and Aunt Norah; we arrived early so had
a front row seat.[2] The King passed so close to us, that I could hear what he

was saying to the D. of Con. They were both wearing the Brigade uniform – it was all quite exciting, and I enjoyed it so much as you can imagine. Gerald stood right in front of us for ages, and twiddled his sword when he saw us!

1. Prince Arthur William Patrick Albert, 1851–1942, third son of Queen Victoria, first Duke of Connaught and Strathearn, colonel of the Regiment of Grenadier Guards, governor-general of Canada 1911–16.

2. Hilda Potter née Meiggs, 1877–1940, Gerald's mother, a.k.a. "Mum," was born in London to American parents. She was an accomplished pianist and held frequent literary salons. Norah Allfrey née Meiggs, 1877–1961, was Hilda Potter's sister.

5th June 1936   London S.W.7.
G. and I went to see the 4th of June celebrations at Eton – there was such a blockade of cars we couldn't get near the place, and had to give up as we were dining at the Guards' Boat Club at 7.30 – Christopher Jeffreys and wife (Lady Rosemary) had us to dinner.[1] I had never met her before, and liked her so much – he is a darling. Lots of people were dining there among them Nan McGowan and Dermot Daly whose engagement has been broken 3 times, and she has just returned from Morrocco [*sic*]![2] We went on to the Fireworks after Eton – thousands of people sitting on the banks of the Thames. It looked so pretty with a full moon just over Windsor Castle in the distance, and the little Eton boys rowing up and down the river. We saw lots of people we knew, and some celebs. we didn't. I bumped into Raymond Massey, and was of course thrilled.[3] The Duchess of Sutherland was sitting next to us on the grass.[4] All the college buildings and flowers were lit up and it looked lovely – we spent an hour getting out of the parking space and were back in London about 1.

Guy Drummond came in to see us yesterday just after we had left – was so sorry to miss him.[5] Also had cards "pushed" by M. et Madame Slavko Y. Grointch (!), Envoyé extraordinaire et ministre Plenipotentiaire de Sa Majesté le roi de Yougoslavie – all this on the card, and draped in black – she is a silly woman from West Virginia but I suppose I shall have to return the call –

G's on picket, and to-morrow I shall lunch with him "on guard" — He told me that he would write to you to-day to tell you his news — he has sent in his papers. I hope you won't be disappointed — I was at first, but am not in the least now, as I am so glad to think he wants to work — I think his disposition and liver would both be ruined if he stayed in much longer! — He is going to take a business course, and has practically got a job — though I better not tell you about it until it's certain. He seems very pleased with the idea of working. He will still be on the Reserve of the G.G. so it isn't completely leaving the Army — [6]

1. Christopher Jeffreys, 1907–40, was a captain in the Grenadier Guards. From 1938 he served as personal assistant to Lord Gort and was later killed in action. Rosemary Jeffreys née Lady Rosemary Agar, 1908–84, was daughter of the fourth Earl and Countess of Normanton.

2. According to Michael Davie, ed., *The Diaries of Evelyn Waugh* (Harmondsworth: Penguin, 1982), 487, Dermot Daly was the grandson of the fourth Baron McGowan. Daly and Nan McGowan did get married: see ibid., 546.

3. Raymond Massey, 1896–1983, a Canadian born actor and director, was a U.S. citizen from 1944.

4. Fifth Duchess of Sutherland née Lady Eileen Butler, d. 1943, justice of the peace, mistress of the robes to Queen Mary from 1916 to 1921.

5. Guy Drummond, 1915–87, Ginnie's cousin.

6. G.G.: the Grenadier Guards regiment.

25th June 1936
900 West Franklin Street
Richmond
Virginia

I answered Gerald's letter. I <u>was</u> disappointed to have him leave the Army but didn't say so. However, it is not for me to dictate to him. The sad part of this life is that each succeeding generation refuses to use the experiences of the previous one and so humanity goes on through the ages learning the same lesson, like a boy who never gets out of the class in school. I just pray he won't put up any capital and go in with anyone without capital and with experience because the end is inevitable. The other person always takes the capital and leaves <u>you</u> with the experience.

30th June 1936   London S.W.7.

Several people came in to see us in the afternoon – among them Rosa Lewis
of the Cavendish Hotel with *three* dogs.[1] She is *75* – mistress of the late
Edward VII, and asked for champagne. She is the most extraordinary old
character, she knows *everyone* in England, and everyone goes there to see
her – not *wild* lords etc. but very sedate respectable people (and of course
the wild ones too I suppose). She said we must come to visit her at Cowes,
and then remarked "Gerald is so cocky, because he belongs to the Squadron
– well anyway, he married a very lovely girl". So G. beamed that I had 'gone
over' with Rosa!!

1. Rosa Lewis née Ovenden, 1867–1952, was a London society cook and the proprietor
of Cavendish Hotel, which according to her biographer was a "naughty nursery" where
the rich "sowed their spurious wild oats and tippled champagne" while being managed
by their "amoral nanny." See Anthony Masters, *Rosa Lewis: An Exceptional Edwardian*
(London: Weidenfeld and Nicholson, 1977), ix.

12th July 1936   London S.W.7.

I went to Mme. Arline for a treatment and had my neck *bleached*. I thought
this most imperative, as I was afraid people would begin saying I was an
octaroon or *worse*.

17th July 1936   Pink Cottage
                                                        Warsash,
                                                        Hampshire

Thursday morning we went to the Presentation in Hyde Park. The King
presented new colours to the Grenadier, Coldstream and Scots Guards. We
had marvellous seats – it was a wonderful spectacle! . . . Saw masses of people we knew and had a *grand* time. The King, as you probably heard, was
shot at on the way back by some maniac – the whole country was outraged
by it, but no-one seems to know *why* the man did it.[1]

1. According to reports released in 2003, a "lowly caretaker" fancifully suggested a

"mysterious foreign power" had paid him to assassinate the king. The *Independent* reported, "I was paid £150 to shoot the King, claimed caretaker," 3 January 2003, 6.

15th September 1936   London S.W.7.

Little Gerald roared off to his first day at the office on Monday morning – he felt just as if he were going back to school. I thought about him all day, and wondered how he was getting on. He came back about 6 looking quite cheerful and brought Mr. Rattle, his boss, with him. A very nice little man and "gentlemanly", though not exactly a gent. He rather murders the King's english, but doesn't try to be what he's not. I think Gerald is going to like working. In case you don't know he is at present an 'office-boy' in a firm called Rattle, McLellan and Co. – he may be a partner in a yr. or so if he's any good – [1]

1. Rattle, McLellen and Co.: London stockbroking company.

18th September 1936   London S.W.7.

Things (as usual) have been happening thick and fast. Gerald asked Col. Gourlay, his Bank Manager, to come in on Wednesday afternoon – he is a most charming little man, and I had a nice chat with him before G. returned home. Lily made some cocktails which I saw to before he and Mr. Gourlay arrived, and I said "Don't make them *too* strong Lily" – she said "Mr. Potter said I *must* make them STRONG madam". I took a small sip, it was *delicious*, and I asked her what she had put in them? "Everything madam". Well anyway it had the desired effect and all went very well.

6th November 1936   London S.W.7.

Wednesday began struggling over letting the house, as we are trying to let it for a *year*. Also looked for service flats, preferably 2 bedrooms, sitting room and bath, so you could stay with us next Spring. Olive Todd wants to know if you would like a ticket in a private house (for Coronation) which overlooks the route.[1] Tickets are 20 guineas apiece, including lunch. This is about the cheapest one I have heard of so far, so may take 3 — All this expense is ludicrous — Australians and Americans are offering *any* price, so have ruined it for us poor Londoners — one woman is letting hers for £1,000 for one day! We are trying to find a flat for £5 or £6 per week from Feb. 15 to July 1st — I hate to think of you not staying at Onslow Sq. but you see if we let it for a whole year it would put us on our feet and we can't afford not to — I would stay at the P.C. [Pink Cottage] in the summer (and you too I hope) and G. would stay at the Guards' Club and come down week-ends — *Think* of what we would save!![2]

1. Olive Todd: a London fashion salon owner.
2. Gerald and Ginnie moved to the Pink Cottage in 1937.

8th December 1936   London S.W.7.

Mum is going to put me down to be presented.[1] But I don't know if I want to be presented to Queen *Wallis*![2] Isn't all this mess *terrible*? I do hope it will turn out all-right, but everyone is awfully depressed. I suppose it will all be over by the time we see you, but *what* will the outcome be? Gerald keeps muttering things like "It's the end — you mark my words" — O Lord, how *could* a King show such bad taste.[3] The whole thing seems unbelievable to me.

I hope no one will slap G. on the back and ask him how "our Wally" is, will they?

Why can't someone bump off 'the Simp' — and might as well do the same thing to the King. He has gone *crazy* and probably wouldn't be any good without her now. O well, we shall see —

1. After being presented at court as a debutante (or slightly older in the case of Ginnie in Ottawa in 1929), it was customary for a woman to be re-presented after her marriage. According to Angela Lambert, of the 1,657 "general circle presentations" of 1939, one-third were recently married women; see Lambert, *1939: The Last Season of Peace* (London: Weidenfeld and Nicolson, 1989), 8.
2. Wallis Simpson, 1896–1986, later Duchess of Windsor.
3. Edward VIII, 1894–1972, king from January to December 1936, when he abdicated to marry Wallis Simpson.

26th April 1937   26 Cranley Gardens
                                                    London S.W.7.

I took Olive Todd to lunch to-day and happened to have with me a white
ostrich fan and feathers for Court that Betty [Pearson] had loaned me (very
kindly) but they were *very* old and torn and dirty, and O. Todd took one
look at them, and said she wouldn't let me go in them – anyway, she has
loaned me some fresh ones, and veil – *also* a lovely palest pink feather fan
– *and* a very pretty tiara. It's paste, but nobody'll know and it's very pretty.
Thence to Jay's to buy Court gloves and to the jewellers to see about the
ear-rings, insurance, etc. and back to Gerald's – so now I am ready for the
event next week. I do wish you were going to be here, though it wouldn't
be very interesting just to see me go off in my cut and made over wedding
dress. I am going to have the train made into a little coat afterwards –

London is getting *messier* every day – awful decorations, terrible traffic,
hundreds of lavatories in the park, and swarms of *Australians*, etc.

3rd May 1937   London S.W.7.

London becomes more crowded every day – lots of colonials and toughs,
but fortunately quite a few Eastern potentates to lend glamour.[1] Kensington Gardens is now closed (much to George's disgust!) and has become the
temporary home of hundreds of troops.[2] The lavatories are hideous, made
of corrugated tin!!

All the main streets have now finished decorating themselves – some
are rather nice, others are tawdry to a degree with bits of crêpe paper, cel-
lophane, bunting hanging in limp strips, and imitation gold crowns – why
they can't *ban* everything but flowers and flags and have it all uniform, I
can't imagine.

There's been a lovely haze the last few days that makes one remember
that an english summer day is hard to be beat (if we could just have more of
them). The bushes and trees in the parks, (glimpsed through the iron-bars
and lavatories) are in full bloom – and makes me long to be in the country.
Bench says the tulips are coming up at the cottage and I have asked him to
send us some.[3]

Thursday Mum and I go to Court, and I am getting rather nervous about it. I hope I won't tread on my train, or drop my feathers, or feel sick. I am wearing *everything* I have, but hope my good jewellery will not make my false tiara look funny —

1. More crowded in anticipation of George VI's coronation.
2. George: Gerald and Ginnie's dog.
3. Bench was the gardener at the Pink Cottage.

(approx. 17th) May 1937[1]   London S.W.7.

We had some sandwiches and sherry before we started, and there were several relations and friends to see us: Joan and fiancé, "Aunt Jo" Potter, "Aunt Norah" Allfrey — and my pal Margie [Rawlings][2] — Mum looked sweet in a lovely dark red-dy lace dress over gold with a fan to match, and a *beautiful* tiara (which belongs to the Allfreys) — I wore my silver lamé wedding dress (with the sleeves cut out) and the Court train cut shorter — and a very pretty diamond tiara (borrowed!) — Then I wore my big brooch, also the diamond ear-rings and Maltese cross (Potter heirlooms) and some cultured pearls added to my real ones which I bought the other day — (cheap!)

We roared off in a large Daimler with chauffeur and footman (hired for the evening) and then drove down the Mall — the traffic was so thick that we moved by inches, and were able to see people in the next cars, all dressed up — Hundreds of people lined the streets to see the 'feathers' go by — We drew up next to the Spencer family (they have 32 Onslow Square) who were there en masse — About 7.30 when the gates were opened we all drove into the forecourt of Buckingham Palace — and waited until 8.30 — when we alighted from our car — The biggest thrill I got was going up the long staircase flanked with soldiers looking like statues, as I felt I was in an Alexander Korda film! — There was then another wait before our turn came — just as we were about to enter the throne room one of the old boys in the bodyguard fell *crash* with a din so the atmosphere was rather *tense*!

I made my two little curtsies, and then Mum and I managed to get a good place in the long hall in order to have a good view of the King & Queen. When all the presentations had been made they walked through the hall — first the bodyguard, then the gold sticks in waiting walking *backwards*, then the King & Queen. They were so close I could have put out my arm and touched them, so I had a very good look! She is very pretty, so much prettier than her photographs — and is very *gracious* and charming. He is *very* good-looking, and I quite lost my heart to him — he's not as tall as I had thought, but *such* a nice face — rather lean and bronzed as if he'd been to the riviera — Then came the Duke and Duchess of Kent, I had *never* seen her before, and I thought she was *perfectly beautiful*, and terribly smart.[3]

Mum and I went to supper where we consumed a bit of champagne and sandwiches — and then left. I couldn't help wishing that Uncle Cyril hadn't got divorced (he had to leave the body-guard on that account) as we would have had the 'entrée' in the Throne Room and wouldn't have had to get there until 9.30!![4] After I dropped Mum in the car, I went in to see Gerald (at 12 o'clock!) in the nursing-home — he seemed to be pleased with the way I looked —[5]

I didn't have any pictures taken, so hope Boogie won't be annoyed — But it seemed silly to have a picture taken in my wedding dress! The Associated Press were here at 7 that evening to photograph me — I didn't tell them that I would be going away at 6 — so I managed to avoid an awful snapshot —

I was very lucky over the Coronation seats, as I had made no plans to go but Hugh Cholmeley very kindly gave me two tickets in the Regimental stand, so I asked Olive Todd to go with me, as she had loaned me the feathers and veil, and a lovely fan to go to Court —[6] I stayed at her flat the night before — and when the day dawned — we arose and dressed and had our breakfast (at 5 A.M.!) and left before 6 armed with coats, a rug, sandwiches, cigarettes, and hot coffee and whisky! We were in our stand at Hyde Park Corner at 6.20 so we had a good long wait, but there was always lots to look at — as many of the Abbey guests passed our way — also the private coaches — the Londonderrys' coach was all yellow with a driver and two footmen all in yellow and gold, and magnificent horses — then there was one pale blue, and so on.[7] In the early hour of the morning, it seemed so unreal and just like a dream of Fairyland. Later the Kents passed going from their house in Belgrave Square to the Palace — The children were with them, and they held up little Princess Alexandra —[8]

Later Miss Todd and I wandered around, had a little coffee etc. The service was broadcast over the radio — The procession didn't reach us until nearly three – but we were so excited we never felt tired. The Indians were marvellous in their glorious uniforms. The Canadian Mounties got *lots* of applause, but the Guards got the most as usual (says she proudly). Hugh C[holmeley] and Alec Lockwood and several others were in the procession.[9] Queen Mary was in a lovely coach with the two little princesses –[10] When Princess Elizabeth passed 145 Piccadilly (her late home) she *hung* out of the carriage and waved frantically, and Queen Mary had to pull her back! Then came the Kents, and the Gloucesters, and finally the King and Queen in a huge gilded affair – and a few officers from every regiment in the Empire behind them. The Duke of Kent and D. of Gloucester were riding immediately behind the coach – not in the carriage with the Duchess.

When it was all over I felt limp with so much emotion, and we walked home in the rain – It began just at the end of the procession, and then poured – After I had had a rest and some tea, and listened to the King's speech at 8 – I came home – and after late dinner walked over to see Gerald, and tell him all about it. He had listened over the wireless all day – did you hear it by any chance?

Thursday night I dined at a club in Pall Mall with the Woodwards, and we walked around for hours to see the illuminations. No cars were allowed in that area, so the thousands of people walked in the streets, and sang and danced. We heard the 'Last Post' at the Horse Guards' Parade, then walked down the Mall to the Palace and yelled "We want the King" along with 200,000 other people – They appeared on the balcony of the floodlit palace – he was in Guards uniform (red) and she in a white dress – and they looked *marvellous*! I've never heard such *cheering* in my life. Afterwards we walked in Trafalgar Square and up Piccadilly to see all the sights.

I went again on Saturday night to see all the places I had missed, and on Monday afternoon drove with Aunt Mobs in an open taxi to see the decorations in the 'city' so now I feel I have 'done the Coronation'!!

1. This letter was written to Ginnie's grandmother, Virginia Fendley Dickinson.

2. Joan Audrey Potter, 1914–84, later Verey, was Gerald's sister. Jo Potter, previously Reid, was Gerald's aunt by marriage.

3. George, Duke of Kent, 1902–42, was brother of George VI. Princess Marina, Duchess of Kent née Princess Marina of Greece, lived from 1906 to 1968.

4. Major Cyril Charles Hamilton Potter, officer of the Order of the British Empire, d. 1941, was a director of Linley, Messel and Co. stockbrokers. He acted as Gerald's guardian following his father's death in 1917.

5. Gerald had contracted rheumatic fever in April, a severe form of rheumatism and a bacterial infection, marked by high temperature and inflammation of joints, often leading to osteoarthritis later in life, which in Gerald's case it did from ca. 1967 onward.

6. Captain Sir Hugh Cholmeley, fifth baronet, 1906–64, Grenadier Guards officer and Lincolnshire landowner.

7. Sir Charles Vane-Tempest-Stewart, the seventh Marquis of Londonderry, 1878–1949, secretary of state for air 1931–35, air commodore 1935–49. His wife was the seventh Marchioness of Londonderry née the Honourable Edith Chaplin, 1879–1959, founder and director-general of the Women's Legion during World War I. She was the first woman to be awarded the Military Order of the British Empire.

8. Princess Alexandra Helen Elizabeth, 1936–, from 1963 the Honourable Mrs. Angus Ogilvy.

9. Alec Lockwood, 1907–ca. 1990, a lieutenant colonel in the Irish Guards during World War II, and a farmer.

10. Queen Mary née Princess Victoria Mary of Teck, 1867–1953, wife of George V.

2nd September 1937   *Montreal*

Foster came in Monday night and asked about you and Gerald, and after getting all the news of your health and the casualties, delivered the following Phillipic [sic] – that it is well-known that the English have rheumatism because of their <u>diet</u>. That the French were in the trenches in water for four years and <u>didn't</u> have rheumatism from the dampness. That <u>you</u> don't have rheumatism from dampness. That Germans don't have as much (rheumatism) as the English. They drink as much but that German beer is made from <u>hops</u> which don't give you rheumatism and that English beer is not made any longer from hops, but the bitter flavour is inserted from some other process. As long as Gerald drinks English beer, he will have a <u>return</u> of rheumatics. He says the English are the only people who persist stubbornly in believing it's their climate which gives it to them. According to him it has been proved a fallacy. I simply pass on what he said, because it <u>may</u> be right. You might ask Bevan.

About the teeth, he says you <u>must</u> have a lot of calcium every day if you want to stop the disintegration. <u>Only</u> calcium will do the work. He told me to *tell you that you must take a large glass of orange juice (which you do) but also that <u>one apple</u> has as much calcium as 6 oranges. If you could manage to eat two apples a day, or even <u>one</u> you would be much less apt to have another abscess. I also pass this on to you. You might as well do it – it won't <u>hurt</u> you –*

21st November 1937   Warsash

We had rather a *blow* on Friday. Gerald received a letter from Barclay's that they were forced to reduce his income for the time being – It seems the lease of some building has expired, and 'until such time as it can be re-let' they are cutting down the monthly income – They never warned him about this – it came 'out of the blue' – I bet old Cyril [Potter] is cursing as well as he has 1/2 shares in it. Well let us hope it's *re-let* again. With things as they are, I don't suppose they'll get as much money, but as they got quite a tidy sum before it ought to make *some* money – In the mean time we have started an 'intensive economy programme' – no more entertaining, no more wine, etc. Gerald is going to see Gourlay about it, and find out what it's all about. He is giving up the shooting next year, and the boat ought not to cost as much this year – (What a perfectly charming year 1937 has been!) Every time I say this something *worse* happens, so please *cut*.

26th November 1937   Warsash

We listened to the broadcast of King Leopold on Thursday morning[1] – he was speaking to the 52 Royal Inniskilling Dragoon Guards as their Col-in-Chief. He *seems* very sweet, and tremendously popular here. London has been pretty snappy lately with *3 Kings* visiting George VI. Pretty good effort for these days and times. By the way, I am fascinated over the mystery of "les cagoulards" in France but no one seems to know what it is all about – [2]

Everyone agrees that it's a "good thing" the D. of Windsor didn't go to America, as they realize how difficult it would have been for the U.S. I am told or "they say" the Duke was given 3 days to leave Germany! – Did you see "the Simp" opening a charity bazaar in Paris? Isn't it divine??! So much for *Court Circles* –

1. Leopold III of Belgium, 1901–83.

2. Les cagoulards: Comité secret d'action révolutionnaire (CSAR), a revolutionary Fascist French group formed in 1936. Anti-Communists supported by rich industrialists comprised the organization, and they were named Cagoulards by the group's opponents, "cagoule" being the French equivalent of a Ku Klux Klan mask.

14th December 1937   Warsash

I received your grand long letter this afternoon – as far as I know everyone seems to think it's grand that Fat-Boy Gort was made C.I.G.S.[1] – *think* of being *General Viscount* Gort, M.C., V.C. and D.S.O. (*three* times). He *must* be a clever soldier. He put Gerald up for the R.Y.S. [Royal Yacht Squadron] you know, besides telling us of a good cake, and a good *jam*, so I'm all for him!!!

1. John Standish Prendergast Vereker, 1886–1946, was the sixth viscount from 1902. He had been a World War I hero and served as commander in chief of the British Expeditionary Force between 1939 and 1940 and as field marshal in 1943. C.I.G.S.: chief of the Imperial General Staff.

10th March 1938   *Hotel New Weston*
                                                                            34 East 50th Street
                                                                            New York

You see by the enclosed from the paper that your action in renouncing your American citizenship was considered <u>news</u>.[1] It didn't make the front page as Barbara Hutton's did, but there is the consolation that the communists won't be insulting about it.[2]

1. The cutting from the *Herald Tribune* reads, "Renounces U.S. Citizenship. Mrs. Virginia Stuart Reynolds Potter, wife of Gerald Edward Winter Potter, a British Army officer in the Royal Military Barracks at London, filed in United States District Court yesterday formal notice of her renunciation of American citizenship. Mrs. Potter is a native of Richmond, Va. Her marriage to Mr. Potter took place in London on March 5, 1936." According to Ginnie's unpublished autobiography, "I was married to an englishman, my children would be english, and I wanted to really belong and to be allowed to vote."

2. Barbara Hutton, 1912–79, was heiress to the Woolworth fortune. One of her seven husbands was the actor Cary Grant.

17th March 1938   *Richmond*

Florrie said I must tell her something to make her feel young.[1] *So this is what I said from a feeling of pure impishness. "Yesterday a voice (was) over the telephone saying 'Is this <u>Miss Daisy</u>?' – of course a negress from the past.*[2] *It turned out to be one Suzie, who had a daughter named Ree, whose grown son works here and who would like <u>me</u> to speak to him. They were from Nana's negro slaves, and this is the pedigree: Hugh, son of Ree, daughter of Susie, daughter of Emma Rainey who <u>belonged</u> to Nana, she in turn daughter of Mammy Suky who was Nana's nurse – so I wound up, 'He is the <u>great-great</u> grandson of Mammy Suky whom <u>we knew</u>.'"*[3] *That finished her completely.*

Hugh has beautiful manners and is quite good looking. They are all well brought up. How the world has changed. Nana inherited 100 slaves and a large property and coal mines. Now look at her. <u>That</u> is what war does to people.

The enclosed will tell their own story. You were <u>front-page</u> news in all the Metropolises – and your story was told over on the transcontinental <u>radio news hours</u>. Pleas. Conquest said he was transfixed to hear "Virginia Stuart Reynolds Potter who married an officer in the Grenadier Guards in London 1936 gives up her American citizenship" coming over the wires. You may not be a plutocrat but that doesn't seem to make any difference. I was horrified. I can't go on the street without being challenged about it.

1. Florence Dickinson Stearns, 1872–1958, was Bougie's sister. She was a poet and president of the Poetry Society of Virginia between 1936 and 1945.

2. Daisy: Bougie's childhood name.

3. Nana: Virginia Fendley Dickinson, 1849–1941, was Bougie's mother. For her Confederate memoir, see "Confederate Money: A Memoir of the 1850s and 1860s," ed. Angela Potter, *Southern Cultures* 9 (Winter 2003): 88–98.

20th March 1938   *Richmond*

I just asked Stuart if anyone had asked him about your renouncing your citizenship and he answered, "Not more than a thousand people". It certainly created a furore.

Of course, this war talk is running me slightly crazy – I don't care how many Germans and Italians kill each other, but I am frantic lest we all have to get in the mess –

29th March 1938   *Richmond*

I forgot to tell you that you figured in "News of 10 years ago" about three weeks ago – something about your being a débutante and going to Montreal to be presented by your aunt! I suppose they considered your importance in the light of your front page début when you renounced your American citizenship. As Huntly says, "Once on the front page, always on the front page" –

Friday night we heard the negro contralto, Marian Anderson, sing in concert.[1] Everyone in Richmond came in and after removing their wraps, looked up in the gallery to see if they could locate their cooks and butlers. Matthews of the Glee Club was in a box. She is the most exciting singer I've ever heard – good looking, well dressed, very dignified and a magnificent artist. It was a real artistic event. She has been beautifully trained, sings German with marvellous diction and Italian, and she was born in Lynchburg –

1. Marian Anderson, 1902–93, a contralto, was in 1955 the first African American artist to sing with the Metropolitan Opera Company.

30th March 1938   Warsash

I nearly collapsed when I received all the clippings – heavens! I feel very badly now that I ever did it, as people have probably worried you to death over it – and asked you hundreds of questions – Did they think it *very* peculiar and were they *incensed* at the idea? What was the reaction, and what did you answer?? I suppose Helen Adams thinks I have sunk to the depths!![1]

I feel that, after all, I have made a great mistake in leaving a country where I seem to be front page news – for a *much* smaller country where the only time I have ever appeared in print was because I did a wee-wee at the Royal Yacht Squadron! It's too sad! –[2]

1. Helen Adams, 1880–ca. 1970, was a retired teacher who was resident at Chesterfield Apartments, Richmond. She is also referred to as "Little Playmate." This was a coded expression used by Bougie and Ginnie to imply women with lesbian tendencies toward them. Ginnie's "Little Playmate" was Sister Griffiths.

2. This refers to an entry in the *Times* "Court Circular" column. According to Ginnie's unpublished memoir, she and Bougie visited the RYS and "in those days one had to write

one's name down if one went to the Ladies' Annexe to change or have a 'wash and brush up'. The next day . . . we read to our astonishment [that] among those visiting the Royal Yacht Squadron was Mrs. G. Potter and Mrs. Stuart Reynolds. . . . Boogie said 'I never thought I would have my name in the Court Circular for just doing a wee-wee.' "

11th April 1938   *Richmond*

I had two skits on the radio lately and to-morrow am speaking over W.M.B.G. — something about the Guidance for Rural Youth.

    There isn't much news — nothing going on in Holy Week — I must go down to Gloucester soon.[1] The painting is finished and I am having to buy a new stove — I have become so stingy lately that I begrudge any money spent on anything — even clothes — I fear it is only a passing phase, but I am a bit apprehensive about the way things are going and want to get all the securities possible out of the country — Stocks went up a trifle today and Saturday but everyone has the jitters about what those idiots in Washington may do — However the opposition won a victory over Roosevelt on this Reorganization Bill. Harry Byrd of <u>Virginia</u> is now being mentioned for the 1940 President.[2] Virginia has made such a brave fight against Roosevelt that it is very much in the public consciousness now —

    1. Stuart Reynolds owned a weekend cottage at Gloucester Banks, Virginia. The house was struck by lightning and burned down in 1945.

    2. Harry Flood Byrd, 1887–1966, was governor of Virginia 1925–30 and a U.S. senator 1915–25 and 1930–65. He was an opponent of desegregation.

4th June 1938   *Richmond*

This afternoon we went out to "Miniborya" to a rural festival, dancing and puppet shows.[1] The Greeks, Bohemians, Italians, to say nothing of the Anglo-Saxons, cavorted on the lawns and we sat on the ground and watched them. We were supposed to dance ourselves after supper. There was a sort of cafeteria, but knowing Huntly, I thought he would prefer a sit down hot meal, so we came away early. I had on a thin dress which became so crushed and weary-looking after sitting about on the ground that I was glad to remove myself and it from the landscape. Huntly was pursued by Helen [Adams], so he was

anxious to leave, but it really was quite pretty — a bit "Hey ho, the holly" sort
of thing, and of course Americans look so floppy when they are being "Anglo-
Saxon" that it is a little dispiriting, but on the whole, it was wholesome.

I am knitting furiously on something which develops as it goes, and I have
no idea what it will turn out to be. There's an element of uncertainty about it
which is positively exciting.[2]

1. Miniborya was a large house south of Richmond built in 1899–1900 by J. Scott Parrish and used for public functions. The house was demolished in 1973 and the site converted to an apartment complex. See Jeffrey M. O'Dell, *Chesterfield County: Early Architecture and Historic Sites* (Chesterfield County Planning Dept., ca. 1983), 331.

2. At this time Ginnie was pregnant with her first baby.

15th October 1938[1]   *R.M.S. Empress of Britain*
                                               Canadian Pacific

I have just come inside from the Promenade deck where I stood waving an
enormous dinner napkin — I hope you and Gerald saw it — I both heard
the firing and saw the smoke — I tried to think I saw you — But with only
the lorgnettes to aid my inadequate eyes, I could scarcely recognize the dots
representing you and Gerald —

You know that in order to leave without making a fool of myself, I must
become a bit wooden and put thinking *out of the question — else I couldn't*
stand it. But I am not as miserable as I thought I should be, because you are
now much better and stronger, and you are going off on a trip of your own,
and I shall now begin to think of the next time *which I sincerely trust may be*
soon —

There isn't anything much I can say in this letter. We have all been through
quite a lot of anxious moments together and we know how we feel about it all,
so it is better to leave it at that. In spite of our anxiety and strain, I loved being
there, and seeing so much of you — I don't know if I can make you understand
how much I love and admire you — and how wonderful I think you are, and
sweet, but if you don't know it by now you never will.

1. This letter follows the summer during which Ginnie's first baby died on 3 September.

17th October 1938   Warsash

Needless to say we were désolés when you left us on Saturday, Boogie. You looked so sweet and *snappy*. . . . I walked quickly away and we drove off in topspeed — it is *grim* but I think much better than to wait until the boat sails, and see that awful ever-widening gap between the dock and the boat!

Will write again before we leave for France if have time but the only boat sailing on Saturday is the Bremen and as G. says "don't send your letters on that damn line" —

15th November 1938   Warsash

Good Heavens, *what* a year 1938 has been — friends dying, everybody ill, etc. and now those blankety-blank Germans are being more brutal and horrible than ever. I do hope it won't lead to another crisis —

We got all dressed up [Wednesday] evening (Gerald had on *new shoes* and I wore the black lace) First had some oysters at Driver's and came to the sad conclusion that they aren't as good as french ones — then went to the Command Performance at the Coliseum — supposedly a sort of top-notch variety show for the King and Queen. We had excellent seats with a good view of the Royal Box. The King looked bored except for the comedian turns; the Queen was all in lamé and diamonds and looked very nice; the Duchess of Kent looked *divine* as usual. The show was rather disappointing — and so was the audience — saw only a few friends — Gary Cooper was there with his wife — We went on to the Savoy for supper, and had a few dances and came home —

24th November 1938   *Richmond*

The papers here continue to be very gravely excited about the jews in Germany and their plight, but someone tonight told me after having had a family of Semites next to him all summer at Virginia Beach, he felt that Hitler was doing the only thing you could do with a jew. I hope they won't all come over here, but I should also like to annihilate Goebbels, the little sick-looking sadist.

Florie's book had a boost in sales today when I bought six — and I was much embarrassed when Florie told me about it with great éclat, not knowing that

I was the purchaser[1] *— I felt rather mean, but she would have felt worse had she discovered who it was. Poor Florie will never understand why the world doesn't acknowledge her as the great genius she believes herself to be —*

Blessed are those who expecteth nothing.

1. Florence Dickinson Stearns wrote *Strange Dimension* (New York: G. P. Putnam, 1938), a poetry anthology dedicated to Bougie.

30th November 1938   *Richmond*

Huntly went to the St. Andrews ball which astonished me, but I was really astonished when he told me he had bought another Pisarro and was thinking of a Bracques — He has gone modern up to the neck —

23rd February 1939   *Montreal*

I heard Jan Masaryk speak yesterday — quite brilliant and a little sardonic.[1] *Lesley had his cheque and I went up to meet him, but as he and "Julia" [Drummond] were having a quarrel about Chamberlain I drew back at the last moment, as he looked irritated and I didn't think it was a moment to have him meet anyone else attached to the Drummonds —*[2] *She is a great advocate of N. Chamberlain's and he, naturally, isn't as enthusiastic. However, he isn't at all bitter — That is wise of him — and I must say he impressed me.*

I was wondering if Gerald couldn't work up some sort of export-import business. England is going to make a drive, I see, for business with the colonies and the U.S.A. and they have a new treaty with America and are working on revisions with the Colonies — They have to fight Japan and Germany economically and the U.S. is now so furious with Germany, that she is ripe for more business with England — if she survives her internal troubles —

1. Jan Masaryk, 1886–1948, was a Czech diplomat and politician. He was chargé d'affaires to the United States 1919–22, Czech ambassador to Britain 1925–38, and foreign minister 1940–45, while his government was exiled in London, and 1945–48 in Czechoslovakia.

2. Sir Neville Chamberlain, 1869–1940, was the British prime minister 1937–40. He favored appeasement toward Hitler and Mussolini, with whom he negotiated the Munich

Agreement in 1938, and resigned in 1940. Jan Masaryk was the son of Tomas Masaryk, first president of Czechoslovakia. The former's antipathy to Chamberlain was presumably the result of the Munich Agreement between Chamberlain and the French and Italian leaders, in which large parts of Czechoslovakia were ceded to Germany. Six months later the Germans took over the whole country.

3rd March 1939   Warsash

My last letter! – which I trust will catch the "Queen Mary" to-morrow. I am hoping for a calm sea, and a speedy voyage on the Ile de France. I'll telegraph you as soon as I arrive in New York and will catch the first possible train to Montreal. If the boat docks in N.Y. on Tuesday the 14th I suppose I'll catch the night train to Montreal unless there's one before. I am not looking forward to the *damn* crossing, but it will be wonderful to think that every hour is taking me nearer to the New World and Boogie/Daddy/Buncle –

22nd May 1939   Warsash

I suppose you read that General Goering is trying to reduce – they now call him the "chevalier sans beurre et sans brioche"![1] Isn't' that lovely.

1. Reichsmarschall Hermann Göring, 1893–1946, commander in chief of Luftwaffe, was known for his obesity.

28th May 1939   Warsash

We have heard many vague rumours from various old Grenadiers etc. that the reserve officers are going to be called up for 2 or 3 months training – we were also told that they would probably be called up about June 15th (!!) I haven't dared breathe lately for fear this would happen to Gerald – as here at last (if no war) we can *both* enjoy ourselves this summer – and have a good time together racing the boat, etc. so it was with relief that I read a letter from the regimental adjutant 2 days ago that Gerald will probably be called up on August 15th – thank goodness – *after* Cowes, the Fastnet and most of the racing, etc. As yet have no idea where he will be stationed but if London we could shut this house up end of September and I could live in London for a month or so which might be fun.

1st June 1939   *Richmond*

I am sending this entirely by air from Richmond to Southampton (at least I think so). Stuart is to take it to the P.O. tomorrow and get the proper stamps etc. The clipper leaves Saturday morning. I want you to tell me <u>when</u> you get it, and we can then tell whether it is worth the difference between 5 cts. and 30. You are allowed 1/2 oz. – hence this special airplane paper.

I shall be glad when the King and Queen are safely home again. I may go up to Washington to see the excitement on the 8th. I also hear that they will pass up the Main Street of Alexandria on the 9th on their way back from Mt. Vernon to Arlington where the King will put a wreath on the unknown soldier's grave.

I want to order you and Gerald some more films – but don't know the size. They are selling Their Majesties' tour through the English Speaking Union – Size 16mm and size 8mm. If you could send me the size by cable perhaps I will put in my order at once. That is, if you want it. I think it will be interesting. It will include the Canadian and American journey and their visit to Hyde Park to the President and the World's Fair. There is another of the Golden Gate International Exposition in San Francisco.

*4*th June 1939   Warsash

Gerald is going up for one night as he must get his uniform out of storage. He has been called up for training to the 2nd Battalion Grenadiers, and is on duty beginning August 15th for from 2 to 3 months. It is a damn nuisance, but we are very relieved it isn't June 15th (Reggie West and several others must go then) as it really would be maddening to have *this* summer messed up too![1]

Gerald will be in camp at Pirbright – about an hour's drive from here – so I suppose he can go back and forth from here. I had thought of spending October in London, as I just thought he would be stationed there.

1. Reginald Alston-Roberts-West, d. 1940, a Grenadier Guards officer.

9th June 1939   *Richmond*

This will be mostly clippings, I fear, as there are so many of them. No room for a letter — Their Majesties have been a great success in Washington — The weather was so impossibly hot that we didn't have the grit to go to see them, as it meant a long hot drive and standing around for hours — Huntly had a nasty accident on Tuesday — was thrown by his horse which fell — and on Huntly — I was frantic and hustled him to a doctor. Fortunately the Xray disclosed no broken bones, but he had painful bruises, and standing about was impossible for him — We had to be content with numerous radio transmissions — We could hear the people cheering and the bands playing etc — quite exciting — We stood up so often for "God Save the King" and the Star Spangled banner that I am exhausted. How they bore the heat I don't know — We have all been worried to death about the King in his uniforms — Everyone seems to be delighted with them and it is a comfort that so far (touch wood) no mishaps — The only ugly thing was a performance by the head of the Irish R.A. — who was locked up — What asses the Irish are — I cannot bear them — A few backwoodsmen from obscure places have said something about 1776 — but they were all unimportant. I think the visit has done a lot of good. I have ordered the films for Gerald's camera —

I will sail about the middle of July — perhaps July 19 — on the Queen Mary — God willing — I mean Hitler! Huntly wants to go too — What about a yacht for us? for two weeks perhaps or ten days — Gerald will want to race Carmela so we would need a sailor of course.[1] I told you to get a boat if you could — But you haven't said anything about it. If it is feasible, and possible as to mooring etc. get it — because it would be much more fun — Then I could go off somewhere on a trip, and if Gerald <u>has</u> to go for training, you could go on the trip also — We will pay the expenses —

Sunday night —

Everything has gone on with the King and Queen quite satisfactorily. They have captivated all who saw them and heard them. Thank God, they are now safely on their way to Canada sans mishap as far as we know —

Miracle of miracles, after years of writing ads and sending in poems and guesses etc. Florie won a prize of $500.00 from Proctor and Gamble — <u>soap</u> manufacturers! She got a telegram from them, and they had an agent go to the grocer who sold her the soap to verify the sale. He was given $25.00 and then Florie was asked how she <u>felt</u> when she received the telegram, and received

$10.00 for that. Isn't it amazing? Now it only remains for her to win the Irish
sweepstakes and all will be well!

1. *Carmela III*, a yacht bought by Huntly Drummond for Gerald in 1937 and sold in
1946.

31st August 1939[1]   *R.M.S. Empress of Australia*
I wanted to send you a Marconi but we are under Admiralty orders and no
one has been able to send any messages. The Captain at whose table I am sit-
ting again, doesn't know himself where any vessels are, as there have been no
communications whatsoever. A tramp ship and two whales caused the greatest
excitement yesterday — we have had to darken portholes, and there have been
no lights on the decks — very cautious is the Admiralty. We have had broad-
casts from England though and, so far, everything seems to be static. *That's*
better than war.

I was absolutely wooden when I told you and Gerald goodbye, and I have
tried ever since to keep my mind off the thing which is on every one's mind
and on this ship. Their tongues. I have managed very well because I have
been reading every moment when I haven't been talking to someone — "The
Last Chronicles of Barsetshire" have been a tower of strength to me — and has
amused me no end. I have slept very well and managed to keep cheerful, and I
am sitting next to an Austrilian [sic] *on deck who is so optimistic and cheerful*
that he helps me. His wife embroiders and never speaks except to reproach
him for talking too much. Yesterday on deck late she said to him, "You have
run everyone away" and I replied "No, I am still true to him" —

At our table are Col. and Mrs. Wallis and her mother, a Mrs. Carson — also
Mrs. Willie Hendric of Hamilton. She reminds me of May [Drummond] —
the same grand gestures, and even looks like her when May was at her fullest
period. She dominates the table when she can. *She never can when the Captain*
is present because he demands that everyone listen to him *attentively. He is a*
most conceited man — Mrs. Hendric on those occasions, murmurs, "Ah, yes —
wonderful — Ah my dear Captain, as the Bishop was just saying to me . . ."
The conversation usually gets round to Royalty before the meal is over — This
is the amusing part —

Darling I hope this letter will reach you promptly and will tell you in my inadequate way how much I loved being with you and Gerald, and how much you mean to me — I hated leaving the Pink Cottage, and severing all the chances of seeing you. I couldn't <u>think</u> and didn't want to — I shall always remember you both waving goodbye. I thoroughly enjoyed my visit in spite of its rude interruption. I shall continue to write to the P.C. until I have a reason to change. I <u>hope</u> that no reason will present itself — Give my love to Gerald please — I shall write him soon, but not on this boat because he would not be able to read it.

As I told you, I put £400 in that joint account. If you should need it there it is, and if you don't, well it can be used for something — If all this awful business blows over, you might still go to St. Jean-de-Luz later, or to Paris on some of it. If Hitler can keep the world waiting on his merest whisper, he will, so the part of the world opposed to him will have to become <u>used</u> to being upset while he holds the nations of the Earth in thrall. It's so grotesque that it seems impossible — but the "great gray greasy" Teutonic mind is fertile manure for such as he — If we could only say "abracadabra" and whisk all the loathesome fat, beer drinking race off the earth, we could be at peace once more —

This boat has almost every nationality on earth aboard her. Most of them <u>dreadful</u>. But the staff has been wonderful —

1. Bougie spent her last prewar visit to England from mid-June to the end of August.

War Letters
September 1939 – December 1941

3rd September 1939

c/o Mrs. Verey
Ruscombe
Twyford, Berkshire

Dearest Boogie and Daddy

I have not cabled you as we were asked not to cable, telegraph or telephone unless absolutely necessary. I am so glad to think you have arrived. I have heard nothing but suppose you are safely ensconced at Drummond St. I kept putting off writing to you from day to day as never knew my plans from one hour to the next – and now it has been a week since you left. I am so terribly relieved to think that you are home – and thank Heavens we never went to France and also T.H. you managed to get a cabin in the boat!!

I am terribly sorry to think you shall be worrying about me and *please* forgive me for not going to America with you. I feel I must, and want to stay here, and you must *try* and not worry. Only rats desert etc. and I would hate to be called that –

Well Sept. 3rd seems to be a fateful day in my life!![1] Isn't it strange to think of a year ago?!

---

1. On 3 September war was declared, and on the same date in 1938 Ginnie's first baby had died.

4th September 1939 *Montreal*
My Darling Ginnie

*I shall just keep writing you, and maybe you will get some of my letters.
I cabled you yesterday. They couldn't guarantee any delivery. I can't* think
*very much – and I am trying to keep myself well in hand – by being calm,
in fact,* wooden. *I had hoped against all signs to the contrary that war might
be averted. I sent you a letter by the* [name crossed out]. *I only learned on
Friday that she was followed by two German submarines for a long distance.
An army plane brought the Capt. the news the first day. I must remember the
censorship –*

6th September 1939 *Montreal*

*I am going to number my letters, so you will know whether you are receiving
all of them. You might do the same. I sent one back by the Australia and one
to New York hoping it would get somehow to England.*

*Canada is going into the war – Potty has gone from his job – Stevie Cantlie
is also going to camp immediately.*[1] *Potty was in here in his kilts last night.*[2]
He hopes to come again before he is sent on to the permanent training camp.

*Everyone is perfectly calm and a bit grim about it, but perfectly deter-
mined. All sentimentality about the "kind" German people who don't want
Hitler, has been cast aside by most people. After all these years, I have everyone agreeing with me. I wish it were possible to bring the States in now, but
I suppose that is outside probability – too many dissenters. I shall not enjoy
going back – and if it gets too painful I can come back here and work.*

1. Steve Cantlie, Canadian Army officer, b. ca. 1907, killed in action during World War II.

2. As a captain in the Black Watch of Canada regiment, Pothier Doucet would have worn a kilt as part of his uniform.

10th September 1939 Twyford
I am afraid this letter is only the second since war was declared but I have
been so busy I have hardly had time to breathe – I was so relieved last week

to discover that we were allowed to send cables and do hope you received mine saying all was well – Thank you for your cable sent on arriving in Montreal. I didn't receive it until the Tuesday as it followed me about but I was very glad to get it – and yesterday I rec'd 2 letters from you – one written on the boat, and the other sent via Air Mail and marked No. 3 – so I hope to receive no. 2 some day.

On the Tuesday Gerald and I drove over to Twyford to see Mum and Joan – as Gerald thought then he might not see them again – Philip rushed in for a minute, he is now a *major* in the Territorials! and poor old G. is still a junior subaltern![1] We drove back in darkness for the last few miles; it's frightfully difficult so I shan't do any more 'black-out' driving than absolutely necessary.

On the Wednesday after I dropped Gerald at his billet, there was an air raid warning, and I was stopped half way home and parked the car and went into a garage-cum-shelter where I had to wait an hour which was most annoying as I hadn't had any breakfast. Otherwise it was quite amusing because of the 'types' and the funny things people said – 2 small girls giggling in a corner, 2 men chatting about feeding pigs and 2 boys playing darts on a picture of Hitler. (There was a picture of Adolf in a paper one day saying "Wanted: for murder, treason, etc." and since then it has been posted on every troop train, etc.) When I returned to the Bush Hotel I found everyone eating breakfast in their dressing-gowns as they had been dragged from their beds for the warning. Well the raid consisted of 2 or 3 German planes 100s of miles away that did no damage and were brought down.

On Wednesday afternoon I came over to see Gerald who was 'on picket' to find him with a temperature of 102°, and shaking like an aspen leaf – so I finally managed to get him into bed and got a doctor. . . . The old fool of a doctor said he had sunstroke, but as he got no better he was completely foxed. Luckily one Dr. Brady from London was in these parts on Monday and so saw Gerald – now he seems to think Gerald has slight rheumatics and an infection of the throat, and the 'old fogey' thinks he has pneumonic tendencies. Anyway he is better to-day than he has been for a week.

You can picture me having started my "war work" by being a *nurse* as I have to bath him, change sheets etc. etc. It is awful that he can't stay with his company poor darling which consists of: Capt. Jack Harrison (who nearly drowned in Cowes week), Charles Villiers (*very* nice – he is married to Rosemary Seymour's sister) and "Wakey" Chandos-Pole – then the 4 servants and over 100 men.[2] He is absolutely désolé that he can't go with them, it is such *rotten* luck that he should get ill now. Nearly *all* his friends went to-day! They all go to the place you heard about for a fortnight or so – and then go to War – you can probably guess where!!

1. Henry Philip Verey, 1909–84, was Gerald's brother-in-law. He was a lawyer, a Territorial Army officer in the Royal Berkshire Regiment, an honorary colonel of the regiment from the 1960s, and a deputy lieutenant of Berkshire from 1966.

2. Jack Harrison, 1908–63, was later a colonel in the Grenadier Guards. Lieutenant Colonel Sir Charles Villiers died in 1992. Major John Walkelyne (Wakey) Chandos-Pole, 1913–94, was aide-de-camp to the viceroy of India between 1938 and 1939.

12th September 1939　　　　　　　　　　　　　　　　　　*Montreal*
Yesterday Canada declared war on Germany – and twice today troops have gone by (Highlanders with bagpipes) and three truckloads of men in khaki singing, preceded by a siren horn!! Everyone seems to think that in a short space of time the U.S. will change her neutrality laws – Then, I think later she will declare war. I do not see how she can keep out. About 100 of the Dogs of Germans have been arrested here – one man across the street on Drummond. They deserve their fate. Residence on St. Helen's Island in winter is almost too good for a German.

14th September 1939　　　　　　　　　　　　　　　　　　*Montreal*
I had a letter from Hilda [Potter] *yesterday dated the 29th August. Will you please thank her and tell her I will answer some time soon, although there isn't much point in it now, as any news I might have can be transmitted through you – it appears to be more certain to send letters by the Clipper Ships and one leaves N.Y. every Saturday and another from here on Thursdays. As there seems to be a rather strict censorship in England and France we only get general news.*

There is quite a different feeling about war this time everywhere – no excitement – just an acceptance of it. Potty came in yesterday and said there were lots of men coming up from the States to enlist. I gather that Roosevelt will try soon to get the neutrality laws changed there. Well there is <u>one</u> American who isn't neutral, and I have no intention of trying to be in any way – If I can't stand it, I will rent my flat and come up here and work.

Canada seems quiet. I hear the Black Watch going down Drummond Street every morning and the sound of the bagpipes sets all my MacGregor blood boiling – and I long to get at some fat German's throat. My hatred of that race has gone to such fever heat that I don't know how I shall sustain it if the war lasts any time. But my hatred of them is <u>not</u> because they are at war – It is a profound distaste for their very being – their language, looks, fat, attitude of mind, thick headedness, sadism, coarseness – <u>even</u> their literature. I cannot stand <u>anything</u> Teutonic, and the sooner they are swept from the earth the happier I will be, only I had rather have the brutes inhabiting central Europe than have anyone I care about paying the price for defeating them – as much as I hate them. I can truly say that the only thing I like about the Germans is their music – and some of that is too sentimental – Wagner and Shubert [sic] for instance. You had better not tell this to Hilda! She will think I am crazy – I get so wrought up about them that the only antidote for me is to laugh at myself.

Darling, once more, if there is anything in my power to do, let me know. Money, food, anything which it is possible for me to contribute. I shall be very economical and save something for emergencies.

21st September 1939   *Montreal*

This may be my last chance to write you by the Clipper Ships. I shall then begin by sending them by any boat which will take them. As I wrote you a few days ago, there is nothing very much of personal affairs to report save that "we are all well and hope you are" as the niggers all say in their letters! But yesterday Huntly sent to the Red Cross in England a cheque for £10,000. I don't feel that my poor contribution would look like much beside that, but I thought that when they make their appeal, you might contribute something from our joint account in both our names. I <u>must</u> find something to do, or I

shall not be able to get through with it, so I shall try the Red Cross in Rich-
mond if they are going to send supplies to France – not unless they are. Wasn't
it wonderful of Huntly to do that? He said that nothing had been done here
because they were preparing their <u>own</u> appeal to the public and he wanted
England to know that some one here had their immediate call for help at
heart. I am glad he did that right away.

Kossatkine tried to enlist yesterday and was turned down. I think his feel-
ings are hurt! He thinks it's because he is a <u>Russian,</u> but I think he must be
nearing 40 and they want younger men. Everyone is fed up with Mackenzie
King.[1]

I went to lunch with Hugh Wallis' wife and her mother and Mrs. Arthur
Morrice on Tuesday. They have a very sweet house on top of the hill above
Côte des Neiges – a very good lunch which I fear gave them trouble as their
cook went down on the Athenia, but, undaunted, is now on her way out aboard
something else. Mrs. Morrice said the voyage on the 2nd Empress of Britain
was horrible. They ate with their life belts beside them, and slept with them
beside the bed. In the 3rd class they were <u>fined</u> on one of the boats, I forget
which, for not having them every moment. The windows and portholes were
painted <u>black</u>. It must have been cheerful. I am glad I didn't wait because I
had a passage on that boat as you may remember. The Morrice family were
in Biarritz when they got the command to leave. They drove 1400 miles ac-
cording to her – it <u>must</u> have been kilometres – in two days, and crossed the
Channel in a boat designed to carry 300, with 1200 people. They were even
packed in the life boats! We were saved all that. I keep wondering about the
Gilmours and I have never heard a word from Moky – and I am rather wor-
ried about them.[2] *I am sure though that Billy can take care of himself.*[3]

1. William Lyon Mackenzie King, 1874–1950, Canadian Liberal prime minister 1921–30 and 1935–48.

2. Gerna Merle Gilmour, 1909–87, later Akerman, was a Canadian concert pianist, a recitalist, and an interviewer for the BBC's overseas services 1940–65. William (Billy) Gilmour, d. 1959, was Gerna's father.

3. The Gilmours escaped from France in 1940, but Maurice Bisdom (Moky) remained in France throughout the war.

24th September 1939   Warsash

We spend most of the time making A.R.P. curtains etc. and Gerald is having a super-air raid shelter built – and anyone in these parts can use it – and I can use it if I ever want to come back here.[1]

We hear very little news, I don't see why everything should be *quite* so hush-hush but doubtless there's a reason for it. The B.B.C. is *so* dreary that it is really laughable, and everyone is making fun of it. We listen to the wireless in the evenings – most of it in German! on Saturday night we heard news given in English in Rome – then Budapest – then Hamburg – and then something called Radio Warsaw! The Germans have switched the wavelength and broadcast propaganda supposedly from Warsaw in every language. It is really very interesting to hear them all, and the German ones are terribly funny. They tell of Polish atrocities to German women and children – or they have a man telling of the "Berlin night-life" – the wonderful succulent dishes, good wines, etc. in restaurants – gay music – happy laughing faces etc. It is so ridiculous that it keeps us amused. They understand the English not at all and the violent speeches and arguments are puerile –

1. A.R.P.: Air Raid Precautions.

28th September 1939   Warsash

Yesterday's news was *charming* was it not? First the fall of Warsaw – then the announcement that income-tax is increased 2/- in the £ making a total of 7/6!! How the British people stand it I don't know. We'll be paying nearly 50% now – Whew – a man with income of £100,000 will pay *£82,000* in tax!! Glad I haven't £100,000! Tobacco is now 24/- a pound ($6.00?). 1 bottle of whiskey is 13/9. Well, let's hope it helps in giving us a quick and glorious victory! – I think they were wise to put it up in one swift blow, rather than gradually dribbling up the threepences and sixpences.

I saw in the paper a day or so ago that a generous Canadian has anonymously sent a *huge* sum to the Red Cross. I must say I was *staggered* when you told me who it was. How simply marvellous of him! I can hardly take it in.

Gerald is out laying bricks in the air raid shelter, and I have been making more curtains. If there are to be any officers stationed near here we shall offer them the house for baths, etc. It will be nice and cold, living in a tent, for the poor things later on.

I listened to Roosevelt's speech for one hour, and finally turned it off. I think you are probably right when you say it is better after all to be *here* instead of so far away.

I shall send the Red Cross something in our names. Thank God for the j. account. I will not call on it until necessary, but please don't feel I am *needy*, as I shall let you know if I am!

29th September 1939   *West Haven, Conn.* [1]
You can understand that it is almost impossible to write here — so this will only be a note. I hope that Gerald is making progress towards a quick recovery. I am so sad that he is ill, but I don't like to think of him in France either, so, which ever way I turn I do not seem to find much comfort. America is the only country where the news isn't censored and we get the wildest rumours, to which I pay no attention.

I saw Alice [Reynolds] *yesterday. She has had the grippe too and is rather pathetic, but still has spirit.* [2] *A Mlle. Caneau!? french teacher was present, and I launched into the Germans knowing I was on sure ground I do not think she had <u>dared</u> say as much, and she thoroughly enjoyed herself. Her father fought at Verdun and she said she was a bit disillusioned because of having to do it all over again. I said because you and the other Allies were weak enough to let the job go unfinished last time. This time one can't tell anything because of Russia, but things happen so fast that I am not going to form any false ideas if I can help it — There is great opposition to a change in neutrality but only the opposition is vocal. It is rather certain to be changed — I shall use all the meagre influence I have to help the cause.*

I told Alice that it was a war for civilization and Christianity and no decent person could afford to keep out of it in some way — I <u>lambasted</u> Lindberg [sic] *for whom I have conceived a violent dislike.* [3]

Madeleine sends her love and says I must tell you that I have <u>told her what to think</u>. I'm afraid I have. It isn't ladylike but I can't help it.

1. Madeleine Nason's home.

2. The "grippe" is influenza.

3. Charles Lindbergh, 1902–74, U.S. aviator and supporter of the America First Committee, formed in 1940 to discourage U.S. participation in World War II.

14th October 1939   *Richmond*

It was not surprising that Warsaw fell. That was inevitable, but they won't have such an easy time on the Western front. I feel now that there has always been something prophetic in my hatred of the Germans – that of all their hideous crimes, the worst one they have committed is to let the Bolsheviks into Western Europe. When Russia was ruled by the upper class that was different, but this man Stalin is the arch butcher of the ages – He and Hitler are such fiends that words fail to convey any meaning.

Stuart and I both go about spreading what we can in the way of "propaganda" as we see the Cause. There are a lot of boneheaded people in this place, but even if they seem foolish and ignorant, they are all in sympathy with the Allies. They don't understand a great deal and at times it is difficult.

26th October 1939   *Richmond*

We have all been in a rage with Lindbergh, but I think he isn't worth the excitement, so I have stopped talking about it.

Tomorrow, Nana celebrates her ninetieth birthday, which is something of an embarrassment to Aunt Florie, as she is afraid people will count and come to some conclusion about her own age.

12th November 1939   *Richmond*

I sent you no. 20 by air-mail on Saturday (yesterday) but as I am never certain that those Lisbon bound missives reach you, I also sent off something like this into the blue. The British steamers aren't advertized and the American ones are no longer allowed into warring nations' ports –

I suppose the Nazis will use the attempt on Hitler's life as a reason for raping some neutral country – the world seems to expect it. The papers are

even forecasting it. They have deceived the world a few times too often – Even
if they ever told the truth now, no one would believe them – only they have
never been caught at it yet! That is one thing they haven't tried – I must say
that for 25 years I have tried to get people to listen to me about the German
character, but it never occurred to me that they could go so far <u>beyond</u> every-
thing horrible of which <u>I</u> might have imagined them capable. It is because no
Anglo-Saxon <u>could</u> think of such brutalities – That is why I failed to accuse
them <u>adequately</u>.

29th November 1939   Windsor

You told me a long time ago to send some money to the Red Cross in your
and my name. As Huntly had given such a large sum, I thought it would be a
good idea to send small sums now and then to worthy causes. Consequently
have paid out the following and do hope that you agree with my ideas, as I
can help people I know are in need –

    Gerald has sent £10-10-0 to the Grenadier Fund
    I have sent: £1-0-0. (Grenadier Guards Comforts)
    £1-0-0 Red Cross
    10-0 Warsash Knitting League for Sailors
    £1-0-0 cigarettes for the troops
    10-0 Tuberculosis stamps!
    £10-0-0 Mrs. Spence (lost husband on 'Royal Oak')
besides three quid to Gladys Godden. I shall send clothes etc. to Grenadier
Comforts from time to time.

30th November 1939   Windsor

We are shortly leaving Windsor as there are several new companies to be
formed, and they are to be stationed at a race-course near London. Gerald is
to be made a Company Commander (though is not being made a Capt. . . .
scandalous).

    At the moment the officers in Gerald's Co. are: Rupert Bevan, the
Duke of Northumberland, Lord Stanley (Derby's grand-son) and one other
though the names are changed nearly every day.[1] Northumberland has

suggested that the officers and their wives live at his house which is only a few miles away.[2] But everything is still very much in the air, as no one knows who is going etc. and his house has no servants, only 2 caretakers as he hasn't lived in it for 2 years. We'll have to get a cook etc. and I gather that I am to live there and do the catering etc. for them. It would be very nice to be with Gerald but I don't see how I can go unless at least one other wife turns up to help me and keep me company.

Tuesday afternoon Gerald and I and John Glyn, Stanley, and Northumberland drove over to the "Barracks" and then in the black out tried to find the way to the house from there.[3] We drove around and around amid factories and villas etc. and suddenly saw the walls of the estate. Once inside the lodge gates we might have been in the heart of the country! A mile or so drive through a beautiful park to the house, and gardens down to the Thames. There *were* several thousand acres, but I believe he only owns about 300 of them now. The house, one of the show places of England, was built in 1400, and as far as I could see in the fast falling night, perfectly beautiful. We looked at the various rooms he thought of using for the mess and would open up 10 or 12 bedrooms all in one wing. We went into some other rooms that have been more or less shut up but the ceilings were all perfectly beautiful – one long gallery entirely Adams the whole ceiling, walls etc. and the panelling. All the pictures, old furniture and valuables have been stored for the 'duration'. I should love to have seen them. We were home about 6.30 and I felt tired from walking.

While writing this I hear that Russia has invaded Finland – o Lord, what next? Wonder what this last move will lead to – I just don't *think* about it!

1. Henry George Percy, 1912–40, the ninth Duke of Northumberland from 1930 and a Grenadier Guards officer, was killed in action at Dunkirk. Baron Edward John Stanley, 1918–94, from 1948 the eighteenth Earl of Derby, was a major in the Grenadier Guards. Edward George Villiers Stanley, 1865–1948, was the seventeenth Earl of Derby, member of Parliament West Houghton Division of Lancashire 1892–1906, secretary of state for war 1916–18, and ambassador to France 1918–20.

2. Syon House, in Middlesex, is eight miles from central London and is the seat of the Dukes of Northumberland. Originally a medieval abbey, it was redesigned in 1547 and again in the eighteenth century.

3. John Glyn, director of Glyn Mills and Co. Bank.

3rd December 1939   *Richmond*

Tonight, I am meeting, of all people Mary Wingfield Scott, to tell her some ancient history of Richmond.[1] *She is getting up an exhibit for the Valentine Museum, and she was interested in Nana's stories about the school she went to in Richmond nearly 80 years ago, and in Jefferson Davis, President of the Confederacy, who used to ride by on his horse! It makes me feel like a centenarian.*

1. The author Mary Wingfield Scott, 1895–1983, wrote books including *Houses of Old Richmond* (Richmond: Valentine Museum, 1941) and *Old Richmond Neighborhoods* (Richmond: Whittet and Shepperson, 1950).

9th December 1939   The Berkeley
                                                                   Berkeley Street
                                                                   London W.1.

Wednesday I lunched with Phyl and Clive Dawson – they were up here for a few days. Then met Gerald who went to play squash and to buy 10 mouth-organs for his men! Parkinson gave him 2 left shoes so he played squash in bare feet. I forgot to say that Tues. evening Gerald arrived looking different – on close examination, I realized he was a *Captain.* He is *acting* Captain *unpaid,* but still a Capt. and the 3 pips on his shoulder looked very good to me! They may take away his rank if he no longer becomes a Co. Commander, i.e. if he went to France without his Company, but I hope not – and after 3 months he *should* be paid. He also was wearing a large mourning band (!) but wasn't quite sure whom it was for! Typical – Apparently Princess Louise died last week –[1] I had not seen it in the papers.

I haven't seen the papers to-night, but isn't it marvellous how the Finns have been holding out? I don't discuss politics and war much in my letters on account of censors. Perhaps my epistles sound as if I didn't know there was a war on!

1. Princess Louise, 1848–1939, was Queen Victoria's youngest daughter and the only one to marry a commoner (the ninth Duke of Argyll, governor-general of Canada 1878–83). She was also a sculptor.

17th December 1939   *Richmond*

Just before I started this, we had news over the radio of the scuttling of the
Graf Spee – now there are only two more of the beastly things prowling about
the night seas dealing death to whom they may send to the bottom.[1] *I would*
have preferred to have the G.S. done to death with British gunfire, or _towed_ *to*
Scapa Flow but this is better than nothing.[2]

1. The battleship *Graf Spee* was scuttled by its German commander on 17 December
1939 following the Battle of the River Plate.

2. Scapa Flow was a naval base in the Orkney Islands during World Wars I and II.

20th December 1939   12 Sloane Terrace Mansions
                                                                          London[1]

Gerald has a new soldier-servant who has been a Grenadier, a policeman,
and a chauffeur-valet to Sir Miles Lampson in Egypt![2] He is *terrific* apparently and a real Jeeves. He is making Gerald slightly clothes-conscious
which is all to the good, and G. announced the other day that he couldn't
let Chivers see a certain pair of torn pants, so I rushed out and bought some
new underwear for the birthday! Chivers stands over Gerald in the morning, coughs and quietly says "Pardon me sir, but I think it is time you arose".

Am told the American press is very anti-British. Having said the English
were *yellow* not to fight in '38, they now say "Dirty dogs, you are plunging
the world into war". Is this true? What do they want, hummingbirds?? And
they are so *proud* of being a peaceful nation. My Godfrey, don't they think
we want peace?

I wonder what the Parlour Bolsheviks (like Weesie) think of Russia
walking into Finland? Well it's all terrible – this chaos – but it is certainly
very interesting. I see the Columbus scuttled herself off Va. this morning.[3]

1. The home of Hilda Potter and Norah Allfrey.

2. Sir Miles Lampson, 1880–1964, was the first Baron Kinearn. He was high commis-
sioner for Egypt and the Sudan in 1933 and the first British ambassador to Egypt 1936–46.

3. The German liner *Columbus* was scuttled to avoid capture by a British destroyer.

8th January 1940   *Richmond*

About the U.S. being anti-British – It is not true – they are about 95% pro-British I should say – save for a few Germans and the Communists. I should be entirely for the Allies. That they do not wish to go to war is another question – some people I know think we should be in it to the limit. But that is not the way Governments behave – You know well that if France and England had gone for Germany when she went on the Rhine against their promises, the world wouldn't be faced with this situation. That is the way governments behave, and we will behave exactly the same way – not do anything until we have to. Sometimes it works and sometimes it doesn't. In the meantime, our fleet is in the Pacific where England's fleet is negligible, and although Congress has been very greedy about payment for war materials, at [least] we are letting England and France have what they want, knowing that Germany can't get anything, and, save for a protest now and then, do nothing about England's taking what goes to the "other party". In other words we want to go through the motions of being neutral and we know all the time we aren't. Don't let anyone say we are anti-British – that would be fatal for England. We want to do everything we can to keep the English Speaking countries as loyal to each other as we can.

We are going to spend an enormous sum to protect the Pacific against Asiatics and if we can remain together (the democracies I mean) and France and England can face the East and we can face the West – and keep the Atlantic free – well that is a far seeing policy. England of course has the harder task now – But I am certain the U.S. cannot afford to let the Huns win –

I have written to the Embassy to find if I can send hams and sugar –

10th January 1940   London SW1

Well, my little fat boy has gone and I expect you can imagine how I am feeling. He is in France by now though of course I don't know *where*, However I will be able to work it out by his letters as we have an intricate code which I have learned by heart so I won't have any "incriminating papers".[1]

It was a beautiful day which made it worse really as the Pink Cottage looked so sweet and he had to say good-bye to the P.C. and George and me, but managed to smile and wave a cheery good-bye. He went with 2 very nice brother officers and several sergeants so that was a help.

1. According to Ginnie's unpublished memoir, Gerald wrote, "My dearest one, the skies are grey since I left you," which she found very touching until she realized it was code for "ten miles north of Lille."

7th March 1940   London

Well, well, well! I had 2 cables this morning forwarded from the Pink Cottage and you could have knocked me over with a feather!! I was still a bit sleepy when I opened them, and thought at first I must be dreaming!!! I can't get over Huntly having told you my 'news' [of pregnancy] but I hope he did the right thing. I left the decision to him, so he must have thought it was best to tell you – but as I managed to keep it a secret all this time, it seems rather a shame that now you will have these last few weeks of anxiety –

8th March 1940   Montreal

I sent you a cable when Huntly told me about your news. I try to be as plucky as you have been. That's all, and I am _not_ of course. Huntly was so enchanted that he couldn't keep it and couldn't do his work all day on account of having to keep it until he came home at tea time.

First, I want to say that I am grateful to you for _not_ having told me. I don't think I could have got through the winter – I could have stood it had it been _me_, but not for you. That's what being your mother means. As I care more about you than any other one thing in the world, what happens to you devastates me in a way which nothing else does. And you are wise enough to know that –

I can't afford for your sake or mine to be too sentimental, and I am sure you also understand that. Strange, but before your news came, I had written Gerald the day before that I had spent 27 years trying to keep "Life" away from you, and, of course, it may have been the wrong thing to do but whatever I have done, _you_ have proved yourself equal to all that _might_ happen, and are *"bigger" also, than anything which might happen to you – and that <u>should</u> be, and is, my reward –*

Potty has been chosen to go to the Staff College at Camberley and leaves here on the 12th of this month. He expects to arrive about the 28th and wants to look you up <u>at once</u>. I haven't said anything <u>yet</u>. He is going to Ivry with us today.

10th April 1940   8 Park Street
                                                                   Windsor
                                                                   Berks

I am so sorry to keep you waiting in suspense like this but Baby Dumpling shows great reluctance to be born. I hope to Heaven I won't have to wait for five long weeks like poor old Joanie [Verey] did.

Well – were you *stunned* by the news of Germany invading Denmark and Norway? Isn't it incredible? I have been listening to every broadcast with bated breath, but so far the news is rather a jumble and can't make out what is going on. I hope it doesn't mean that Gerald will be popping off to strange places again, but I don't *think* so. Anyway let's hope "B.D." arrives before he leaves.

3rd May 1940   Windsor

Needless to say, I am very thrilled indeed with my infant![1] She is very sweet and I only wish you could see her. I suppose she is hideous really, but not to me!

Had very few pains (and not at all bad) then Maxwell and Sister decided forceps would have to be used – the anaesthetist arrived in 1 minute – I had a *lovely* smell of gas and oxygen and was out like a light, the baby was born at 1.30 P.M. Saturday afternoon – I came to about 2.30 (not quite sure when really) and there was "Baby Dumpling" on Sister's knee! I just couldn't believe my eyes!!

"Baby Dumpling" weighed 7 1/2 lbs. at birth – she has dark blue eyes rather wide apart, beige fluff on her head, fat cheeks, a nice pale skin, the usual squshed [*sic*] nose, flat well-shaped ears, a pretty mouth – lovely little body and is gradually growing around rather *large* hands! O yes, fair eyebrows, and rather long brown lashes – my description probably makes her sound much too beautiful, but have tried to convey what she looks like.

I have received to date 9 cables, 18 telegrams, 55 letters, 27 boxes of flowers, and 15 presents for 'Baby Dumpling' – which is very very nice – (and pretty good for wartime) Huntly suggests I call B.D. Narvika.[2] The news is a bit grim at the moment, isn't it? The Navy was certainly wonderful in Norway, and the public seem to think we should have overwhelmed the Nazis on land as well –

1. Jennifer (Jenny) Rosemary Virginia Potter was born 13 April 1940 and eventually became a photographer.

2. This name refers to naval battles at Narvik, where the British attempted to capture the ice-free port. These culminated on 13 April, the day Jenny was born.

11th May 1940   Windsor

Baby Dumpling is four weeks old to-day, and she's a very beautiful baby. She weighs 8 lbs. 10 ounces – a gain of 5 ounces in the past week. I am still feeding her though she has a bit of Cow & Gate tinned food as well. She smiled for the first time on Thursday, also had her first outing, so it was a gala day for her, if not for the rest of the world!

We went for a short drive in an open Victoria, the sun was beautifully warm – we drove down the Long Walk in Windsor. I have never seen a more beautiful Spring – chestnuts, lilac, everything is at its height. Could anything be more remote from war than driving down an english lane in a Victoria??

Gerald, you will be very glad to hear, is *safe*. Not long after he returned to France, he drank some fluid from a bottle of whiskey – it turned out to be Pyrene (fire extinguisher). He was quite ill for a week, then was sent to hospital for X-rays and is lying safely there, and feeling almost all-right! So Sister Griffiths and I hope he will drink some more![1] I think he must have a special guardian angel – the Finnish Peace Pact was signed the night he was to sail – and now, having very foolishly drank Pyrene, he is safely behind the lines when the Big Push begins!![2] His letter rec'd tonight says he is on the mend.

1. The nurse Miss H. Griffiths was hired to assist with Jenny's birth and postnatal care.

2. The treaty of Moscow signed on 12 March 1940 ended the Finnish-Soviet war, which had begun on 30 November 1939. Both the French and British governments were preparing to send an expeditionary force to assist the Finns, in which Gerald would have taken part, but the peace treaty was signed before the force departed.

19th May 1940   Windsor

I hope you received my cable that I sent last week, and that by now you have received some letters *since* the arrival of Dumpling. When I heard from Gerald that he was being detained at hospital, I was very relieved, as prefer him to be in hospital than at the front, although I am sure he is furious. I have had another letter from him since sending your cable – telling me that he hoped to be released in a few days, but of course *I* am hoping that he's still there. So far he's been very lucky, so I pray his luck may continue. It seems rather feeble to write *my* news, when this terrible battle is being waged. Everything else in the *world* pales into insignificance when one thinks of the struggle, the tragedies, the heroism that is now taking place in France. From what I read in the papers it looks as if the isolationists in the U.S. are being shouted down, let's hope the Americans will send planes and then more planes to the Allies.

It looks as if before long, civilians here are going to have a taste of what war is like – there is only one thing to do, and that is to be a *fatalist*! I have thought of how *for your sake* I would like to get away – wouldn't one look silly though to run off when other people can't, and rush to a place of safety only to be knocked down by a taxi! So please try to be fatalists. It makes me very unhappy to think that you are probably worried about me – but it is only for your sake and Gerald's that I worry about myself! As for Gerald I hope his "guardian angel" (that kept him from getting to Finland, that kept him from *breaking his neck* when he fell on the ice that time in France, that sent him off to hospital just before the Blitzkrieg came etc.) is still looking after him!!

Baby Dumpling and I are flourishing. She was 5 weeks old yesterday and now weighs 9 lbs. 2 ounces. She is *so* pretty now – o Lordy! how I wish you could see her!! The photographs have arrived, and I'll send one off tomorrow.

Its 1 A.M. so must get to bed and will post this in the morning. I am terribly well, in fact never felt better. O how I wish you could see your adorable grandchild. All these years I have wanted a baby – now I've got one – and the damn Blitzkrieg comes along, and I can't show her to you. Still, let's hope we'll all be together soon, won't it be wonderful?

Isn't it *incredible* to think the Bosches [*sic*] should be in France again? What was the reaction to Churchill as P.M. in U.S. I felt so sad for Chamberlain, still I suppose it was better to have a "man of action" –

3rd June 1940   *Richmond*

The Red Cross work here has increased by leaps and bounds. Among the people I doubt if there are many isolationists – Everyone wants to help except the German population and the communists and they are being watched and reported on. The German here has left. It was interesting to note that living on the <u>same floor</u> with him was the local F.B.I. agent (alias [?]). I made up my mind that I would not live here under the same roof with him, and told the management as much – I had the satisfaction of being told that they didn't want him back. He is a rather miserable-looking individual, and <u>some</u> people think him innocent. I do not think <u>any</u> one of them is innocent and I "go" on that basis –

I had a sweet letter from Gerald telling me about the Pyrene. God bless it, and the mere thought of his being there [Dunkirk] at all absolutely "floored" me, and I showed my first sign of weakness –[1] But most of the time I am able to face what I have to do – Funny, I find I have to be alone a great deal. I must be more religious than I <u>thought</u> I was.

Dr. Calisch rang me up with tears in his voice to thank me. He is Treasurer [of British War Relief Richmond]. *The funny part was that I was rather ashamed of not having given them more. But I decided I would give a certain part of my income <u>each</u> month to war work, instead of giving it all at once – I have very few expenses this year because I am not going abroad and I want to*

do everything I can to help the wonderful men and women who are fighting
this war. It is a drop in the bucket but if <u>everyone</u> would do the same it would
reach staggering proportions.

1. The British Expeditionary Force (BEF) in France was positioned on the Belgian border, around Lille, but was forced to withdraw toward Dunkirk. The evacuation of British
and French troops from there began on 26 May and was completed on 3 June. Gerald was
wounded defending the Dunkirk perimeter in the Battle of Furnes on 31 May.

6th June 1940   Warsash

[I] was wondering what had happened to Gerald who was in hospital in
France, but kept writing to say he was leaving for the front. Of course I
hoped that he wouldn't be allowed to go! as he had been so ill from drinking "Pyrene" in mistake for whiskey – he vomited every hour for nearly a
fortnight, and was really very lucky not to have died of it.

We worked [on the Pink Cottage] in the day – listened to the 9 o'clock
news over the wireless – then did the black-out etc. and went to bed steeped
in gloom. It has been a ghastly fortnight, but I never believed so many of the
B.E.F. [British Expeditionary Force] would be saved. It is really wonderful
that they weren't all annihilated, you can imagine how I felt knowing that
Gerald was probably there, and that most of our friends were in the thick
of it all!

Saturday I returned from a shopping expedition to hear the telephone
ringing. It was to say that Gerald was back in England! – slightly wounded
but safe. I burst into tears with relief. O God, isn't it wonderful that he came
back – I know I am very very lucky indeed, but it is very hard to realize
that so many of our friends have gone.

Mabs Busch came to see me Saturday afternoon, also Colin and Mary
Gray – She is expecting a baby any minute. They were all three so thrilled
to hear about Gerald. We telephoned the hospital Saturday night as had
heard he was to have an operation that afternoon, but could get no information about him. I was afraid he was going to lose his right arm and that
they had kept it from me, but he never had the operation after all, and I
gather there is no danger of the arm going now. He had a bullet that went

straight through his arm near the shoulder, breaking up the bone a bit, but luckily bullet went through the *middle* of his arm-bone, so didn't shatter the edge.

Mum went to see him on Sunday – and I spent all Sunday trying to *think* how I could get to him, as was still feeding the baby – didn't want to leave Sister [Griffiths] here alone and didn't want to drag the baby around England – As we had already started weaning her I decided to give it up for good, and Sister bound up my front with adhesive tape, and gave me lots of salts. It wasn't as bad as I expected but felt very hot and thirsty in this extremely hot weather we are having.

Got everything ready to go off on Monday morning, and made all arrangements for food etc. as was leaving Sister here alone with the baby. Then waited for Mum's telephone – she rang up Sunday evening, to give me news of him – that he was exhausted but getting along well – and wanted some clothes etc – as he had *nothing* – not even soap or pyjamas and they hadn't had time to bath him. She also said that he was of course heartbroken over the death of several of his best friends – then Mum told me that Christopher Jeffreys had been killed – and poor dear Reggie West – and George Northumberland. O God, isn't it awful? George N. was a charming person and a *real* gentleman if I have ever met one – it makes one think the world doesn't make sense when you see fat jews going to their businesses, and men like these 3 mentioned getting killed.

Feeling quite numb, I packed up Gerald's clothes and a small suitcase for myself – and got into bed prepared for sleep, when I heard the sounds of gunfire. We got up again and wandered about for an hour, but it was *very* far away I think and died down after a bit, so at 2 A.M. we crawled into bed again. Sister was up at 5.30 and at 1/4 to 7 woke me to get my *bust* ready for the journey! I caught the 9 o'clock train from Southampton –

It was so wonderful to see Gerald, and he looked *much* better than I expected, and had been washed and shaved and was quite hale and hearty considering. He is altogether wonderful, and we tried not to mention our friends that have been killed but talked about the P. Cottage and B. Dumpling. He was in hospital when the Blitzkrieg came, and was rather weak as he had lost over a stone and was on a milk diet. He was told to return to England but refused, gathered together a bit of kit – and started out for the village where his Battalion was — They had of course left it days before, and it had been bombarded twice since, but he *found his equipment*, made a Company of some guardsmen that had got left behind — and made for the front line. He fought for 56 hours on end, and had to take over a company in place of Christopher when he was killed. The commanding officer Jack Lloyd was also killed —[1] When he was wounded he was put into an ambulance, which was twice shelled on the way, also when they arrived — He was twice shelled *walking* onto the destroyer — Luckily he didn't get onto the hospital ship as that was sunk, but *walked* to the destroyer, and was twice bombed on the way to England where he was put into the hospital train! and there he was sitting up looking quite normal — What a man! He seemed to be rather worried that he needed an enema so badly as "*days* ago I was just going to relieve myself when the damn lavatory was blown up" —

He is so anxious to have news of the 1st Battalion, but nothing has come through yet, and I am dreading the news. He showed me his tin hat which had been grazed by a bullet. You will probably want to write to Rosemary Jeffreys, her address is Burkham House, Alton, Hants. She asked me for your address a few weeks ago as she wanted to congratulate you on being a grandmother, but don't know if she did.

Lally, and Vera Sinclair turned up to see Gerald too.[2] The poor French officers looked longingly at Gerald who was surrounded by a harem! The little man in the next bed speaks no english, I bought him some washing things, and am trying to find out the address of his one friend in England —

Took Lally and Vera back to London in "my car", dined with Mum — then met Pothier for an hour or so (he is now working in London) — I stayed the night with Mum, went to see Gerald again on Tuesday — had 'high tea' with Mum — caught the 7.30 train for S'ton [Southampton] — and was home soon after ten.

1. Lieutenant Colonel John A. Lloyd (Jack), d. 1940, a Grenadier Guards company commander.

2. "Lally" (also "Lallie") is Aline Mary Burge née Potter, later Butler, 1912–2002, Gerald's sister. She was a sculptor.

9th June 1940   *Richmond*

Somehow, I have not been able to write since I received your cable – only I dispatched one to you in return. I hope you received it – I realized where Gerald was after I had his letter and I spent a horrible week, waiting – What a magnificent feat the B.E.F. succeeded in accomplishing – The whole world held its breath – It was the most dramatic event in all the world's history, I think – I spent my time as usual, evenly divided between praying and working – I haven't read anything for weeks – I simply cannot do it. It is cowardly of me, but I must live, anyhow, until this catastrophe is over, one way or another.

I am going to take a course in making Red Cross surgical dressings in order to be a supervisor. They are badly in need of them here – and that is something I <u>can</u> do – so I might as well do what I can – No one here is <u>enjoying</u> life –

Everyone in Richmond practically has rung me up about you and Gerald. <u>Carrie Washington</u> was wonderful.[1] *She said she had her <u>church members</u> praying that "God would rain down blessings on all my family" no matter what else He found to do. She was so dramatic that I wept – and she wiped her eyes with the corner of her apron – Dear old Carrie – I shall never be able to discharge her now. She said she always prayed for us before she ate. Such loyalty and devotion is very touching, to say the least, and all the cobwebs left in the corners of the rooms don't matter!*

1. Carrie Washington was Bougie's maid.

12th June 1940   Warsash

Mussolini is playing a nice stab in the back isn't he?[1] I hope a few Abyssinians get hold of him before he's through, as they will know *just* what to do with him!

I am so thrilled that the U.S. are sending planes, etc. Lets hope they get here before long. André Maurois spoke over the wireless about France last night, it sounded as if he were crying, it was frightfully sad –[2] But Duff Cooper gave a damn good speech about the Italians, it was grand!![3]

The weather is *glorious* as it has been since middle of April!! The Pink Cottage is covered in roses, the hay is being cut in the surrounding fields, George is rolling over and over on the lawn, Dumpling is "gurgling" in her pram – and the Germans are nearing Paris – O LORDY let's hope they don't get there –

1. Italy declared war on Britain and France 10 June 1940.

2. André Maurois, 1885–1968, was a French writer and novelist.

3. Alfred Duff Cooper, 1890–1954, was from 1952 the first Viscount Norwich and was ambassador to France 1944–47. As minister of information from 1940 to 1941, he would have given the speech referred to.

23rd June 1940   Warsash

Things happen so quickly these days that it seems almost futile to write, knowing how very stale my news will be by the time you receive it. "As we go to Press" France has capitulated, the terms will of course be very hard indeed, I will never be able to understand what happened to make the French decide against 'fighting to the end'. Now it seems we have no ally except the U.S. support – and this little island seems very small, but I am sure we shall fight to the end, it would be terrible if we didn't –

Gerald is continually badgering me to go to America, I am so touched by his unselfishness in wanting me to go away and take our baby with me, when he knows the odds are against his seeing us again. He keeps after me about it, and I know he wants me to go for my sake and especially too for *yours* – But put yourself in my place – he wants me to go very soon – he won't be well for weeks more I am sure – this means that I shall leave him here alone and wounded – living in the P. Cottage until he is well enough to fight! How *CAN* I do that? For your sakes, I want *so much* to go, but I cannot leave him while we can still be together – He keeps saying that I am American, etc. and that he will be well very soon – and all the things he can think of to persuade me to go. Sister G. gets so overcome by his unselfish attitude she starts to *snuffle* – I am sure that you will think I am right in staying here – How can I see everyone giving up everything, and think of my own security. As I have said many times before, I am *perfectly miserable* for YOUR sakes – I shall try and do the right thing and the sensible thing – *Please* do not worry about me, as I know I shall be all-right. It is as safe here as anywhere, and we have the finest shelter you have ever imagined –

Sister and I distempered it pale green – It has a carpet, comfortable chairs, a fire, and a cot for Dumpling etc. We are keeping rabbits, and Bench has made some hutches.

3rd July 1940   Warsash

I just feel completely numb when I think about France which is just as well. It is too much to take in isn't it? O Lord why should they have been totally lacking in leadership at a time like this? de Gaulle seems a good man – as Algy Dawson says "at least he's *under 80* which is all to the good".

Well, your grand-daughter was christened on Friday – and do not fall flat, but at the *last moment* we decided to call her Jennifer! I do hope you aren't disappointed about it – but she *looks* like Jennifer, and it seems *right* somehow – and it sounds very 'cutesey' with Potter, don't you think? She is such a sweetie, and full of smiles, that Jennifer Potter suits her very well.

Her *full* name is: Jennifer Rosemary Virginia. It's an awful mouthful but I wanted to call her after you and Nana, and Jennifer Va. doesn't go, so threw in Rosemary after R. Jeffreys!!! – She is of course still 'Baby Dumpling'.

Nannie is short and fat, about 50 with henna'd hair, and glorious set of false teeth, and her name is Violet! The baby adores her as she has a gentle touch and an ample bosom! She is rather *grand* for the Pink Cottage (as she has been with the Princesse de Faucigny-Lucinge, the Duchesse de Coromandel, Lady Mercy Dean and others!!), but I think she's going to be all-right when she settles down. Nannie takes quite good snaps, so we shall send you some as soon as possible.

I received a telegram from Gerna [Gilmour] in the middle of the christening tea-party, and she telephoned me the following day. She and Billy are in London where they have taken a small service flat for the time being. They escaped from St. Jean with their lives and 1 suitcase each.[1] I have suggested they come and stay down here at the Golf Club if they want it –

We have warnings now and then of course, but we all retire to the shelter where one feels *very* safe, so don't worry.

1. The town of St.-Jean-de-Luz near Biarritz in southwest France, where Ginnie and Gerna had attended school in the 1920s.

8th July 1940   *Richmond*

First I would never exert undue pressure to persuade you to come to America if you felt it wasn't the right thing or if you didn't want to. I can put myself in your place, and I know that you would be very unhappy — I only said occasion might arise when it would be <u>the best thing</u>, and <u>if</u> it did, I want you to know that I will be ready for it, or even to take <u>any</u> Potter who might wish to come — Let us hope the day never comes. Please explain this to Gerald —

We are arranging here through the English Speaking Union to take English children. One woman is taking <u>50</u> — Mrs. Cocke of "Claremont" — Many people have said they wanted them. I think this is the most unselfish service we can do. I can't take any, situated as I am at present, but shall offer to put up some money for support. Also I may put something more in j.a. [joint account] *because the <u>more</u> American money <u>spent in England</u> now, the more it helps the war — You could spend it where it would help. I shall consult the B. of M.* [Bank of Montreal]. *I consider that England is fighting for the world and that includes America and I want to do my bit.*

I read a paper yesterday for the first time in about two months — News trickles into me just the same — and <u>other people</u> force me to hear the radio, because everyone has one and they keep them going constantly. I am heart broken about the French débâcle, and am very much embarrassed as well as I promised Jeanne Johnson and Edith Ragland to help with the relief work in France. Now, I have no desire to do so, as I prefer to give my entire effort to England — I shall have to make a compromise with them — It is very sad, but I can never feel the same about France again, I fear — I realize that the people themselves are not wholly responsible for their rotten politicians — and I don't want to do them an injustice, but, when the "heart" goes out of a thing, only the shell is left. Either I should have wished to die before this war, or live long enough, now, to see some of the cruelties avenged, and to see England victorious, to see America help, and France risen from her bitter infamy and shame. That would be a good end. Well, all this is idle to speak of, now —

There is only one issue, and one objective – Sometimes, the news over here is fantastic. I try not to see it, nor believe it if I <u>do</u> see it.

Everyone is well – and when I last heard from Huntly he had just got his new Lagonda from England. He was caught <u>by one day</u> in the meshes of the new 80% tax on luxuries! He wanted to give the money to England and that is why he ordered the English car – now he gives 80% to Canada as well. His income tax is now 69% of his income – However, he doesn't mind, and he says people are satisfied with it.

21st July 1940   *Richmond*

Thank Heaven we have finished with the two political conventions. Decent people are disgusted with their antics. It is traditional to make a circus of it, and they did not depart from their silly custom. I am deeply concerned about this country – It seems to be dancing a "danse macabre" in the face of inevitable consequences, but things are going on – There is a quiet movement underneath all the nonsense – As usual, I have joined everything which points to preparation – The other day I had a telegram which said, "Please wire President to try to stop isolationalist trend at Chicago" (that is where the Convention for Roosevelt's nomination was held) so I sent it, saying what they told me, and adding "Country behind your foreign policy. We are in deadly peril." I am beginning to feel quite intimate with Mr. R. as I wrote him a letter not very long ago. I joined something called "Committee to defend America by helping England" – It is a nation wide thing, with a unit in Richmond. Mr. Sands is Chairman and many people I know are in it among them, Morris Pinckney.

22nd July 1940   Warsash

Who do you think we had for the week-end?? Gerna and Billy Gilmour!! They arrived from London on Friday afternoon, and we put them up at the Golf Club. Gerna left Paris in her car a few days before it fell – and had to drive alone, and all day and night down to St. Jean de Luz – they escaped on a Dutch boat from Bayonne – a boat to hold 700 passengers, and there were 4000 on board. She and Billy, John Gilmour, Val and her husband and

2 yr. old baby sat on the floor of the lounge – they were over 3 days getting here and had practically no food. Naughty La Touche was on board also. Val and her baby returned to Canada.

John, Val's husband and G. and Billy have a flat in London for the time being. They both looked very well, but were very glad to have a peaceful few days at Warsash. Gerna is very worried about her beau Miguel of whom she has heard nothing. They were *very* lucky to get out of France – though of course their car, furniture, etc. is gone. She gave Isabelle Baignol her car though of course they can't get any petrol, but she *might* be able to sell it.[1] It was difficult to get food at St. Jean even when they left. God knows what it must be like in France now.

June 23rd

Didn't have time to finish this yesterday and have been busy all day until now so hope to get this letter off to-night with luck. It's a beautiful night so I suppose we can expect a warning but hope they don't come for a bit. It's an awful bore going to the shelter but we feel we *must* always go, as it would be silly not to use it. It does give one a very safe feeling and it's nice and cosy when you get there but hard to make up your mind to get out of your warm bed in the middle of the night. It would be useless to tell you that we never have warnings because you must know that we do, but usually we don't even *hear* any planes in the distance and as we ALWAYS go to the shelter you need never worry for our safety.

1. Isabelle Baignol, later Basterretche, had been Ginnie's chaperone when she was at school in St.-Jean-de-Luz.

9th August 1940   Warsash

We are all very thrilled about the air-battle which took place yesterday and 60 or more German planes were brought down. Wasn't it wonderful. We listened to a German broadcast later and they announced that they had lost *one* plane!?

As I 'go to press' the Italians are marching into Somaliland. This war makes one good at geography if nothing else!

I suppose there is much excitement going on in the U.S. now over Mr.

Wendell Wilkie vs. Roosevelt.[1] Who are you voting for? I will be glad when the November elections are over! But the U.S. certainly seem to be doing a lot for "the Ally" now, isn't it grand? And thank God.

This time last year we were racing at Cowes (in a gale of wind, but still racing). How far off it seems! –

1. Wendell Wilkie, 1892–1944, was a Republican presidential nominee in 1940. After the election he became Roosevelt's ally and supporter of Lend-Lease and traveled to Britain in 1941 as his representative.

19th August 1940   Warsash

Gerald went to —— Hospital this morning to have his Medical Board and they told him to come back on Friday. So that's something! For now I know he'll probably be with me for another week at least – then he'll be sent to —— where we were last Autumn.[1] (I am censoring my own letters to save the censor trouble!)

There is no use to deny the fact that we have had raids, as you will of course have heard (some kind people are bound to tell you!) that we have had several raids in the past week. *But* I hope you have also read that people in shelters have always been untouched so please keep in mind that we have about the best shelter in England and we always go to it when we hear a warning. Gerald looks through the glasses at the fun, and refuses to let me come up and watch. At night the searchlights are *lovely*, and the R.A.F. is absolutely *glorious*. Those young men who fly in Spitfires and Hurricanes and fight the Nazis must be superhuman, and I am lost in admiration of them. Yesterday they "bagged" over 100 German planes – it is incredible – I want to tell you that the British information about German losses is very conservative. I realize that you must wonder *what* is true and what isn't, and of course you probably get the Nazi news first as the English are such awful propagandists. One day we had an Air Force friend in who told us that the losses (of German planes) announced on the B.B.C. were very conservative – and told us how many he knew of that had been shot down that day. Later the wireless news corroborated his statement. Fifteen minutes later, having heard the R.A.F. had shot down 80 or so, we got on to Haw-Haw on the German wireless who announced that the Germans had lost ONE plane –[2]

I have just heard on the 1 o'clock news that *140* Nazi planes were shot down yesterday –

In spite of having S —— [Southampton] on our right and P —— [Portsmouth] on our left I think this particular little corner where the P.C. sits is very safe, so DARLINGS I do hope you don't worry too much.

Wednesday Pothier arrived to spend a few days with us, as he had his first leave since he came over here. He looked very well, and it was grand to see him. He looks just like a doll in his plaid trousers, cutaway khaki jacket, and natty little tam o'shanter with a coy bunch of red feathers tucked on one side! The three of us plus George went for a long walk to show Potty around.

The next day was lovely and sunny. We went for walks, sat in deck chairs in the garden – there were quite a lot of raids on that day so we didn't need to think up anything to entertain our guest as we had several free shows. We had our tea on the lawn under the trees, which was very pleasant and we could quickly pop down into the shelter if the necessity arose.

Rosemary Jeffreys and her Nannie have started a Nannies' Fund to buy a *Spitfire* and all Nannies are giving and trying to collect so I shall send them something from you –

1. Probably Pirbright Camp in Surrey, the Brigade of Guards' depot.

2. William Joyce, 1906–46, Sir Oswald Mosley's deputy in the British Union of Fascists 1933–37, fled to Germany in 1939 and was dubbed "Lord Haw Haw" for broadcasting pro-German propaganda over the radio.

12th September 1940   Warsash

I went up to Maidenhead a week ago to stay the night with G. at the Boat Club to try and discuss plans. He and Sister had both been persuading me to go to the U.S. but when I got to the Boat Club, Gerald said he didn't think it was a very propitious moment to go and suggested my taking a house near Windsor. I couldn't find one, came back here, and thought perhaps the best thing for me to do was to go to America for the winter, leave Jennifer there, and come back here in the Spring. As the flying-boat people said they couldn't give me a passage until December unless I had *pull*, I thought I would send Huntly a cable. Now Gerald has rung up to say he thinks he has found a house complete with servants, nursery and A.R. shelter. So that will be marvellous! The only thing I felt I really couldn't stick was to be here alone through the winter with Nannie who is the most *tiresome* old B. imaginable and absolutely *helpless* about anything not connected with the baby.

Since writing this letter poor old London has had a go of indiscriminate bombing and with the invasion expected at any moment, it is better not to make any complicated plans!!

I have had a touch of flu, thought Jennifer was going to get it but she is all-right now, sacked Nannie, Gerald has found a house at Datchet, Sister is helping me get there and we are to move on Monday. God willing, wind and weather permitting, and Hitler allowing, we shall be there next Monday. The address is

Black Potts, Datchet, Nr. Windsor

I packed Nannie off yesterday morning, and was very relieved to see the last of her. She was *windy* and difficult besides and I feel a *new woman* now that she has gone. Sister and I are taking turns looking after B.D. and it is such fun. Sister has been about the best friend to me that anyone could be – and has helped me sort out all my problems, helped to pack up and will see me installed at Datchet and settled with a new Nannie before leaving me.

The house has a married couple living in that go with it, also a gardener – and every modern convenience including A.R. shelter Gerald says. So I may even look after the baby without a Nannie for a bit. She is *so* adorable that I want to be with her all the time!

I loathe leaving my own home, but know that I would be miserable here alone in the winter, and Gerald is frantic when he can't get on to us to know how we are.

I will be able to arrange the U.S. trip so much easier from there, and when things are a bit more settled I think it a good idea. God knows I want to see you *so much* that I *ache* when I think about it, and I shall certainly come if possible later on. I am very glad I didn't go before. I couldn't ever feel happy that I had left Gerald here still wounded, and I shall never regret being here to see the courage and patience of the British Public. No one could possibly believe it unless they *saw it* with their own eyes. From all the grumbling and inefficiency that went on at the beginning of the war, the change over to this grim determination is incredible. I am speaking of the civilians as the heroism of the R.A.F. etc. goes without saying.

29th September 1940   *Wild Thyme Cottage*
                                                                  Lac Chatillon
                                                                  Ivry
                                                                  Province of Quebec

I have had 2 letters from E.S.U. and several from Olive Todd, and they seemed so enthusiastic about my little gift in dollars that I shall buy something further, I think, now, while it is needed – In every letter which I write to friends I say, "If you want to help England, buy British. It is next, in importance, to airplanes and munitions – and it is one way you can help". I even sent a letter to Martha Bianchi to ask her to influence Alfred Hampson to order his winter clothes from Joce who has a representative in this country.[1] *They will all laugh at me for a while, as they used to, when I inveighed for years against the Germans; and then, after a while, they will begin to think of it seriously, and will do it, and tell me about it. The whole world is like that, so I suppose I am also.*

Naturally, there is no gaiety in Montreal – There has been a big campaign for funds for Red Cross and as I have been up here all the time, save during that week, I haven't had much chance to see many people –

1. Martha Dickinson Bianchi, 1866–1943, was Emily Dickinson's niece and literary heir. She was an author and poet whose works include *The Life and Letters of Emily Dickinson* (Boston: Houghton Mifflin, 1924). Bougie and Bianchi had been good friends from about 1925. Alfred Leete Hampson, d. 1952, was Martha Dickinson Bianchi's secretary and collaborated with her on the publication of Dickinson's poems. He was the heir to rights of publication of Bianchi's Dickinson manuscripts and to her house the Evergreens (next door to Emily's house) in Amherst, into which he moved in the 1920s. He married Mary Landis in 1947, who lived in the house until her death in 1988.

28th November 1940   Black Potts
                                                                        Eton College
                                                                        Windsor

Nannie arrived [Thursday] afternoon. She's about 60, a dear old soul, by
name *Rosie Moon* (and her sister's name is Mrs. *Catchlove* – the other letter
I posted for her was to a Miss Mutton).[1] Well, I think Nannie Moon is
going to be a success. The secret is she has been with nice people and is
well-mannered and doesn't keep complaining and asking for this and that
like old Violet did. She is *kind* and intelligent and we were so relieved and
amazed that I said to Sister, "Perhaps she murdered her grandfather" and
Sister said, "I am sure she's *wanted* for something! This is too good to be
true."

1. Rose Moon, 1880–1963, was a professional nannie employed by the Potter family
from 1940 to 1962. Nannies were generally known by the name of the family that employed
them; thus Moon became Nannie Potter.

7th January 1941   Black Potts

The bunnies are flourishing. A bomb dropped at the front gate of the P.C.
No one was there at the time. Not a single window broken, wasn't it marvellous? As you have probably read, the Guildhall in London has gone, and
several Wren churches. One alternates in mood from thinking "How horrible that all these beautiful buildings should be destroyed by these damned
Vandals" etc. etc. or "When the war is over there may be a Bigger and Better
London" with more parks, broad streets, fewer slums, etc.

We have been fearing the worst re. Gerald's income as his property in
Manchester might have gone and puff! goes the income. Well the worst
has not quite happened – a few incendiaries were dropped on the bldgs.
but an ancient caretaker was able to put them out, so that only the top floor
is damaged. This will be I suppose about £500 each for G. and Uncle Cyril
in repairs. It does not matter so much about the income, as one can live
on less, the only tricky bit is paying income-tax for the yrs. before, when
one's income has become so much less. However as he has been a Captain

for nearly a year and a half, they *may* give him a Capt.'s allowance soon. Having been wounded, I think he was reverted to a lieutenant again, until he came back here, thus losing Captain's pay.

At least he no longer has an overdraft. I persuaded him to sell some capital some time ago, as it seemed silly to me to go on paying interest on an overdraft! We have let the Pink C. to Mabs Busch – and Ella is here, so we have no expenses there except Bench and our 'dig-for-victory' garden, so it's no more expensive for us to live here except rent which is reasonable.[1] We have use of all the vegetables, and gardener's wages thrown in and I have started a real no-waste campaign. No coal fires until the afternoon. Any old bones to make soup, with veg. from the garden – when the bones are boiled, they go to the salvage. Every bit of paper goes in a bag which is collected. All potato-peelings and scraps go to the Ansons' pigs.[2] Envelopes are used again with the aid of small bits of paper and some glue. This war has taught me that I was about the most *wasteful* person imaginable!

1. Ella Packman was the maid at the Pink Cottage.

2. Viscount Thomas William (Bill) Anson, 1913–58, a major in the Grenadier Guards, was son of the fourth Earl of Lichfield. Viscountess Anson née Anne Ferelith Bowes-Lyon, 1921–80, was niece of the late Queen Elizabeth the Queen Mother. In 1949 Anson became Princess Georg of Denmark.

29th January 1941   Black Potts

Wendell Wilkie and Harry Hopkins are now in London – wonder why W.W. is here?[1] Have you ever heard of the new U.S. Ambassador to London, J. Winant?[2] Roosevelt seems to be doing his best to stir people up. Tell him to *hurry*. Was it Jo Kennedy who said, "Let's give Britain all possible aid short of help"?

1. Harry Lloyd Hopkins, 1890–1946, headed the Works Progress Administration from 1935 to 1938 and administered the Lend-Lease program.

2. John Gilbert Winant, 1889–1947, was governor of New Hampshire 1924–26 and 1930–36. He was U.S. ambassador to Britain 1941–46.

9th February 1941   *Richmond*

I have been trying to write this letter for four days. It is a hard one to write because it has to convey to you some sad news, and I hate to tell you. I decided that I wouldn't cable you because I saw no reason in telling you, when you couldn't do anything.

Darling Nana has gone. She died last Tuesday, February 4th at about 2 o'clock in the afternoon. We thought she was going to get well. I worked in the British War Relief all that morning, planning to go to see her in the afternoon. I was sent for while I was having lunch here, and when I arrived she had been dead for 15 minutes. I never saw her again. I didn't want to remember her as different from what I had been used to – The doctor was with her, and she had a marvellous nurse who was as good as gold to her. She just stopped breathing. Her heart couldn't stand the strain of the influenza. I saw her the day before and she looked sweet in a little blue dressing gown and a pink cover and blankets I had just bought for her.

I can't take it in that Nana has gone. Even though she was very old, she kept her calm sweet philosophy always. Her mind was clear, and her hearing as good as ever. She often told me that the radio you gave her had given her more pleasure than anything – She followed all the serials from day to day.

You know that she adored you and in some way I connect you two in my mind always. You were always so sweet and tactful with her. I am glad of that.

Darling, I hate to have to give you bad news now. But you would have to know sooner or later. We couldn't keep Nana always and we were fortunate to have her so long. I find it strange to think that I no longer have a mother. I wrote you last week at this time telling you of her illness. But I had every idea that she would recover –

I am sending this air mail and shall write my usual regular letter and send it by boat.[1]

1. No letters reflect Ginnie's grief at her grandmother's death, but there is reference to a cable sent on 23 March 1941 in which she no doubt expressed her feelings, as she was very fond of Nana.

9th February 1941   Black Potts

There was a terrific "do" in Barracks that afternoon, an annual cocktail party and about 300 guests invited. I spent most of Friday trying to think up something to wear and in the end chose among my 'gorgeous garments' ye olde black velvet coat and skirt vintage '37. Having no hat (!) I put a green velvet turban twist around my locks and, armed with Huntly's silver foxes, felt I could face the party. (Thank God for the silver foxes.) Left Mrs. Hartley's and went into Barracks where Gerald met me at the steps. Everything was done slap up – red canopy, sentries in red and gold, and champagne flowing. It sounds rather awful somehow to go to a big party in the middle of the war, but I think it did everyone a lot of good and cost practically nothing (as the champagne had been lying there ready for such an occasion!).

The King and Queen were there and Major Goschen introduced Gerald and me and we had quite a long chat and she said, "Isn't this fun? I haven't been to a party since before the war!" and asked us all about Black Potts as Major G. said we were living on a "diminishing island".[1] She is so natural and human and easy to talk to and of course perfectly *charming*. The Ansons, Alsops, Heneages and Co. were all there – a smattering of Eton masters – a few of the "oldest inhabitants" of Windsor including Audrey Alsop's grandmother, who was once the *mayoress*. She wears a red wig and has a hook nose is known as "the copper horse". Then there was a smattering of "Court Circular" and a bit of the R.A.F. and many odds and ends. A very good party and a fine time had by all.

In the end we traded in Myfanwy for a 7 yr. old Bentley – not a thing of beauty but it seems to better understand its motive in life, i.e. it RUNS – So now we have "Benito the Bentley" and hope she won't let us down. G. thinks it's an "investment" – I for once agreed!

1. John Alex Goschen, 1906–77, the third Viscount Goschen, was a colonel in the Grenadier Guards. Black Potts was sited on an island in the River Thames and was prone to occasional flooding.

21st February 1941   *Montreal*

As you may imagine I had a very trying time before I came up here. Nana's
death was a shock to all of us, because we thought she was getting well. She
looked sweet and pretty up to the time she died. I always think of her as a
young girl, and never as an old woman of 91. Do you remember the story of
her early life she wrote for you? I think I shall edit it and have it published just
for private consumption if you don't mind.[1] *She has been writing in a diary*
lately and Florie said there was a lot about you and the baby. I haven't seen
it. Fendley and I will look after Florie of course.[2]

1. See Angela Potter, ed., "Confederate Money: A Memoir of the 1850s and 1860s,"
Southern Cultures 9 (Winter 2003): 88–98.

2. Fendley Dickinson, 1873–1945, Bougie's brother, was involved in the tobacco business
in Richmond.

27th February 1941   Black Potts

We had a letter from Laurence Olivier who wants to take on the Pink Cottage, but I think Mabs has just gone there.[1]

1. Sir Laurence Olivier, 1907–89, from 1970 Lord Olivier, English actor and director.

23rd March 1941   *Richmond*

We left Montreal on Wednesday March 29th via C.N.R. I came straight
through to Washington. Stuart stopped in New York to go to a British War
Relief meeting. They are trying for 10 million dollars this year – there are 700
branches in the country. Yesterday they sent $300,000 off to England. Nellie
Bryan was very glad to have us come home, because she had been "holding
the fort" for Stuart and Scott Parrish who has been in Florida.[1] *Stuart had his*
picture taken with Mrs. Roosevelt – we have teased him considerably about it.

I had a letter from Huntly yesterday who had been lunching with the
Minister of Justice of Luxembourg! who told him that when he escaped from
L——— he had to shoot two Germans dead in order to get into his house to
rescue his wife. He says there is no hope of their ever being anything but bar-

barians, that they always have been and always will be, and that there are at least one million men in Germany whose business it is to murder – sweet race!

1. Nellie Bryan was a contemporary of Bougie. J. Scott Parrish, d. 1945, was the owner of Miniborya and the Chesterfield Apartment block in which Bougie lived.

29th March 1941   Black Potts

Wed. we went to London as I have decided to give away a lot of the things that are in the Depository so had to see about that. . . . We went to see "Philadelphia Story", then back to the 500, and Laurence Olivier came in to tea to see about taking the P.C. I was disappointed that he didn't bring his wife (Scarlett O'Hara) with him, as was dying to meet her.[1]

It's good news about Jugoslavia isn't it?[2] I hope they'll be able to stand out against the Bosch [*sic*].

1. Olivier was married to Vivien Leigh, 1913–67, film and stage actor.
2. Following the Italian invasion of Greece in October 1940, the Yugoslav government led by the regent Prince Paul was bullied by Hitler into signing a tripartite pact with Germany and Italy, which Yugoslavia eventually did on 25 March 1941. This produced popular demonstrations against the Axis in Serbia and Slovenia. A coup in Belgrade on 27 March abolished the regency and declared that King Peter II had come of age. Since he was known to favor the Allies, this event was presumably the good news to which Ginnie refers. However, Hitler, much insulted by the coup, attacked Yugoslavia on 6 April 1941, the same day that he invaded Greece. The Yugoslavs surrendered on 17 April 1941.

6th April 1941   *Richmond*

I don't go out "socially" but there have been innumerable meetings this week. Tuesday I lunched with the Board of the English Speaking Union, for Sir Evelyn and Lady Wrench –[1] They are very nice, but look like "picked chickens" after months of going around the United States on a lecture tour. I think she is cleverer than he is – Also she is the sister of the Comm. in Chief, General Brooke – some extra to her credit.[2] There were 24 of us men and women – I ordered the lunch, which I thought was quite good. Lady Wrench ate the

baked potato only — That afternoon there was an exhibition of St. Mémin
portraits at the Valentine Museum.[3] I was asked to the tea but didn't go — St.
Mémin was a frenchman who positively smeared the State of Virginia with
his portraiture done on <u>pink</u> paper about 150 years ago. They aren't "great
art" but are quaint and very valuable here now because of their uniqueness
and the historical value to Virginia.

Stuart is now the "big shot" in the War Relief for Britain in Virginia and
went to South Boston to organise a branch and address a mass meeting Friday.
He has made quite an impression, both here and in New York. Scott Parrish
said everyone in New York was very taken with him — It has done a good
deal for him, too — Evidently all he needed was a boost and some praise from
the public and he was off!!

Since I came home I haven't done any outside things but have just finished
my 26th sweater —

We are boiling with rage at the strikes, and wondering when the Govern-
ment is going to take over the industries producing war materials. I must say
Mr. Roosevelt is a very reluctant dictator — All his enemies accused him of
wanting to be one. This is his big chance, and the public is prodding him, but
he hangs back — I am certain that Hitler's latest prisoner Mussolini would
like the job — as he is out of one now —

1. Sir Evelyn Wrench, 1882–1966, was founder of the Overseas League in 1910 and the
English Speaking Union in 1918. He and his wife traveled on a lecture tour of Canada, the
United States, New Zealand, and Australia between 1940 and 1941. Lady Wrench, companion of the Order of the British Empire, née Hylda Brooke, d. 1955, was honorary controller
of the Overseas League from 1918 to 1949.

2. General Sir Alan Brooke, 1883–1963, was from 1946 the first Viscount Alanbrooke,
chief of the Imperial General Staff 1941–46, commander in chief of the Home Forces 1940–
41, and field marshal from 1944.

3. Charles B. J. Fevret de St. Mémin was a French artist and aristocrat who fled France
following the Revolution and lived in Richmond 1807–8.

7th April 1941   Black-Potts

Well, now we have another ally i.e. Jugoslavia and let's hope to God that
the Bosch [*sic*] won't overrun their country. Everything looks a bit muddled,

but I don't suppose one can really know what's happening – so we can only hope and pray for the best.

The new budget came out to-day – it is now 10/- in the £. The very rich will pay 19/6 in the pound (that is to say an income of £66,000 a year will be reduced to £5,000) – Some humorists have remarked that it might be a good idea for the very rich to pay 20/- in the pound, this would enable them to draw dole!

As for my doings – on Tuesday (the 1st) I went up to London as I decided to get a lot of stuff out of storage to give away to bombed families. I sent some to soldiers in the regiment, others to people in the East end that Sister knew. I gave away 5 servants' beds, complete with pillows, blankets and covers – also the servants hall furniture, a few chairs, kitchen utensils, some old clothes, etc. It cost £3 to get it out but I couldn't bear to think of the things just sitting there not being used – Our good furniture seems to be in good condition which cheered me.

12th April 1941   *Richmond*

I sent you a cable on Thursday about Jennifer's birthday. I sent a cheque for "Wings for Britain" in her name and Huntly is so taken with the idea that he now wants to give all the rest of the money for an extra Spitfire and name the Spitfire "Jennifer Potter" – but I don't know if it will come off really. However, once he gets an idea like that, he usually goes through with it – Don't tell him I said anything about it, because I am not really certain yet. But I hope he does, and I trust that it will take its toll of the enemy –

19th April 1941   Black-Potts

First, I must thank you for your cable of Easter greetings and wonderful birthday present for Jennifer. She will be very pleased when she is older to know that "she" contributed something towards Wings for Britain, and asks me to thank you a thousand times. In the paper on Friday, I read the following: – "Spitfire 'Jennifer' given to Wings for Britain Fund by Virginian to mark birthday of girl named Jennifer, daughter of U.S. soldier" –

Wasn't that extraordinary as Jennifer is such an uncommon name (*in* the U.S.) – Thank you so very much, Boogie darling –

21st April 1941   Black-Potts

Pot left soon after lunch to report, but doesn't know where he is being sent.[1] Gerald and Fiander (the soldier servant) left at tea-time as G. is going on a course with the R.A.F. School of Army Cooperation. He has just rung up to say he is getting along all-right. I am so pleased to think he has the chance of doing this course, as am sure he will do it very well as he is so interested in it, and he hopes it may lead to other things.

Jennifer is beginning to notice everything, she is thrilled by the trees, and the boats, and Egbert the swan – It is all so beautiful, and so perfectly sickening to think that the whole world is at war on account of these filthy Germans – I wonder how Hitler enjoyed his birthday – there are lots of things that I would have liked to give him, including castor oil. If he could see the spirit of the English people after they have been bombed, he might be a little dubious about a German victory. I would love to know what effect the R.A.F. bombing has on his people –

1. "Pot" is a nickname for Pothier Doucet.

1st May 1941   Black Potts

I was flabbergasted when you said in your last letter "Huntly is thinking of giving *another* Spitfire" as didn't know he had given one! and how marvellous of you to give all that money for a mobile canteen! You and Buncle are truly marvellous.

The War Weapons Week of Windsor begins in a few days, and I shall buy Jennifer some National Savings Certificates from you to swell the Windsor coffers. She has already got about 8 certificates bought by the pennies put in her bank in the Nursery! besides the 50 that she rec'd when she was born (from you)

2nd May 1941   Black Potts

On Monday I had a busy time trying to find someone who might mend
the car, as it needs certain repairs and G. will need it when he returns here
– then did my weekly shopping bout. Housekeeping is somewhat "*sim-
plified*" by war-time menus, though it's a bit more difficult to 'ring the
changes' – At least one *remembers* what is needed, as the shopping list begins with the rationed foods – then you go through the list of certain foods
you want and *may* get. I can recite them in my sleep! We are very lucky
to get all our potatoes, vegetables, lettuces etc. out of the garden and eggs
from the Anson-Potter chickens. We get certified milk for B. Dumpling
and there's cereals, greens, broth etc. for her, so do not worry about her!! Of
course there's a scarcity of oranges, but she drinks the juice of swede turnips
which smells awful but she seems to like it! There was a consignment of
oranges which arrived in England a short time ago. The shops here had
signs out "no oranges" which was as far as *I* got to buying any! The first
english tomatoes were being sold at 10/- a pound. Now this raises a point.
Should one refuse to buy them, as we are asked to *save*, or should one help
the growers, and should one buy them if you can afford it in place of something the poor could afford? Query – I compromised and bought 1/4 of a
pound for Jennifer! We have rhubarb and spring onions in our garden, and
the broad beans are on the way – Old Brown is a wonderful gardener and
keeps everything as neat as a pin. Anything we have left over goes to Eton
College –

Had a long letter from Aunt Jo to-day who sent Jennifer a lovely little
dress. Their flat in London was bombed, and Betty [Pearson] was sleeping
there alone at the time and luckily escaped injury – but had to pick her
way out in the dark down 3 flights of stairs which must have been slightly
'impressionant' but I know the old girl has plenty of guts. A. Jo has been
up, getting what's left of the furniture removed –

5th May 1941   *Richmond*

*I am wondering if you know all the excitement which resulted from my small
gift on Jennifer's first birthday, to Wings for Britain? Huntly became so intrigued with the idea of the money I sent in Jennifer's name, that he rushed off*

and put up all the rest of the $35,000 necessary to purchase a fully equipped plane complete with 8 guns and named it "Jennifer" – so that a Spitfire will be roaring about named for your baby. I began to get telegrams and notes while I was so ill, and I hadn't much strength to take it in. Huntly remained anonymous, and so did we all as far as that is concerned, but McConnell was also intrigued with the idea, so the Star had a front page article which said that relatives of "Jennifer" had given a plane – and said it was on the occasion of the baby Jennifer's first birthday – [1] *Then several people wrote me and told me how wonderful my gift was – They knew it must be me, because they knew I had a grandchild named Jennifer.*

The article was copied on the front page of the Richmond Times-Dispatch. Lewis Warren wanted the story, but we refused – [2] *No names appeared thank God – but you can imagine my embarrassment when I had only given 1/35th of the money – Then Huntly wrote me and asked me please to let it go because it had proved to be such an appeal and such good publicity that he hoped I would forgive him – Then Beaverbrook sent a cable and wanted the story with names for England.* [3] *Huntly refused that – I think he is a bit afraid of what you and Gerald might think. But we have remained anonymous – only Jennifer's first name has appeared.*

We decided that if it did any good as far as contributions are concerned that the rest wasn't serious – I see by the latest clippings that it has spurred contributions and different people are sending in different amounts – I forwarded a snapshot of J. to Huntly who showed it to McConnell, who was enchanted with it and rushed off with it and it appeared on the front page of the Star – smiling in the pram! It said, This is Jennifer, sweet and smiling, whose parents have given a Spitfire, etc. etc.

In a few days I received a letter addressed thus:

> *Miss Jennifer –*
> *Friend of Britain*
> *Virginia*
> *U.S.A.*

no name, not even Richmond. The postman met Stuart in British War Relief and said, "Can you give me any information about this?" and Stuart said, "Yes, it is mine" – Did you ever hear of such a coincidence in your life? [It was from] *some woman who was asking for a photograph of Jennifer, saying she had framed the newspaper picture. It began to H.R.H. Jennifer – and said she had fallen in love with her! 3 verses of poetry addressed to her. When I get a chance I shall copy them, and save the priceless original – The paper had given the impression that Jennifer was a <u>Virginia</u> baby, so I wrote back on an addressless piece of paper, and thanked her for the poem, said I had no photograph of the baby – that she was an English baby, not Virginian – that her mother was Virginian and her father English – that her relatives <u>must</u> remain anonymous, and signed it "Friend of Britain". If she writes again to "Miss Jennifer", I shall not answer –*

I hear now that every State in the U.S. is being asked to contribute a plane – The money has been collected in Virginia, Kentucky and New York I think.

Well, "it's an ill wind" and "we" seem to have started something which is bearing fruit, but I shall <u>never</u> believe another newspaper story –

1. John Wilson McConnell, 1877–1963, was owner of the *Montreal Star* and a governor of McGill University. A philanthropist, he donated one million pounds to Wings for Britain in World War II.

2. Lewis Warren was a *Richmond Times-Dispatch* journalist.

3. Sir William Maxwell Aitken, 1879–1964, was the first Baron Beaverbrook. Canadian born, he was the proprietor of the *Daily Express*, *Sunday Express*, and *London Evening Standard* newspapers.

15th May 1941   Black Potts

Sunday Gerald and I had a grand long walk. . . . It was so far removed from the war that it seemed strange to think how much poor old London has suffered recently. As you have of course heard, Westminster Abbey and the Houses of Parliament were hit. The news of *Hess* being in Scotland has amazed the world, I give no comment as I do not understand it at all! – 1

On Monday morning I rec'd your April 13th letter that Huntly was *thinking* of giving a Spitfire. Tuesday morning I rec'd much-appreciated packet from Dionne – and then a cable telling me that Buncle had bought a Spitfire to be named Jennifer Potter – needless to say I was flabbergasted and tremendously thrilled – and can't resist telling everyone I see about it. It really is wonderful of him! I have also rec'd a cable from him, and shall send him one to-morrow – What a man! –

On Tuesday I went up to London . . . to lunch with Pothier at the Carlton Grill. It was very amusing there, as among others lunching there I spotted Beaverbrook, Rex Harrison, Lupino Lane, Hore-Belisha and the Duke of Sutherland – *not* all at the same table!![2] Potty had to rush off early to his job, so I joined Patsy and Babs – then to Parfitt, etc.[3] Tea with Sister and caught the bus back. I went to my corsetiere thinking a new corset might not be a bad idea! – but found the building non-existant [*sic*], so that was that! The shop you bought your silver tray from has recently been hit, in fact has caused a nice "diversion" of traffic, as most of the shop was in the middle of the street.

1. Rudolf Hess, 1894–1987, was deputy führer to Hitler from 1932. To universal astonishment, Hess flew to Scotland on 10 May 1941 and demanded to see the Duke of Hamilton with a view to arranging peace talks with King George VI. He was ignored and imprisoned as a POW in England until 1945, and as a life prisoner following the Nuremberg trials.

2. Reginald (Rex) Harrison, 1908–90, was an English theater and film actor. Lupino Lane, 1892–1959, a.k.a. Henry George Lupino, was a variety and pantomime performer and creator of the Lambeth Walk dance. Leslie Hore-Belisha, 1893–1957, was a Liberal who as secretary of state for war established the British Expeditionary Force. George Granville Sutherland-Leveson-Gower, 1888–1963, was the fifth Duke of Sutherland. He was lord steward of the household to King Edward VIII in 1936.

3. "Patsy" is Patricia Evelyn née McCalmont; "Babs" is Jacqueline Lockwood née Mayer, 1909–86, from ca. 1972 Colvin.

27th May 1941   Black Potts

What a lot of things have happened in the past year – War, Jennifer's birth, Gerald being wounded, the collapse of France, the start of the Blitzes, dear Nana's death, your operation, and everybody being ill.[1] Quite a neat little packet! You wouldn't think so much could be crammed into one year! How is Huntly, do tell me about his health when you next write.

We were very depressed to hear about the Hood – but good news to-day about the Bismarck, isn't it? I hope things aren't as bad as they sound in

Crete. Have you read "Black Record" by Sir Robert Vansittart.[2] If not I will send it to you. He's a man after your own heart, Boogie.

1. Bougie had an operation to remove her gallbladder.

2. Robert Vansittart, *Black Record: Germans Past and Present* (London: Hamish Hamilton, 1941). Sir Robert Vansittart, 1881–1957, was the first Baron Vansittart of Denham. He was permanent undersecretary of state for foreign affairs 1930–38 and chief diplomatic adviser to the foreign secretary 1938–41.

6th June 1941   Black Potts

Since I last wrote, we have had the sad evacuation of Crete, I wonder what the Germans will have annexed, by my next letter! –

The great topic of conversation this week was the *clothes* rationing! It really is funny to have to buy a handkerchief with a magazine coupon! As I haven't had any clothes since Sept. 1938, I am going to look pretty shabby before this war is over! Luckily I ordered a winter coat a month ago, so went to London to see about it on Tuesday – lunched with Pothier, then to see Parfitt, and back home.

I don't like to *ask* for anything, but would be terribly thrilled with some more Nylon stockings – I wonder if it would be *allowed* if you sent them in a letter? English stockings are rotten as you know and are 2 coupons a pair. We get 66 coupons per year, so think the best thing to do is to go without! and wear woolen ones in the winter.

10th June 1941   *Richmond*

We went [to Gloucester] *alone, which I was glad of, for although I am really well, I find that you don't recover from operations <u>nervously</u> for some time, and in that little cottage you can't get away from people. The weather was perfect and I sat on the porch and <u>sewed</u>, and watched the birds! It is now a paradise for them and there are many varieties – robins, thrush, wrens, blackbirds, catbirds, woodpeckers and many I don't recognise, but the most interesting are the mocking birds with their imitations. I heard one giving an exact imitation of the quail ("Bob White"), only the mocking bird's note* *was much sweeter than the original. There was a full moon, a little misty, but bright enough, to encourage the mocking birds to sing at night.*

I went into tea, where five of us had a "dogfight" about Mr. Roosevelt. I take the stand that, although I have disapproved of him for eight years, now we are in danger and he is the "leader", and we mustn't do anything to divide the country any more than it is divided already. I think we should stop talking, and all do what we can for the common good, which is a fight for freedom and ideals. We are beginning to realize that the fascists and communists have made very great inroads in our body politic, and patriotic people are demanding that these disloyal people be punished wherever they may be found.

Huntly is at Government House today, paying a visit to the Earl of Athlone and H.R.H. Princess Alice.[1] He is having a social "spurt" – most unusual for him – He even took the Louis Auberts to Chatillon for the week-end and last week had lunch with the Chinese Ambassador and Dorothy Thompson![2]

The "Woman's Who's Who in America" keep writing for my life history, and I am so discouraged when I read the questionnaire and so ashamed to admit how little I have done and how really <u>uneducated</u> I am (as to degrees, etc.) I don't answer. Then, they come at me again! It is absurd that I should be included in such a volume. You are my only real achievement, and I don't think I can say that.

1. Alexander Frederick William Cambridge, 1874–1957, was the first Earl of Athlone, son of the first Duke of Teck. He was personal aide-de-camp to George V 1919–36, to Edward VIII in 1936, and to George VI 1937–52, and governor-general of South Africa 1923–30 and of Canada 1940–46. Princess Alice, 1883–1981, was the Countess of Athlone and the daughter of the Duke of Albany (Queen Victoria's first son), first cousin to George VI. She was the commandant in chief of the Women's Transport Service.

2. Dorothy Thompson, 1894–1961, was a writer, journalist, and broadcaster. In 1934 she was expelled from the *New York Post* Berlin bureau after criticizing Hitler and his government.

15th June 1941   *Richmond*

As to War activities the past in Virginia is being obliterated – The Government has taken over an enormous tract of land in Chesterfield County, between Richmond and Petersburg – and that includes the houses my great

grandfather built – "Auburn Chase" now known as "Bellwood's", because
many years ago a Canadian farmer named Bellwood bought it and made
a dairy farm of it. Also the land known as "Kingsland" where Nana's house
was and my Uncle William Gregory's place has been bought for a large metal
factory.

I was interested in your reading. I am about to finish Ambassador Dodd's
Diary, U.S. Ambassador in Germany from 1933 to 1937 –[1] *It finished in Sept.*
1938 in America. It is <u>*very revealing*</u> *– his* <u>*private*</u> *diary in which he shows*
plainly that everyone in the diplomatic corps <u>*knew*</u> *what was going on in*
Germany – they seemed powerless to stop it, but why, oh why? We had very
stupid politicians – This world can never be the same again, but let us hope
that even though we shall all be much poorer, we can have some idea of true
values. Southerners are used to poverty, so that part doesn't worry <u>*us*</u> *much –*

Our politicians have carried us to the brink of destruction and our chil-
dren's children will build up the new world from the ruins. Man never learns
anything from one generation to another – I have always thought we were
the stupidest of all the animals.

A letter this morning from Huntly – He seems to be on the jump but his
greatest worry seems to have been what <u>*clothes*</u> *to wear to Government House*
– A luncheon for 40 with our Sec'y Knox to talk about <u>*loans.*</u>[2]

1. William E. Dodd Jr. and Martha Dodd, eds., *Ambassador Dodd's Diary, 1933–1938*
(New York: Harcourt, Brace, ca. 1941).

2. William Franklin Knox, 1874–1944, secretary of the U.S. Navy 1940–44.

23rd June 1941   Black Potts

On Friday 13th I went to see Anne [Anson] and her 6 day old daughter and
found both *extremely* well. The baby weighed 6 1/2 lbs. and is *too* sweet.
It seems that H.M. [King George VI] has asked to be god-father [as Anne
is the Queen's niece] so I think the baby will probably be inflicted with the
name "Georgiana".[1]

Sunday morning we were of course electrified by the news that Germany
had marched into Russia, and have been *hanging* over the wireless ever
since. I get awfully *muddled* when I start thinking about it all –

1. Lady Elizabeth Georgiana Anson, b. 1941, from 1972 Lady Shakerley, the director of Party Planners.

29th June 1941   Black Potts

I think Richmond people are marvellous to keep giving money in this way. I was enormously impressed to hear of Mrs. Kelly Evans (in your letter to Olive) giving a whole Spitfire and very pleased to think that the "Jennifer" has boosted contributions! Sometime I hope you will send me the poem that was written, and either send or save for me, the clipping with picture that was in the paper so that I can paste it in her book. I always tell everyone about the "Jennifer" as like them to know how much is being done, etc. Nannie, I am sure is thrilled over the idea.

23rd July 1941   Black Potts

I do hope you are feeling really well by now – I am wondering if you will be going to Canada soon as it must be terribly hot in Richmond. I was very thrilled to receive the cable from Huntly telling me about the second Spitfire to be called Boogie. Huntly is really *incredible*, how *can* he go on giving away all this money. It looks as if he will be living on bread and water soon –

On Friday July 10th Bill and Anne [Anson] had their daughter christened in the tiny little 12th century church of St. Mary's Wexham just near their house. It's a sweet little village just off the main road of villas and factories, and quite a surprise to find it there. It was a *grilling* hot day, and it seemed so nice and cool inside the church – I was going to get all dressed up and at the last minute, felt I looked like a "plush horse", so while doing my shopping I grabbed a 6/6 white hat to go with a simple little afternoon dress. The only people there were the godparents; two old aunts of Bill's; a few 'retainers'; the Queen and the two Princesses and ourselves – so I thought it very sweet of them to include us. Elizabeth Georgiana screamed the whole time she was being christened, and Patrick (aged 2) murmured "Patrick mustn't speak" through the entire service to the great amusement of the Princesses.[1] The Master of Forbes (a cousin of Bill's) stood proxy to the King and the other godparents were Major John Freeman, Princess Cröy and Juliet Peel.[2] They had a small reception at the house afterwards, and I was thrilled to meet the Princesses as I had never seen them before. Anne A. is *so* full of natural charm and poise and introduced everyone very nicely, and told the Queen how we shared *chickens*, so I said something to the effect that it was the first time I had ever gone to the Anson household without taking our swill. . . . After a glass of champagne we thought we were going to blow up, so I suggested a swim at Black Potts and later Bill and Anne and her sister Diana and the three godparents came here for a grand swim, and we all had supper together.[3]

I think I told you in my last letter that we had decided to take on Black Potts for the duration, and let the P. Cottage for same – and decided to use some of our furniture that is stored in London. Having given away a good deal, and sold some, and with stuff sent here we'll now only have to pay about half the storage fees – Now that we know 'where we are' we are going to breed rabbits, ducks, geese and chickens like mad and DIG DIG DIG for Victory. At least Dumpling is easy on the fishmonger's bill as Fiander usually catches a little fish for her after supper and she has it for lunch the next day!!

The garden is in great shape – after a month of drought the rain came just in time. We have been picking the redcurrants and making jelly etc.

1. Patrick Anson, 1939–2005, was from 1960 the fifth Earl of Lichfield. He later adopted the name Patrick Lichfield for his career as a society and fashion photographer.

2. Captain Nigel Ivan Forbes, b. 1918, was Master of Forbes and the twenty-second Baron Forbes.

3. Diana Bowes-Lyon, 1923–86, from 1960 Somervell, was Anne Anson's sister.

26th July 1941   *Richmond*
I am getting through this war by skimming over the surface of things – I can't let myself become sentimental because I am <u>afraid</u> of what it might do to me. I don't think I have ever known what <u>fear</u> was before – for God's sake, don't <u>love</u> Baby D. as much as I love you – There is a terrific pathos in the <u>maternal succession</u> in our family. I have tried to edit Nana's story, which she wrote for

*you – and I can't even read it! I don't feel that way about the men. I suppose
because I am a woman and don't understand them. But they are <u>supposed</u> to
be brave and strong – That's the way they are bred – I don't mean that I am
not sympathetic to them. I am, and always get on well with them but I don't
feel the same poignancy about them – Maybe the whole thing hinges on the
fact that <u>you</u> are a woman and you are the person I have always loved the
most.*

    *I should be <u>mush</u> if I saw B.D. of course. You will understand that if I don't
wax very <u>personal,</u> it is because I can't <u>allow</u> myself to give way to anything
which may undermine the fight I am putting up to remain calm and reasonable – In the meantime, I am always in the <u>fight</u> for something – Now, it
is the "Fight for Freedom", a propaganda organization designed to fight the
influence of the isolationists, the Wheelers, the Nyes, the Lindberghs, in other
words, the defeatists.[1] It is designed to influence people to uphold the President's foreign policy – I am writing to all our Senators and Congressmen to
ask them to <u>impeach</u> Wheeler. He is a <u>traitor</u> – Lindbergh is only a "stooge"
and a fool – We are planning a mass meeting in the Mosque to bring before
the people some of the issues at stake.[2] I think [Wendell] Willkie will speak
for us. His "speech" is deplorable, but he is <u>honest</u> and very earnest, and he
has proved his generosity in upholding Roosevelt –*

    *I hate all this, but I feel I <u>must</u> do it. <u>Someone</u> has to do it – and I have
always talked so glibly about how I would do anything to try to defeat Hitler
and the Germans, and <u>now</u> is the time – Russia seems to be doing well, so far
– touch wood! Wheeler is the American Quisling.*

    *Sunday we went home from Gloucester, where I am now – to go to "Mini-
borya" to a party for officers from a British auxiliary cruiser stationed at
Newport News for repairs – It was a wonderful party – and Scott [Parrish]
did everything to make them have a good time. Tuesday Claire McCarthy
staged a dance for them in their camp near Petersburg, on Swift Creek. They
said that camp was a godsend to them – They seem to like Richmond. There
will be more coming and we must organize ourselves in order to give them
some touch of "home" – Drive them over to Richmond, and show them some
attention – I always ask them to use their influence <u>at home</u> to see that Germany is not forgiven for this war. I have not found one yet who showed any*

disposition <u>not to</u> – I wish all Englishmen felt the same way Churchill seems to about the enemy.

I am reading Shirer's "Berlin Diary" –[3] *It shows up in no uncertain light the unconsciousness of the politicians in those fateful years – the silly belief in Germany's "good intentions". Germans <u>never</u> have good intentions.*

There is a destroyer in the York today – there is immense activity across the river and all around the neighbourhood – Camp Sustis at Lee Hall on the James River, Camp Ft. Story at Virginia Beach, huge barracks at the oiling station and mine depot across the river, Hampton and Newport News and Norfolk a seething mass of people – steel nets across the entrance to this station. It isn't a secret – Anyone can see it who goes down to the bay, about five miles from here – Camp Lee at Petersburg – an enormous tract of land between Richmond and Petersburg requisitioned for a permanent quartermaster's dept. My great grandfather's house has been torn down – and Nana's old home site bought up for a huge steel factory, just below DuPonts enormous one at Falling Creek – All up and down the James now, below Richmond, there are factories and camps. All the old landmarks are disappearing.

I am putting everything away in the cupboards in my flat because it is to be re-decorated, and I have all your latest letters in the highboy – <u>very few</u> are missing. I have received, eventually, nearly all of them. I have been lucky. Much mail was lost from the U.S. in May – Some of mine may be missing –

I am gradually getting much stronger and, now, go in swimming before breakfast down here [Gloucester] *– It was lovely today – Lady Drummond is dying slowly, which is distressing to Huntly – How much better to go in a moment as dear Nana did – Huntly as always is a tower of strength. An article came out in the "Star" about the "Boogie" – he had to spell it with a 'u' – which said that it was an intimate family nickname, denoting a <u>sprightly nature</u> which nearly embarrassed me to death. Huntly is a darling, but this war is going to his head a bit! Don't you love "Jennifer" and "Bougie" swooping over Germany and blowing up a few Nasties. Lady Davis' "King's Messenger" bagged 4 Messerschmidts* [sic] *–*[4] *I hope Baby Dumpling and I do as well – We wanted the plane named "Virginia" for <u>you</u> and <u>me</u> but there was already one named that. Huntly insisted that the world's best German-hater <u>should</u> have a Spitfire named for her –*

I still cannot recover from Hess going to England – Does anyone know why? –

1. Burton Kendall Wheeler, 1882–1975, was a lawyer and Democratic senator for Montana 1923–47. He was an extreme isolationist. Gerald Nye, 1892–1971, senator for North Dakota, suggested that many American businesses had much to gain by being involved in the war.

2. The Mosque Theatre in Richmond was later renamed the Landmark Theatre.

3. William L. Shirer, *Berlin Diary: The Journal of a Foreign Correspondent, 1934–1941* (New York: A. A. Knopf, 1941).

4. Lady Henriette Marie Davis, b. ca. 1880, lived in Montreal and Paris. According to Ginnie's unpublished memoir, in 1930 "Lady Davis . . . had had the monkey gland operation and was bent on dancing every night. . . . As she was much older than my mother I felt it was a bit strange to say the least." Monkey gland operations, supposedly rejuvenating to the recipients, were popular in the 1920s. See Roy Porter, *The Greatest Benefit to Mankind: A Medical History of Humanity from Antiquity to the Present* (London: HarperCollins, 1997), 568.

1st August 1941   Black Potts

On the Wednesday evening Gerald and I were asked to a small dance by T.M. [Their Majesties] at the Castle. We went first to dine with Bill and Anne [Anson] – Peter and Patsy Evelyn were there too, and the Allsopps, and we all went on together.[1] I wore ye olde black lace, knowing that black wasn't the 'right thing' but not having any other choice. It was the most marvellous party I have ever been to! – about 100 guests, all young people as it was really a dance for P. Elizabeth and sister. It was a glorious summer night, and one wandered about on the terrace, overlooking the lovely garden etc. We were 'introduced' in a large room, walls covered with green moiré and beautiful paintings. The ballroom was panelled in red moiré – more beautiful pictures by Reynolds etc. – supper room off that room, and a little bar in a sort of Gothic rotunda off the upper room. The Queen looked lovely in white with gold and silver sequins, and the little Princesses in adorable long fluffy white dresses, with blue sashes, the bodice slightly spangled in blue and silver. H.M. said she remembered meeting me at the christening; I was so busy curtseying to 4 people that I found difficulty in answering! We danced to a marvellous band – then wandered on to the terrace. The whole scene looked like a film of old Vienna or something. I have never seen so many beautiful women – and the men of course all in uniform, mostly blue with flashing buttons and medals (Gerald one of the few in khaki, as his "blue" is stored and he refuses to wear it in wartime).

We had supper about 11.30 – a motley array of 'waiters' some in bright red, some in various uniforms. An enormous painting of Queen Victoria hung in the supper room. She gazed down at us all in what seemed a rather disapproving look! that we should be enjoying ourselves. It was all very informal and delightful and I enjoyed dancing so much. Danced with Nick Villiers, Pat Britton (both good dancers) and several others, also the ones on our party.[2] We then had a few Lambeth Walks and "Boomps-a-Daisies", also a "Paul Jones", one of which I danced with the host [King George VI] (who is incidentally a very good dancer). About 2.30 the party broke up and all streamed into the supper-room for a sandwich and a drink. We missed getting a chair, so went into the little bar. By this time I felt almost suffocated, as it was completely airless in the tiny bar. It *was* a very hot night and no air could get in once the black-out was up. I began to feel a little peculiar, and rather trapped as I *couldn't* get through the supper room, and began wondering if I had better walk into the pantry. I began to realize that it was no good, I *must* have *air* so murmured something to Anne and Patsy [Evelyn] and Diana [Bowes-Lyon] and began to make for the nether regions. It was just as well that I did for the next thing I knew I was being *carried* along a long dark passage by poor old Gerald! with Bill and Peter [Evelyn] trying to assist! – I was laid on a bench, while one scarlet-coated lackey brought a cushion, and an equerry (I think P. Legh) put a piece of ice down my neck!![3] I then felt quite all-right but felt rather a fool at my dying duck act, but thank *Heavens* no one saw or knew but our little party.

We then realized it was too late for us to say good-bye, so retreated through anterooms etc. and came out at the top of the big staircase. Anne, Patsy and I sat on a bench while the others went to get our coats and the cars. At this moment the entire Royal Family appeared on their way to bed, and looked rather surprised to see us! Anne murmured something about waiting for the car – and we all thanked them for our lovely time and left.

The next morning people kept ringing up to know how I was, then Mum rang up from Twyford. Diana (Anne's sister) was staying at the Castle so explained why we were standing at the top of the staircase, and they were all so sorry etc. etc. so I feel I am only famous for one thing: having fainted in awkward places. You remember the last time was in Piccadilly Circus!! I wouldn't tell you this story if I thought it would worry you – but I assure you I have *never felt better in my life* than I do now. I always feel faint when I get in an airless place, and I suppose I always will.

It is such a funny story that I felt I must tell you about it. I do hope it's all right for me to tell you about this party but as it happened a long time ago I am sure it must be all right.

1. Major Peter George Evelyn, 1909–43, a Grenadier Guards officer and master of the Surrey Union Foxhounds, was killed in action.

2. The Honourable Nicholas Hyde Villiers, b. 1916, a Grenadier Guards officer.

3. Lieutenant Colonel the Honourable Sir Piers Walter Legh, 1890–1955, was equerry to the Prince of Wales 1919–36 and to George VI 1936–46.

4th August 1941   Blackpotts

Saturday morning I went off to collect another hen and 12 baby ducks that we have just bought. The "farm" is growing apace – we now have 18 ducks, 2 hens, 4 geese – also a rabbit who has just produced *12* babies – then there are the chickens at the Ansons, and more rabbits which we are bringing up from the P. Cottage. They take a bit of looking after when they are young and G. is busy making coops and hutches out of an old boat-house we broke up.

We were given 4 tickets by the manager of the Windsor Repertory theatre to see the 1st night of Ivor Novello's new play "Breakaway" last night, so we took Bill and Anne – I didn't think it a particularly good play but it was very amusing and very well done. Afterwards Novello made his usual gushing speech – then we went to the bar where we saw a very motley crowd of actors etc. and had a few giggles.[1]

I went to London this morning as I had to see several people including G's Bank Manager and Parfitt. Then met Gerna and Pot for lunch, did a little shopping and went to see Fantasia, Walt Disney's new film. I am dying to know what you think of it – I loved the music of Stravinsky and thought the film very good in spots, but disappointing and didn't like it as well as his "Pinocchio" which was very 'gemutlich', a style in which he excels –

Thank you a million times for the marvellous presents, all of which have arrived. I cannot begin to tell you how grateful I am, or how thrilled. It is terribly sweet of you, darling, and the whole thing so well thought out. I shall send you a cable in the morning thanking you for 'Christian present' so that you will know it has all arrived. The first thing to happen was a note from the customs that one pair of nylon stockings had arrived in an envelope and had been seized as they didn't have a green label or something – but if I would pay 4/3 plus 6D clearance fees plus 6D postage etc. I would receive stockings. This I did forthwith as nylon stockings are worth their weight in diamonds. I was down to my last pair which I kept for best, otherwise I wear anything I can find i.e. woolen, cotton with darns in them, silk of *odd* colours etc. The nylons are really wonderful and out of the 3 pair you sent last winter I still have 1 1/2 pair left, having bought no others. There is *no point* in buying English stockings (which not only cost 7/3 but are 2 coupons) as they usually run the first time you put them on and I positively *refuse* to waste the money – so I feel it is 'nylon or nothing' and you have SAVED MY LIFE.

On Monday to my *amazement* one V[irgini]a. ham and the bacon turned up. I just cannot believe it! It is just too, too wonderful. We are going to cook the ham *at once* as we just can't wait, and can hardly wait to eat the bacon too! We haven't seen ham for *months* and certainly not Va. ham. We are luckier with bacon as we get 4 oz. per head each week which is pretty good really. Fiander eats most of it for breakfast, I have to give him *something*. We are going to boil the ham, and then cover with breadcrumbs etc. as you suggest. I see in the paper that parcels from U.S. are going to be prohibited in future which I suppose is only *right* as it isn't really fair for some to get things when others can't – but at the same time, I must admit that I am very pleased you managed to get this wonderful lot off to me. Thank you *so much* for all your thoughtfulness and trouble.

1. Ivor Novello, 1893–1951, Welsh actor-manager, dramatist, and composer.

15th August 1941   *Montreal*

Monday we drove over [from Great Barrington, Massachusetts] *for the day to Amherst to see Martha Bianchi – Martha gave us cocktails and had Alfred* [Leete Hampson] *to do the honours, and an old Col. Lawless, former Canadian, to meet us – She has had servant trouble and had no cook so we lunched in the "Lord Jeffrey". Both Helen* [Adams] *and Delia* [Carrington] *were very impressed with Martha and the family things and Emily* [Dickinson]*'s history etc. and I think they enjoyed it.*[1]

Your sweet note with Jennifer's signature was <u>grand</u> – I give you the medal for being the world's most adorable child and I ask nothing more. I am completely satisfied so darling Ginnie, if the skies fall, and the world is made over, and everything else is in flux, I have the knowledge that "integrity" is possible, and that in some way I am connected with it, so I can be <u>serene</u> in the midst of war – We have lived, and shall go on living as long as it is feasible to live, and even the thought of your being alive is enough for me, as long as <u>you</u> can see something worthwhile –

Today we know that Churchill and Roosevelt met – a very stupendous meeting in a way –

1. Delia Carrington, a Richmond contemporary of Bougie.

28th August 1941   Blackpotts

Simply delighted to hear that Laval was shot, wish they had done a better job of it.[1]

1. This incident refers to the attempted assassination in Paris of Pierre Laval, 1883–1945, the French prime minister and foreign secretary from 1931 to 1932 and again from 1935 to 1936. He was the vice premier of Petain's Vichy Government until December 1940 and the chief instigator of collaboration. He was executed in 1945.

4th September 1941   Blackpotts

We have been catching a lot of rats, and so far have got 6 big ones, so have partly avenged the death of Chloë's 4 babies. I have to shut them [rabbits]

all up at night now, and it is quite a job persuading them to go to bed, especially Milly's 12 babies who are very sweet and tame, and just *won't* go into their hutch. How I'll ever eat the cute little things I don't know. I won't mind eating the geese or the ducks, because they are so *silly* and *dirty* – and their pens have to be cleaned out continuously. The rabbits on the other hand are very "tidy" and do their "do-dos" in one corner of their runway! Our record so far is:

    2 rabbits eaten
    8 (buck) rabbits sold
    4 killed by rats
    1 died
    6 rats killed
    and 4 eggs

Not a very productive farm so far! though Milly's 12 babies are my pride.

Tuesday morning after dealing with the farm, etc. I left here before 10.30 and roared into Windsor to start my W.V.S. (Women's Volunteer Service) work at the new British Restaurant they have just opened for factory work-ers etc.[1] I was put at the hot plate dishing up food – a very warm job, so am looking forward to doing it in the winter!! It is also very hard work but I rather enjoy doing it, as have been very anxious to do something of the kind. We served 295 lunches and then the food gave out. I helped clean up and left there at 3.30. Then went to the chiropodist who successfully treated that place on my foot, and walked home, buying all the rat-traps I could on the way!! Got home at 6 just in time to feed the creatures, finished at 8, supper and so to bed.

After lunch [on Wednesday] I bought a much needed corset (3 coupons), a pair of walking shoes (5 coupons), a country hat (no coupons) and a W.V.S. overall, and returned by the 4.45 bus just in time to start mincing the swill again.

You would have laughed at me to-day. I was very annoyed with one wait-ress, later discovered it was Lady Kavanagh (who has been ringing up to ask me to lunch etc.) so didn't dare tell her who I was![2] I work at the hot plate with Lady Wigram one day and the other with a cheery soul whose hus-band mends Green Line busses![3] The manageress is Mrs. Laycock (Angela

Dudley-Ward) who tells me her children are in Vancouver. She is terribly attractive – another waitress is old Mrs. Carteret-Carey aged *80* who is known as the "Copper Horse" – it is a very funny motley crew!! –

1. The Women's Voluntary Service was founded in 1938. British Restaurants were established to provide low-cost, nourishing meals. For further information on British Restaurants, see R. J. Hammond, *History of the Second World War*, vol. 2, *Food* (London: HMSO, 1956), 352–421.

2. Possibly Lady Kavanagh née May Perry, who married Lieutenant-General Sir Charles Kavanagh in 1895.

3. Probably Lady Wigram née Nora Chamberlain, daughter of Sir Neville Chamberlain. Lord Wigram was lord in waiting to George VI and deputy constable and keeper of the king's archives at Windsor Castle.

12th September 1941   *Montreal*

Thursday, Dora and Dorothea took us to lunch at a new place on Sherbrooke St. called the Salad Bar –[1] *Dora is going off to college in Vancouver – Dot has just taken an exam in* <u>*Trigonometry*</u> *– and is, herself, going to Vancouver for two weeks – It is a strange family! Last night they came in before their train, and we all listened to Roosevelt's speech about shooting the Germans* <u>*on sight!*</u> *Hooray! Wish I could. I wonder what the "Jennifer" is doing – don't know if "Bougie" is in the fighting yet. Huntly murmurs every now and then something about one named "Ginnie" – Wouldn't it be funny to see Bougie, Ginnie and Jennifer swooping down on the Nazis – something after the manner of Walt Disney – Well, in a way, I thought very much as you did about "Fantasia", but I thought a little better of it than you did – I liked* <u>*most*</u> *of it, but didn't care about the one when Micky was nearly* <u>*drowned*</u>, *the Sorcerer's Apprentice one – thought it was overdone. I liked Stravinsky also –*

1. Dorothea (Dora) McNiven née Millar, b. 1921, was a Canadian cousin. Mary Dorothea (Dot) Millar née Drummond, 1900–1985, was Dorothea's mother.

27th September 1941   *Richmond*

We started off [from Montreal] on Thursday in the car, and motored along [Lake] Champlain and to the lower end of Lake George which might have been an Italian lake in peace-time. Finally we landed up at Kingston on the Hudson for the night – a nice hotel with a garden in the back – About 8.30 we heard some people talking about <u>lights</u> as we sat inside reading papers, so Stuart remarked "I think there are Northern Lights" – I rushed out, and there they were not just in the North, but <u>everywhere</u>, green curtains moving in the West, the Aurora in the North, <u>streamers</u> of pink in the East and overhead pools and shafts of light <u>jumping</u> all over the heavens. I never saw <u>anything</u> like it in my life. They lasted until about 1 a.m. – I thought it might be very cold the next day, but there was no change in the weather at all.

The second day we went through lovely country and spent the night in York, Pennsylvania. The third day to Frederick, Maryland, thence to Leesburg, Middleburg, Warrenton, Fredericksburg and home – We missed out both Baltimore and Washington. All the way we ran into Army trucks and signs of war. You see more soldiers in Virginia than anywhere. Night before last the 29th Division passed through here at <u>2 a.m.</u>, and they were still going at 4 p.m. yesterday afternoon! – moved bag and baggage to Fort Bragg, North Carolina.

28th September 1941   Blackpotts

Mrs. Fiander left just 2 weeks ago and since then I have been doing the housework, the cooking, looking after 52 animals, and working for the W.V.S., so haven't put my foot off the island except for working in the restaurant –[1] On Tuesdays and Thursday I work from 11–3 dishing up food at a hot plate in the British Restaurant run by the Women's Volunteer Service. It is very hot work, so will be lovely in the winter! We serve over 300 meals a day and they cost 8D or 10D. On Wednesdays and Saturdays I spend the morning cleaning and disinfecting the geese, duck and hen houses, raking the runways etc. etc. I shall start a manure factory soon as a sideline!

On Wednesday last (17th) Pothier came over for the afternoon for his afternoon off. I said he could come but explained I would be very busy so he set to and helped me. I managed to clean the house, get lunch and turn out the geese pens etc. before he arrived. Then we minced swill and prepared the food. I got him to carry water to the duck pond for me. If you could have seen him in his immaculate plaid trousers and highly polished shoes roaring along with a wheelbarrow full of water that sloshed over him at every bump in the path, and slipping on the mud and nearly getting wet through in his effort to help me with what he called the "Gunga Din Express" you would have laughed! Then we had half an hour to spare before feeding the animals, so we went for a row in the dinghy!! We then cooked supper and washed up and he had to leave. Not a very restful afternoon for him I am afraid.

I was just beginning to say to myself "Est-ce que ca n'en finit plus ALORS" when I at last got a cook! She came yesterday afternoon, and calls herself Bella and as yet I don't know how she'll turn out – but at least it is something.[2] Poor old Nannie was beginning to show the strain, as with Jennifer sick and all the extra work I realized she couldn't keep it up much longer. She has worked like 2 blacks and has been absolutely marvellous, but as she hasn't been able to get outside the house for weeks I was getting very worried about her – I sent her out for a walk with Jennifer the minute Bella arrived and she was so pleased to see the other Nannies again. I celebrated the occasion by having my hair done! after the W.V.S. to-day.

I know it must make you laugh when you think of me in the animal world! If I'm not trying to chase a rabbit which has got loose in the wrong pen, I am bathing a duck's eye! I keep track of all the rats caught (!) and the eggs produced. Then went to clean out the shed and uncovered a nest of baby mice! My poor sick duck has died. George has hurt his paw. I think Brandy has got fleas. O lord, she has just done another wee-wee. O my God. Sometimes I half expect to wake up in the morning with an asses head on my shoulders like Bottom the weaver.

The conversation at Blackpotts is ridiculous – there's me saying "Bad dog" and "Quack-quack". There's Jennifer who can only say "Ta". There's Bella who never speaks and there's Nannie who when she does (speak) gets everything muddled – it's all rather like a Trappist Monastery. (Nannie told me to-day that a large fomentation of planes had bombed Italy!)

1. Lavinia Fiander, b. ca. 1921, was the wife of Gerald's soldier-servant. She was helping out at Black Potts prior to being called up for war work.

2. Isabella (Bella) Zeyde was the Austrian cook at Black Potts between 1941 and 1945.

2nd October 1941   *Richmond*

I have been quite busy this week trying to get things straightened up for the winter – I am active in something called <u>Fight for Freedom</u> and we are going to Washington next week to have my photograph taken on the steps of the Capitol under the Virginia flag, when we shall all join in rededicating the 48 States to Liberty as in 1776!! It is all very ridiculous, but this sort of bunk seems to mean something in this country – I shall be caught in a cringing attitude! but I am willing to do <u>anything</u> which will advance the cause of fighting this war as soon as possible.

    Last night I heard a marvellous speech by Stringfellow Barr, who fear-lessly accused us of all the things of which we are guilty.[1] Everyone applauded him. That's the strange part. Whose fault is it? We don't know. Perhaps the leader's, but I am not certain. Anyhow, the taxes have started. My income is to be about 1/2 next year. I am struggling with Trust Companies and lawyers. Thank God I have saved a little and can share that. My trouble is that I pay in two countries, but can't remove my capital from Canada by Government order – As for my personal needs – they are slight. I am going to Pangman as much as possible – so don't worry – I refuse to be defeated![2] I shall not be able to give anything to Chinamen, Greeks, Russians, etc. but shall try to carry on with England!

    Well, I am going off to an executive meeting of Fight for Freedom now – There isn't much to write about, but we had a whole army in our midst last week. They took from 1 a.m. until the following afternoon at 4 to pass through the streets. Mrs. Willingham, who is an enthusiast, stayed up until 5 a.m. to watch the show –[3] I didn't see any of it, but Carrie [Washington] reports she saw a second lot today. Carrie has an admirer whom she tells me is <u>very affectionate</u>. What that means for Carrie, I don't know –

1. Stringfellow Barr, 1897–1982, was a professor of modern European history at the

University of Virginia from 1924 to 1937. He was president of St. John's College, Annapolis, from 1937 to 1946 and president of the Foundation for World Government from 1948 to 1958.

2. Mr. Pangman was manager of the Bank of Montreal, Waterloo Place, London, where Bougie and Ginnie held a joint account, into which Bougie placed funds for Ginnie's use.

3. Martha Willingham, manager of the Chesterfield Apartments in Richmond.

6th October 1941   Blackpotts

Isn't it wonderful what the Russians are doing? Do you think the Germans have lost 3 million men (killed, wounded and prisoners) in the Russian Campaign? If so it is COLOSSALE [*sic*]. I suppose we will be Communist after the war but that is 100% better than being Nazi. It looks as if the Americans may be in the war before the spring. I suppose your taxes are going up and up from now on. Is petrol rationed in the U.S. as well as Canada? Well let's hope that the war won't last forever and that some day we will be reunited again.

12th October 1941   *Gloucester Point*
                                                                    Gloucester County
                                                                    Virginia

This is a period of rest for me after a strenuous time in Washington as a <u>delegate</u> to "Fight for Freedom" – It was a thrilling meeting – representatives from all the states – some heads of labour unions, representatives from youth organizations etc. Bishop Hobson from Southern Ohio is the active Chairman. There was a banquet of speeches, and the last day, the resolutions were sent to Congress – We asked for the immediate repeal of the Neutrality Act, and added that if Hitler "reacted" we wanted war – and <u>now</u> – I found I was a <u>conservative</u> in comparison with some of the others – It was a fiery crowd, and they <u>refused</u> the amendment striking out – reference to war – Lindbergh's <u>mother-in-law</u>, Mrs. Morrow helped write the resolution –[1] When scornful things were said about the Lindberghs, she never changed countenance! She is wonderful –

We hear that the "America First", a subversive organization for which Lindbergh speaks is losing ground rapidly – and the last poll taken shows

that 70% of a cross section of the population wants <u>action now</u> — I have been writing letters, signing people up and distributing cards to be sent to Sen. Connally about the Neutrality Law, for ten days —[2] It is a nuisance to have to do these things, but it seems to be the way people want it, so one <u>must</u> take the trouble. Tuesday I went to Washington. I was asked to go to the Skyline Drive over Blue Ridge Mountain — I was dying to go, because I have never been and it was a beautiful day. Also I was asked to meet Capt. Tuck of the "Illustrious" (British aircraft carrier) whom I hear is most attractive — All my engagements seemed to come the same day —

The roads and streets here are filled with soldiers — There is a problem in the Norfolk area — 300,000 soldiers near a town of less than 200,000 — They are trying to look after them, but the poor things have nowhere to go when they are on leave — The distances in this country make it impossible for most of the men to go home for weekend leaves —

It is sad to see people growing old — I have thought lately, since seeing Bessie Drummond and Lady D. and all the others that those young heroes who go out and meet death so gallantly, and are killed, have had a supreme experience and they are going to escape rheumatism and all the beastly things. <u>However</u> I don't want to see anyone I love die, nor do I wish to myself — so it only works for someone <u>you don't know</u>.

1. Elizabeth Reeve Morrow née Cutter, diarist whose second daughter married Charles Lindbergh.

2. Thomas Terry Connally, 1877–1963, was a senator for Texas 1928–52 and chair of the foreign relations committee 1941–46 and 1949–50. He supported the lifting of the isolationist arms embargo of 1939 and the Lend-Lease Law of 1941.

21st October 1941   *Richmond*

We were quite gay over the week-end — Saturday, Gracie Fields gave her usual sprightly performance for British War Relief.[1] Stuart and Murray Forbes-Bayliss brought at their expense 110 British sailors from one of the ships — They filled one end of the Mezzanine, and sang all the choruses with Gracie. At the end, a little monkey-faced stoker, with a bald head and tufts of hair sticking up on the sides, leaped on the stage. He was feeling no pain,

and Murray had been holding him by the seat of his trousers for some time,
but with one gargantuan wrench, he freed himself and made a dash for the
stage and tried to kiss Gracie, who parried his advances with tact and skill.
He did a dance, and arm in arm they skipped off – The audience thought
it was arranged, and broke into a thunderous applause – I was asked to the
party afterwards at the Williams', Katherine's mother – but little Playmate
[Helen Adams] had been doing her <u>worst</u> all day – and I had ended up in
a Berserk rage which gave me a headache, so I went home and Stuart went
alone. He came in about 2.30 and had "lost all his strength" the next morning.

Last night, we went to the Philadelphia Orchestra in the Mosque – I now
live in the Mosque half the time. Eugene Ormandy conducted a beautiful
program and, once more, British sailors were present, as well as Army men
from Camp Lee near Petersburg –[2] *After the performance, we went to a large*
party for Ormandy at Quincy Cole's – about 150 people. I knew everyone there
and it was quite nice.

1. Gracie Fields (originally Stansfield), 1898–1979, was an English music hall and cabaret singer. She toured extensively during the war, giving concerts to troops.

2. Eugene Ormandy, 1899–1985, was born in Budapest, settled in the United States in 1921, and was the musical director of the Philadelphia Orchestra from 1938 to 1980.

1st December 1941   Blackpotts

Gerald has a marvellous new job – connected with air force and army liaison, and is going to be a MAJOR. I will write you what I can about it when I see him and glean more about it.

Virginia Stuart Reynolds (Ginnie), 1920s. Photo by Foster Studio, Richmond.

From left, Virginia Stuart Reynolds (Ginnie), William (Billy) Gilmour, Virginia Dickinson Reynolds (Bougie), Huntly Drummond, Gerna Gilmour, and unidentified man, Casino de la Pergola, St.-Jean-de-Luz, France, 1920s.

Chesterfield Apartments in
Richmond, where Stuart and
Virginia Reynolds lived from 1920.
Virginia remained there until her
death in 1966. Photo by Angela
Potter, 1998.

Ginnie and Bougie at Ivry, 1932.

Virginia Reynolds at Ivry, 1933.

Virginia and Stuart Reynolds at Ivry, 1930s.

Virginia Reynolds (Bougie), 1935. Photo by Foster Studio, Richmond.

From left, Stuart Reynolds, Virginia Reynolds
(Bougie), and Huntly Drummond at Wild Thyme
Cottage, Ivry, 1930s.

Pothier Doucet, Montreal, 1934.

Marriage of Virginia Stuart Reynolds (Ginnie) and Gerald Potter at the Guards Chapel, London, with Grenadier soldiers forming a guard of honor, March 1936. Photo by Keystone Press Agency, London.

Ginnie Potter, 1930s. Photo by Wallace Heaton, London.

From left, Gerald Potter, Ginnie Potter, and Virginia Reynolds (Bougie) on board Gerald's yacht *Carmela*, ca. 1937.

Black Potts, the wartime home of the Potter family near Windsor. Photo is from the 1940s.

Gerald and Ginnie Potter at the Pink Cottage, Warsash, Hampshire, ca. 1937.

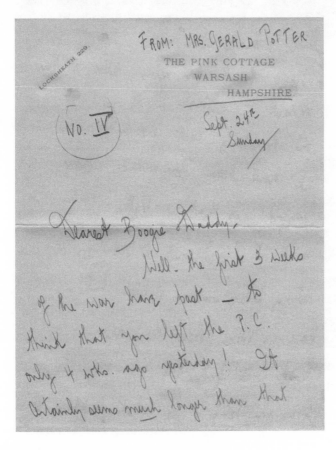

A letter from
Ginnie to Bougie,
1939.

Gerald Potter in the uniform of a
captain in the Grenadier Guards,
ca. 1940.

A letter from Bougie to Ginnie, 1941.

From left, Ginnie Potter, Jenny Potter, and Rose Moon (Nannie) in the vegetable garden at Black Potts, 1942.

Huntly Drummond, n.d., probably post–World War II.

Bougie Reynolds, Ginnie Potter, and Jenny Potter
at Wild Thyme Cottage, Ivry, ca. 1948.

Florence Dickinson Stearns when
she became vice president of the
Poetry Society of Virginia, 1949.
Photo by Foster Studio, Richmond.

Greenmarch, the Potter family home from 1949 to 1984. Photo by Jenny Potter, 1954.

Ginnie Potter with her daughter Angela at Greenmarch, ca. 1950.

Gerald Potter, ca. 1958.

Virginia Reynolds (Bougie), 1964. Photo by Jenny Potter.

Ginnie Potter (left) and Jenny Potter at Black Potts, 1990. Photo by Angela Potter.

War Letters
December 1941—August 1945

14th December 1941   *Richmond*

You may imagine that we have all been a little hectic since 2.22 p.m. Eastern Standard Time Dec. 7th, exactly one week ago — I have just come home from the Allison Building on Main St. where we are actively engaged in making a card index of Richmond's citizens, zoning them and placing them in their proper districts — This has to be done now for use in case of emergencies — The Richmond Citizens League which I started by a meeting in the Woman's Club over a year ago for the purpose of getting the city cleaned up is now the agency for assisting, with volunteer workers, the Mayor and his Police Dept.[1] So much for that.

Also on Friday evening, I met with Helen Adams and Leslie Jones and three people from Washington to decide what to do about "Fight for Freedom", now that we <u>are</u> fighting for just that. Naturally we think our function is over, but we shall keep in touch with our membership and preserve the files, in order to use them for other purposes. The agreement was unanimous that we shall have a peace offensive, when the war is over, and we are <u>victorious,</u> which will <u>do</u> something about Germany — <u>I</u> hope something very drastic. I have always said that I would go "on the stump" for the purpose of dealing out to those poisonous brutes what they have <u>always</u> deserved. It will be <u>my day</u>, and I hope I shall be alive for it.

I bought a crèche from Cole's for decoration this Christmas and opened it up to examine it, to make sure that all the figures etc. were there. On the bottom of the <u>Virgin</u> was printed "Made in Japan"! —

Everyone is quite calm here about the war. A few old women spend all their time listening to the bulletins over the radio, but they aren't good for much else – We have a large Red Cross drive beginning today etc. etc. So at last America is at war – Now we shall see what we are capable of doing. The manner of attacking by the Japanese was certainly "made in Germany" –

1. The Woman's Club of Richmond was founded in 1894. For further information, see Sandra Gioia Treadway, *Women of Mark: A History of the Woman's Club of Richmond, Virginia, 1894–1994* (Richmond: Library of Virginia, 1995).

18th December 1941   Blackpotts

So many things have happened since my last letter that it leaves one breathless. America has not only gone to war with Japan, but with Germany and Italy and Rumania as well! Whew – I cannot possibly know until I hear from you, but somehow I imagine that most Americans were rather relieved when things came to a head. At least now they know where they stand and that there is only one thing left to do – and that is to fight like hell – I am longing for your first letter telling me of people's reactions etc. To think that California has been blacked out and that New York had a warning. It seems incredible!! I am wondering if you will start having rationing too. I hope I will not ever have to worry that you are living on the 7th floor!! The night U.S. war was declared we had Dick and Frances Westmacott to supper and we missed *hearing the news* because we *hadn't finished our supper.* We then sat about and talked (incidentally said that we didn't think Japan would fight – they were already doing it!!) until about 20 to 12, when Dick and Frances left. Gerald said he was going to wait and hear the news, and I said I was much too sleepy and went upstairs and just as I was stepping into my hot bath, Gerald called "Come quickly, Japan has attacked America". I rushed downstairs clad in a bathtowel and *burst into tears* and said "Do you think Boogie and Daddy will be all-right?" Gerald had to get out the Atlas and persuade me that you were really rather far removed from the scene of action, and what did I suppose you felt about *me* who had been living on a rather small island that had been continually bombed, and for some time had been more or less alone against half the world, so then I saw his point and felt quite pleased.

The evening of the party Beryl Saunderson took R. [Rosemary Jeffreys] and me to the theatre and supper afterwards. Gerald was back for the day on Wed. and pushed off again after dinner. He had some military business to do near here in the morning. I think I told you that he is now a major – the rank may only be temporary but the lovely part is that I don't think he can ever be made a lieutenant again! He has done very well in Army Cooperation, and is now stationed near C. [Camberley] (where he was living before we were married). It's difficult to explain, but it's the Bomber Support for the Army and he is second in command. He has worked hard to get into Army-Air Liaison, which interests him so much and I am so thrilled that he has done so well.

28th December 1941   *Richmond*

We have all been so excited about Winston Churchill's being here that we scarcely thought of aught else. He came to <u>*Richmond*</u> *in an army bomber from "somewhere" and took the train here to Washington. We have just heard over the radio that the news of the German General who was supposed to have landed in Ireland, is a sort of hoax. The Japanese have begun putting out the sort of news that Haw-Haw began two years ago, but the news* <u>*is*</u> *bad from the Pacific. However, we shall hope to get them in the end –*

Tomorrow I am starting to work again on the Civilian Defense card index system.[1] *That will soon be over – and I shall then do something else. I should like to find something which would contribute* <u>*directly*</u> *to the discomfort of Germans and Japanese, such as making bullets etc. but I presume that I am a bit ancient for that, so I shall have to content myself with Red Cross or such things – very boring. I shall have to do my bit in buying Defense bonds, so I am investigating buying them as a co-owner with Jennifer. They mature in 10 years and they would be very good for educating her at that time – A bond for $93.00 matures at $125.00, $2,000 would be $2500, and $4000 would be $5000 – I don't know how much I can do because I am trying to stretch over as much ground as possible now while the dividends are coming in – At any rate, I shall have to do* <u>*something*</u> *soon –*

Yesterday I saw Walt Disney's "Dumbo", the flying elephant which I loved, and the day before went to "Great Guns" with Laurel and Hardy. My brain is atrophied, and my taste is growing more childish daily – But, frankly, with nothing in the offing but wars and rumours of wars, I only like the comedies –

I actually went inside Fendley's house the other day. I was delivering a Christmas present and Marian came to the door, so I had to go in. She was rather flustered. The house is very <u>neat</u> – and hopelessly middle-class – I shall never understand how he could do it, but he seems to be <u>delighted</u>, so it isn't "my funeral" –²

We are being rationed on <u>rubber</u> and I doubt if we can go often to Glouces-ter. We shall have to go and <u>stay</u> and use the car as little as possible. No more motoring to Canada – "We're in the Army now". Walter Winchell's New Year's toast to the Jap Navy was – Bottoms up!³ I never told you about Wal-ter Winchell's column mentioning <u>Jennifer</u> – It was merely a rehash of the articles about the Spitfires –

1. According to Mary Martha Thomas, the Civilian Defense Program was "authorized to create a Citizens' Defense Corps. These volunteers acted as air raid wardens, auxiliary firemen, emergency medical corps, nurses' aides and messengers." See Thomas, *Riveting and Rationing in Dixie: Alabama Women and the Second World War* (Tuscaloosa: University of Alabama Press, 1987), 82.

2. In 1940 at the age of sixty-seven, Fendley Dickinson had married his second wife, Marian Koch (1899–1954), who was descended from a German immigrant family, much to Bougie's disapproval.

3. Walter Winchell, 1897–1972, was a journalist and gossip columnist. His column titled "On Broadway" appeared in more than eight hundred newspapers from 1929. He was a regular radio broadcaster from 1931 to 1935.

2nd January 1942   Black Potts

I have been listening to the 9 o'clock news, and very sad to hear of the fall of Manila. But I don't suppose we can expect much except defeat in the next few months, until things really get going. I hope the U.S. navy will emerge again, after this first staggering blow they have had. It's funny to think that

Churchill has been in Washington and Ottawa over Xmas. I wish I could have gone with him on his official tour!!

Tuesday things began to look UP and I had recovered from state of irritation due to lack of sleep and bad plumbing! – I went in to work at the British Restaurant, and to my joy heard that Angela Laycock's husband was reported safe and well –[1] Was thrilled to read of his exploits in the papers – he was in the Commando [unit] that popped in at General Rommel's H.Q. in Libya. He (Col. Laycock) arrived back after 41 days in hiding, with only a goat to eat and a few berries and their iron rations during that time. Angela expects him back in England shortly. Everyone at the W.V.S. was so gay and cheery, I think the customers must have thought us crazy. When I returned home, I found 2 letters from you, so it was a real banner day –

1. Major General Sir Robert Laycock, 1907–68, succeeded Mountbatten as chief of combined operations 1943–47 and served as governor and commander in chief of Malta 1945–59.

9th January 1942   Black Potts

As for our news, where were we? O yes. Last Saturday I took Anne Anson's place at the Restaurant as she and Bill had gone away on leave – they did not go to G[lamis] after all as I thought, but to Bill's home in Staffordshire, which is a trifle pompous I gather from Anne.[1] Bill's family have just sold nearly all their jewellery (including a "fender" like Lady Astor's) and a lot of good furniture and china at Christies'. When Anne returned, she found that "Aunt Elizabeth" [the late Queen Mother] had bought back a beautiful Crown Derby service and given it to her, so she was very touchée.

The news in Russia is very heartening, isn't it? Not so good in the Far East but I hope things will get better soon. Am longing to receive your letters on the subject. I see that U.S. Forces may be sent to England – I hope this will include a few Richmond friends! (Perhaps this sounds *selfish* but if they have got to go somewhere I hope they'll come here.)

1. Glamis Castle, Scotland, is the seat of the Earls of Strathmore, family of Queen Eliz-

abeth the Queen Mother, who was a daughter of the fourteenth earl. Shugborough Hall, Staffordshire, is the seat of the Earls of Lichfield.

19th January 1942   *Richmond*

This is Stuart's and my wedding anniversary. Certainly had we not embarked on the stormy sea of matrimony on a snowy day 34 years ago, I should have been denied the acquisition of the world's sweetest and most adorable daughter. Unlike Nana, who used to attempt to put a curse on me by saying, "I hope that you will have a daughter who will be as naughty as you are". I say "I pray that your small Jennifer will be as charming as you are".

I also hope very much that she will <u>not</u> inherit my disposition which, if full of verve, is not a sweet tone. I was born <u>furious,</u> and I am <u>still.</u> Just as furious as the day when, at the age of two years, I went to have my photograph taken, and was <u>not</u> allowed to cross my legs! I am furious with the enemy as I have <u>always</u> been with the beastly German race − I am <u>furious</u> because of separation and frustration. It keeps me from being <u>sorry</u> for myself − the rages I get into!! but no one could call me <u>sweet</u> and I hope that Jennifer is like you and not like me − They say these things skip a generation − Where I got the burning flame within me, God knows, but it burns there as fiercely as ever − and the churning up on the inside afflicts me when certain things are done, said, looked or insinuated −

25th January 1942   *Richmond*

We are now rationed on sugar, and I am wondering if I can send any more − Perhaps I can from Canada − I am thinking of going up there about February 12th − Florie wants to send you some Citrus Concentrates. Helen Norman loved hers − and banana flakes − there are a good many concentrated foods now, which is handy and they take up small space −

We consider the affair at Pearl Harbour a national disgrace, but at least it frightened this enormous, and unwieldy nation, and although it has handicapped us in the East, we will make a more or less united effort now, come what may −

This place is simply teeming with soldiers. There are two huge camps near here, and one enormous one at Bowling Green – innumerable ones down near the cottage, and Norfolk now has a population of about 300,000 – Just after Pearl Harbour over 1/2 million men were moved from the East – The railroads lived up well, and scarcely anyone knew until it was accomplished – The pact with South America turned out a bit of milk and water – but at least something was accomplished – I can't tell you how thrilled I am with the Russian Campaign against the Germans – We know now that Lindbergh was only shown a few old bits of junk, and the poor boob believed Stalin. He must have laughed up his sleeve, or roared like the Tartars in the Chauve-Souris in "Letter to the Sultan" – [1] *I shall never forget that "acrid Asiatic mirth" Ha! Ha! Ha! Ha! Ha! Ha! Ha! Ha! in a descending scale. Do you remember it? What a complete failure that poor pro-German Swedish nut has made of everything since he flew the ocean going East. He even got his wife to write something called "The Wave of the Future" which has made her the object of scorn and laughter.* [2]

About any danger to <u>us</u> – I can't imagine that there would be any particular reason for Richmond being <u>bombed</u> but this national disgrace in Hawaii has scared us all and we aren't going to take any chances. We are to have a trial black-out soon – I imagine, knowing R'd., that it will be fairly <u>comic</u>. All I am going to do is turn out all the lights and go into <u>the hall</u> with a chair and my knitting! I am on #38 sweater. I did one for the U.S. Navy and was pursued by a jinx, so decided that the Bon Dieu meant for me to knit solely for the British and am back on British Navy work. Also I found that they were giving out tons of wool to other people for the U.S.

Don't worry about us – we are quite all right. It will be a long time before the Japs can get to Richmond – and the Germans are rather busy in Russia. Vive la Russie. I grow angry when I think of your giving your fur lined coat to the wretched Finns – The only thing which troubles me is – what is the World going to do with the <u>Russians</u> if they whip the Germans. But one problem at a time!

1. *Chauve-Souris* is an opera by Johann Strauss usually referred to as *Die Fledermaus (The Bat)*. Bougie is referring to the "Laughing Song" sung by Adèle, others, and the chorus.

2. Anne Spencer Morrow Lindbergh, *The Wave of the Future: A Confession of Faith* (New York: Harcourt, Brace, 1940).

27th January 1942   Black Potts

[Monday] evening I listened to a talk about Gen. Lee on the anniversary of his birthday (and your wedding anniversary) and felt all Southern and wanted to sing Dixie – I am so thrilled that my country is at war (is this wrong of me?) and am thrilled to know that there are Americans in N. Ireland now. I pray for some sort of REAL Anglo-American unity after this war.

Tuesday after W.V.S. Gerna [Gilmour] arrived to stay and Gerald also came for the night. Gerna and I had a long walk on Wed. afternoon in the crisp newfallen snow, and helped Nannie push the pram; it was rather heavy-going as the snow was quite deep. Black Potts looked lovely and Gerna was thrilled with it, and wanted to give a lot of bread to the birds and the swans (you can just imagine) and I had to restrain her! That evening we listened to Solomon's concert over the wireless – [1] He does play beautifully and Gerna is lucky to be studying under him – Gerna left Thursday morning. I put her on the bus and then went on to the Restaurant.

1. Solomon Cutner, 1902–88, an English pianist always known by his first name, toured for the forces during World War II.

1st February 1942   Richmond

You want to know what the reaction to a declaration of war was. Here, it was taken very quietly, but naturally everyone was stunned by the dreadful blow at Pearl Harbour which you now know about. It appears that in spite of repeated dispatches from Washington neither the Generals nor Admirals seemed to take it seriously. We know we will pay a heavy price for their criminal negligence. Some people think that it was all a part of the same pattern. I could go on indefinitely about that because, as you know, I have always been very vocal on the subject of this war, and the part we should take. I have always thought that we should have begun to go into it from the start. The trouble has been the Administration's weak position with labour. Roosevelt knew, but he didn't dare say, because he had to be elected first. He went as far as he dared go, asking for repeal of neutrality, and the arming of Guam. This Congress absolutely refused, so he had to give in, because he didn't dare make a cam-

paign issue of it. The whole truth is, as I see it, that had not Japan attacked, as she did, with such force in the Pacific, we would have gone under as France did, in another year. Until you take in that this is a world revolution, and that you don't know whether your "brother" is your friend or your enemy, you cannot understand what is going on. France had so many people who hated the Republique that she couldn't put enough into the fight. All the persons in high places, with few exceptions, preferred Hitler's "New Order" to people like Blum.[1] It is a great pity that he ever got to power and gave them a reason. We were all stupid about Spain, not beginning to take in that the Dictators were using Spain as a proving ground. Now, it stands out with clarity. Russia, China, England and the U.S. are, whether they mean to be or not, on the side of liberalism and the so-called "Rights of Man" – Germany, Japan and Italy, God help those poor boobs (the Italians) are trying to establish a feudal state of being, with the gangsters which represent them (in the case of Germany and Italy) in the saddle. Japan seems to be in the hands of the reactionaries and the Army.

These two groups are in a global death struggle. Because of our labour situation, Japan got in the first blow, and a serious blow it is. We are fast becoming an arsenal from one end of the country to the other. Living as I do in a kind of backwater I don't see very much, but, every now and then, vast numbers of Army trucks go rattling through Belvidere Street – the lights blink and everything stops for them to go speeding across the main arteries of traffic. One movement took 24 hours. They were routed in a roundabout way so as not to paralyze the usual traffic. I heard them, but didn't see them.

The only thing which has touched us so far, is the rise in food prices, not serious yet, the additional income taxes and the fact that I had to be finger printed and have my picture taken to go on a permit to fish in the York River. I found that positively amusing. It looked to me as if all the thugs in Virginia assembled with me to be fingerprinted. There were a few octogenarian women tottering on their feeble legs, men with beards, roustabouts of all kinds and then – me. I was escorted in a most Chesterfieldian manner by Mr. Nicholson, my next door neighbour in Gloucester who makes the night air hideous with his accordion and his natural speaking voice (St. Louis) to a position of advantage. He sponsored me. I can't get over it, but I shall be forced to be nice to him from now on –

Many passenger trains have been taken off. We are rationed on sugar, and can't get any rubber – so we use our car with great care with an eye on the future, and a reservation about how much we may be able to use it for going to Gloucester. Stuart has gone completely <u>moral</u> on me – and refuses to buy spark plugs, fan belts, and rubber tubing. He says it is <u>hoarding</u>. Several days ago I saw a small, slight figure, positively tottering under a consignment of the above articles, and it was Bessie Morris! having it all put away in the <u>safe</u> downstairs in the lobby – I wish you could have seen Virginia Massie's face behind the desk. Bessie is our A #1 joke in the Chesterfield –

I am definitely committed to Red Cross in St. James Church on Friday. I am a supervisor but prefer making the dressings to telling other people how to do them.

I am so anxious to see you and Jennifer that I dare not dwell on it. I shall write about her another time, as this is a fat letter already and I have difficulty getting it in the envelope – I was interested in all your news and what you tell me about people. How sweet of "Aunt Elizabeth" to buy the Crown Derby. What about my buying <u>you</u> something?

I keep all your letters. Someday you might want to do something with them.

1. Léon Blum, 1872–1950, was the first socialist prime minister of France from 1936 to 1937. He was imprisoned by the Vichy government and released by the Allies in 1945.

8th February 1942   *Richmond*
Having <u>refused</u> to stop, look, listen for two years in a time when any sensible creature had to <u>know</u> that we would have to go to war – in fact I should say that for the last five or six years any intelligent person must <u>feel</u> that the thing was unavoidable, we, <u>now</u>, are going "hay wire" curbing everything. There are no <u>pins</u> – no one can buy <u>any</u> rubber. Everyone has gone out of the city and now there are no tires for the cars they <u>must</u> use. Sugar is rationed and so on, ad infinitum. The <u>billions</u> are tossed about in Congress like so many balls, without a murmur – Everyone not working is hissed at as a "parasite" and then there are long arguments about who is a parasite, and why – Tonight, we go on "war time" and tomorrow night Richmond is to have a trial "black out". I am to rush to my apartment, lower all the Venetian blinds, put out the

*lights, open my front door. I am warden for the 7th floor! On my floor there
is a man with ears and a long face named Gallagher who is either a spy or a
super criminal, if his looks mean anything, and a woman who has been pro
German throughout and who scarcely speaks to me because I have said in
no uncertain terms what I thought! so it is going to be pleasant for me. No
doubt Dick Osterloh is fire war warden for the building and is busy as a bee
going to meetings! It is like children playing "fire department" — All the old
ladies are just as scared as if it were real — I can't imagine that either Japan
or Germany would single out Richmond for a blitz, even if they could reach
here with enough load to do any damage. But I suppose it is all right to be
prepared for the "charming scout" Germans —*

*Last Monday I worked on Civilian Defense down on Main St. with El-
eanor Barton, and in the afternoon went to see "The Vanishing Virginian",
written by a Richmond woman Rebecca Yancey Williams about her father
Capt. Bob Yancey of Lynchburg.[1] It is a <u>thin</u> picture, but very well done, and
reminiscent for me, of the lazy, safe days of the late 90s and early 1900s before
the 1st war. The negroes in it were the best part of it. I should like for you to
see it.*

*Wednesday I was Chairman for one of those Literary Luncheons. I had
a little man named Stevenson from Richmond University who made a good
talk about "Ancestral Voices" — meaning English poetry. The only trouble
was that he was ill with laryngitis and I think most people found the voices
remained ancestral and didn't come beyond the platform. He was a nice man
and really had a good message for us. His wife was like a faun which had
become frightened by human contact. I managed to calm her down, and sent
<u>him</u> to the dressing room to rest after lunch — before the speech —*

1. Rebecca Yancey Williams, *The Vanishing Virginian* (New York: E. P. Dutton, 1940).

9th February 1942   Black Potts
Since my last letter I have received yours of Dec. 28th (no. 38) with the
lovely letter from Edna Catlett enclosed. To-day I had a pacquet from Dionne's, and also a letter from Huntly with clipping about the Jennifer Spitfire being in action. This is very thrilling news indeed, and I do wish I could

get hold of the Canadian pilot, as I should like to ask him here for a visit. So will see if Gerald has any ideas on how I could catch up with him. It would be grand to meet him. Isn't it thrilling that he has downed six Germans, and I hope the "Boogie" has done as well –

17th February 1942   Black Potts

Friday the 13th was certainly a bad date as far as the news was concerned, as we heard about the Scharnhorst and the Gneisenau.[1] Then on Sunday the news that Singapore had fallen – It is all too GRIM for words, but I feel the situation is bound to improve in the next few months. Gerald is getting very restive to have another crack at the Bosche [sic]. His new job isn't nearly as active as he had hoped, but he has always felt that cooperation between the Services is so important that he must do everything within his power to improve that situation – When he's doing worthwhile things he enjoys it, but if he has to sit back on his behind for long, he would prefer to be back with the Regiment as he misses both the men and the officers. I read an article the other day, which I have cut out, of a man in a certain crack regiment who requested to be sent on Active Service overseas – and was refused – then tried to join the Parachutists – and was refused – then asked to be transferred to the Navy and was refused – "He then took to crime" – Their time will come, I am sure but how often they must feel a sense of frustration and stagnation.

I went up to London on Saturday to stay the night. Quite a little fling as I hadn't been there for 2 months. First lunched with Gerna and Billy [Gilmour] in their new flat. They gave me a *chop* for lunch, which I thought was the height of hospitality as I knew it could be their only meat meal for the week – but I think they felt they wanted to do something GRAND in return for the meals they have had here – Gerna has bought a piano with the money she got from selling her grandmother's diamond star!! She then took me to a concert at the Albert Hall to hear the London Philharmonic, conductor Sir Adrian Boult, and soloist Solomon (Gerna's teacher).[2] They played a marvellous concerto for piano by Bliss and Tchaikovsky's 4th Symphony.

1. *Scharnhorst* and *Gneisenau* were German battle cruisers that the British failed to sink as they sailed through the English Channel after their departure from Brest.

2. Sir Adrian Boult, 1889–1983, was musical director of the BBC 1930–42. He conducted the BBC Symphony and London Philharmonic Orchestras.

21st February 1942   *Ivry, P.Q.*

Washington was <u>*seething*</u> *with soldiers, mostly "rookies" going to Camp Meade in Maryland. Some of them were grouped near where I was sitting and one of them caught my eye — He shook some change in his hand and said, "I only have 60 cents". I said, "What do you want and how much?" He sat beside me, and said, "Confidentially, Madam, my pal and I want a pint of whisky between us, and we don't get paid until next week". I gave him the money, and he fled, flinging back a "God will bless you, Madam, for this". On the train there were a good many more soldiers of different descriptions — some Canadians and some, I thought, British Air Force — and some very mysterious looking men. My imagination runs away with me at times — and I felt surrounded by* [G-men?]. *I didn't sleep very well although I had quite a luxurious compartment. The "customs" wake you at 6.30, and you feel there is no especial reason for your having gone to bed — Huntly met us at the train. He limps a little, but I think he is much better. Anyhow he still goes skiing.*

8th April 1942   *Richmond*

Here I am living as if I were on a plantation in ante-bellum days "befo' de War" — I have an old coloured nurse who tells me every day that I am <u>*beautiful*</u>*. She has no idea of nursing but no matter — She flatters me to the point of idiocy. Erma comes every day to clean silver and polish furniture etc., and Carrie, who has a new hair-do and sang in a chorus for the benefit of the old people in the City Home on Easter — I am giving orders every moment from the sofa where the afflicted knee reposes, bound up, and only slightly swollen now. The gardenia bush gives me the slight illusion of the deep south, and when Martha says, "Chile, ain't you too cool in that thin covering?" I am absolutely in the feudal age once more — How different all this is from*

Montreal – where I have to hear every day about the virtues of all the Clan
D. [Drummond] I was a little fed up, but breathe it not in Gath.

13th April 1942   *Richmond*

I am getting on quite well with this tedious thing of not using my knee – The
"Mammy" Martha Bates comes every day and puts me in the tub and scrubs
me. I can do it perfectly myself, but it pleases her to have the illusion that
she is nursing me. Then she tells me that Venus is a slouch to me. Imagine!
and that I have the brains of a female Socrates – only she never heard of him
– These negroes are marvellous for flattery – Erma is here cleaning silver
– Carrie using an electrolux and Martha saying how beautiful everything
is! –

Yesterday I went out for a long drive – Rubber is non-existent here but,
so far, gas isn't rationed. (It is rationed in Canada) and as I must have some
air while I am laid up with this wrenched knee I use the car. Stuart thinks our
tires will last for a possible year and a half.

16th April 1942   Black Potts

Gerald came back for the week-end and we spent a busy time in the garden.
I did some shopping on Saturday afternoon as hadn't been off 'the island'
for a week, also went to see Brown the gardener who is up though still
feeling very weak – [1] However I hope he may be able to come back in a
few weeks' time and do a little work, as we are nearly going mad trying to
get the digging and planting done. We have applied for a land girl as there
is lots more space which *should* be under cultivation – the L.G. [land girl]
will apparently (even if she *does* come) be totally ignorant, but perhaps
Brown will be able to impart a little of his knowledge.[2] Also it seems that
we will have to house her (God knows where!), but the important thing is
to DIG FOR VICTORY, so she'll have a cot in my room perhaps! Anyway
we haven't even *got* her yet, so no use jumping ditches etc.

On Tuesday I went to the Restaurant as usual – and yesterday roared up
to London for a few hours to have a fitting, shop for Jennifer, and had a
hasty lunch with Gerna at the 500 – I bought J. some viyella nightgowns

for next winter – as they are 4 yr. old size I had to give 4 coupons each for them – that is the trouble with having a *large* child, you have to give more coupons – also bought socks and shoes as she is growing so fast I cannot seem to keep her in shoes. Her feet are like "Suitcase Simpson's" – [3]

The new income-tax budget is out, there are to be more taxes on luxuries and on beer, tobacco and spirits, but thank Goodness the income-tax hasn't gone up – Gerald has put the car up for sale but I don't imagine he'll be offered much for it, as petrol for civilians is being taken off the market after June – so if he isn't offered a good price for 'Benito' I expect we'll put her up somewhere for 'the duration'.

1. Mr. Brown, ca. 1866–1942, was the part-time gardener at Black Potts.

2. England's Women's Land Army was founded in 1916 to attract women to work on farms. By 1943 more than eighty thousand women had signed up as land girls.

3. This is probably a reference to Harry "Suitcase" Simpson, 1925–79, a Negro League baseball player, so called by virtue of his playing for seventeen different teams.

21st April 1942   *Richmond*
Travel is difficult now – such crowds – troops moving all the time and you can hear great vans rumbling along the streets here, carrying soldiers. It looks more and more like an all-out to try to defeat the enemies – and none too soon. What a world – and all the time we must defeat the enemies from within – The pro-Germans, the pro-Vichyites, the opportunists, the plain thugs – The life-time prisoners from the Oklahoma prison want to be allowed to do suicide service in the Navy – I am all for it. They would get their thrill and do some service for the country –

There are a great many negroes in the service and it is difficult to get good domestic servants –

Stuart is very well and cheery – He seems to have found himself and is now deputy controller! of the Control Board for Civilian Defense, and says his promotion has been so rapid that there is nothing to prevent his being a General in a few weeks!

Well, if "we" can stave off Hitler and Co this summer, his goose is cooked and I pray hourly that this may come to pass. He and Laval will make a move for peace this year I am certain — We must see that they don't get it. I never thought I should become enamoured of Joe Stalin, but, now, I even admire his moustache, and the cruel look I have always disliked in his eyes looks kindly, like the brooding, paternal expression in the face of a philanthropist. Such is human nature!

23rd April 1942   Black Potts

Many thanks for letter #51 written March 20th which arrived yesterday — it seems so funny to think that now *you* can't get things like hairpins and corsets — Old things that you have tucked away and forgotten all about give you a *big thrill* now when you find them. I came across an old scarf, a pair of cotton stockings, etc. the other day and felt as if I had discovered a gold mine. The wonderful parcel from Rose arrived on Monday — some pure gold in the form of 5 cakes of soap, 1 dozen razor blades and 2 prs. of socks and an adorable blue cardigan for Jennifer. It's the most *extraordinary* thing but it was *exactly* what I wanted for B.D. as she needed socks very badly and the cardigan is *just* what she needs for the summer. It was a really *inspired* parcel. I rushed at once and had a very *lathery* bath! Gave Gerald 1/2 the razor blades and he was thrilled — and kept the others for my verucca calcas!

Gerald got back about 6 — in terrific form and very thrilled because he had had an intensely interesting week. He had been staying at an aerodrome where the Commanding Officer was a great friend — and it was in a part of the world he loves, and he ran into several old friends, etc. One afternoon he went on an operational flight to France and they bombed Cherbourg — so naturally I was very interested to hear all about it (but am glad I didn't know beforehand) — His job has been very interesting lately as he has been to so many of the various aerodromes, and made friends with a lot of the pilots.

Tuesday was what one might call a slightly hectic day. I was up at 7, first saw to the goslings, then fed the broody hens, the ducks, the chickens, the geese, watered all the new plants, and opened the frames. Then dressed in my best bib and tucker and left at 9.30 — picked up Anne Anson, also Peter and Patsy Evelyn (who were staying with the Ansons) and together we went to see Princess Elizabeth inspect the Grenadier Guards in the quadrangle of Windsor Castle. She has just been made Col. of the Regiment, owing to the death of the Duke of Connaught. The King and Queen and Princess Margaret Rose were there too, and it was all most impressive. I saw quite a lot of people I knew. Rosemary [Jeffreys] was there with Mark, also Sir George, and Lady Cantelupe.[1]

We are going to call the goslings "Adolf" and "Elizabeth" as they were born on either April 20th or 21st (we are not sure which) –

1. Mark Jeffreys, 1932–86, was from 1960 the second Baron Jeffreys. General Sir George Jeffreys, 1878–1960, was aide-de-camp general to the king 1936–38 and member of Parliament for Petersfield 1941–51. Lady Dorothy Cantelupe, d. 1953, was the widow of Viscount Cantelupe and married Sir George in 1905.

20th May 1942   Black Potts

We realized that something was going on in the goose-pen as there was a bit of tapping and cheeping and the gander (or the "old gentleman" as Nannie calls him) was walking up and down outside the pen – he wouldn't eat or sleep, I have never seen such an anxious father. The next day we saw 4 baby goslings had hatched out – and later the 2 geese, the gander and the 4 babies were swimming about in the pond. These 4 goslings have been called "Blood, Toil, Tears and Sweat" (extract from Churchill's famous speech). They are certainly not much toil or sweat as we can't go near them at the moment as Mamma Goose won't allow it, so we just have to let them fend for themselves, and hope they'll be all right.

At 5.30 I had to meet Miss Lucy Tomkins, the Land Girl – she has had a month's training and before the war was a shop assistant – her home is in East Dulwich, London.[1] She seemed to think she was going to a big estate where there would be lots of other L.G.s and that she would be billeted with other L.G.s. We got lost looking for the billet, and when we arrived found it was a tiny private house – the owner had a screaming baby in her arms, and over the bawling of the infant we tried to make arrangements. The owner said she wasn't expecting us so soon, and the only stick of furniture in the tiny room was a bed! Miss Tomkins was getting gloomier and gloomier about the whole affair, and at this point, a thunderstorm burst. I brought her back here to show her around in the pelting rain, and fed the animals – then took her back – By this time, I was exhausted with L.G.s and everything else and told Gerald we must go to a cinema, so we went to see Robert Young and Hedy LaMarr in "H.M. Pelham, Esq", which we both enjoyed enormously – and we had a cold supper when we returned.

Tuesday morning la Tomkins turned up – still steeped in gloom – I showed her animals etc. and left her to do some digging – Gerald was off to his new job in the West of England, and Fiander was packing up all the equipment etc. Then to see Bella about L.G.'s lunch, Fiander's lunch, Gerald's lunch etc. and left for the British Restaurant. I was a waitress and in a frenzy of energy I broke the record by serving 69 lunches.

[Today I went] to dressmaker's [in London] to discuss possibility of one summer dress – and found myself sitting beside one of King Zog's sisters.[2] She is the eldest of the three, is about 4 feet 6 – very plain, aged about 45 – and had on a large powder-blue hat decorated with a large cabbage rose – a small creature nearby was her "A.D.C." or some member of the retinue – He was *slightly* taller with enormous ears and hair standing on end, and looked exactly like a soda-jerker in a hick town in North Carolina complete with pencil and fountain pen clips outside his breast pocket! –

I returned by train to find Miss Tomkins awaiting me on the doorstep to tell me that she had been to see the W.L.A. [Women's Land Army] and that they were billeting her in a hostel for L. Girls quite near here – and she thought she would like to stay after all!! So *all being well*, she is moving from the minute room to-morrow morning and going to this hostel, then coming here to report as soon as she is settled. I am holding my breath until she arrives to-morrow, for fear there is some hitch and no room at the hostel—— I do hope she will stay and be a success because we are so anxious to *cultivate* much more, and there is unlimited space for animals and vegetables. Two full time gardeners could find plenty to do here, so you can imagine I was somewhat dismayed at the dismal thought of having it on my own! As soon as we are a little under control with the vegetables I shall try and spruce up the rose garden, which is rapidly becoming a jungle.

I really love this house – I love seeing the boats go by, I love the *view* – I love seeing the wild duck, and the pheasants and the old heron, and dear old Egbert the swan. We also have a cuckoo with laryngitis, and a nightingale —

1. Lucy Tomkins worked at Black Potts from May 1942 until May 1944.

2. Ahmed Beg Zogu Zog, 1895–1961, was the king of Albania from 1928 to 1939. He was expelled by the Italians in 1939 and moved to England.

22nd May 1942   *Richmond*

There has been a wave of optimism over here recently, but in the last few days the officials in Washington have warned us that the German Peace Offensive was on its insidious way, so we are made to believe that it is unpatriotic to give in to a feeling of optimism. So here goes my only "lift of the spirit" in some time — in with aluminium and rubber and sugar and cuffs on men's trousers and unlimited railway travel etc. etc. Very amusing. We can't even be gay! I hear that New York is the black hole of Calcutta as far as enjoyment is concerned, and that the Maine coast is infested with "enemy aliens" — Martha Bianchi believes England is the safest place to live in now! which idea is a comfort to me certainly.

6th June 1942   *Richmond*

Thank Heaven that Heydrich the Hangman has died of the bullet holes placed in him by the brave and daring Czechs —[1]

On Monday I went up to Florie's and played bridge with her and Mr. and Mrs. Richard Reynolds.[2] *He is head of the Reynolds metal company, and is a power in the International metal companies such as Aluminum etc. He made himself rather interesting about international cartels and big business. They are enormously rich but very simple. Also they are rather ordinary but I liked them. She is like a little bird chirping on a high key and he looks exactly like one of the municipal water-plugs, which one sees on street corners. That is his shape. You aren't allowed to park within 6 ft. of them and personally, in this instance, I had no desire to get too near, but strange to relate, he writes poetry, and so does she, and that is how Florie got so intimate with them.*

1. Reinhard Heydrich, 1904–42, head of the Nazi security service, was involved in planning the "final solution" of genocide. Hundreds of reprisal executions followed his assassination near Prague on 27 May by Free Czechs parachuted in for that purpose.

2. Richard S. Reynolds Jr., 1908–80, company director and author of *Opportunity in Crisis: The Reynolds Metal Story* (New York: Newcomen Society in North America, 1956).

14th June 1942   *Richmond*

Lady Drummond died on Wednesday. I thought of sending you a cable, but Stuart said it would be in the Times, and so I just hoped you would see it and send Huntly a message. I don't like to send any superfluous cables. I spoke to Huntly over the telephone and he said he was quite all right and that he considered Julia's death a release for her and for all the relatives who have been watching for her death for so long – He was going up to Chatillon for a few days, but he will have quite a lot to do, I suppose, about subsequent arrangements. I wish that he would go to live in her *house. There is an oil shortage and he changed his furnace about 2 years ago from coal to oil.*

I went to a negro *wedding at 6.30 – The "contracting parties" were the daughter of Maud the waitress here who calls me "darling" – She married a Sergeant in the Army, who is stationed at Camp Lee – It was all very nicely done, by an* undertaker *– The bride wore a blue dress, and had a maid of honour so "light" as to cause you to wonder. Eight people (white) from the Chesterfield were there. I was so overcome by the pathos of it that I cried. A large fat negress sang a song at the end called "Because" – I didn't know what the inference was – I was quite dressed up in one of my best frocks because Mrs. Willingham said Maud wanted us to dress. I felt so much dressed that I was forced to keep on the velvet cape and wield an enormous fan which I got at a bullfight in San Sebastian! I thought at one time that I was going to illustrate "Death in the Afternoon" – We took up so much room in Maud's tiny house that I whispered to the other 7 'white sisters', "Let's go home so* they *can enjoy themselves". They all agreed.*

We have just landed another A.E.F. in Ulster, and we routed the Japanese at Midway, and have had M. Molotov, so maybe things will "shape up" with decision soon –[1] *Our great menace seems to be Hitler's U-boats, which appear to be numerous – But we will find a way, I have no doubt.*

"They" want me in the filter centre which means airplane spotting and all that goes with it. I may go, but I can't imagine that at the moment either Japan or Germany are in a position to do much damage in <u>Virginia</u>. If they do, they are supermen – I also feel that it is my duty to go to Canada for a visit on Huntly's account. He is going to begin to feel the blows soon and I am capable of cheering him. I shall find out what I can about the centre this week, and see if I think I can be of use – there are hundreds of younger women now doing all sorts of jobs, and I don't want to do anything, just to <u>say</u> I am doing something useful. I can always go on knitting and making Red Cross dressings and giving money as long as that lasts! – but I would love to make bombers and bullets for Hitler's minions – However, I can't, so that's that. Our production seems to be ahead of schedule, and all we need is <u>ships!</u> and more ships.

Now, we are scouring premises for rubber. I found a rubber sheet and some hot water bottles and sent them to the receiving station. We are rationed on sugar and soon, tea and coffee, and of course rubber and gas – It makes quite a difference to us not to have the car when we want it, but nothing like that matters of course – All that matters is to <u>win</u>.

Saw an amusing item in the paper from Fredericksburg – "Japanese bee-tles attack Chinese elms" – The Japanese are very thorough.

1. A.E.F.: American Expeditionary Force. Vyacheslav Mikhailovich Molotov, 1890–1986, was the Soviet prime minister 1930–41 who negotiated partnership with the Allies following the German invasion. He served as foreign minister 1939–49 and 1953–56.

24th July 1942   Black Potts

Margie [Hart] told me that they had had an American to dinner one night, and asked me if he was typical or peculiar. He arrived 3/4 of an hour late, made no excuse, gave flowery speeches about the simple little meal she produced, told long-winded stories at which everyone had to listen, and if anyone spoke waited for them to stop and began all over again; and then *wouldn't go*. I said he was perhaps the typical American BORE – whereas the typical English BORE would have arrived *early* (before one was ready) and remained boot-faced throughout the evening, drinking and eating everything that was offered and rather taking it all for granted, making no effort to ease the conversation, and also refusing to go.

I am terribly anxious to give *hospitality* to any Americans over here, as I think it *so important* that they get a bit of home life, and get to know English people, but it is difficult to know *how* as I could only have them when Gerald is not here (owing to the lack of room) and when he *isn't* here, I could only have one man at a time – to be in the tiny dressing-room off my bedroom!! I am thinking of going to the English Speaking Union and putting my name down – as perhaps they would be able to come for the day on Sundays –

1st August 1942   *Gloucester Banks*

The gas rationing over here is very mysterious – only 17 out of 48 States are rationed. . . . I do not have to tell you that it makes a great difference in our lives – more here – because we have none of the services England has – For instance you cannot get to Gloucester by train or boat and the service from the C. & O. railway is negligible –[1] *There is a bus once a day from Lee Hall, but the bus on this side only comes to Gloucester Court House –*

Night before last I had a very satisfactory talk with Vice-Admiral Halsey, who organised the attack against the Japs in the Marshall and Gilbert Islands.[2] *He is a grand old sea-dog with the blue eyes and rather beetling gray eyebrows – He is here for some treatments, having heard about Warren Vaughan in the last.*[3] *He seems to have done the trick for Adm. Halsey. He certainly did nothing for* <u>me</u> *– I wouldn't have come from Petersburg to go to him – Halsey seems absolutely confident that we will win – and I took a great fancy to him, because he loathes the Germans as much as I do, and says they must be exterminated as a race. He is scornful of their U-boat warfare along our coast – says they don't torpedo anything but helpless merchant ships and tankers. It appears they can cruise for about 3 months before they have to return – Also he says the Americans are not soft as people said they were – and that they are having splendid training – He fought Germans last time and this time Japanese – He says they are "vermin" – and that neither the Germans nor the Japs are the supermen they pretend. It was balm to my soul to hear him talk. No one knows how frightened I was about the U.S. from* *last August until Dec. 7th – I was afraid we would go the way of France – German propaganda was at its height. The Japanese did us a favour to attack in that way at Pearl Harbour –*

1. C & O: the Chesapeake and Ohio Railway.

2. William Halsey, 1882–1959, U.S. fleet admiral from December 1945 and commander of the South Pacific force October 1942–44.

3. Probably Dr. Warren T. Vaughan, 1893–1944, immunologist and president of the American Association for the Study of Allergy from 1940.

24th August 1942   Black Potts

Yes I think you are right – the attack on Pearl Harbour brought the U.S. to her senses overnight. It was a terrible tragedy for the people involved, but I now see that nothing else would have made her declare war. According to Mary [Bishop], the U.S. was decidedly anti-British, or was, when she was last there.[1] I expect they still are but at least they are more anti-Jap and German than anti-B.

The wireless has just announced that Mr. Churchill has returned from Moscow and points east.

I expect the Canadians were very thrilled to get in a scrap at last, after all this waiting – and I hope they killed a lot of Germans at Dieppe. I was very alarmed when I heard of the sinking of H.M.S. Foresight [destroyer], as it was Bobbie Fell's ship, but have just heard that he is safe and well.[2] It was sunk in that big convoy on the way to Malta, when the Eagle [carrier] and Manchester [cruiser] were sunk.

1. Mary Bishop née Hill, Ginnie's contemporary from Richmond.

2. Commander Robert (Bobbie) Fell, 1907–90, a Royal Navy officer and Gerald's cousin-in-law.

7th September 1942   Black Potts

When I returned home I found Bella in tears. It appears that Rosa has (somehow) had a letter that her mother and father and little brother aged 13 have been sent to Poland.[1] O Godfrey, isn't it awful? I didn't know what to do or say so did the *only* thing I could think of — that was to offer them a stiff drink. They have really behaved very well, considering — But it must be *ghastly* for them, to wonder what is happening to their own family. What *can* it be like in Poland now? a veritable Hell-on-Earth, I should think, and the food situation in Europe must be too terrible (that is, for the occupied countries).

1. Rosa lived at Black Potts but worked in a local munitions factory. She was the niece of the Austrian cook, Isabella (Bella) Zeyde.

16th September 1942   *Montreal*
Last night Potty came in to dinner — He may be going today — I sent messages by him — One thing I shall have to ask you, I wanted to fix him a present, but he said he had everything he needed — so I told him that I wanted you and him to have a grand "binge" in London and the cost will have to be paid by you. I will reimburse you when I forward your Christmas present. I hope that is all right. He will see you as soon as possible.

I had a request to take over the Committee for Fine Arts, for the camps near Richmond. What on earth do you suppose that is? It sounds absurd — The Army is having to teach the men to be tough, and to think solely of winning this war — and here come the sentimental females with projects of the opposite idea. There is no room for "Fine Arts" in this mad world at present — At any rate I shall investigate when I return — I want to make <u>bullets</u>, but I must have a definite job when I return — I haven't been fit up to now with all the accidents and operations etc., but am all right now — touch wood. Red Cross work is all right but not particularly satisfying to me.

20th September 1942   Black Potts
I am so sorry to think that you can use the car only a little — and hope you'll have enough to get to Gloucester now and then. Gerald will be able to use his motorcycle until Nov., after then I don't know how he'll get back — as *all* Green Line Buses are to be taken off this month and with no cars the trains will be impossible. I am getting very fond of my bicycle, and have

no desire to go anywhere anyway so the new travel regulations don't worry *me*, but it must be too dreadful for people that have to get about, and who try to get back to their homes occasionally –

Funny that you should get only 1 oz. of tea, and here we get 2 ozs – and we are not rationed for coffee! (but I expect we will be soon). Also, we are not rationed for fish (when you can get it) or vegetables or "condiments", or bread. I think Lord Woolton is *absolutely marvellous* the way he has managed food rationing in this country.[1]

1. Frederick James Marquis Woolton, 1883–1964, was from 1939 the first Baron and from 1956 the first Earl of Woolton. As minister of food 1940–43, he took charge of food organization. He was a member of the War Cabinet from 1943 to 1945.

10th October 1942   *Richmond*
Speaking of the Dickinsons – there is a whole chapter in Van Loon's new book called "Lives of Great People", about Emily Dickinson. There is a new novel called "Come Slowly Eden" (not Anthony!) by Laura Benet about Emily and Alfred Hampson is getting out a book about the family.[1] I think that both Florie and I appear in it. Anyhow, I will buy these books and keep the whole collection for you. I have about six already and there is a history of Amherst which features [our] great grandfather who founded the College.[2] It was because of that that my grandfather had to go out into the world to make a living and that is the reason we are Southern. His father gave away all he had to promote the establishment of that college – And that gentleman was also Emily's grandfather – I must bestir myself to get together some family history for Jennifer, who will never know it unless I do it –

No one knows what Wilkie means. Most people are furious with him, but it appears to be some kind of abracadabra because Roosevelt smiles and says nothing – I seem to hear Churchill gnashing his teeth, but as R. and C. are quite good friends. I can't imagine R. sending a live talking machine around the world without consultation. Well, no one knows anything.

1. Laura Benet, *Come Slowly Eden* (New York: Dodd, Meach and Dodd, 1942). Neither Van Loon's nor Hampson's books are cataloged in the Library of Congress.

2. Samuel Fowler Dickinson, 1775–1838, was a lawyer and a founder of Amherst College. For further information, see Richard B. Sewall, *The Life of Emily Dickinson* (London: Faber and Faber, 1976); and William S. Tyler, *A History of Amherst College during the Administrations of Its First Five Presidents: From 1821 to 1891* (New York: F. H. Hitchcock, 1895).

19th October 1942   Black Potts

Yes, the "antagonism and disunity" of all the peoples on this globe is a very depressing thing. But when you get it even in your own household (the terrible *prejudice* of one nation to another) it makes you realize that it could never be otherwise. Bella won't eat mutton because she never ate it before she came here! Gerald, of course, is completely insular. Then one day last year when Potty was here we were sitting on the lawn, and across the river we saw a man with a long grey beard, dressed completely in green except for a yellow silk skull-cap and pink gloves, and he was carrying a large mauve cushion. Potty said, "I think he's a fifth columnist from Mars" — We called Nannie to see if she saw what we saw (we thought for a moment that we had both gone crazy) and Nannie, quite unmoved, dismissed him by saying "I think he must be a foreigner".

I hope I haven't told you this little story before — but I laugh at it every time I think of it, because it's such a wonderful eye-opener on what any nation thinks of any other nation. There is a wonderful sequel to this story. Not long ago I saw the 'Green Man' again, in a busy main street. He was riding a bicycle and there was a very near-accident when one car tried to pass another, and I caught my breath waiting to hear the crash, which fortunately didn't come. The green man passed so close to me that I could hear him muttering to himself, "Americans, americans all over the road — all driving on the wrong side".

26th October 1942   Black Potts

Isn't the defence of Stalingrad glorious? One wonders how much longer the Russians can hold out. And now we have bombed Genoa and started an attack in Egypt — so the news sounds a bit better on the whole don't you think?[1] I am wondering if any of our pals are involved in this new attack in the Middle East. Gerald is of course furious that he is not with them.

1. This offensive marks the beginning of the Battles of El Alamein.

1st November 1942   *Richmond*
Williamsburg is a seething mass of humanity – sailors, soldiers, construction engineers, negroes and scholars – It all looks weird against that rebuilt 18th century background.

6th November 1942   Black Potts
The news is certainly thrilling. The paper says we have taken 9000 prisoners in Egypt and captured the leader of the Afrika Corps. I hope it will be a marvellous victory and will satisfy the arm-chair strategists who have been clamouring for a "second front".

Mrs. 'My Day' has been rushing about the country and seems to have squeezed an enormous amount of activities into a few days.[1] The reaction to her visit seems to be a good one, as far as I can make out from the papers. She is to speak in the 9 o'clock news on Sunday night. She paid a visit to Canterbury, and missed quite a big raid by 24 hrs. It was a pity in a way she wasn't there for the raid (this is in *my* opinion only) not of course that I wish her the slightest harm, but it would have made a vivid impression, that she could impart to Americans on her return.

Rosa received a telegram from an aunt in Switzerland yesterday saying "Sorry. Dets from parents. Kurt is with them." It doesn't make much sense, and the poor thing is of course frantic with worry. I keep telling them it must mean "no news from parents" – but if *from* and *of* have the same meaning (as de in french), I expect it must mean "death of parents". She has sent another telegram, asking them to write, but I expect it will be some time before they hear anything. It is too pathetic – I think I told you that she had heard a month or so ago that her mother and father and 13 yr. old brother had been sent to Poland. I am glad Rosa keeps busy. She works in a factory nr. here, also has short-hand lessons 2 or 3 nights a week, and goes to London for week-ends usually, and stays with a friend.

1. Eleanor Roosevelt's newspaper column "My Day" was widely syndicated and her left-wing views regarded skeptically by the Right.

8th November 1942   *Richmond*

On Tuesday, we ended our War Relief and Community Fund by "going over the top" to the tune of $62,000 extra. We raised about $930,000, which is good for a population of 160,000 white people. I didn't work for it, but Stuart is one of the Trustees, representing British War Relief, and I gave 4 times as much as I ever had – dividing 3 larger amounts between England, Russia and China – Half those amounts between Holland, Greece, Fighting French, War Prisoners and United Services –

9th November 1942   Black Potts

I am so thrilled over the news I can hardly contain myself – [1] Isn't it marvellous? We were so excited when we read the papers on Thursday morning – since then I have listened to every broadcast and read every paper from cover to cover. The number of prisoners we have taken seems almost incredible; I feel I am dreaming and will wake up and find it was all wishful thinking. I wouldn't believe it until I saw pictures of von Thoma etc.[2] I loved the story of the Italian General who, with quite a lot of men, surrendered to 2 English Officers. The officers said they were awfully sorry but they didn't have time to capture them – but if they would walk to a certain place, they could wait for the next train to Alexandria!

Of course I was thrilled when I read of the American troops in Algiers, Casablanca etc. When I was in Algiers (back in '27!) it seemed so *remote* from anything American, and it seems so extraordinary to think of the U.S. troops being there.[3] Hitler's speech was grand, too! when he talked about "that perfumed A. Eden" and "that jew Roosevelt" and that he didn't want to continue in Stalingrad as it was pity to sacrifice so many more *Russian* lives!?[4] It is all too marvellous, and I hope this is the 'turning of the corner'.

Sunday was a lovely day, crisp and sparkly. After feeding animals etc. we took Jennifer for a walk. We listened to Mrs. Roosevelt's speech after the news. I think she was speaking to *America* as she gave a long description of the black-out here (?) etc. etc. As a broadcast *to* the U.S. I think it was quite good – she has a nice voice, though it seems to lack personality and is a bit 'thin'. She has made a very favourable impression here as far as I can understand.

Rosemary [Jeffreys] and I talked far into the night – I think she is so thrilled to be away from the atmosphere of Burkham where one's knitting is put away at 10 and everyone rises to go to bed that she can't resist staying up. We had lots of laughs telling each other various stories. She is very funny about her family. Her mother (who was lady-in-waiting to Queen Victoria) was a daughter of Lord Strafford – old Lord S. first married a Dane (Rosemary's grandmother) and when she died he married Cora Colgate (of Colgate Toothpaste).[5] She was always known in the family as "Cora Countess" as she killed off old Lord S. and then married a man much younger than herself, but still called herself "Cora Countess".

Pothier rang up to-night – he is meeting me in London on the 19th to bring me the trunk (hooray!) and we are going to a theatre and dinner. I can hardly wait to see trunk as you can imagine.

1. This refers to the Operation Torch landings in North Africa following the Allied victory at the Battles of El Alamein.

2. Wilhelm von Thoma, 1891–1948, director of Germany's Mobile Forces from 1940 and commander of the seventeenth panzer division in 1941, was captured in North Africa in 1942 and remained a prisoner of war until just before his death.

3. Ginnie had visited North Africa on a trip with her Parisian school.

4. Anthony Eden, 1897–1977, was the first Earl of Avon. He was British foreign secretary from 1935 to 1938 and 1940 to 1945 and prime minister from 1955 to 1957 but resigned following the Suez crisis. He was noted for being good looking and a stylish dresser.

5. Rosemary Jeffreys's mother was the fourth Countess of Normanton née Amy Frederica Alice Byng, d. 1961. Jeffreys's grandfather was Henry Byng, the fourth Earl of Strafford, 1831–1900, equerry to Queen Victoria from 1874. He married first the Countess Henrietta Daneskiold Samsoe, and second Cora Colgate.

16th November 1942   Black Potts

The news is certainly thrilling these days isn't it? As we go to press the
allies have taken Bone and are pushing into Tunisia; the 8th Army has
captured or killed or wounded 75,000 men and the Germans have taken
over Unoccupied France – I wonder what else will have happened by the
time you receive this letter. I confess I am a little muddled over the French
Fleet, also Darlan – [1] I should think he was a bit of a "mugwump", but I
cannot make out who the F. Fleet are loyal to, perhaps no one? There is one
thing that is certain in this changing world, no matter *what* happens, one
can rely on Pétain to protest. It really is funny – every day the headlines
are different, but the sub-title is always "Pétain protests" –

Sunday morning the church bells rang to celebrate the Battle of Egypt.
It was lovely to hear them again. Jennifer was thrilled with them, Bella just
bored and Nannie started on a long preamble as her "dear father had been
a bell-ringer for 50 years" etc.

1. Admiral Jean Darlan, 1881–1942, was foreign minister and vice premier of the Vichy
government. Darlan switched his loyalty to the Allies but was assassinated on 24 December
1942.

20th November 1942   *Richmond*

*Since I started this letter another letter has come from you dated Oct. 26 – you
sent a clipping about "My Day" and the court circular announcement about
Mrs. R's first dinner party. There is a jingle going the rounds about her here
– "Eleanor, Eleanor where have you been? I've been to London to visit the
Queen – Eleanor, Eleanor, what did you there? I frightened a Messerschmitt
out of the air".*

*Yes, the news now is much better and the African successes have sent every-
one's spirits soaring. The Russians have been magnificent – In fact, everyone
has done very well – Mussolini is so pathetic now that you cannot hate him
– You can only have a contempt for him.*

23rd November 1942   Black Potts

I had a very nice letter from Florrie, please tell her I'll write soon – and 2 packages, one from *Rose* containing: E[lizabeth]. Arden powder, sponge for B.D., sugar and Lux, and another from you containing: banana flakes, egg powder, concentrated orange juice, sultanas and butter. A thousand thanks Boogie darling. We are going to give Jennifer the banana flakes to-morrow, but I intend to steal a spoonful or two when no one is looking.

I joined Lyell and Pothier at the Ecu de France for lunch (on Wed.) and afterwards we sent you a cable, did a little shopping etc.[1] Lyell showed me the photographs of his small daughter aged 3, she looks perfectly adorable – I had tea with them, went back to dress – and went with Pothier to see "The Importance of Being Earnest", which we both adored – It was *beautifully* done – some of the same cast as we saw in Aug '39 i.e. Edith Evans, Peggy Ashcroft and Gwen Frangçon-Davies – Jean Cadell took the part of Miss Prism this time, and the 2 men were John Gielgud and Cyril Ritchard.[2] C. Ritchard was incredibly funny, the first 'straight' part he has ever had as he is usually in revues etc., but he was wonderfully cast. I think this play was the high-light of my holiday. There is really nothing better than a witty play well acted and I got such a kick out of it. We then went to the Savoy to meet Lyell, and the 3 of us had dinner and danced and had a *marvellous* time –

1. Lyell Doucet, 1911–91, Pothier Doucet's brother.

2. Edith Evans, 1888–1976, an English actor, was made a Dame in 1946. Peggy Ashcroft, 1907–91, an English actor, was made a Dame in 1956. Gwen Ffrangçon-Davies, b. 1891, was an English actor. Jean Cadell, 1883–1967, was a Scottish actor. John Gielgud, 1904–2000, was knighted in 1953. Cyril Ritchard, 1898–1977, was an Australian-born actor and comedian.

29th November 1942   *Richmond*

Well this week has been so exciting in the war zones that all else fails to interest. The Russians thrusting back the Germans, the events in North Africa, and the fleet at Toulon blowing itself up, if one can believe the news. No <u>official</u> confirmation has ever come to us but I don't suppose there is any doubt *about it. There is a wonderful article in the N.Y. Times by Saint Exupéry of "Flight to Arras" exorting all Frenchmen of whatever creed, to forget their quarrels and come to the assistance, wherever they can, of the United Nations. De Gaulle is coming to see Roosevelt and I am a bit "leery" of what he has to say – Anyhow, Hitler won't get the fleet and we pray that France may redeem herself from now on –*

On Friday, I went to the dinner given by the Virginia Education Association in the John Marshall Hotel – I should never have thought of doing this if it hadn't been for Lord Halifax, and his speech –[1] It was rather dramatic listening to the British Ambassador telling about the news we had just received about the scuttling of the French fleet, as all of us have wondered since 1940 what would become of it. I enjoyed it and had various and conflicting emotions on the subject –

Today I am awaiting the broadcast by Winston Churchill after having gone to church and eaten my lunch –

H.R.D. [Huntly] has announced his intention to resign as Pres. of the B. of M.[2] I think he will be made Chairman of the Board – I am sure he hates to give up, but thinks he should.

1. Viscount Halifax, 1881–1959, the first Earl of Halifax from 1944, served as viceroy of India 1926–31, leader of the House of Lords 1935–38, a member of the War Cabinet 1939–40, and British ambassador to the United States 1940–46.

2. B. of M.: the Bank of Montreal.

30th November 1942   Black Potts

The news is *very* heartening isn't it. Wonderful to think the Germans are being attacked at Leningrad, at Moscow, in Libya and in Tunisia. Somehow I never thought Sfax and such places would come into the world news. Someone (I think it was O. Todd) said they were interested to read that Bougie had been occupied by the Americans without opposition! – and Gerald rang up too one evening to inform me of the storming of Bougie –[1]

The farm is going well. I want to eat a goose soon, but I can't face killing it and plucking it and cleaning it if I am going to eat it! so am trying to find someone who'll at least kill it for me. Miss T. [Tompkins] won't go near them and Bella is terrified of a mouse, so they aren't much help. I am very disappointed over the 6 pullets I bought last Spring. One has already died and to-day a sad thing happened. One of them laid an egg *but* it had such a struggle to lay it that most of its insides fell out as well. I think it is called a 'prolapse' in the poultry world. I couldn't bring myself to kill the wretched bird, so went off in search of help and luckily found Butler (a groundsman at Eton College) who very kindly came and wrung its neck for me. So we are going to have a chicken to eat! Whoopeee! The ducks and geese lay eggs for a couple of months in the spring only, so I am going to kill off most of them – and we are fattening up some drakes and a gander for Xmas and keep the ducks (female) and geese for laying in the Spring.

1. Sites for Allied landings in the North African campaign included the coastal town of Bougie in Algeria.

7th December 1942   Black Potts

The U.S. has been at war just a year, and certainly seems to have made great strides towards victory in that time. I hope the Tunis business will get finished off fairly soon. The Germans seem to be fighting hard, so I expect it'll be some time before that can happen. Wasn't it pathetic to think of the French Fleet scuttling their ships at Toulon? I confess I wish that Darlan the mystery man was still in France! Didn't you think Mussolini's speech was funny? I loved to make a mental picture of the "Englishman in evening clothes (!) sitting down to tea at 5 o'clock" who was really "a barbarian painted blue" if you undressed him.

Thank you very much for the Dorothy Thompson and Walter Lippman clippings. There seems to be a lot of intense feeling about the 'British Empire' in America just now. I suppose it was originally started by German agents, and it will be some time before it dies down. It strikes me that the greatest difference between the English and the Americans is that whereas the Englishman is a master of *understatement*, the American is the reverse, and this is where they always misunderstand each other and are irritated by each other.

Col. White told me a funny story; he has to censor the men's letters and the other day he couldn't help reading one rather carefully which said: "Say Jake – take my advice and get into the army right away and get yourself sent to England as fast as you can. You'd be surprised what you can get for two chocolate bars over here." The English Tommie hasn't a chance when the Doughboy turns up with chocolate and cigarettes – and perhaps even an orange!! – and of course lots more money. I cannot see why they had to send coloured troops over here, as the poor things must be so miserable, and so cold – and there's nowhere for them to go and worst of all no coloured girl-friends! However, I expect the Chiefs-of-Staff have their reasons, unknown to me –

There has been a lot of talk in the papers about the Beveridge report – by one Sir William Beveridge.[1] I confess I don't understand much about it – but *Nannie* is tremendously interested as Sir William is marrying Mrs. Mair next week, and Nannie was with the Mairs for about 12 yrs.[2] Mr. Mair "passed on" a few months ago, and Nannie has been anxiously watching the papers as "I always felt she would marry *Will* one day"! –

1. Sir William Beveridge, 1879–1963, was a British economist and civil servant. He was the author of the Beveridge Report, which formed the basis of Britain's welfare state.

2. Janet Mair née Philip.

14th December 1942   *Richmond*

All ski trains have been taken off from Montreal. Huntly "gave up" at the *wrong time! I shall suggest his going up to stay for a while – He was made* *Chairman of the Board of the Bank, so he will have a morning's work, anyhow.* *I am sorry for him, because he is so used to work that leisure means nothing* *to him – I am so used to leisure that I can't take work seriously! What a* *difference. I am on my 51st sweater, and I do some war work, but not enough. I* *am always in search for something which I can do, which is essential. I refused* *to give my time to watching the skies for enemy planes which certainly won't* *come as long as they are being kept too busy in Europe and the Pacific. I prefer* *to stick to Red Cross dressings. There are so many young women working on* *canteens etc. that it is absurd for me to compete with them. I shall stick to Red* *Cross. But I have another plan now – which I shall tell you about if it develops.*

31st December 1942   Black Potts
Gerald has now gone to his new job – he is extremely busy, but thrilled that
this job was offered him. He is commanding the Support Company of the
Guards Armoured Division. It is about twice the size in men and officers as
the ordinary company, so he won't have much time on his hands. He rang
up last night, and says he can't get back for a month or six weeks – so I may
go there and spend a week-end with him fairly soon, but a long journey in
an unheated train in the middle of January is certainly a labour of love –
(I may be maligning the railway, and long-distance trains *may* be heated,
I wouldn't know).

6th January 1943   Black Potts
I am sorry to hear that you are so short of coffee, and wonder if I ought
to send you some?? It seems so funny to think that we can get plenty here!
It's the ONE thing besides bread and potatoes, that *isn't* rationed! – reason
being of course that so few people in England drink coffee.

10th January 1943   *Richmond*
Thursday evening, we went to "Die Fledermaus" – The last time I heard it
you, Gerna, Billy Gilmour and I were in the old Opera House in Vienna! They
(Viennese) aren't allowed to play Strauss' old tunes any more – It makes me
sad to hear them, but the company was quite good and the settings modernistic.
It is almost too light.

The British War Relief has 40 sailors up from a "new" ship which has
just come in – forty more to arrive next week. They do very well by them
and people take them in their homes – and try to make them have a good
time, if possible. Usually the poor sailors want a good bed, good food and for
the rest, they wish to be let alone to a large extent. Stuart usually takes them
sightseeing, but I don't know if we shall be allowed to do that now, since the
new order went into effect last Thursday: No pleasure driving.

11th January 1943   Black Potts

Miss T. and I cleaned up the farm this morning, and divine pullets laid *8 eggs* yesterday and 7 the day before! I am pickling most of them, while they are laying so well – and then shall give away a few to various people who would appreciate them. The egg ration is now 1 a month each, so you can imagine how *much* they will be appreciated – and realize how *terribly* lucky we are to have such good laying hens. It is really *wonderful* to think of the food we do get in this fourth winter of the war, and my admiration for Lord Woolton knows no bounds – He has done, and is doing, a marvellous job.

The news is certainly more encouraging, but there's no use being too optimistic about it. The Americans are certainly doing wonderful things in the Pacific, but it looks as if it will be some time before the French mess is cleared up in North Africa. They bombed Kairouan [in Tunisia] a few days ago – I wonder if they hit any of those awful little men that eat glass and stick swords through their mouths – that upset me so much when I was there aged 17.[1]

1. An undated press cutting titled "Air Mails by Sea" enclosed with this letter reads as follows: "The Postmaster-General reminds the public that the difficulty in arranging for the conveyance by air across the Atlantic of air mails for Canada, the United States, and beyond is greatly increased during the winter months, and much of the correspondence has recently had to be forwarded by sea. Every effort will continue to be made to dispatch as much as possible of the correspondence by air, but no guarantee can be given that the prepayment of air mail postage on correspondence for the North Atlantic Air Service will result in acceleration compared with the transit time of correspondence prepaid at the ordinary rates of postage for transmission by sea."

17th January 1943   *Richmond*

Believe it or not we are sitting in this room with several windows open, and the thermometer outside stands at about 70° at 8.45 p.m. Inside, it is 77° – It has been warm for several days, but not as torrid as this. Sunday is so full of good radio programs, that it is difficult to do anything else – I always dislike going out on Sunday because of John Vander Cook at 3 p.m., Tomlinson on South

America, Shirer on Germany, "We, the People" etc. etc. but today we patron-
ized the Symphony from Washington at 3 – We can't use cars for pleasure, so it
is more convenient for those living in outlying districts to go to the Symphony
in the afternoon. Before lunch today Mrs. Victor Williams brought two British
sailors in here for a drink. The Misses Williams have been putting them up
for three days – must have been gay for the "jolly tars" – they all remained
to lunch in the Chesterfield and Mrs. Williams took them to the concert. I
liked the program very much – Beethoven's 7th Symphony, something from
Glinka's Ludmilla, Smetana's Moldau Suite and some waltzes from Richard
Strauss' Rosenkavalier –

Tuesday went to hear Horowitz play –[1] *He was as nervous as a witch, and*
I couldn't blame him, because in my life I have never heard such coughing –
a wave of it flew over the audience every time he came to a soft and delicate
passage – and a wave of pain across Vladimir's face!

1. Vladimir Horowitz, 1904–89, Russian-born American pianist.

31st January 1943   Black Potts

As soon as May left, I rushed and turned on the wireless to hear the 6 o'clock
news, only to discover that my clock was slow and I heard something about
Goering's speech in Berlin and a raid – so at 9 o'clock I settled down with
my coffee and cigarette to listen to it from the beginning and just as Big
Ben was striking Pothier rang up to say hello. I rather hinted to him that
9 p.m. was *not* the hour to say hello on the 10th Anniversary of the rise of
National Socialism in Germany! He knew nothing of aforementioned raid,
apparently. I spent the rest of the evening trying to get various stations,
and at least heard Lord Haw-Haw which was very funny – and finally at 12
o'clock heard the news that the R.A.F. had bombed Berlin at 11 a.m. (and
for an hour had "kept the Marshal from the Mike") – goody-goody – and
again at 4 the time for Goebbels to read Hitler's proclamation. One wonders
why Adolf himself failed to speak.[1]

1. Hitler became demoralized over Germany's capitulation at Stalingrad.

7th February 1943   Black Potts

Well, there have been big things happening in the world this week. Church-
ill and Roosevelt at Casablanca, Churchill's visit to Turkey and to Tripoli
(I have just been listening to a broadcast of his reception there by the 8th
Army) and the Russians advancing on Rostov; and the sacking of Ciano and
Grandi by Mussolini etc. etc.[1]

Rosa stayed home from the office as the river was rising steadily – I
sent Miss Tomkins home as she looked so jittery and was doing nothing
but getting in the way and irritating us all anyway. I had to bring in all the
chickens as she "doesn't like feathers". She borrowed my boots as hers leak,
and then got them wet inside – some land girl –

In the meantime Gerald rang up to say he was coming home for 48 hours
leave! What a time for the poor man to choose! He arrived cold and tired,
left his car at the local garage and had to wade in carrying his suitcase. I
was very glad to see him and felt a bit less cut off from the world.

The next morning there was 3 feet of water in the garage and drive –
and about 1 to 2 feet in the main road. The island of B. Potts was completely
submerged except for the house, the barn and 2 sheds by the house – and
about 1 or 2 feet of lawn in front of the house. Rosa of course couldn't go to
work and Miss Tomkins rang up to say it was much worse, and she couldn't
get here and gleefully went off to London.

Gerald however was not deterred as he had an important conference in
London at 11. He went off completely dressed as Guards officer with buttons
and leather shining – the only difference being he had no trousers! He
had a pr. of swimming shorts and carried a little suitcase containing towel,
trousers, shoes and socks and important military papers. I *wish* you could
have seen him striding off into the icy water, puffing at his pipe. There had
been a heavy frost, so I can assure you that the water wasn't warm!!

He lunched with Mum in London, and was home about 6 bringing the
milk and papers, which he had collected at Butler's. The next morning he
went off in tweeds and tweed cap, but still without trousers – and he looked
just like the goalkeeper in a French football game. Butler turned up with
the milk having borrowed some hip-boots.

About 4 that afternoon, Anne Anson turned up!! She just waded in! Her
thin little legs were shocking pink from the cold water. Some people might

even forget to ring you up to see how you were getting on – I just couldn't get over that Anne had *come* to see how we were. It was foolish of her, as the current was quite strong in places, also she might have caught cold, but she is certainly full of spirit.

1. Count Galeazzo Ciano di Cortellazzo, 1903–44, was Mussolini's son-in-law and Italy's foreign minister until 1943. He conspired to overthrow Mussolini and was sentenced to death at the Verona trials. Count Dino Grandi, 1895–1988, was minister of justice from 1939. He planned the resolution leading to Mussolini's downfall, was dismissed in 1943, fled to Brazil, and returned to Italy in 1973.

3rd March 1943   *Montreal*
We are beginning meat rationing in the U.S. this month – 1 3/4 lbs. a week – In April the ban on pleasure driving will be off with 2 gals. a week. That will give us about 125 miles a month – that means we can go to Gloucester once a month if we don't do anything else with the car –

28th March 1943   *Richmond*
Heard from Martha Bianchi last week. Her book about our family and Amherst isn't out yet, but she says she has played <u>me</u> up rather strong –[1] *Boogie may go thundering down to posterity, yet – I shall be terrified to read what she has written.*

1. This reference is probably to Bianchi's unpublished autobiographical memoir, now in private possession, a copy of which is held with the Bianchi papers at Brown University Library, Providence, Rhode Island.

11th April 1943   *Richmond*
Nellie Bryan asked me to change my morning work in Red Cross on Thursday to afternoon – There were four supervisors and two people at work, so I got down to making bandages again, and began a conversation with an old woman who told me the history of her life – She had lived in Indian Territory,

and her stories were blood curdling. You may remember that what is now Oklahoma was that same Indian Territory. No white people could buy land. You could lease it but you were surrounded literally by Redskins. The movie called Cimarron was the story of her early life.[1] At least, her early life was like Cimarron – I remember that it was shown here, and it is the name of a river, which I didn't know – Well the old girl turned out to be the most interesting person I have talked to for ages!

1. *Cimarron* (1931), directed by Wesley Ruggles, was set in Cimarron County, Oklahoma.

9th May 1943   *Richmond*

On Monday, I went as usual to hear the lecture at the Club. We had a gentleman from the deep South with an Alabamian drawl, and he was rather a lightweight, but every now and then it is nice to listen to an "honest to God" Southerner, because they are much freer of "issues" than the Yankees and the Westerners – God deliver us from the strange notions coming out of the middle West –

16th May 1943   Black Potts

The bells have been ringing to-day to celebrate the North African victory. Isn't it thrilling that the Huns have been driven out of Africa? and that now we have five times as many German prisoners as they have of ours? General von Arnim has arrived in England by plane –[1]

We have been celebrating at Black Potts too! On Monday three baby goslings hatched out under a broody hen, and have been given the names of Winston, Franklin and Joseph. George has had a bath for fleas, and the kitchen has been painted!

1. Generaloberst Hans-Jürgen von Arnim, 1889–1962, was commander in chief of the German Army between March and May 1943. He was held in British captivity in Tunis from 12 May 1943.

23rd May 1943   *Richmond*

Yesterday was Playmate's [Helen Adams] *birthday so I took her out to lunch*
– and last night I went down to the Misses Cookes' apartment to play bridge
– Nellie [Bryan] *was fourth – There wasn't much play, as Nellie talked <u>all</u>*
the time – Her sister Mrs. Grant had the Windsors to dinner when they were
in New York – [1] *Nellie said Berta had submitted her list to the Windsors and*
they had left out her best friend, Mrs. Dykeman – I would have seen "Wally"
in Hades before I should have submitted a list of my dinner guests to <u>her</u> –
I shouldn't have minded him so much but, after all, he is only the Governor
of Nassau now, and if he wasn't willing to meet my guests I shouldn't have
asked them (the W's). We don't do that sort of thing here, and I see no reason
for doing it for the W's – It would have been different had it been the King
and Queen – Anyhow that would have been attended to by officials. I think
Berta was an idiot – It makes me <u>furious</u> –

On Wednesday Huntly is getting his L.L.D. degree in company with Sir
William Beveridge <u>against</u> whose ideology he has written a pamphlet, which
has had rather wide-spread notice – He cannot bear the old boy – and writes
that he would <u>refuse</u> the honour were it not too late to do so – Nannie will be
interested in hearing that Sir W. and your uncle are receiving twin honours –

1. The Duke and Duchess of Windsor.

24th May 1943   Black Potts

The *war* news is wonderful isn't it? The North African campaign over, the
bombing of the dams in the Ruhr, bombing of Sicily etc. etc.

Jennifer helped me feed the animals – she *loves* "helping" me – the
incubator goslings are going on well – The 3 goslings which hatched out
under the broody hen are named Winston, Franklin and Joseph. We have
at least found names for our 2 tom-cats born in the barn – they are Hess
and Messe (the Italian Gen. who arrived with Von Arnim). We don't know
how Messe is pronounced – but are content with Hess and Mess. No one
ever hears anything of Rudolf Hess these days, I wonder how he's enjoying
the war?[1]

1. Hess was held in British hospitals until the Nuremberg trials.

30th May 1943   *Richmond*

We aren't allowed to use any gas now, save for very necessary things — Food is difficult, although everyone has enough — The main thing is the trouble connected with it, and servants are scarce also — The Chesterfield is inundated *with outside people. It isn't much like "home" — But we are lucky, and have no complaints. There has been a famine of potatoes — and* hominy *has taken the place of the "spud"! However, we have new potatoes now, and people regard them as a great delicacy.*

Tuesday Red Cross as usual. Stuart had to go to a fire and gas drill. He came into the room where we were playing cards with his gas mask on — Everyone roared. Gas masks are not seen very often here — so they are the subject of laughter — They do *make people look like pigs, of course — But* you *know what they look like!!*

Wednesday Huntly got his L.L.D. degree from McGill along with "Will" Beveridge. The photograph of it is very grim. I wrote him yesterday and addressed the letter to Dr. *Drummond — Lady B[everidge]., Nannie's old time acquaintance was present at the ceremony — She has a pleasant, but surprised, look. Wednesday afternoon, two meetings about the Officers Club.*

You will notice that we now have a number — #20. It is supposed that using a district number like an arrondissement will expedite the distribution of letters.

All the rooftops of buildings belonging to the Extension Depts. of William & Mary College are filled at this moment with bathing beauties taking the sun — Stuart said just now, "That's what they call higher education" — They now own seven *of the houses around here, and they seem to spend their time in bathing suits.*

6th June 1943   *Richmond*

You will notice that there is a #20 after Richmond. That is our district. We are divided now into districts. I gather it is a national movement — as I had to write 5, to the agency Bank of Montreal, New York —

On Friday I went to a really Victorian lunch in the Commonwealth, cer-
tainly pre-war — Drinks, turtle soup, boiled salmon, breast of chicken with
asparagus — an ice and a large orange cake! with candles — Masses of roses
on the table and at each plate! Sweets to match the orange effect — It was for
Mattie Dickinson's birthday and was given by her sister, who still wears tea-
gowns and high heeled shoes, and gasps for breath in a "straight jacket" which
pushes her anatomy into something looking like a concealed water melon — [1]
She said it was her last public appearance for "the duration" — She couldn't
get a taxi and no one can use their cars for pleasure driving.

We are all furious about John L. Lewis but holding our breath lest those
idiots in Washington won't pass the required anti-strike legislation — [2] *Roo-*
sevelt and Lewis are having a war all on their own — We are all wondering
who is going to win out. The general public and the Press are much inflamed
on the subject —

I have just bought Trevelyan's "Social History of England". [3] *I am now at*
the Caxton period, having finished the age of Chaucer. It is not light reading
but very interesting.

It is gratifying that the French seem to have made a sort of truce. No one
here seems to understand — I think de Gaulle must be difficile — My "af-
fection" centers upon Giraud somehow — [4] *Let us hope the General staff is*
right in predicting the downfall of Germany for sometime in 1944 — It is now
almost 4 years since I saw you — I had a very strong premonition when I said
goodbye at the Emp. Australia that night, but I wouldn't admit it. Something
kept saying inside me "At least five years". I was wooden. Well, darling, I've
"done" four years — and I am making no more predictions, just so you are
safe, and as contented as one can be under the circumstances —

1. Mattie Dickinson is probably not a relation. Martha Dickinson Bianchi was sometimes referred to as Mattie, but she neither had a sister nor lived in Virginia.

2. John L. Lewis, 1880–1969, was president of the Union of Mine Workers of America
1920–26. He called a nationwide coal strike that resulted in increased union membership
and higher wages for members.

3. G. M. Trevelyan, *Social History of England* (New York: Longmans Green, 1942).

4. General Henri-Honoré Giraud, 1879–1949, was the French officer in command of

the Seventh French Army who was captured by the Germans but escaped in 1942. He was difficult to work with, and his position as commander in chief of local French forces was abolished in 1944.

13th June 1943   *Richmond*

I have just been reading an article about character reading from hand writing. There were examples of Hitler's, Mussolini's and Stalin's — Mine looks more like Stalin's!

Yesterday I went to the movie of Mission to Moscow — very magnificently photographed —[1] *Some of the historic characters were quite good, some ridiculous. Molotov and their Ambassador to the U.S. quite good — Stalin looked like a "Kentucky Colonel" after too many mint juleps in a kind and mellow mood — The President Kalinin was more like the picture of an ancient Chinese philosopher who had long since given up the world and wasn't on any speaking terms with the Devil, than like a modern Russian — But on the whole, it was entertaining. Walter Huston took Davies' part — obvious propaganda. The way Americans are able to learn to love the Kalmuk overnight and to see only virtue in the Chinese is amazing. Well — I shall do nothing to try to break anyone's dreams as long as they are allied to us —*

    1. *Mission to Moscow* (1943), directed by Michael Curtiz.

19th June 43   *Miniborya Farm*
                                            Chesterfield County
                                                          Virginia

The pictures of Jennifer taken at the party came last week. To me she looks quite pretty, although you say she isn't — She has a personality, and looks as if she was "master of her fate". Both Stuart and I think these last ones are much the best looking. Do you think she looks a bit like May [Drummond]? *She is that big blond type and I compared her picture with a baby one of May, and it looked very much like her — As May was a very handsome woman and considered a great beauty in Montreal when she was at her best, that isn't* *so bad — There is no trace of <u>Dickinson</u> I am glad to say because, whatever they may be, they are <u>not</u> beautiful. I had one beautiful cousin, who was so conscious of her looks that she made an ass of herself — and that is worse than no looks —*

The world which we must live in after this awful war will, of necessity, be a very different one from even the one you came into — There will be new ideals, and new opportunities. Many places will be opened up and exploited, I think, and a great shifting of populations — My idea is that Germans must be made to work on rehabilitating the wreckage they have made — and that the Anglo Saxons be given the chance to re-industrialize the world. I hope the Russians may be kept busy re-building their own fatherland — All this must come if we win, and, now, it looks very much as if we shall — However, we must wait for events on the Continent. It is strange that the Germans aren't developing their Russian offensive so far. Is it because they are afraid of the Anglo-American one? One can't tell anything, because they are so busy trying to fool each other. Straws show in the wind which blows — The dismissal of Von Papen in Turkey, <u>if</u> it is true, must mean that he has been a failure there recently, and that Turkey <u>may</u> assist us —[1] *<u>Why</u> is the border closed? All that is fascinating, and the things concealed are more interesting than those in the open —*

It is <u>very</u> hot — I am sitting on the porch writing. In true Southern style the house is closed <u>tight</u>. There are bowls of magnolias, which are in bloom now. The huge tree beside the house is a mass of large white blossoms. That is my idea of the South in summer — closed green shutters and bowls of magnolias — We eat in the outside dining room, and I notice that the table is set for a buffet luncheon — Evidently the whole Scott P. [Parrish] Jr. family is expected for lunch —

1. Franz von Papen, 1879–1969, was a diplomat and politician instrumental in Hitler's election as chancellor in 1932. As ambassador to Austria from 1934 to 1939, von Papen helped to plan the Anschluss. He was appointed German ambassador to Turkey in 1939 and remained there until August 1944, when Turkey broke off diplomatic relations with Germany, so the report to which Bougie refers was presumably untrue.

21st June 1943   Black Potts

I was much impressed to read that Huntly has been given the degree of Doctor of Law by McGill University – just as I was writing to congratulate him, I saw in the paper that Bologna University, Italy had given a D. of L. degree to von Ribbentrop.[1] I have been trying to compose a little poem to the effect that some universities make intelligent choices, and some don't etc., but after using a lot of paper (for salvage), I have come to the conclusion that my muse has deserted me, and I had better not waste any more paper!

One thing cheered us – just at dusk when we were going to bed, we heard the drone of bombers and went out to have a look – I counted over 50 with my naked eye. It gave one quite a thrill to think they were off to give a lot of trouble to the Hun! They certainly seem to be pounding the Hell out of Germany now. It is wonderful to see *our* planes going off – the last time I had seen so many planes, they were German ones coming *in*! It is wonderful to think how things have changed since then. I used to try and identify the various planes, and thought I was quite good at it. One lazy summer afternoon back at the P.C. I was lying on my back on the lawn, looking through field-glasses and had Gerald's little models in a pile beside me. I thought I was getting quite proficient, and was sure I knew what they were – just as about 100 bombers zoomed overhead and I was patting myself on the back, I suddenly saw puffs of smoke etc. and DID I RUN? A brilliant bit of plane-spotting!

1. Joachim von Ribbentrop, 1893–1946, the German ambassador to Britain 1936–38 and foreign minister 1938–45, was hanged as a war criminal following the Nuremberg trials.

11th July 1943   *Richmond*

Two days ago the all out offensive against the Axis in Sicily began – It makes me regret never having seen Taormina before the cities are destroyed, which no doubt will happen, unless the enemy gives only slight resistance.[1] Well, the sea and the sky and hills will be there anyhow.

I have been working at the Ration board helping to get out the new ration books. I went twice last week, and the first time sat beside a <u>blind</u> girl who

*was folding the books. The second time, I sat opposite a <u>one</u>-armed woman,
who did the whole thing with that one hand. She told me they wanted to take
her picture because (she said) of her infirmity! I said, "No, you are mistaken,
because of your spirit" – I have been trying to find something for Florie to
do which is useful, so I asked her to fold the ration books. She told me yesterday that she <u>had</u> gone, but that it exhausted her! Fendley's wife goes to Red
Cross on Thursdays, and she said she would place a bet that Florie wouldn't
do it!*

1. Allied landings in Sicily began on 19 July 1943. Taomina is a picturesque resort northeast of Mount Etna, on the east coast of Sicily, and did not fall into Allied hands until early
August.

18th July 1943   *Richmond*
*In your last letter you were expecting Gerald, and Bella was going for her hol-
iday with the bride and groom! That was a minor tragedy, and the thought of
you cooking for two weeks sent me into a frenzied sympathy, because cooking
is as foreign and unknown to me as the Sanscrit texts in the Upanishads, more
so really because I have read some translations of those.*

    *Tuesday Red Cross and work on ration books. I folded 1000 an hour for the
first hour, and went a little more slowly after that, as streams of water were
running from my anatomy and my efficiency was impaired by it. I have been
taking some tablets which Stuart says the Foundry men take for restoring
certain body salts, due to over perspiring. Anyhow I had enough strength left
to play bridge with Lewis Warren, and a Mrs. Thompson, whose husband is
a Colonel (West Point, regular Army) –*

    *Yesterday there was a grand parade – gasless, the best Richmond has ever
had. It was very amusing and spontaneous. The bullocks driven by the Governor went a bit prima donna in front of the Commonwealth and got up on
the pavement, causing consternation among a group of pickaninnies – I en-
close newspaper account. I kept thinking of how Jennifer would have loved the
ponies and the goats etc. It was really absurd to see the old family "buggies"
and one brougham, and one French provincial cart with enormous wheels, etc.
I had no idea there could be so many of those in existence and so many horses.*

In the good old days my father had trotting horses, which aren't as spec-
tacular as some of the other varieties! but the "sulky" yesterday gave me a
feeling of being back in the days of a wonderful black one we had from the
"blue grass" Kentucky breeding grounds. It was called "Dusky Queen" or
something equally obvious but I loved the silky coat and the slender ankles,
and the defiant eyes of that animal. No one since Papa has ever cared anything
about horses in my life at least, and so gradually all "horse sense" has been
drained from my environment – I will say the odour from all the animals
on that steaming hot day was rather strong, to say the least. But neither is the
smell of petrol very nice –

29th July 1943   Black Potts

Since last writing to you Benito has fallen from grace in Italy – wasn't
it wonderful news? It is amusing to read the various reports from all the
countries regarding where they think he has fled – Germany: Mussolini is
in Spain; Spain: Muss. in Switzerland; U.S.: Muss. has committed suicide.
I wonder where he really is? Well, the news is pretty encouraging, thank
Goodness –

My darling 'old boy' left Saturday morning. Of course I don't know when
he actually sailed, or from where – or where he went to – but anyway he
left B. Potts on Sat. morning.[1] It is perhaps unnecessary to say that I felt
steeped in gloom. We had such a lovely time on his leave, and he had been
in his very best form. He certainly was in radiant health when he left –
and had been most amusing. I was so glad that he had seen so many of his
friends, and think that he was very pleased that many of them had taken
the trouble to come and see him. I will send you a cable when I know his
address, so that you can perhaps write to him. I expect Daddy will know
the best means of writing from the U.S. Here the best thing is to send an
air letter-card which costs sixpence.

It has taken me some time to get used to the idea of his going away
– now I have you two thousands of miles away in the U.S. and Gerald, I
suppose, somewhere in the Mediterranean, so thank Goodness I have *Jen-*
nifer! I spent the week-end after he left wandering around in a daze mostly,
but wrote a long letter to you and several others – Anne came in to dine

with me on the Sunday evening, the best person in the world to cheer one up.

1. Gerald left for Tripoli, from where his regiment sailed to Salerno to take part in the Italian campaign. He was commanding No. 2 Company of the Sixth Battalion of the 201st Brigade of Grenadier Guards. For details of Gerald's involvement, see Nigel Nicolson, *The Grenadier Guards in the War of 1939–1945*, vol. 2, *The Mediterranean Campaigns* (Aldershot: Gale and Polden, 1949), 361, 370.

28th August 1943   *Ivry*

Huntly's staff, which now consists only of François, Nellie [Clark] *and Sarah Higgins, the Irish maid, is very efficient.*[1] *The house looks better than it ever did, and Sarah is a perfect whiz. Nellie does the housekeeping, and he tells me that his bills are 60% of what they were before – The food in Canada is very good. There seems to be no shortage, although they are rationed. The situation in Richmond is very bad, as we have about 20,000 extra people descending on us from nearby camps every weekend, and the hungry sailors and soldiers eat up everything. I am perfectly willing to have them get it, but I do appreciate the good food now that I can have it – and am enjoying it to the full! I understand why people talk about food now – I get enough to make me quite fat, but it is highly unsatisfactory. I know that you have the same experience. I am very glad that you can sometimes have one of your own good animals, and some fresh eggs –*

I hear that Mr. Churchill caught a trout 20 inches long yesterday! He did better than I did! No one knows just where he went, but I am glad he is having a few days holiday. I thought he looked very tired in his last pictures. He is going to broadcast Tuesday. The reception which Roosevelt got in Ottawa was quite thrilling and Mackenzie King made the best speech of his career – He is a very dull person usually when droning on in his monotonous way –

Darling, I think of you every hour in the day – I long so to see you that I dare not give way to my feelings on paper – It is better, also, that I have never seen Jennifer, or I should have an added desire which might be too much for me – You have been so wonderful about telling me all the details, that I can visualize all of you, almost as if I were there. It isn't the same thing, but it is

*as satisfactory as it could be under the circumstances, and I am very grateful
to you –*

1. François was Huntly's chauffeur, and Nellie Clark his cook.

8th September 1943   Black Potts

I have just heard the wonderful news that Italy has surrendered. We were
all helping in making a new run for the chickens when Rosa came home
with a rumour about Italy, so long before the 9 o'clock news, we were sitting
tensely around the wireless to be sure of hearing it. (I am now hoping that
Gerald has gone to Italy – in his last letter he said he would write from
Rome.) I have had two letters from him lately, in the first he had been
suffering from sunstroke, but must be all-right again, as the letter rec'd to-
day didn't mention it. It was written on Aug. 31st – pretty quick work! The
heat sounds too ghastly for words and I am praying they will have gone to
a cooler clime and more civilized part of the world – I am wondering if
you are still in Canada, and how long you are staying – and hope you have
all had a good time at Ivry.

13th September 1943   Black Potts

I am glad you got away from that awful heat in Richmond, it must have
been too terrible. What a pity you couldn't have sent us some of it. I can't
bear to think that the summer is practically over – We have had a plague of
flies and mosquitoes, I am bitten from head to foot – When I close the shutters at black-out time, I hear a tremendous drone going on overhead and
think it's the night bombers until I realize it's mosquitoes. I feel I mustn't
complain as it's only about 1/50 as much as our soldiers are enduring in
the Mediterranean. The insects out there must be too awful, and like you
with the heat in Richmond, I don't like to complain about my bites, but
just scratch quietly to myself! I see an expert says the plague of insects here
may be due to all the "static water tanks" placed all over the country in
readiness for incendiaries.

I had a form to fill out from the Labour Exchange – what each person in the house was doing etc. etc. so decided to go and have a talk with them, and see if they thought I was doing the right thing, and if they preferred me to release the land girl. I couldn't seem to find anyone to talk to, and felt rather like Charlie Chaplin in that film where he wants to go to prison, and can't find anyone to arrest him![1]

To tell you the truth, I was hoping to have a baby, and am *very* much disappointed that it is *definitely* off! I thought it an excellent opportunity with Gerald away, and having this nice house for the duration etc. etc. I simply cannot think of any reasons *against* the idea, except that possibly you wouldn't have been pleased – I have saved all the clothes, equipment etc. so didn't have to worry about that – even had a Doctor on tap – in fact everything was in order – except the baby! so cannot help feeling somewhat *flat* as I was so hoping to have one – O well, perhaps it's just as well that I didn't, you never know –

1. Probably *Modern Times* (1936), directed by Charlie Chaplin, in which Chaplin's character, having spent an enjoyable time in prison, is reluctant to be released and anxious to be rearrested.

28th September 1943   Black Potts

On Thursday morning the blow fell. I had had no idea that Gerald's battalion was in the thick of the fighting in Italy until I received his air-letter-card written on Sept. 13th. I gather they have had a pretty ghastly time, but Gerald's letter was wonderfully cheery in spite of it all. Since then one casualty has followed another, and I feel it is *weeks* since I saw that letter. The second in command in G's company, John Hermon, has been killed; also Ian Brown (who has been here several times) and Michael Ridpath (whose brother Tom was killed in Tunis). Francis Wigram has also been killed (the most attractive and far the nicest of the 3 children, and I gather the favourite child). I feel terribly sorry for Lady Wigram, I hear she is being simply wonderful. I had a very sweet letter from her in answer to mine; she said that in his last letter he was "sorry he hadn't gone to G. Potter's Company" and had been sent to another when he got out of hospital.

In Gerald's letter he tells me not to worry but I find it difficult to follow instructions! He has "been buried once, but apart from a few squeaks am intact". Bill [Anson] said in his letter to Anne that Gerald was being absolutely marvellous, and he had seen him "standing in three feet of water firing a Bren gun from his hip". Can't you just see him? It cheered me up a *little* to hear Bill's news of Gerald and I feel very proud of him.

5th October 1943   Black Potts

I had a letter from Gerald to-day dated Sept. 17th – He sounds as if he were still in good heart and good health, thank Heaven – He says "I smell like Hell, but my figure is too, too divine, my dear". He had just "shot a pig which the boys are going to eat for dinner to-night" – he also says "I am not allowed to say what we are doing, but we have been pretty busy for the last few days". A wonderful understatement! – I think I told you that he had been "buried once, but emerged completely black, and quite intact".

12th October 1943   *Richmond*

Tuesday October 5th I worked in Red Cross, and lunched with Marie Boushall in the Commonwealth. Kept an engagement later, with Helen [Adams], and went to a movie – "The Constant Nymph" with Charles Boyer in the lead – quite good I thought, but Joan Fontaine as the nymph ran about so much that you <u>knew</u> she would die of heart disease before the end of the play.[1]

Thursday Red Cross again and at 6.30 to have drinks with Mrs. Thornton Lewis and her daughter Alice Botts. Their nice old Georgian house near the White Sulphur has been taken for headquarters for a War Prisoners Camp. Mrs. Lewis says the Italians were delightful and very happy to be there and that they walked about quite freely, and smiled, and gave cheery greetings as you passed. Unfortunately they have been taken away and the Germans have come, and they are grim, and cross looking, and very defiant.

I am going to finish this homely narrative in my next letter, because I must dress to go to an early dinner in the Commonwealth – The occasion is the beginning of the Annual Campaign for the Community Fund and Allied War

Relief drive. I am a solicitor on the special gifts committee – I loathe doing it and am no good at asking for money – or anything else –

P.S. The meeting tonight was a great success. Will tell you about it all as I progress towards my goal. We are going to raise between $900,000 and a million dollars in Richmond – Our Governor made a strong speech for Anglo-American friendship, which got wild applause – This was in connection with the British War Relief item – He told me afterward that the travelling Senators' report was a bit of abracadabra.

1. *The Constant Nymph* (1943), directed by Edmund Goulding.

21st October 1943   Black Potts

No more news of Gerald since his letter of Sept. 28th but I gather they are now 'resting' for which I am truly thankful. Pothier seems to be tearing through Italy and having a wonderful time.[1] I had a letter yesterday written on Sept. 30th –

Someone asked me to-day how long it had been since I saw you and I told them "exactly four years, one month, and 28 days" and I miss her more every day – I hope this dreary separation will end sometime in the near future – Thank Goodness I am not intuitive, and did not realize how long it was going to be – you say you *felt* "five years" at the time you left. I hope that was correct, in that case there is only 10 more months to go!!

1. Pothier Doucet was taking part in the Italian campaign as second in command of the Perth Regiment.

24th October 1943   *Richmond*

Tuesday Red Cross as usual and the beginning of the drive for funds for the Community Fund and War Relief. They had about 3000 people for dinner – the food was bad enough to give me indigestion for several days. I am working in two units – the "Special Gifts" – and the Chesterfield. It is an "eye-opener" – to see what people give, and what their idea of giving is. So many say "I can't

give because I am <u>buying</u> war bonds". Then I say, "Saving is the opposite of
giving" – They seem utterly surprised, never thought of it. We are having
a hard time – as we must collect an amount just short of a million dollars –
which is a great deal of money in so small a place, but if those who can afford
it would do their part, the money would be easy to get. The rich ones are the
stingey [sic] ones, and they have no <u>vision</u>. I gave three times as much to the
other nations as I gave to my own community, which is my idea of the state
of the world. I think I am almost unique in that point of view. Frankly I don't
understand other people's mental processes – we <u>must</u> get the money –

1st November 1943   *Richmond*
By the way, speaking of talent – You certainly have a flair for writing, and it
will be well if you examine it. It isn't literary, but it is <u>clear</u> and <u>simple</u>, and
gives a perfect picture. That is a <u>gift</u>. Everyone remarks on it – It is direct, and
good writing, so <u>do</u> take it seriously. Don't try poetry – I think it is definitely
prose style – You may laugh at me, but I mean it. The story of your island in
this war would be a good story –[1]

1. The island referred to is Black Potts, rather than Britain as a whole.

5th November 1943   Black Potts
I am so sorry I didn't agree with you about "Watch on the Rhine" and
wonder if I am losing my grip when I don't have the same taste as you.[1] Do
you remember the time I chose Xmas cards in New York and you chose the
same card for me in Richmond? and Huntly's remark that it would have
been a coincidence if we had chosen different cards? I must say I didn't
enjoy Watch on the Rhine much – thought the direction, sequence and
tempo poor – I never think films of plays are very good – I can see that
it would have been a good play – all the horror of Nazism brought to one
American drawing-room, but it loses the whole point in a film.

1. *Watch on the Rhine* (1943), directed by Herman Shumlin.

7th November 1943   *Richmond*

I worked in Red Cross Monday, Tuesday and Wednesday on filing "working hours", a most tedious business and absurd. Monday at six I had to go to the "Victory dinner" of the War & Community Fund. We went over the top $56,000, collecting $1,050.000 which was excellent for a place in which there are only 190,000 white people in what is known as the Metropolitan area – The band of the John Marshall High School blared forth as every team reported gains, and an enormous bell was rung. It was quite exciting at first but by the time they had read out dozens of reports I was a bit weary. I was seated at the Special Gifts table and we were the last to report. "We" raised $550,000 of the total, in fact 55% – I wish you could have seen me marching about the Grays Armoury, preceded by the band, with a large red feather decorating my ample bosom –

19th November 1943   Black Potts

Soon after I wrote to you, I had a letter from the Regimental Adjutant telling me of Gerald's exploits and how well he had done – I was of course thrilled to hear this. They intend sending out a 'narrative' about it ("they" being the Regimental orderly room) when all the details are collected, and I am anxiously awaiting further details. In his letter to me, the Reg. Adjutant quoted a letter from the Commanding Officer of G's battalion which said "Gerald Potter in particular distinguished himself in this attack by arriving 3/4 of an hour before he was expected to do so, and catching the Boche with literally his trousers down".[1] I am of course thrilled that my old boy has done so well, and am very proud of him – I rang Mum to tell her the news – she was delighted too –

When I had a temperature of 102° and was feeling at my lowest, the blow fell and I learned the sad news that Gerald is now in hospital in Italy suffering from rheumatic fever! I expect you can imagine how upset I was at hearing the news – the one thing that I have dreaded the most, as Gerald is so incredibly strong otherwise and I wasn't at all worried about his getting ill out there – except that he might get that damnable rheumatic fever – Anne Anson rang me up Tues. evening (not knowing that I had flu) to tell me that she had had a letter from Bill from Hospital saying that Gerald had just arrived — She thought I would be so pleased that he was out of it for the time being — which of course I was — and then she said, "Don't worry, he isn't wounded — he's just got rheumatism".

I had a day's reprieve as rec'd messages from both A. Mobs and Mum the next day that they had heard from Gerald (in a letter written Nov. 5th) saying that he had lumbago and had left the Company for a few days. However yesterday I had a letter from him written on Nov. 10th saying he had rheumatic fever. He is frantic, poor darling, that he'll lose his place in the Battalion, and miserable at being parted from his men and his pals. My one hope is that he says his temperature has gone down and that the pain isn't spreading — so I *pray* that it may be only a relapse and not the real thing. If I hear any better news about him, I'll send you a cable — His address is:

> Major Gerald Potter
> Grenadier Guards
> c/o 92 General Hospital
> C.M.F.

1. Gerald distinguished himself by leading his company to the top of Monte Maggiore, to the northwest of Naples, taking the German defenders by surprise and capturing the territory.

26th November 1943   Black Potts

I had a letter from Gerald this morning written on Nov. 17th saying he was feeling quite all-right and hoped to be leaving hospital soon. Wonderful news for me, as I think by the time he returns to the B[attalio]n. they will be having a well-earned respite. They have had a *terrible* time, and Gerald is of course terribly depressed at the casualties — there is practically nothing left of his company of which he was so proud. The officers have all been killed or badly wounded, and there are only *20* men left. Isn't it terrible? and I can imagine how dreadfully he feels about it, poor darling — I am sure he wishes he had been there, but thank God he wasn't!!!

28th November 1943   *Richmond*

Gerald mentioned our Officers Club and said he would like to partake of a "tenderloin" in it. I don't like to disillusion him, but tenderloins are now in the class with the Dodo, and all the Club serves is sandwiches, champagne and beer – also soft drinks. There is no kitchen, there <u>are</u> no cooks – and there isn't even a connection for an electric stove. Withal, it fills a need here, is very gay and attractive. I am now about to become permanent House Chairman – I hate being in responsible positions, and my idea of bliss is the idea in Anatole France's "La Chemise" – my favourite story in all the world – I suppose I might have been a pompous, large chested Club Pres. People have the mistaken idea that I am an executive – All I want to do is lie down in the grass under a kind blue sky! But now one <u>must</u> do something useful.

I'm sorry to say that many Americans do chew <u>gum</u>! and I suppose chewing the thing may be a comfort in war time. I have a vision of an enormous Army of Americans advancing on Germany, chewing gum, and maybe using it as a sort of secondary ammunition – It <u>would</u> be funny – Berta Trigg says the Germans retreated in the last war when they saw the sweaters the Americans were wearing, knitted by their women folk! For Heaven's sake don't let Jennifer become a <u>chewer</u> of gum, although I have always been told it was good for the teeth!

5th December 1943   *Richmond*

Everyone over here began to get excited about a "terrible epidemic" called "<u>cat</u> fever" – People sort of looked you in the eye with a jaundiced expression and said, "I think I have cat fever", or "Isn't this cat fever awful?" – The bubble burst yesterday when the "medicos" announced that cat fever is "short" for <u>catarrhal fever</u>, which is what the medicos call the <u>common cold</u>! Really Americans are absurd. Speaking of absurd Americans, I have just written to Lord Vansittart. I finished his book about the Germans – "Lessons of My Life" –[1] Word for word, chapter by chapter, it is <u>exactly</u> my idea about Germany – and I was so overjoyed that he had said it, that I wrote to him. I didn't have his address, but sent it to his American publishers with a proper

stamp for England and asked them to forward it. How I should have loved it
if I could have been the author of that book –

On Monday to the Club lecture – someone named Wolfe, just back from
England, one of the best we have had, but not optimistic about an early end
to hostilities. Delia lunched with me – and afterwards she bought a book for
me called "Under Cover", and I bought Vansittart's book at the same time. I
am now going to begin reading "Under Cover" – about the isolationists and
5th columnists. England seems to be a bit peeved about the release of Oswald
Mosley [2] *– But, on the other hand, our papers are so sensational, that I don't*
trust their news always –

1. Robert Gilbert Vansittart, *Lessons of My Life* (New York: A. A. Knopf, 1943).

2. Sir Oswald Mosley, 1896–1980, was founder of the British Union of Fascists and a member of Parliament from 1918 to 1931. He was interned until November 1943, when he was released because he was no longer considered to be a threat. He resumed activity with the BUF in 1948.

17th December 1943   Black Potts

I had a letter from Gerald on Tuesday written on Nov. 30th saying he is much better, and hopes to rejoin the Battalion by Jan. 1st – they are 'resting' and re-forming at the moment. I think they have had a pretty ghastly time – I think I told you that soon after Gerald went to hospital, his beloved company was practically wiped out, and every officer killed but 2, and they were seriously wounded – I can imagine how Gerald feels about it, but for myself I think he had rheumatic fever at the right moment! I hope he recovers completely, because I cannot imagine the poor old boy being sent home because he's not well enough or young enough. There was a rumour rushing round Windsor (quite unfounded) that he was on his way home. I just cannot imagine what would happen if he *was* sent home. He would be like a lion in a cage. He is as strong as a horse, and has an incredible consti-tution – and wrote that he never felt fitter in his life – but unfortunately he would always have a tendency to get rheumatic fever again, I should think – and I can imagine how it maddens him. He is gnashing his teeth at his inactivity, but says whenever he gets low, he thinks of his 2nd in Command, who is in the same hospital – he has lost one leg poor wretched chap, and they think he will have to lose the other as well – [1]

The last news I had from Pothier he was still in hospital with jaundice. On his right there is Lord Tweedsmuir and on his left an American Col. named Lehman, and they are known as the "three jaundiced Colonels" – I had hoped that Potty would be coming back here for Christmas, as originally intended, but when he recovers he is being given a job out there – he's going to be G.1. (Ops) to the 1st Cdn. Corps and his address is simply:

> H.Q.
> 1st Cdn. Corps
> C.M.F.[2]

1. Captain Ralph Howard, d. 1958.

2. Pothier received a general operations staff appointment. G.1 was concerned with personnel and disciplinary matters.

25th December 1943   *Richmond*

It has been a sad week for me because I had a telegram on Wednesday that Martha Bianchi had died of "flu" in a hospital in New York – Like Nana, her heart gave out. Alfred Hampson just sent me a message saying "Martha has left us" – I sent him one, asking for details and he replied that they had a service for her in the Church of St. Mary the Virgin in New York – very High Church – I didn't realize that Martha was so very "high" – and they interred her in the family plot in Amherst that afternoon Dec. 23rd – There is no one left now in Amherst. I don't know what Alfred will do about her affairs – nor how she has disposed of all of Emily [Dickinson]'s things, and the manuscripts. As Emily is a national figure of a certain importance I wonder what may happen – Perhaps Amherst College will take over – Her grandfather founded the college (my great grandfather) so it would be logical for Amherst to get the collection, but I don't think that Martha wanted that – I have written to Alfred. I pray that she didn't include me as one of the Trustees of the Emily Collection as she once said she wished to do. I don't want the responsibility, so I am rather nervous about it until I know certainly that she did not. I am very sorry for Alfred. I was surprised at her age – 77 – She seemed much younger and had not a gray hair. That is more than can be said of me.

So Eisenhower is to be in supreme command of the invasion. That is very tactful of the English. I hope he may prove adequate –

28th December 1943   Black Potts

Jennifer, Nannie, Reid [Dunn] and I had our Xmas dinner together and ate Randolph's turkey with all the trimmings, and had a Christmas pudding with "brandy butter" (made out of whiskey and my week's butter ration).[1] We staggered from the table, and wished that all the children in Europe could be having a dinner like that. We drank a toast to "absent friends", then at three we listened to the King's Speech, and to the National Anthems of all the Allies, including Ethiopia – Having given the animals their Xmas meal, we went for a walk, and played with Jennifer until her bed-time – then had some very good cocktails and a *very* small supper.

The best thing of all was receiving a letter from Gerald written on Dec. 9th, saying that he was much better! He seems to think he'll rejoin the B[attalio]n. by Jan. 1st, but I think he's being very optimistic – I don't like to think of him being in hospital, nor do I want him to be in the fighting, so *hope* he's convalescing at some charming resort!

1. Reid Dunn was Ginnie's contemporary from Richmond.

11th January 1944   *Richmond*

I am anxious to find out what is going to become of Martha Bianchi's effects. I pray she didn't name me as a trustee of Emily [Dickinson]*'s things, manu-scripts, portraits, furniture and the like, as she threatened to do. I have heard nothing since the funeral. I think Alfred Hampson is swamped with arrange-ments etc.*

16th January 1944   *Richmond*

You seldom see nice big wood fires now, and I really love them. Dorothy says they shut their drawing room off most of the time, and try to keep the rest of the house warm, because there are serious shortages of coal and oil — Southerners are so cold all the time, they mind that more than anything I think. We get plenty of food, but a good many things are lacking. Fish and oysters are expensive because of labour shortage, and the meat is poor and scarce — very little beef and lamb — There is pork. In fact, the market is now glutted with it because the farmers find food for the livestock so expensive they kill the hogs — It is all very complicated and difficult, and I am sure we don't do it as well as Lord Woolton has for you. However, I can only eat a certain amount of pork, so having the market glutted does me no good. I eat too much, though, in spite of all this!

I had a letter from Alfred Hampson last week saying he wanted my help and advice about Martha's plans. I am very sorry about Martha because, somehow, she appealed to me more as a relative than most of my other kinsfolk. All of Emily's original manuscripts and all of Martha's possessions are involved, but I don't want to be drawn into anything, because I fear what is needed is someone to put up some money to establish a shrine for Emily. I don't see how I can do that now, with almost everything "frozen" and the future uncertain. I spend a lot of time trying to keep what there is for the succeeding generations!

Carrie Washington tells me she has been invited to become Mrs. James Gregory of Chesterfield. As Nana's relatives were named Gregory and lived in Chesterfield, I fear that some bar-sinister in the period après la guerre will make me some connection of Carrie's husband. Well, I have had relations very inferior in charm to Carrie! I hope she won't be foolish enough to take on a second husband. . . . Everything is becoming so mixed up socially that I have no idea where or what or who anyone is any more —

17th January 1944   Black Potts

No letter from you since I last wrote, and as I have spent a rather domestic week, I haven't much news to tell you from the 'Black-Potts front' — but this morning I received a letter from Gerald written on January 7th — and in the letter there was very thrilling news indeed! i.e. Gerald has been awarded the Military Cross! I am terribly thrilled and excited about it as you can imagine and very proud of him. Isn't it wonderful — I sent off a cable to you this afternoon, as I knew how pleased you would be to hear it, and trust you will pass the news on to Huntly, as I know he will be very pleased, too.

6th February 1944   *Richmond*
Friday I had a letter from Potty and yesterday (Saturday) one from Gerald, dated Jan. 21st — that is very good — just about two weeks — He was answering one from me, written Dec. 20th. In it he said, "You will probably be as surprised as I was to hear that H.M. the King has been good enough to bestow on me the Military Cross. What for, I am not quite clear" — There spoke the true Briton —

7th February 1944   Black Potts
I was very distressed to hear about Martha Bianchi, and how depressing for you to receive the news just before Christmas. Poor old Alfred will be lost without her — I wonder what will be done with Emily Dickinson's things —

11th February 1944   *Richmond*
I had a letter yesterday from Lord Vansittart! After I read his book, I wrote to him, and told him I regarded his philosophy and ideas about the Germans as more nearly mine than I could possible hope for — He sent his answer by air mail, and wrote quite a long letter, and seemed highly pleased to have my praise. It may ease your mind to know that I did not mention having any relatives in England — I am taking the letter for Huntly to read —

I am re-reading Tolstoy's War and Peace — After descriptions of Borodino and the like, I decided that men are incurable and that the only thing for women to do is to strike as in Lysistrata to refuse to have children certainly. But, now, they seem to be having more than ever — At least about every other young woman I see appears to be going headlong into motherhood —

14th February 1944   *Montreal*

*We had a very comfortable journey up, but as we had to do last year, once
more, we were forced to change in N.Y. because the Montrealer was so late
getting to N.Y. that it couldn't go as far as Washington – It wasn't bad, though
– the train was late, and we felt hungry so we went into the dining car – There
was a black Harlem negro sitting at one table – I had to wait, and I made a bet
with myself that I, the only Southerner, would be placed opposite the negro. I
<u>was</u>. I took it like a man – and gazed out of the window. He turned out to be
an actor with a troupe from California going to – of all places – St. Sauveur
as entertainers.[1] How have the pure Laurentians fallen – giving way to cheap
tap dancers and bogus senoritas – One girl with a chenille mantilla gave the
impression of being au Mexique but I heard her tell the immigration officer
she was born in Chicago! I am sure she is the true love of a <u>gunman</u>.*

1. St. Sauveur-des-Monts, a resort northwest of Montreal in the Laurentian Mountains.

20th February 1944   *Ivry*

Huntly had a dinner [Thursday] *evening before the Russian ballet – 12 guests
including the three Drummond women and their husbands – the Kosatkines
and Mme. Frankowska – a Polish lady – quite attractive. We <u>dashed</u> off after
a good dinner, which included turkey etc. and Veuve Cliquot and liqueurs,
to the St. Denis Theatre. Huntly had a box, and directly opposite us Their
Exs. the Gov. General and Princess Alice sitting in the Abe Broughmans' box
– If you have never heard of Abe, he is a rich Jew, who has become very
prominent lately. The proceeds from the Ballet went to Russian Relief, and
the Soviet Ambassador was present also – The British and Soviet flag decorated the proscenium – at the end, the orchestra played O Canada, God save
the King, <u>and</u> the new Russian hymn, which supplants the Internationale.
Mme. Frankowska had to stand up for the Russian anthem and told me afterwards that <u>nothing</u> would surprise her again, after having done that, as she
cannot stand Russia, especially the U.S.S.R. breed. I said "Maybe you might
be surprised if you had to stand for the Horst Wessel" – "Not even that", said
she, "after tonight" – There were several Russian uniforms which excited
Kosatkine no end –*

28th February 1944   Black Potts

That evening we all had pancakes for dinner as it was Shrove Tuesday and
someone gave me a LEMON!! The first one I have seen for about four years.
They gave it to me for the pancakes, but I divided it into five slices, and
everyone decided what they would do with theirs! Nannie put hers on her
pancake, Jennifer had a *small* glass of lemonade, I had mine in my tea Wed.
afternoon and so did Bella and Rosa.

2nd March 1944   *Montreal*

*I am forwarding two very American books – I bought them for you and now
I have read them. I am not overenthusiastic, but it is something to read at
any rate. Alexander Woollcott stories aren't as good as the ones in "Which
Rome Burns" and "So Little Time" is a best seller, but a bit too American in
a certain sense to please my artistic taste.*[1] *It is very New Englandy – But
the satires are good – the one of the foreign correspondent, Walter Newcombe,
particularly good – Maybe it will amuse you –*

1. This book is possibly Alexander Woollcott, ed., *As You Were: A Portable Library of
American Prose and Poetry Assembled for Members of the Armed Forces and the Merchant
Marine* (New York: Viking Press, 1943). It is unclear what the second book is.

16th March 1944   Black Potts

After lunch I started on the trek to St. Mary's Hospital at Roehampton and
after changing from bus to bus and having my ticket punched and punched,
I arrived about 4 to see Ralph Howard, who was 2nd in command to Gerald.
He is a charming person with a grand sense of humour – and certainly full
of guts, and I was delighted to meet him at last and congratulated him on
receiving the D.S.O. He had had an operation the day before, so I felt I
shouldn't stay very long but planned to see him again in another week or
so. He's going down to Devon for a few weeks shortly, and when he comes
back, hopes to get his new legs – I have asked him to come for a week-end
here as soon as he's well enough. He commanded G's company when they
were cut off from the rest of the B[attalio]n. in that awful battle (this was

after G. had gone to hospital) and directed from a stretcher. I suppose it was a long time before he rec'd aid, consequently he lost both legs, poor man. It's a crazy world when some men are so gloriously brave, and others rifle the remaining belongings of men that have been killed fighting for them.

20th March 1944   Black Potts

Great news of Gerald! I had a letter written on March 10th saying the B[attalio]n. was resting. I am so thrilled that at last they are having a much-needed and well-deserved rest. He tells me that they are in very comfortable billets, with electricity and even water, and a bar. I have yet to hear *how* he got his M.C. but I think it must have something to do with a little party which took place some months ago, and which was written up in the regimental newsletter – "the capture of a mountain was allotted to the ———, and G's Company carried out the assault straight up the steepest face – A dead silence followed the barrage, while distant commanders strained their eyes through their glasses – at last figures were seen moving far off on the top, and uncertainty as to their identity was dispelled by the notes of No – (G's) Company call carrying clean across the valley on a *German* bugle – the surprise was complete – The enemy some of them only partially dressed, making off as best they could." Quite a lot of prisoners, guns, etc. were captured – It can't matter my telling you this *now*, as it all happened a long time ago, but thought you would appreciate the dramatic effect of the German bugle – Can't you see the old boy standing at the top?

3rd April 1944   Black Potts

On Thurs. to the B.R. [British Restaurant] as usual. Friday I went up to see Mum, as I hadn't seen her for ages – She's looking very well and in pretty good form, in spite of busy days and noisy nights. We lunched at the little hotel near her late flat – the road was blocked on account of the egg that fell the night Gerna was dining with John and the d'Ivrys – and their kitchen ceiling fell in – and small wonder as it was very near – One house was completely demolished, and miraculously the occupants all escaped – As I passed by I saw that the walls on either side of the house were still standing, the middle was a mass of rubble, but on the third and fourth floors up, some dresses were still hanging on pegs against the wall – It was an extraordinary sight!

1st May 1944   Black Potts

On Saturday I had a message that Gerald was on his way home, also a letter that Pothier was arriving at any minute. All very exciting and I tried not to talk of my thrilling news to Patsy [Evelyn][1] – Also had a letter from the Land Army that they were taking away Miss Tomkins for work of more national importance. My head was in a whirl – That afternoon Pothier rang up!! having just arrived by plane from Casablanca – so I asked him to come to B. Potts the next day – and again sat up late talking to Patsy when I would so much rather have sat down and written a long letter to you, telling you all the exciting news –

I then went to the Restaurant and to the W.V.S. office to tender my resignation as with Gerald on leave and then full time on the land, I don't see how I can work at the Restaurant for some time to come – I then met Pothier for lunch. . . . I was so interested to hear all about Pot's adventures and experiences. He had to go back to duty the next morning – 2 days' leave since last June seems a bit hard! and he was furious to have to go back so soon – He is now G1 (liaison) to the 1st Canadian Army – and is stationed at Cdn. H.Q. not far from where he was last year –

I arrived at Black Potts at 3.25 and at 3.30 GERALD arrived. It was marvellous to see him again, and I was so relieved to find him looking so well, and in such good form. He is thinner, very sunburned and his hair is grey – which gives him quite a distingué appearance – Unfortunately his teeth have gone on the blink owing to rheumatic fever, trench mouth, to say nothing of the appalling conditions in which he has been living – they are all loose and wobbly, and several of them have got to come out. He brought some gin, and rum, some soap, some scrubbing soap, and some washing-up powder! also a wooden cigarette case, and some lovely handkerchiefs with my monogram embroidered on them, a doll for Jennifer, and sweets for Nannie, Bella, Rosa and la Tomkins. O yes, and a lot of lemons packed in a German mine-case! – When the Bn. arrived, they were met at the station by a band, and inspected by "the Colonel" – and I was sorry I had missed this! but would probably have been pretty emotionné to have seen it – [2] We had a very good dinner, and wandered about trying to get unpacked – Fiander looks very well, and was beaming at the thought of seeing his wife and new baby –

1. Patsy Evelyn's husband, Major Peter Evelyn, had been missing, presumed dead, since 1943.

2. Princess Elizabeth, who became Queen Elizabeth II from 1952.

12th May 1944   Black Potts

Miss Tomkins left for good, for work of "more national importance" on Friday, so now I am a land girl. I don't quite know how I shall cope with 2 acres of vegetables and 35 animals, besides the housework, shopping and various other things, but so far I haven't done much about it as, with Gerald on leave, parties etc., the garden will just have to go until his leave is over! –

Tuesday poor old Gerald had to have two teeth out, but seemed quite unperturbed and we drove over to Aylesbury to have lunch with Aunt Mobs, who was of course thrilled to see him again, and gave us a marvellous lunch – Afterwards we saw Mrs. Lee (who is living in the other half of the house) – her daughter Betty Hare (alias Philadelphia Lee, alias Gabrielle d'Esteve the actress) was there.[1] I had never met her before, and was so glad to meet the famous Betty at last. She is terribly attractive and was very funny about the "stately home" [Hartwell] which is now full of Americans. Betty goes over now and then to entertain them, as she works for some American Red Cross Entertainment thing – The Commanding Officer of the "stately home" comes from North Carolina, and the other day he said to her, "From my bedroom in your late house, I have a lovely view of the yard". Betty said, "My God, *les pelouses* with a *lake* in the distance is now called a *yard*" – [2] She likes the Americans there enormously, and I should imagine it is mutual.

Yesterday Gerald went to London for a meeting of the R.Y.S. [Royal Yacht Squadron] at Claridge's – he said he was the only member there who didn't have to be carried in and propped up by several people – and Sir Philip Hunloke was made the new Commodore –[3] Then he had lunch with Ralph Howard, and they ended up by G. pushing Ralph's chair around to Rosa Lewis who is just about half dead and quite ga-ga now, but gave them some champagne (!) I had a busy day while G. was away – trying to dig, also getting off a few letters –

1. Betty Hare, b. 1900, English actress and singer.

2. *Les pelouses:* the lawns. According to Peter Ackroyd, " 'garden' – otherwise 'garth', 'yerd' or 'yard' – itself springs from a root word suggesting enclosure and protection." See Ackroyd, *Albion: The Origins of the English Imagination* (London: Chatto and Windus, 2002), 411.

3. Major Sir Philip Hunloke, b. 1868, sailing master to George V during the 1930s and commodore of the Royal Yacht Squadron 1943–47.

24th May 1944   Black Potts

Many thanks for your April 16th letter #8 which arrived last week, and for #9 (April 23rd) which I received yesterday – Thank you also very, very much for the two books you sent me, very sweet of you and I shall look forward to reading them when I get the chance! Gerald had an air mail letter from you yesterday posted in Montreal on March 11th – It went to Italy and was sent on to him here. It is torn, burnt, stained (frottée, usée, dechirée) and stamped across the front in red ink is written "Salvaged from an air crash" – I feel it should be kept, and shall put it in my 'book'.

Ralph Howard came to stay with us [for the weekend] – We put up a bed in the study for him, but it was all a little tricky as there is no bathroom downstairs. He has a man to look after him until he gets his new legs, and Wilbraham carried him upstairs for his bath. It couldn't have been easy as Gerald tells me Ralph was 6 feet 2 – I think I told you that Ralph got the D.S.O. in Italy when he commanded the company that got cut off, and that he lay on a stretcher in the *snow* on top of a mountain for several days and nights before help reached him, and that he was wounded in the arm on the 1st day of the attack – It is amazing that he is still alive. Gerald tells me he was *superb* and cannot see why he didn't get the V.C. We went off to a cocktail party at Betty Lee's, and Ralph insisted upon coming too – had dinner here, and put the old boy to bed early –

Pothier came over on Friday for the day. He had spent the day before with Mackenzie King and had quite an interesting time.

2nd June 1944   Black Potts

I spent Friday morning standing in a queue for the new ration cards – Gerald went off about 6.30 and Jennifer and I waved large white handkerchiefs as he and Fiander went by in the train. He will only be away for about a month, then I gather he is being sent back to Windsor to train young officers for a bit. He is surprisingly enough quite philosophical about it, as he realizes he is not yet fit enough to live in a slit trench, but needless to say he has *applied* to be sent somewhere *active* when the 2nd Front begins, but I don't think anyone will pay any attention to his application!

6th June 1944 *D. DAY*   Black Potts

Well here it is – D-Day!! all very exciting but rather agonizing – My stomach keeps turning over and over at the mere thought of it – Gerald thank goodness is safely in Scotland at the moment, so I don't have to worry about him – I am not so sure about Pothier's movements as naturally he could not tell me anything, but find it difficult not to worry –

We were back [from London] at 5, and consumed a large tea, since when I have done nothing much but listen to the wireless and rush out now and then to watch the planes going over – They went over in droves last night flying quite low. I fell asleep with the roar still going on, and when I woke up this morning, it seemed to be still going on. I had a feeling *something* terrific must be happening –

11th June 1944   *Richmond*

On Monday we went to a party at the Morgans where I ate Lobster Newberg and cheese besides various other things, and became a casualty by 10 a.m. Tuesday morning on the fateful June 6th – In other words I had something

which gave a fair imitation of ptomaine poison – Stuart was ill also, but no one else that we know of succumbed. It was just like me to be ill on D-Day – if not exactly "H. Hour" – At 5 a.m. Tuesday June 6th I was awakened by the frantic ringing of the chimes of St. James' Church – One of the hymns was "For those in peril on the Sea". I had been too sleepy to recognize the others – I knew instantly, of course, what it meant – Somewhere a dog was howling – I didn't want to wake up and so I said a very sleepy prayer for the success of our troops, and tried to go back to sleep. However the extras began to come out and there were quite a few radios going full tilt, so sleep was impossible – I didn't want to <u>think</u>, because I try hard not to get nervous about what is going on – Stuart slept through it all, and didn't know anything until 8.30 – Well, it has started very well – and let us pray that it goes on as it has begun!

I have described Tuesday but I wasn't so ill that I couldn't listen to the radio, and I heard De Gaulle and the King, also Roosevelt's prayer which I thought a bit messy, not nearly so good as the King's. R. always uses too many words to express what he means to say – that is an American failing, and annoys me, although I think the fault is <u>mine</u> as well as his. That doesn't make it any better for me –

14th June 1944   *Miniborya Farm*

I am just beginning to realize how vague I have been about facts all my life, but there is <u>one</u> fact I am not vague about and that is I want to see you again – I have been thinking of how on earth I could accomplish that – It is going to be difficult to get passage from East to West after the War, with all the soldiers and various kinds of people surging from side to side of the Atlantic, and I am wondering if you couldn't make application for transport to Canada! not for now, of course, but for later – perhaps by Air – You know that I am not what Americans call "Air-minded" (an atrocious vulgarism), but I shall be terrified of floating mines and contraptions of every kind lurking about in the Ocean, as left-overs from the beastly Hun – My imagination has always been overdone. I should be willing to fly over to see you if I could secure passage –

I imagine, though, that I won't be very popular as a visitor, after the hordes of doughboys have swamped "the Island" – The latest joke over here is about that. Four reasons why the English don't like American soldiers – They are – "overpaid, over-decorated, over sexed, and over there" – However I like the one about the "big three" better – Stalin asked Roosevelt if he had territorial ambitions after the War – "No" said R. – Then to Churchill – "Have you?" "Yes" was the answer – Stalin: "What do you want?" "London", said Churchill – I suppose that is a stale joke, and it may have originated in England – Je ne sais pas! – but it is witty.

Monday we had a very creditable parade to start our 5th War Loan. I must subscribe. I now have over $20,000 in bonds – Canadian and American, and I am having a hard time keeping my savings above the water line, but I am not spending much for useless things and living in the most obnoxious middle class way – Maybe even middle class is a bit of bragging – However I lack none of the fundamentals and I should be ashamed now, to have any of the luxuries – so I am able to do the few essentials –

Two wild looking notes from Alfred Hampson – I can't make him out – or what may be the fate of all the manuscripts of Emily [Dickinson]*, nor the family portraits, china furniture, etc. – He tells me nothing –*

24th June 1944   Black Potts

Fifteen minutes after I had finished the letter to you, the warning went – I went to bed and was surprised not to hear the all-clear until 9.30 the next morning. Warnings and all-clears went on all through the morning, but it was not until I took Jennifer to dancing class that afternoon that I heard of the new weapon, the pilotless plane, or "doodlebug" – [1]

You will I expect have read of the doodlebugs by now. They seemed very unpleasant at first, and horribly uncanny, but I don't suppose any worse than the ordinary plane – It's difficult to write owing to the censorship, as I am always terrified of saying anything I shouldn't, but at least I *can* say that there is absolutely no reason for you to worry about us –

1. "Doodlebug" was the British nickname for the V-1 pilotless bombs aimed at southern England from June 1944 until January 1945. Around ten thousand were launched, of which a third landed in London.

25th June 1944   *Richmond*
Mr. James Gregory (Carrie Washington's fiancé) sat in the audience [at Carrie's concert], *smiling in a very approving way at the chorus with Carrie so
prominently placed –* "Mr. Gregory" *is very nice looking with a lofty look,
which savages so often have. In fact, I thought he was quite distinguished looking. He and Carrie are pure negro, which I like so much more than the very
disconcerting mulatto type – I always find myself wondering whose ancestors have strayed from the straight and narrow way – One girl was almost
as white as I am with long pale hands – I can't take that! It implies too much
– There is so much pathos in the implications that it disturbs me – and too
much reproach –*

1st July 1944   Black Potts
I wrote to you last Saturday evening – on Sunday morning Pothier came to
stay for a 24 hrs. leave – He is a little tired of this hanging about, as there is
nothing for them to do until they move – and when that will be they don't
know, so they get away whenever they can – After an enormous Sunday
lunch we looked at the papers, and then settled down to do a bit of work –
We raked the lawn, chopped wood, brought in coke etc. and stopped about
7.30 for a hot bath, a lovely drink of Pimm's, dinner – and the news, and
heard of the Fall of Cherbourg. How wonderful that the Americans have
captured it – Everyone seems to be very optimistic about the Invasion and
things seem to be going pretty well, in spite of the terrible handicap of the
weather which has been *appalling*. It has been blowing hard ever since D-
Day (or so it seems) and how they ever managed to get the supplies over
there, I can't imagine – We hear planes droning night and day –
   I spoke to Gerna last night. She sounded very cheerful, but as a "con-
noisseur" of raids, having lived in London for four years, says she minds
the latest type more than the good old-fashioned kind.

23rd July 1944   *Richmond*
*I was rather unhappy at the mere thought of a cast in the hot weather, knowing
from experience how uncomfortable it can be! Everyone was very sweet to me,*

and I received gifts of all kinds, including fruit, sweets, books, magazines etc!
Helen Reed sent me "Anna and the King of Siam" which I had wanted, and
when I wrote to thank her (who had herself had a broken hip last winter) I
said, "The only virtue I can see to be got out of my accident is that I listened
to the Democratic National Convention for the first time in my life and now
I know that I can take any punishment and so it is a relief to realize I can go
on having these accidents without any injury to my morale" — [1] *Really, you*
never heard such a display of "bunk" and sentimental nonsense in your life.
Old hardened politicians fresh from orgies of graft practically wept over their
candidates — They had no trouble nominating Roosevelt but they really were
"in labour" over the Vice-President — The South staged a revolt — as they
have become anti-Roosevelt and very anti-Wallace — [2] *However, they won't*
vote for Dewey so it amounts to nothing at the moment. [3] *They finally rejected*
Wallace and got Senator Truman. [4] *I don't know much about him, but they say*
he is very good at Foreign Relations. They were afraid of the idealist Wallace
because so many people seem to think that Roosevelt is very tired and may
not last out another 4 years.

As for me, my mind is made up — For me, the war and the arrangements
for Peace are the most important of the issues — Roosevelt knows the most
about those things, has the widest vision and the most experience, so I shall
vote for him. I don't trust the Republicans not to sabotage the Peace, as they
did after the last war — and all my energies must be used in doing my bit for
world co-operation.

1. Bougie had sprained her hand and chipped an ankle bone in a fall.

2. Henry A. Wallace, 1888–1965, an agricultural economist from Iowa, was appointed secretary of agriculture in 1933 and was to be the Progressive Party presidential candidate in the 1948 election.

3. Thomas E. Dewey, 1902–71, was the Republican presidential candidate in the 1944 and 1948 elections.

4. Harry S. Truman, 1884–1972, a U.S. senator from Missouri 1935–45, became president upon FDR's death in 1945 and served until 1953.

12th August 1944   Black Potts

Isn't it wonderful that *some* of the towns in Brittany have been spared. I
was so relieved that Mont St. Michel didn't have to be blown up – now that
the Americans are nearing our beloved Chartres, I am holding my breath!
The Americans are doing marvellously, aren't they, and it is incredible how
far they have advanced in the last few weeks – Everyone seems to be very
optimistic about the war. I hope "they" have a right to be so cheerful about
it. But I hate to think of all the young men that are still to be sacrificed
before it's over – and personally I can't see how it can end before the spring
– Also I am not terribly keen to hear about these rocket bombs![1] You probably heard Churchill announce that 800,000 houses in London have been
damaged by Doodlebugs – Gerald is *very* optimistic about the war, and he
usually seems to be right in his guesses – so let's hope he is this time too.

[Saturday] evening I dined with Audrey and John Vernon-Wentworth
and met a young man in the Reg. who insisted on escorting me home – I
offered him a drink, and he stayed until 1 a.m.! He was very funny telling
me about his experiences in N. Africa. At one time, after leaving hospital
there, he had a liaison job with the Americans and wore American uniform – liked them enormously except for one or two occasions. Once when
a young American said "What are we going to do with the God-damned
British after the war? How are we going to *use* them?" They didn't know
he was english until he opened his mouth!

1. The first v-2, or rocket, bomb landed in Britain on 8 September 1944 in Chiswick, in
southwest London.

13th August 1944   *Richmond*

*All the mothers are upset about an epidemic of infantile paralysis, mostly in
North Carolina, but so many children went off to camps in the N.C. mountains, and are quarantined until it passes. However, life goes on very quietly –
and at least we don't have bombs and black-outs. There is nothing to complain
of except the awful anxiety –*

*If this war in Europe ends this year – I am wondering if you can't come
to America. I doubt if I should be allowed to go there for some time – Would*

*you fly? I think I might get up the courage to do it after the war – Planes
are so different now – Gerna was so disgusted with me for refusing to fly to
Buda Pest from Vienna, and said I kept you in cotton wool. Well, you haven't
been in cotton wool lately. Personally, I should like to have you in it now, but
you might not wish to be in it, as one doesn't "grow up" – But why grow up
if you can avoid it? Unfortunately, one can't avoid it forever, because Life is
violent – I can't get over how violent it is – All the country we knew so well
– Angers, Vitré, Caen etc. must be in ruins – How awful – I just try not to
think of London – But we have had Armageddon – and looked it in the face,
and are defeating the enemy evidently, so the worst may be over – I pray God
it is – but I made no predictions, nor boasts, nor do I think too far ahead – I
just long to see you at the earliest possible moment – that is all –*

21st August 1944   Black Potts

Wasn't it thrilling to hear of the landing on the Riviera. I get on the floor
and gaze at my atlas when I listen to the 9 o'clock news, and am so thrilled
that most of Normandy and Brittany have been liberated. Wasn't it wonderful that Chartres Cathedral wasn't damaged?

24th August 1944   Montreal

*The news is so exciting now that I can scarcely contain myself, but I shall not
be happy ever until I know the Pas de Calais area is freed, and those bombs
stop falling over England. My always vivid imagination runs riot, and you
know I am very good at having an awful apprehension about you. If I knew
that you were safe at Black Potts, my enthusiasm over the liberation of Paris
and large sections of France might run riot, but under the circumstances, I sit
like a graven image and send both formal and informal messages spinning in
the direction of le Bon Dieu – Yesterday hearing the Marseillaise gave me
quite a thrill, but I didn't hear or see any demonstrations.*

*The U.S. Government has built a large air base near the Mingan River
[in Eastern Quebec] and there is great excitement about that. Of course the
Canadian Government will take it over – It is in a direct line to Goose Bay
Labrador, which is the short taking off place for the other side. All this has*

been a secret until now, but it isn't any longer, so maybe the censor won't mind. It may *make the Mingan property more valuable − Huntly has let the U.S. officers fish it this year −*

Today the papers say there is fierce fighting in Paris. It appears that the Germans made an Armistice and broke it. Honourable creatures, the Huns!

I had a letter from Gerald this week, describing Hawick which he said was "pronounced as in expectoration" − He said you were noble to go up there. I think so too − I do hope he may be sent to another place − but not into the fighting until he is fit −

4th September 1944   Black Potts

in the 6th year of World War II

So much has happened in the world since I last wrote to you that I am breathless! Isn't the news wonderful? France nearly liberated, and to-day the news that Brussels has been liberated. It is simply *thrilling* − It is marvellous to think the war with Germany *may* be over in a few months. I get quite weak at the thought there is a possibility of seeing you before another year has passed − perhaps as soon as next spring??

Bill A. [Anson] has just rung up and tells me it was announced over the wireless half an hour ago, that we have entered Holland. Hooray! Hooray! I shall 'close down' and listen to the midnight news − and will write again in a few days −

6th September 1944   Ivry

Early Tuesday morning about 12.45 I was lying in bed struggling to get to sleep − and had almost lost consciousness when suddenly I heard a low rumbling sound, the house gave out a cracking noise, and then the whole room began to tremble. I knew there was an earthquake. It didn't take me long to leap from the bed and put on my slippers. By that time the trembling had ceased, and I listened for the others to make a sign − Stuart, in the room next to mine, gave several groans and turned over heavily in bed − He didn't realize what the matter was − Huntly slept peacefully through it all − Only François and

I realized what was taking place – In Cornwall, Ontario a million dollars of damage was done, and women fainted, according to the paper – The quake was felt as far South as Delaware, and as far West as Wisconsin – It was very spooky. I looked out of my window and the fog was so thick I couldn't see the lake, and the awful rumbling was eerie – In the midst of it the 4 loons began their weird calls to each other – My imagination began to work and I saw myself rushing from the house only to fall in to a yawning abyss in back of the house – There were two more quakes, but not felt here – one at 4 a.m. and another about 7 – I fell to sleep finally between 2.30 and 3 – Well, I suppose doodlebugs are worse, but there is something a bit awe-inspiring about an earth quake –

19th September 1944   Black Potts

Sunday night there was a relaxation of the black out. Owing to the arrangements here, it only made a difference of one window, i.e. my bedroom window. I now only have to draw the curtains, and no longer have to put up the blackout material. In London there was a warning soon after black out, so people that had torn theirs up had to sit in the darkness –

19th September 1944   Montreal

Huntly missed helping to confer a degree on Churchill and Roosevelt at Quebec by being at Chat[illon]. A contingent of Governors went down on Saturday. I am sorry he missed it. He would have loved seeing Churchill. Huntly is now a D.C.L. of McGill and an L.L.D. of Lennoxville, but no one calls him Dr.! He looks very well, but had an attack of arthritis in his shoulder yesterday, which is better today – Too bad he has to endure that. He has been lucky, though, to have lived this long with no serious illnesses –

There are two conventions here now – the conference on U.N.N.R.A. [sic] and one on Hormones at the Ritz.[1] The latter seems so frivolous after Unnra.

We are leaving Friday morning for New Haven and intend staying two days. I expect to stop in N.Y. for a few days, as I haven't been there for five years, and am anxious to talk to Alfred Hampson about Martha Bianchi's

affairs – I shall try to see Margot Holmes who lives in the Waldorf – and a few other people – but I <u>dread</u> the train journeys – and no red caps to carry bags. I shall go very "light" –

I went to see Paul Robeson in Othello last night – a magnificent production – the direction was perfect. Robert Edmond Jones' décor – Robeson and all of them acted marvellously, but the negro tongue is too <u>thick</u> for Shakespeare –

1. Bougie means UNRRA, United Nations Relief and Rehabilitation Administration, which operated from November 1943 until June 1947 to assist refugees in liberated countries.

27th September 1944   *Lexington Hotel*
                                                       New York

I am struck with the fact that you are more conscious of <u>war</u> in Richmond than anywhere else – If you didn't hear the pipes and see sailors and soldiers drilling in Montreal you would never know there was a war – Richmond has been shot to pieces – not any good food, no servants, streets filled with service men – same streets untidy beyond belief – We have an enormous Army Hospital – and about 20 huge camps quite close to us, as well as an Air Base. It being a smaller place than Montreal and New York, it is more noticeable, of course.

I communicated with Alfred Hampson, whom I <u>really</u> came to see, as I wish to know what he is going to do about Martha Bianchi's affairs – I am having dinner with him tonight.

I mailed you a pair of shoes. I hope they are the right size – I had to guess – (There is a new ruling about clothes for overseas). If they don't fit, they may do for someone else, and I hope that you can get the duty or coupons returned. I can send small parcels of food, it seems, sans duty and coupons – Everyone who has seen France says they haven't been <u>without</u> half as much as England has – It makes me <u>mad</u> –

29th September 1944   Black Potts

Gerna very kindly went with me to the station. It bucked me up a lot to
have a little moral support and a few good laughs at dinner with Gerna.
We still behave as we did in the 1920s when we get together, and nearly
always enjoy ourselves. I was very lucky in getting a third-class sleeper, so
Gerna left in a taxi. I deposited my bags on the platform beside the sleeping
car and sat down on them (the bags) to await the arrival of the attendant.
There is something awfully dreary about sitting on a station platform in
the black out. The lugubrious lighting system in that smoky atmosphere
gives a most peculiar effect. You feel you could cut the air with a knife –
At this point the sirens wailed, and a few minutes later a doodlebug went
burbling overhead – I have never heard one so close before – The engine
stopped and everyone looked (or you *felt* they were looking, as you couldn't
see them) a little tense – However it must have glided for *miles* as we never
heard the crash – There were apparently three more after this, though I
must honestly say *I* didn't hear but one more – Anyway we weren't sorry
when the train pulled out.

A third class sleeper is like a couchette in France, i.e. a sort of hermeti-
cally sealed compartment containing four hard bunks – 2 upper and 2 lower
and one is given a pillow – One female over me was going to see her husband who had returned from Normandy; of the second "upper" I gleaned
nothing; opposite me in the lower was a Dutch refugee weighing about 19
stone, and her little girl aged 2 1/2 – The little girl had enormous brown
eyes, and was most attractive though she kept us awake most of the night
asking, "Mummee, vot iss?" I found it impossible to sleep, but about one
o'clock managed to get the window open, ate a few sandwiches and dozed
off now and then, only to be awakened by "Vot iss" again.

I arrived at Hawick at 7.30 a.m. where Gerald met me and took me out
to Teviot Bank, where we stayed before with the Sperlings –

Friday morning we had to get up at 6 a.m., get our breakfast, wash up,
make our beds, dress and leave for Barracks at 7.30. Gerald suggested I
walk up and down outside the Barrack gate (like Lilli Marlene) while he
got dressed in his best uniform.[1] As there was a thick fog, and I was *trying* to look smart, I didn't relish the idea much, so in the end I was smug-

gled into his hut – He got dressed and at 8 we foregathered at the camp gate with 5 sergeants and their wives, who were also going to collect their gongs. As we were all so terribly disappointed not to be going to Buck House [Buckingham Palace], and as there was no certainty of a train getting us to Edinburgh in time for the Investiture, as a great concession two taxis had been hired to take us there – so off we drove into the fog. We hadn't gone many miles before one of the wives came "all over faint" and opened the window wide – A large draft blew down my neck and I was blue with cold, but didn't feel I could complain on account of the faintness, so just sat there quietly freezing.

We stopped at a hotel for a "wash and brush up" before going on to the Palace [Holyrood].[2] I ran into Lord Clarendon, who was of course up there for the "do".[3] On arrival at Holyrood, Gerald and the other recipients went to the right, we went to the left into the long Picture Gallery, where there were seats for about 500 people – but I was about the 499th to arrive, so was in the last row. However, Gerald later reappeared from God knows where, found me, introduced me to Admiral Bromley (an A.D.C., Rupert's father), who produced a chair for me immediately in front of the dais, so that I was able to see very well.[4] We sat there about an hour, while a band played outside in the courtyard –

The King arrived about eleven and the long line of people receiving the medals filed in. Lord Clarendon read out the names, the King pinned a medal on each breast, shook hands with them, and said a few words – and they bowed and walked off. Each medal was put on a red velvet cushion, held by a Naval aide standing beside the King, and Major Harry Stockley (he and Mrs. S. used to live at 8 Park Street [Windsor] at the beginning of the War) placed the medal on the cushion. I didn't know any of the people – there were many civilians (probably locals), quite a lot of Merchant Navy, but very few officers in the Forces, a few "charlie officers" (C for Charlie, O for orange, MMON) and I felt sad that Gerald wasn't there with any of his pals.

When Gerald's turn came, he looked *grand* and I felt very proud of him. The King had quite a chat with him. He bowed and walked well, and looked like something – so many of them seemed incapable of bowing properly – I suppose they were nervous. The band struck up "Carry me back to old

Virginny" (!) and with a click of the heels, Gerald marched off – I couldn't help regretting the fact that we weren't in London, where we could fore-gather with a few friends for a party. I felt very proud of him and wanted to show him off!! I was dressed in all my glad rags, but honestly an old mackintosh would have been more in keeping with the rest of the audi-ence. I wore my only decent number, i.e. brown coat and skirt, brown felt hat, beige blouse and beige gloves. It sounds rather *bleak*, but it is really very nice.

We then went to the L.N.E.R. Hotel (as all the Restaurants were full) where we had a mediocre drink and a filthy lunch – . . . . and returned to Hawick.[5] The last straw was when the Edinburgh Police stopped our taxi for being out of their zone – and I believe there's a lawsuit going on about it – When we got back to Teviot Bank we lit a fire, and made some toast for our tea, and came to the conclusion that Scotland has NO message for either of us. I like the Highlands, kilts, bagpipes, but I really don't care if I *never* see the Lowlands again!

Gerald had Sunday free. We went for a walk, ate, slept and read. He is really very busy and I think was glad of a day's rest. He has been busy training men of the R.A.F. Regiment who have been transferred – He feels rather badly that he can't go with them, but they absolutely refuse to send him, so he is trying to be philosophical, but is bored to tears with his brother officers – and says he never speaks to anyone but Fergus and Jock Rowan, and keeps to his cell and is really living the life of a Trappist monk! –

He took me to the midnight train. I knew the same attendant would be on the sleeper as on Wed. night. His name is Drummond – so was easy to remember (not difficult like William, the waiter!), so when the train pulled in to Hawick, I rushed up to the sleeping car with my *sweetest* smile and said, "Drummond, oh DRUM-MOND, have you anything for me?" He didn't answer, but took my bags – so I hoped for the best, said good-bye to Gerald and was sorry to have to leave him in that God-forsaken hole – I pushed passed someone in the corridor – he turned out to be the Duke of Gloucester – Then Drummond ushered me into a small 2-bunk cubicle which he told me he usually slept in – I asked him where he was going to sleep and he said sadly he would sit up in a chair. So I said I would get into the upper – and there wasn't any reason why he couldn't get into the lower – I slept soundly all-night and Drummond brought me some tea in the morning.

I went to see Gerald's Bank Manager on my arrival in London. When he asked me if I had had a good night on the sleeper, I said, "O yes, I slept with the attendant" – He looked very *embarrassed* and I wished I hadn't tried to make a good story of it.

1. This refers to the first two lines of the popular song "Lilli Marlene": "Outside the barracks by the corner light / I'll always stand and wait for you at night."

2. Holyrood Palace, in Edinburgh, was used for state and official occasions.

3. George Hyde Villiers, 1877–1955, the sixth Earl of Clarendon, was lord chamberlain 1938–52 and had been chairman of the BBC 1927–30 and governor-general of South Africa 1931–37.

4. Rear Admiral Sir Arthur Bromley, 1876–1961, the eighth baronet, was the gentleman usher to the king 1927–52 and to the queen from 1952. Rupert Bromley, b. 1910, was from 1961 the ninth baronet.

5. L.N.E.R.: the London and North Eastern Railway.

5th October 1944   *Richmond*
I had not been [to New York] *since the war, except for one day and night – four years ago, and was anxious to see Alfred Hampson about Martha* [Bianchi]*'s will etc – Finally after telephoning back and forth, Margot Holmes assured me that she had secured me a room in the Lexington on Lexington Ave. and 48th St – just one block from the Waldorf where she lives. I tried to get in there but to no avail –*

[After lunch on Wednesday] *I went "home" to my room to rest before tacking Alfred – which I knew would be rather difficult – He was supposed to call for me at 7.30 – He arrived at 9.15 – By that time, I had lost interest, but evidently he hadn't, as when I met him in the lobby, he folded me in his arms, and said, "You look beautiful". Fancy! He was feeling no pain as he had been to a party – We went to a Russian cabaret, very amusing, but – Alfred was so un-conscious of his surroundings and so emotionné about Martha and about my being "the only Dickinson left" that I think the diners were more interested in us than the show. Every now and then he would take out his handkerchief and weep large fat tears – In between times he was gnawing my shoulder!*

It appears that Martha has left <u>everything</u> to him – family portraits etc. – a clean sweep – but there are complications – She wanted a shrine to Emily established there. There are manuscripts, letters etc. In other words, the situation is dynamite. Some of the letters contain things of explosive nature. Books are still being written about the Dickinsons. They are in effect the American Brontës – I am certain that, if I were not married, Alfred would propose matrimony. He thinks <u>we</u> could make a marvellous thing of the Amherst set-up. The whole thing is rather astounding – He said "Now, Virginia, since Martha's death, you are <u>the</u> Dickinson!" "The King is dead – Long live the King". I wouldn't tell Florie![1] She would <u>kill</u> him I am sure – Well, we finally staggered out of the café at 3 a.m. and the next morning I was in bed with a mild attack of flu. Alfred had made a joke of my Camille cough which had begun sometime in the afternoon – I had planned to go to lunch with Emily Clark and to dinner and to see Helen Hayes in "Harriet" – those had to be called off. I read and drank orange juice, and by Friday I was out again.

Potty writes me that there are many things in the shops in France and Brussels that haven't been seen in London for five years, and that the French aren't starving by any means. "Georges-Paris" said a French friend had just flown back to Montreal laden with <u>silk</u> stockings and Lanvin perfume – England has been much harder hit than any of the others on the Western side. I have no doubt that Poland and Greece have been rather devastated. There is never too much food in Greece –

I left Mrs. Golsan's to go to dinner in the Colony Club with Mrs. Charles Whitman – That is a very charming club – old world – has atmosphere – old ladies in stiff taffeta dresses and old gentlemen whispering in subdued tones in corners – something left over from a dead world –

1. Florence, as Bougie's elder sister and a writer, would no doubt consider herself *the* Dickinson.

21st October 1944   Black Potts

The old boy returns on Tuesday for 10 days' leave and after that is being sent to a new job, which means he may be able to live in.[1] I am delighted he is getting away from Scotland and am thrilled he will be coming home

– but rather wish I had a free week or two *first* to take a few long deep breaths. Perhaps I am getting old?? Thank Goodness they don't consider him fit enough to go on active service for the time being, and after that dreary place ("pronounced as in expectoration") I think he will be glad to do *anything*, and has definitely become a little more philosophical with the years, so I don't think he will go on like a raging bull this time, if he's not sent. (He nearly drove everybody nuts before he got himself sent to Italy!) The household's reaction to the warrior's return was quite funny – they just opened their mouths and said "Oh" – *knowing* that life is about *ten* times more hectic when he is around. G. is one of those 24 hr. jobs! and there is never a dull moment –

1. From November 1944 Gerald commanded the London District School of Street Fighting, where troops were trained in urban combat techniques.

22nd October 1944   *Richmond*
Alex Weddell sent me a book which had my aunt's name written in it – "Margaret Townes, Macon, Georgia 1856" – she was Uncle Arthur Dickinson's wife – [1] *It is French and the first half is about Les Prisons d'Etât – that doesn't seem very cheerful reading for a young lady of her tender age – She couldn't have been more than 17 at the time –*

Darling, it scares me to death to think of "doodlebugs" anywhere near you – I am beginning to think you are right and that this war may drag on in Germany until the late Spring. The Phillipine [sic] invasion was quite exciting – How MacArthur must have loved it.

1. Alexander Weddell, 1876–1948, was a U.S. ambassador to Argentina 1933–39 and to Spain 1939–42. Arthur Dickinson, 1835–ca. 1900, married Margaret Townes, b. ca. 1839, in 1868.

29th December 1944   Black Potts
Gerald had to entertain the King of Jugoslavia the other day when he came to inspect the school [of Street Fighting]. [1] They gave him a bang up lunch

— later he drove G. in his 2-seater (with a couple of detectives sitting in the "dickie") through the streets from Barracks to somewhere else, while his car radio blared forth "Is you is, or is you ain't my baby?" He seemed to have enjoyed himself very much and G. says he is a "very nice little boy".

1. Peter II, 1923–70, king of Yugoslavia from 1934 until he was deposed in 1945.

31st December 1944   *Richmond*

Now for 1945! All we can do is to pray that it will bring a victory over Germany — I must say that the Germans are extraordinarily good fighters and very clever in the bargain. One hates to admit it, but I think it dangerous to be too optimistic. That has always been our tendency. I don't dare say what I really think about mankind en masse. It is better not to express it. I am distressed to hear that Ian Pearson has been given up, and that Lady Glyn's son was killed — Here, the latest casualties are hitting many of my friends, with sickening regularity.

I have been trying to finish the Basic History of the U.S. by William and Mary Beard —[1] It is disillusioning, to say the least and quite boring, but I am persevering because I have always been fairly ignorant on that subject.

I note that Sheila [Child] has a boy — that will please them. As for me, I don't care if no boy is ever born again, and personally, I am delighted that yours is a girl.

I had two letters from Potty. In one he said he hadn't heard from you for some time, and that he wondered what was the matter. He said you had kept his morale boosted. I am sure you have and everyone has written me of your splendid and wonderful spirit — Maybe it won't be long now — Then you can have a well deserved rest from responsibility and nobility — But I can't write of these things. I am afraid to, and being raised up with "blacks", I am superstitious in the bargain.

Tonight I shall drink a toast to you and Gerald and Jennifer and say a prayer that I may be allowed to see you before 1946 —

This is a stupid letter. I want to say so many things, but, somehow, it is better not to say too much — But I do feel that we may be on the last lap of this awful mess — Until that is finished one can only live from day to day —

1. Charles A. Beard and Mary R. Beard, *New Basic History of the United States* (New York: Doubleday, Doran, 1944). The book was revised by their son William Beard in 1968.

12th January 1945   Black Potts

I am beginning the "1945 Series" with no. 1 – the only resolution I made was to write to you more often, and as you see from above, I have already broken it! I "note" that my last letter written, I believe on New Year's Eve – was no 44 which shows I didn't write you *every* week. God knows I hope by the end of 1945, I will not only be able to stop numbering my letters, but will not have to write at all, because we will be together! It is really getting beyond a joke. If anyone had told me in Sept. 1939 that 5 1/2 years would go by before I should see you again, I would have just caved in at once – Let us hope that now it will only be a matter of *months* –

7th February 1945   Black Potts

The Russian news is wonderful, I feel the War may be over by the summer, don't you? and I shall do everything possible to get to the U.S. as soon as I am allowed – Please God, we will all be together by next Christmas at the *very latest*!! I had a letter from Cook's the other day saying that if I was willing to accept a 48 hours' notice and could get an exit permit, passport, etc. and was inoculated for yellow fever, malaria, diptheria [*sic*] (and leprosy?) and paid *£210* per person, I could get to U.S. via North Africa, Gold Coast, Brazil etc. – via plane! I told the man I didn't particularly want to take my child around the world! and I was terrified we might get stranded in "The White Man's Grave" and might be there for years! How *could* one settle one's affairs, store furniture etc. in 48 hrs?? Anyway, I have now filled out a form (though I don't suppose it means anything) for sea passage to Canada – and put my name down for an air passage (*direct* to Canada: £165) for the end of the summer – Also, Olive Todd has given me the address of a man who might help me.

8th February 1945   *Richmond*

How annoying to have the two [uninvited] *American pilots turn up at such an inauspicious moment.*[1] *Like you, I find almost no one has good manners now – Certainly, most Americans have very bad ones – only the older generation is thoughtful – These young things over here have been completely ruined in that way, by an inept idea that young people must be allowed to "follow their bent", to "express themselves". It is called "Progressive Education" – Those who have been subjected to its vicious influences can't read properly, nor write, nor spell anything, nor speak the language, and they have no conception of the niceties of life. You expect to have them put their feet on your best furniture, slap you on the back, and say "Hello" to everyone – I got in a car this morning with a woman I have been working with in Red Cross. She introduced me to her daughter, and she gave me one look, and said "Hello" – It is horrible, but I have to stand it and so I do but it keeps me in a constant state of indignation. It isn't the fault of the young people, but of their mothers – who on earth can these people be? The city is full of them – that's all I know – I don't mind my friends saying "hello" to me – It is the custom here and is a sort of amusing, intimate, informal way of greeting, but a strange young woman I have never seen – on being introduced??*

Don't let the idea that you are getting old because these things shock you, take hold of you – They always shocked you – But I do remember that I was shocked by the fact young people called everyone by their first names, when you were a child. I was utterly unused to that – So, it is true that each generation gets a jolt –

1. Ginnie had made it known that visiting Americans were welcome at her house, but she would have expected prior notice of their visits.

22nd February 1945   *Montreal*

Fendley said to the Doctor, "I think I'll get up now, and go out for some air" – and turned over on his side and died. It was a wonderful way to go – He would have chosen it. Well, he wasn't young and the last years of his life were quite successful and happy, except for Mr. Roosevelt! We have so much of tragedy now, that we just go on, and say nothing.

Potty said you were very entertaining but cold, your anatomy, not your hospitality – That worries me of course. Also, he says Jennifer is sweet, very well behaved and wise beyond her years at times! As long as you get through this winter without freezing and the three of you are living and well, I can stand anything.

I am quite well again – we all are – Huntly as wonderful as ever – We have been lucky – so I can't complain. From the sublime to the necessary! The food here is wonderful. All the meat you want – nothing lacking. You wouldn't know there was a war. Quite different in Richmond – almost no meat, no butter – and everything short –

20th March 1945   Black Potts

I was very sad to think your holiday was cut short – I know you and Daddy badly needed a change and a good rest – and I know how disappointed darling Huntly must have been. What a terrible blow to have Fendley's death come so unexpectedly and then the news of [the death of] Scott Parrish as well – I am so grieved for you dearest Boogie, and send you all my loving sympathy – I feel so helpless being so far away – I am glad for our darling Nana's sake that she died before Fendley – how terrible it would have been for her otherwise. It is awful that I cannot be there to try and comfort and help you in all the sorrows, illnesses and vicissitudes you have had in the last five years – I know you realize how terribly I long to be with you again. I feel that nothing else matters as long as I can see you again, and we are 'hale' enough to have a happy time together – and we could enjoy the "third generation" together. Well, your grand-daughter is pretty tough, thank God – Her naughtiness is very trying but I think she has health and personality and guts!!

I am going up to London to-morrow to have a session with Playmate II, an appointment with the chiropodist, *try* and get a hat, and tea with Mum – but *mainly* to see about a chance of a passage – [1] What I would *like* to do is to get one at the end of the summer – I feel we will be thrown out of this house by then, as our agreement is for the duration only – and Mrs. Fletcher's lease anyway comes to an end in December. I will have to get our furniture out, etc. and get everything straightened out before I leave

— I would like to go to U.S. *now*, but don't know if that's possible, and I feel it would be rather hard on Gerald to leave him stranded and homeless. He *loathes* his present job — of course it is all a terrible anti-climax after doing his stuff, and it is only natural that he should have a reaction. He is pretty fit and well, thank Goodness, but just between you and me, I find this "post-war rehabilitation" more difficult than I thought it would be! He *longs* for the end of the war, and can hardly wait to get out of his scratchy battledress, but after the war, what then? No job in the offing, and so many of his friends have been killed. The "tough guys" like Gerald and Hugh Cholmeley who have been so whole-hearted about doing their bit, will find it harder to settle down than most.

1. Playmate II: Sister Griffiths.

22nd March 1945   Black Potts

How I hate the thought of your receiving all that bad news as soon as you arrived in Montreal. I am wondering what sort of trip you had back to Richmond, and how you are feeling since your return. The good food at Huntly's must have been *marvellous* after the Chesterfield! I felt a bit jealous to hear of the chicken for lunch and *lamb* for dinner!! but you were impressed by our Xmas fare here, and so it goes — Food is a bit difficult nowadays but of course we still have eggs, and in a few months' time will be having peas and beans, and all sorts of vegetables from our garden. We are told the meat ration is going to be cut from 1/2 a week to a shilling. Twopence isn't much, but will make our weekly piece of meat "so small as to be almost repulsive". (1/2 buys 2 small lamb cutlets — I wonder how this compares with yours). Well, what do you think we had last week? *Grapefruit*!! I got one for each book — Jennifer was thrilled as she had never seen one before — they were rather small and sour, but the first for 5 years so tasted like ambrosia to me —

I am simply thrilled to death to hear you have sent me some stockings, I didn't know you could get them still!! I have still got 1 pr. left from the 5 prs. you sent me via Pothier in 1942, or was it 41? I wear cotton or old darned woolen and put on the ONE PAIR when I go to London — and hardly dare breathe, for fear they'll run. Gerald brought me 3 prs. from Italy last year (they cost £2-10-0 each! and didn't wear [last]) otherwise I haven't had any since the 'bumper crop' in '42 – I am told you *can* get "fully-fashioned rayon" in England, but have never seen any –

28th March 1945   Black Potts

Had a long letter from Pothier and at the very end he said "PS. I got an O.B.E." I am so pleased about it, but can imagine how he will dread telling his father about it. Papa Doucet will probably write you reams and reams and bore the Hell out of you, and everyone else and in the end Pothier will wish he hadn't rec'd it!!

6th April 1945   Black Potts

Tuesday afternoon Jennifer went to her first *cinema*! We were asked by Anne to see the "Thief of Bagdad" [*sic*] in glorious Technicolour –[1] It made me feel rather old to be taking my child to the films – and to remember that *we* had once been to Hollywood and seen the set of the old thief of Bagdad [*sic*] – which Anne of course had never heard of! being before *her* time –[2] You remember it don't you – with Douglas Fairbanks – Jennifer was thrilled with the "pretty pictures" and thoroughly enjoyed herself – and we had tea at the Ansons afterwards – When we got home, she told Bella and Nannie about it. "I have been to a cinema – you go in, in the dark and a girl with a torch finds a seat for you – Then you see lovely pictures of a horse that falls to pieces in the air, and a magic carpet that doesn't fall to pieces", and then added "I must take you sometime, Nannie, you would love it" –

Jennifer and I pulled a wishbone the other day – she said "I wish for the war to end" – I asked why and she said "I thought you told me I was going to get a pony after the War".

1. *The Thief of Bagdad* [*sic*] (1940), directed by Alexander Korda and others.
2. *The Thief of Baghdad* (1924), directed by Raoul Walsh.

12th April 1945   Black Potts

The news is so breath taking I find it difficult to take in! Isn't it wonderful to think that the Allies may be in *Berlin* before you receive this letter – How *marvellous* that we are fighting on *German* soil. To-night the Americans have reached Magdeburg, etc. etc. etc. The English on their way to Bremen, the Cdn. 1st Army cutting off the Germans in Holland, and the Russians have captured most of Vienna – Hi-de-hi! –

I saw a bunch of asparagus for sale to-day, rushed in to buy it but re-tired gracefully when I was told it cost ONE POUND. I saw goose-eggs in Fortnum and Mason's at 3/9 each!! I sell mine for sixpence each, as am *not* Queen of the Black Market – and sell them usually for children, invalids, etc.

There have been no rockets on London for over a week, isn't it wonder-ful? but expect the Germans will manage to send a few more before the end – Wonder how Hitler is feeling to-night, and how he will celebrate *his* birthday on April 20th –

15th April 1945   *Richmond*

You may imagine that we are stunned by the death of the President. Some people disliked him, of course, especially the rich ones, because his politics for twelve years have somewhat reduced their incomes. But that might have happened anyhow, and personally, in these last years, I have been one of his ardent admirers – I have the feeling that Fendley might be alive today if he hadn't expended so much ire on account of Mr. R. – My feeling about him was that he had vision and courage, and he worked hard for cooperation among the nations and for the coming Peace, the only thing which really matters.

I was at a little tea party at Berta Wellford's when I got the news. It was very dramatic. There was only one Roosevelt hater present, but I happened to catch the <u>first</u> look on her face, which was one of <u>joy</u>! I wish I hadn't seen it. After the first surprise, she got hold of herself! I suppose people like Roosevelt always inspire either hatred or admiration. <u>No one</u> was neutral about him. The trouble is – what about this poor substitute, Mr. Harry <u>S.</u> Truman! I un-derstand that S doesn't stand for anything, he just likes the sound of S.[1] That is just like the negroes – Do you remember Henry Evel <u>T</u>.? He followed the *plough in Missouri not so many years ago. So we no longer have a "gentle-man" in the White House – and I fear that Princess Martha of Norway will become persona non grata!!*[2]

Recently two books have been published by one Mrs. Bingham, giving the "Amherst" Dickinsons the devil![3] *Her mother* [Mabel Loomis Todd] *was a traditional enemy of my family, and these books have been in the offing for some time, but Mrs. Bingham didn't dare publish them before Martha Bianchi died –*

I can never tell you how much I miss you. I have never found a companion in the real sense. Since I left you or you left me –

I hope Gerald is more reconciled to his job – The war looks almost over in Germany. Even Von Papen has been captured. I wonder where Hitler is, and that rotten Von Ribbentrop – Oh well, they can't last much longer, and now we must begin to worry about the Peace *– I just want to go to some peaceful spot and* vegetate *–*

1. This matter seems much disputed. The most plausible version is that "S." was not an abbreviation, because Truman's family could not decide whether to name him for his paternal grandfather, Anderson Shippe Truman, or his maternal grandfather, Solomon Young.

2. Princess Martha Sofia Louisa Dagmar Thyra of Norway, 1901–54, the second daughter of Prince Oscar Vilhelm of Sweden.

3. Millicent Todd Bingham, *Ancestors' Brocades: The Literary Debut of Emily Dickinson* (New York: Harper and Bros., 1945); Mabel Loomis Todd and Millicent Todd Bingham, eds., *Bolts of Melody: New Poems of Emily Dickinson* (New York: Harper and Bros., 1945).

18th April 1945   Black Potts

I wrote you last Thursday – The next morning (Friday the 13th) Nannie and Jennifer came into my room, plunked the presents down on my feet when I was still asleep and Nannie said "Roosevelt is dead" – a poor start to the day! I was so shocked at the dreadful news that couldn't get up much enthusiasm over Jennifer's presents, and Nannie kept muttering, "Never mind, the other gentleman says he will carry on"?!!! It is really dreadful, and there has been a gloom over everybody in the past few days – Of course I am sure it is the same in America, but most people in England feel they have lost "the greatest friend and ally of England". The demonstrations of the regard everyone feels for Roosevelt have been most impressive – I couldn't help thinking, "Now America will become Isolationist again, and when Churchill dies we will have a Socialist Government in England *so* there will be another war in 20 yrs. time, when Jennifer is 25" –

29th April 1945   *Richmond*

Things are coming very close to the end in Germany, and last night we had a wild rumour [of the end of the war] *which reached the Chesterfield at the dinner hour – I had just finished my dinner when I heard a <u>cowbell</u> ringing in the hall outside my door! It was Mrs. Willie* [Willingham], *who rushed in and threw her arms around my neck and began crying and saying, "I am thinking about all those bombs which have fallen on England". I <u>couldn't</u> do anything because I didn't believe the rumour, but I tried to live up to what was expected of me, feeling all the while that it was "fausse nouvelle".*[1] *Remembering the last war, also, when people went berserk over a like rumour, and three thousands were killed afterwards – I tried to hold down the celebration, and also not to appear as a wet blanket. Well, I was right. That idiot Senator Tom Connally got the news during the San Francisco Conference sessions, and instead of trying to confirm it, he just gave it out as gospel. By the time you receive this, all will be over I am sure. At the moment, I feel that Senator Connally would do better to confine himself to roping steers in Texas where he came from than be serving as Ch. of the Foreign Affairs Com.*

Stuart has gone to New York to a meeting of the British War Relief. He will go to see his sisters in New Haven before he returns. I can think of nothing but seeing you, now. I am very tired of <u>not</u> doing so, as you may imagine –

This last week hasn't been very exciting as to engagements – so I won't bore you – I read at the Poetry Society Wednesday evening. My own two poems, fancy that – Then there were others – and some limericks. It wasn't too awful, but I had dreaded it, I must say –

I see that Thalheimer [sic] *is advertising a service called Convoys Ltd. which insists that I can send parcels to Europe with dispatch through them. I shall investigate it. I should like to get something off to Moky as well as you –*[2] *I mailed a dress to you yesterday. It is five years old, but good. I hope you can use it in the summer – I couldn't find much for the collection for "devastated Europe", because I gave everything I had to England and have bought nothing to speak of for five years — I wish you could see the clothes in the warehouses! Piles of them in 2 large warehouses as high as the ceilings with only narrow lanes in which to walk about. I am going to help sort on Thursday — I rather imagine that many of them will have to be thrown out. I sent some good shoes and sweaters which were not very smart on me — Eleanor gave me two of her mother's — quite new, so I shall use those at Chatillon and that allowed me to give the old ones to the collection. I don't wear sweaters here. Clothes are impossible here now — and food is poor — and we have to carry bags to bring home our purchases just as you have done — There is a paper shortage also — They have collections all the time for magazines and newspapers — and so on ad infinitum.*

How exciting to get the grapefruit — You and Jennifer will have to live on fruit if you come over here to make up for lost time. We get a plenty of citrus fruit, but "yes, we have no bananas" — You see people whispering in corners, and you know they are telling each other where they may find sweets and bananas —

After this war, I am determined to have some fun, before I get to be 70.

1. In fact *nouvelle fausse:* false report.
2. Maurice (Moky) Bisdom van Cattenbroek remained in France through the war.

4th May 1945   Black Potts

We have just heard over the wireless that HITLER is dead! It is difficult to try and take it in — so much has happened in the last 10 days since I have written you that my brain is in a whirl — Mussolini executed, the Americans in Munich, the Russians in Berlin, Hitler dead — and I suppose the war with Germany over in a few days! All the things that one has been waiting to hear for years, and now one can't believe it.

I don't think many people feel elated at the thought of Victory Day — so many people have been killed, so many people's lives wrecked — It has gone on all too long, and there is an extraordinary feeling of flatness. But my God, it is wonderful to think the soldiers won't have to fight Germans any more, and *incredible* to take in the thought that one won't hear warnings any more – I find it hard to believe that the Doodle-bug and Rocket Days are over –

I wonder how long it will be before the Japs are settled, and the *World War* ends?

Five years ago the Blitzkrieg on Holland and Belgium were about to begin – *Five years* since May 1940, and the retreat in France – It seems *decades* ago that Sister and Jennifer (aged 1 month) and I went down to the Pink Cottage from Windsor and the first raids began – By the time you receive this letter, the war in Europe may be over.

Gerald and I are going to Southampton in 1/2 an hour to try and get Carmela fitted up for his next leave as the Solent is now open. Hope to write there or on return from Hamble.

6th May 1945   *Richmond*

This has been a wildly exciting week as to war news. I imagine that we will get the official news of the end of the European war by Wednesday, if not before – Mussolini is dead – and Germany is a shambles – But what has happened to Hitler, Goebbels, Himmler and Göering? – The paper said the Canadian Army had finished fighting and they will be going home soon – It's all so stupendous that I can't take it in. This last 5 years and 7 months has been too awful for words – I can't help wishing I was over there. It is sickening to be sitting here, twiddling my thumbs, with almost everyone I care about so far away – And how long is it going to be before I can see you? The New York Times advertizes the fact that England will begin operating commercial planes by May 15 – In spite of everything we have been lucky – You and Gerald and Jennifer are alive, and so I must not complain.

I am sorry Jennifer couldn't have her birthday party, but of course you were wise. I trust she didn't have the measles – Also, I am very sorry that your friends, the As [Ansons], can't get on together, and feel they must separate. What will she do, and where will they live? Of course, the war has upset a good many people, and there will be a great many divorces. War is apt to do something quite definite to the men who must fight. It makes them restless, I think – they all say their one idea is to go home to their families, but when they finally get home, they are not the same – That may not apply to all of them, but it certainly does to some –

As for engagements, I don't remember having much excitement socially last week. Monday, as usual, I went to the Woman's Club. The speaker was none other than Friederlinde Wagner, grand-daughter of Richard.[1] *She is 27 – very Titian blonde with pretty blue eyes, but a regular German figure and legs – She has become an American citizen and is looked after by Arturo Toscanini – She told us that her mother had espoused the cause of Hitler (I am sorry to say that the mother who espoused the cause of Hitler was English) and at the age of 14 – she ran away from home, after the death of her father and went to S. America where Toscanini arranged to get her into the U.S. – She giggled quite a lot and seemed to have a sense of humour – She even laughed when she told the story of her grandmother Cosima running away from Von Bülow and going off with Wagner –*[2] *Everyone seemed to like her, but I have my fingers crossed when I meet anyone* <u>German</u> *– I had a talk with her and she was quite simple and unaffected.*

1. Friedelinde Wagner, 1919–91, moved to the United States during World War II.

2. Cosima Wagner, 1837–1930, formerly von Bülow, daughter of Franz Lizst, was Richard Wagner's second wife. Hans von Bülow, 1830–94, a pianist and conductor, was Cosima Wagner's first husband.

13th May 1945   *Richmond*

This is a big day for Virginians especially. It is the day the President set aside for prayers of thanksgiving for the Victory in Europe and a rededication for the War in Asia – It is also <u>Mothers' Day</u>*, and for us the Anniversary of the first landing on Jamestown island of that little bank of Englishmen who arrived in those three small boats, which were so tiny that they tied them up to the* <u>trees</u> *on the shore (in 1607) –*

I don't think I can do justice to this past week – The stupendous events and their implications were too much for me – All day long Tuesday the 8th I hung on the radio, and was rather exhausted when it was over – However, I have gone in for Peace propaganda in a big way – and am arranging meetings all the time with speakers explaining the San Francisco proposals, and the

Bretton Woods economic plans – One cannot tell what Congress may do, but I'm going to put my oar in to do what I can –

Tuesday evening I had Dr. Kincaid coming here to speak about the Banks and Fund plans, written at Bretton Woods – I was dead tired from the emotion of the day, but he did it awfully well, and he had some authority as he is the economist from the Federal Reserve Bank. I arranged it all. We had about 50 or 60 people in the main dining-room of the Chesterfield and after it was over Mrs. Willie and I set the tables for breakfast, as the servants had gone home – I fell into bed exhausted –

Several people have written to me to say how they had thought of me and what a relief it must be to me to know that you are no longer in danger from V Bombs. I was touched by that. I must say people have been very interested in you and in the fact that we have been separated so long under these awful circumstances –

The biggest thrill I got was when Churchill ended up his speech with "Advance Brittania! Long live Liberty, God save the King" – We are sad to feel that Roosevelt, who understood the world so much better than anybody else in Washington, and who really was killed by work, wasn't here to know that we were victorious, and to speak to us. All the people I know, at least all the intelligent ones, thank God that Churchill remains to the world – We need someone in the English speaking world with a sense of drama, which poor Mr. Truman lacks. Now that radio is such a form in world affairs, I hope that diction and a sense of how to speak to the masses, will be forced on our politicians as a must, provided they aren't going to use their voices for hideous purposes, as Goebbels and Hitler did.

Thursday I worked in Red Cross. Our gauze has come, finally and we have a huge order to fill in a month. I am very weary of that routine, but I suppose I must keep at it, until Japan is defeated. We hope that war will only last a year – Of course, any personal feeling I had about the War is over with the end of Germany – I have had many bad moments, which I tried to hide. Stuart remained cheerful, which was a help – I have loathed the Germans so long, and now they are biting the dust – Long may they continue to do so!! I have chosen the work on the Peace, as the best part for me of the latter episode of this war and I am better equipped for that –

Today in church, I wept when the congregation sang the National Anthem, *one of the few times when I have even <u>wished</u> to cry – Now it is over, and I have cried twice! Quite a record for me because I never cry, now –*

Florie and I have been very interested in the two books recently published by one Mrs. Bingham about Emily Dickinson, one containing over 600 poems by Emily which that family have kept all this time since her death in 1886 –

Now Churchill is about to speak!! so excuse me for a moment –

3.35 p.m.

That was a wonderful speech – and once more I say – we are thankful for the great Mr. Churchill, especially since we have lost the also great Mr. Roosevelt – What we should have done without them God only knows –

Well, darling, you have lived through, and had a hand in, one of England's (if not <u>the</u>) most perilous and glorious pages of history. To live through it and to know that you are doing it at the time, is an experience which men do not have often. It has been hideous and will be hard for some time, but it must be a consolation to you that you did it cheerfully and courageously – Although you were so situated that you were not called upon to work in a factory nor man an ack-ack gun, you lived up to your part, and I, as your mother, who always tried to protect you from all things hard and disagreeable, am very proud of you – Never forget that – Now, I mustn't say any more – You know how I feel –

To go back to what I was writing when Churchill began to speak – The Mrs. Bingham has also published a book about my family called "Ancestors' Brocades". It is a book written in a spirit of <u>revenge</u>, for there was a feud between her mother and the Dickinsons about a law suit – She didn't <u>dare</u> publish it while Martha Bianchi was alive – so she waited until she died to do so – The Todds (Mrs. Bingham's parents) fastened themselves upon the Dickinsons, and sucked up all the distinction they could from contact with them – Austin D., Martha's father, was supposed to have been intrigued by Mrs. T.[1] Someone must have given her the poems – possibly Austin. All this time they have hidden the poems in a <u>trunk</u>, which they carried about with them, everywhere – The law suit was about a paltry strip of land belonging to Lavinia –[2] She went to court and recovered it from Mrs. Todd. Also, they went to court and proved that Mrs. Todd (who was forced to swear it in court) didn't know Emily, and had never even <u>seen</u> her – Suddenly, now, her daughter after more than 50 years publishes that book trying to defame the character of

Lavinia and Martha's mother.[3] *It is a dastardly business, and of course they had no right to hide the poems. That is where the matter stands and now Florie is writing a criticism of the book, in which she intends to blast their motives, and show up Mrs. Bingham — Well, so goes this merry world — I thought you might be interested in the story of some of your ancestors!*

1. Austin Dickinson, 1829–95, was Emily Dickinson's brother, a lawyer, and the treasurer at Amherst College. For an account of the relationship between Austin Dickinson and Mabel Loomis Todd, see Polly Longsworth, *Austin and Mabel: The Amherst Affair and Love Letters of Austin Dickinson and Mabel Loomis Todd* (New York: Farrar, Straus, Giroux, 1984).

2. Lavinia Norcross Dickinson, 1833–99, was Emily's sister. The strip of land had been left to Mabel Loomis Todd by Austin Dickinson in his will to thank her for editing Emily's poems. Lavinia felt this was totally inappropriate, hence the court case. For an account of the lawsuit by Todd's daughter, see Bingham, *Ancestors' Brocades*, and Richard B. Sewall, *The Life of Emily Dickinson* (London: Faber and Faber, 1976), 229–34.

3. Martha's mother was Susan Gilbert Dickinson, 1830–1913.

16th May 1945   Royal Southern Yacht Club
– V – V – V – V – V   Hamble
                                                          Hampshire

Since my last long letter to you we have had: – a hectic week-end at Black Potts, later 24 hrs. in Warsash to see about getting Carmela into the water again, on our return to Windsor news of capitulation of Germany, two and a half days in London for "VEDAY" and "VE+1" Day – one day to breathe before coming down here for Gerald's leave – I brought *pads* of this terrible notepaper to write *copious* letters to you, and up 'til to-day nothing has happened so far!!

Well, I don't know what your reaction was to the end of the war in Europe, but I feel completely DAZED and find it impossible to take it in – And there is still a war on with Japan, chaos in Europe, a muddle with Russia over Poland. (I confess to complete lack of faith in Russia) etc. etc. so I suppose it doesn't do to be *too* optimistic. But it is *wonderful* to think there is no longer any fighting on the Western front.

No MORE BLACK-OUT!!

No more sirens, bombs, incendiaries, H[igh]. E[xplosives].'s, doodlebugs or rockets! –

I long to have a bonfire of all the black-out materials and boards but Nannie says I "must remember the salvage". The basic petrol ration comes on June 1st, after three years or is it four? And Gerald expects to be demobilized by the Autumn!! I don't suppose he'll be sent to Burma as he's now too old and not A1, so *that's* a relief –

20th May 1945   *Richmond*

I am full of good works just now, being tortured with a strange kind of conscience. We went to a special Peace *service last Sunday – and took our usual drive in the afternoon. It is the only time we can use the car – as we have only 2 gals. a week. I feel I* must *get out in the fields and woods once a week –*

Tuesday, in fact all this week, it has poured raining, and I was especially fed up with it on Tuesday and again on Thursday, when I was responsible for a large and expensive meeting about the San Francisco Conference. It took place in the John Marshall High School Auditorium which holds 1200 people – We got one Philip Cummings all the way down from N.Y. to speak and we had only about 250 staunch souls who braved the elements. I have never seen such storms – wild wind, and lashing rains, with some thunder and lightning. Emma Gray Trigg took me down in her car –[1] As she works for O.P.A., or in other words Office of Price Administration, she has extra gas – The meeting went off very well save for the three fat men who spoke before *the regular speaker began –*

They threaten no more ice cream or desserts on account of the sugar shortage, and so it goes. I really think that Mrs. W. [Willingham] manages very well, but you can imagine that the old ladies here are beginning to howl.

Florie has gone to Norfolk – She won the Poetry prize for Virginia on three sonnets she sent in to the contest ($50.00) which she says she will use to buy her some contraption enabling her to hear. She is very *deaf. This letter seems to be all about* deaf *people – Well –* I *am not deaf –* yet.

I simply cannot take it in that we have defeated the Germans – I hope *they capture Himmler and that cad, Von Ribbentrop – and let us hope that they along with most of the Gestapo will be executed (see Lord Vansittart).*

I keep thinking that maybe I can get to St. Jean de Luz by this summer a year, and that Jennifer can learn to swim and speak French, and I can ride a water bicycle!

1. Emma Gray Trigg, 1890–1976, was a Richmond musician and poet. Her published works include *Paulownia Tree* (Francestown, N.H.: Golden Quill Press, 1969) and *Spanish Pirates and Other Poems* (Verona, Va.: McClure Press, 1973).

22nd May 1945   Black Potts

Monday [7th] I rushed about packing, shopping etc. and caught the 3.42 for Waterloo – met Rosemary [Jeffreys] at Claridge's at 5 – where she had got a room for us (clever girl) – and Gerald stayed at Chelsea Barracks.[1] We had tea and sat down to listen to the 6 o'clock news thinking we would hear the announcement of Victory night, however there was no news – so we went up to our room to have a bath and dress, feeling rather disappointed that we were going out on the wrong night –

We started out to join the rest of the party, determined to enjoy ourselves – Anne's mother had us for cocktails at her house in Charles St. (she lives on the ground floor as the top part has been "blitzed".) Anne's sister Diana was there too and her beau David Bethell (who had been sent to Gerald's school that DAY!); also Tony Nation, an old pal of Gerald's. We then went on to the "Mirabelle" (run by Ernest, who used to be under Ferraro at the Berkeley), where we were joined by Monty Lowry-Corry and his sister Patricia – [2] We had an *excellent* dinner (the first decent meal I have had in London for *years*) and a magnificent Jeroboam of champagne! Ran into Dickie Gillson, who tells me she is off to *Italy* where she is going to do welfare work – We had a very gay time and stayed there until the place closed down – Forgot to say that just before we went to the Mirabelle we heard that the next day was VE Day, so of course everyone starting celebrating at once – We tried to get through to Buckingham Palace but the crowds were too thick – We then planned to meet at the 400 Club in Leicester Square – by this time the crowds everywhere were terrific – and there were bonfires in Piccadilly! Of course we got lost from the others, they never got to the 400 – so G. took me back to Claridge's and returned to Chelsea Barracks.

The next day – VE Day! Rosemary got through to find out about Mark, then I tried to get through to BPotts but by that time all toll calls were off! – but got through to Gerald who had to go down to Windsor anyway to ask him to deliver a message to the family – and he took Anne down to the dentist – He first had a glass of port with Mum and Aunt Norah, then some gin at Black-Potts with Nannie and Bella! Rosemary and I dressed slowly, about 11 the housemaid *rolled* into our room, and said in a thick Scotch accent, "Excuse me, but we have been having a bit of a jollification downstairs, I have only had 4 drinks but the bath-maid has had seven" –

When we got downstairs, Claridge's was a seething mass of people and saw several people we knew. I had Mum to lunch, and Rosemary had her new sister-in-law Fiona Normanton.[3] We listened to Mr. Churchill's speech at 3 p.m. then had to move from Claridge's to the Connaught Hotel where we had luckily got a room at the last minute – there were no taxis, so we began to walk with our luggage, though soon found Myles Knox-Gore driving a Grenadier lorry – and he kindly took our bags to the hotel – We walked down a street where there were several buildings taken over by Americans and were snowed under by bits of paper being thrown out of the windows –

We had tea at the Connaught and at 7 were picked up in Annabelle and taken to Gerald's sitting room at C. Barracks for a cocktail party, and then the same party as the night before dined at the Mirabelle (sitting at the next table to us was a lone couple – the Londonderrys (!), I longed to ask them if they had heard from their friend *Ribbentrop* lately).[4] We had another Jeroboam of Moët and Chandon and enjoyed ourselves very much – then back to C. Barracks for sandwiches, and to "Gerald's" pub the "Dew Drop" in Battersea for beer and darts! The "Dew Drop" is in G's "area" and stands alone amongst a pile of rubble, the only building left in the street still standing – and so to bed –

1. Having written only a short letter on 16 May 1945, in this letter Ginnie recounts the events of VE Day celebrations in greater detail.

2. Montague Lowry-Corry, d. 1977, a Grenadier Guards officer and barrister.

3. The fifth Countess of Normanton née Lady Fiona Fuller.

4. The Marquis and Marchioness of Londonderry, London society hosts, had befriended

Nazi leaders in the late 1930s but ceased their support for the party following Hitler's occupation of Prague in March 1939.

27th May 1945   *Richmond*

On Tuesday, I made a speech before the combined Woman's organisations in St James' Church – Everyone said it was a good one, but it came at the end of a long session, and was full of figures, comparing the last war and this one, so I imagine it must have been a bit tiring. Walter Craigie made one also, but he was able to make a quick "getaway" and I had to remain until the bitter end –

I want to write to Jo Potter, but don't dare because I have had no word about Ian –[1] *Do let me know if you have heard anything – The American papers are trying to acquaint the public with the German atrocities – with horrible stories of Buchenwald and Dachau etc. A man in Colorado was indicted for being cruel to a rat – How can we ever understand the Germans – I hope it makes some impression on them – the masses are so woefully ignorant.*

1. Ian Reid, 1915–84, was Jo Potter's son by her first marriage. He wrote an account of his experiences as a prisoner of war in his book *Prisoner at Large: The Story of Five Escapes* (London: Victor Gollancz, 1947).

7th June 1945   Black Potts

I had one day at Black Potts after the VE festivities in London, in order to shop and have hair done and get everything 'in order' before going away for Gerald's leave – After a mad rush of trying to find sailing clothes and pack etc. we started off on Friday afternoon (May 11th) in Annabelle – G, Anne Anson and I arrived with luggage, eggs, rations, sardines, job sheets and a spinnaker, etc. etc. and drove down to Hamble where we stayed at the Royal Southern Yacht Club. It is a tiny little place on the edge of the Hamble River – *could* be nice but is so badly run – the service and food are quite terrible, and practically no *comforts* of any kind – hence our foresight in taking the sardines, eggs – and even rolls of toilet paper! Gerald was very lucky in being able to get Carmela out after she had been lying on a mud berth for nearly six years! She was in remarkably good condition, *considering* – He went out on Saturday to try her out with a man from the ship yard to make sure she didn't fall to bits, before taking Anne and me in her –

Sunday started by being a lovely day. By the time we got out of the Hamble River it was blowing quite hard – I could hardly remember what to do, and didn't have much 'leisure' in which to refresh my memory – We then got in a bad squall, it was a good test for Carmela who stood up to it wonderfully – as it was blowing half a gale at *least*. When we turned back into the Hamble with that wind and the tide behind us, we rushed up the river like a bat out of Hell. Gerald has some moorings right up at the ship yard at the end of the river, as his own moorings are still 'navy' and can't be used for some time. We were back at the Club about three, they gave us a little *bread* for our lunch, so the sardines came in very handy, also a delicious cake Bella had made us.

I got back to Hamble about seven [on Tuesday], where I joined Gerald and Anne and we dined at the Swan with Eric Lloyd who commands the "Solent Patrol" – We sailed on Wednesday and Thursday and saw lots of interesting things: bits of Mulberry Harbour left over from D Day; landing craft, troopships, and gigantic spools of cable – no one knew what *these* were, but we learned later that they were part of that miraculous oil pipe line that fed the tanks in Normandy –

8th June 1945   Black Potts

I still haven't taken in the fact that the Germans are beaten, whenever I hear a bump or explosion of any sort, my first reaction is to listen for the wail of the siren – then my slow brain realizes that sirens are now 'off' – It is incredible to think that we never even had a pane of glass broken during the 5 years when we were "subject to attack" – Even the Pink Cottage came out unscathed – the nearest damage there was when 25 incendiaries fell in the next field (just beyond our hedge) a few nights before we left in Sept. '40, and a few panes of glass were broken when a doodlebug fell near there one night last summer – The stairs of Mabs' house and part of her ceiling fell in, and she was there all alone – but the thing that really annoyed her was the broken glass and dust in her larder, where she had just put all her jam and marmalade which she had *just* finished making!

Isn't it wonderful to think Goebbels, Himmler etc. are dead? Again I find it very hard to take in. The second the war in Europe was over, the Socialist Party in England started on the rampage – How *irritating* of them to worry about politics *now*, when there is still the war with Japan to finish. I wonder what the outcome will be. How quickly people forget the soldiers that fight for them, and the miracle (?) that saved this island from utter defeat in 1940 – My God, when one thinks how near one came to living under the Nazi hell – and as the Germans hate the English more than any other race, I am convinced that England would have become one large Buchenwald if the Germans *had* defeated us – What a BORE this election is –

Nannie left for her fortnight's holiday. . . . [Thursday] . . . so I settled down to complete domestic life of looking after Jennifer, feeding the animals twice a day, cleaning them out twice a week, watering the greenhouse and spraying the tomatoes three times a day, picking the vegetables, shopping, washing, doing a bit of housework, etc. etc and found the days weren't nearly long enough in which to get everything done –

17th June 1945   *Richmond*

We are now in our worst period of deprivations – food is horrible – and clothes are no good, and expensive. We can't go anywhere because we are patriotic enough not to wish to travel save for going to see Huntly, which I think is quite important to him, and very nice for us of course. We are going to have a little more gas, and shall go to Gloucester if it cools off a little. In the intense heat, we are more comfortable here. You can't get away from the heat in Gloucester, and here you can cool off a bit by shutting out the sun and turning a fan on yourself – We plan to go the 4th of July perhaps for several days if everything is suitable.

Thursday was dedicated to Red Cross, an interview with the Editor of our Times-Dispatch on the subject of our Public Schools – I had an article in

the paper, which has drawn very favourable comment, since it appeared –
The Schools are in a complete mess, and, in the meantime, the children are
suffering. Hairdresser in the afternoon –

I see the censorship is off now, I am glad to say – Well, that beastly wine
merchant (Von) Ribbentrop has been caught, and Lord Haw Haw. If they
could only be certain of Hitler! I cannot believe he killed himself. And fancy
his having married Eva Braun – They are even adding children to that sweet
ménage, in the papers. I don't believe he had any children –

Sunday 17th June 1945   Black Potts
Yes, wasn't it sad that Roosevelt died just before the Victory – As you say,
thank Goodness for Churchill – wasn't his speech on the 13th May wonderful? But *now* what is going to happen with this awful election coming
on? Isn't it dreadful that the politicians couldn't wait until the war with
Japan was over before forcing an election – Churchill led England through
its darkest hours and now that we are "safe", the political squabbling begins. What an undignified shambles – and what will happen if Churchill
is ousted? Can you see (honest) Mr. Truman and Mr. *Attlee* facing up to
Stalin?[1] What a mess this world is in, and it looks as if it will continue to be
for sometime, but *at least* the Germans didn't beat us! *Anything* is better
than that –

Had a letter from Pothier, he is now in the Cdn Occupation Forces, and
is commanding the 3rd "Highland Light Infantry of Canada". He expects
to be given some leave (to Canada) in the next few months.

Gerna tells me the shipping office has told her to "come back in January" – It looks as if my chances to get to you by *sea* next autumn are
pretty hopeless! Oh HELL – However Cook's have written to say they take
"commercial passengers" by air occasionally so this is my one hope – *Please*
let me know in your next letter if you think it all-right for Nannie, Jennifer
and me to come BY AIR.

1. Clement Attlee, 1883–1967, the first Earl Attlee, was leader of the Labour Party
1935–40, served in the coalition government during World War II, and was British prime
minister 1945–51.

24th June 1945   *Richmond*

I am very bored with being stuck, like a spike in the asphalt, in Richmond, for so long — I hear that I can speak to you over the telephone now for $12.00! I am dying to do it. If I could only arrange it beforehand satisfactorily! I shall make enquiries. I should like to hear yours, Jennifer's and Gerald's voices, if possible. Perhaps that might <u>not</u> be possible, but you could at least arrange for you and Jennifer.

24th June 1945   Black Potts

Well, you would think there had never been a war, the papers are full of nothing but the election. How boring it all is! — Every night after the news on the wireless, instead of the usual "War Commentary" we now have an "election speech" — At first, I began to try and listen to them all intelligently, after a week, I just couldn't bear it any longer — Pothier said the Gen. Election here is no better than the ones in Canada and the States — the mud-slinging, etc. I feel heartily sick of it already — I do wish Churchill had been allowed to remain as P.M. in a National Government, until the war with Japan is finished —

Gerald thinks he may be out of the Army!! by September and he is *thrilled*, but I don't quite see what he is going to do then? He wants to look for a house, and move in, in the autumn — but I don't see where the money comes from, and how can we know where we want to live until he gets a job, and as his army pay will soon stop, I feel we ought to lie low for a bit — anyway what is the point of getting a house, just before I go to U.S.? although of course we must have a roof over our heads *somewhere* — If *only* we could stay here until we leave for U.S.! I love this place so much, that I *loathe* the thought of leaving it (*except* to go to U.S.) and the garden is looking so sweet now, and the roses and sweet peas are divine. Did I ever tell you that there are some trees opposite on the river bank that look exactly like the Monet picture that hangs over the mantelpiece at Ivry — I have bought a copy of the picture to keep, it all links up with B. Potts and Ivry — I shall *hate* leaving those trees behind.

6th July 1945   Black Potts

I hope in my last letters I *paved the way* a little for the "shock" I have
for you — I do hope you won't be too upset when I tell you I am going to
have a baby! I have longed to tell you so much, but for your sake, I couldn't
bear to think you would worry about me — and knowing the anxiety you
had last time, I thought it best to spare you. I am counting on this letter
taking about three weeks to reach you — so that when you receive this letter
about July 27th (?) you won't have very long to worry over me, as the baby
is expected in August.

Unfortunately there isn't a room at the nursing-home so I am having the
baby here — At first I thought it was a dreadful idea, but have got used to it
now — and once it's over, it will be nice to be in my own comfortable home
— I only hope Bella will play up well! — I will have to put the nurse in the
dressing-room, so poor old Gerald will have to move out for the time being.
Anyway with "street-fighting" in the week and sailing every week-end,
and a fortnight's leave on board Latifa in August, I thought *that* problem
was well under control.

This week has been somewhat hectic — On Monday Sister Irvine came
to discuss equipment etc. and have a look around. She is Scotch, but luckily
hasn't a very strong accent — as I find a lot of "wee" and burr rather irritating! She also seems to have a good sense of humour — In the midst of
showing Sister I. around Gerald arrived with Fiander and a lot of luggage
— also Rupert Bromley and Dicky King-Smith to have a talk about 'Latifa'.[1]
When they all finally left, I got supper for Gerald.

Saturday.

Didn't finish this last night, as was feeling a bit weary by midnight.
Gerald went off Friday morning, Nannie and I had a busy day — and I went
to have a rather painful interview with a friend à propos of her reputation
(which was *not* a very pleasant task) —[2]

---

1. Dick King-Smith, b. 1922, was the author of more than sixty children's books and
served in the Grenadier Guards during World War II.

2. It was at this time that Ginnie discovered Gerald had been having an affair with
Anne Anson. In her letter of 13 September 1945, Ginnie refers to the above meeting as a
"dénouement."

23rd July 1945   *Richmond*

Your letter #22 written about July 8, telling me the momentous news, arrived July 21. Your letter #20 sent on <u>June 18th</u> arrived <u>this morning</u>, as well as your air letter mailed <u>July 16</u>. Had the June 18 letter arrived in normal time, I should have been prepared – The news was a bolt from the blue and it took me 48 hours to recover! You were very unselfish and sweet not to tell me beforehand, because of course I should have been very anxious – Now I only have a short time to wait. I think that it is better to have two children, perhaps, than one, although I was always satisfied with the uniqueness of <u>you</u>!

Don't think that I disapprove of your having another baby – I am just nervous about <u>you</u>. However, don't worry about my reactions – I have millions of them, being a scion of the super-sensitive "House of Dickinson" –

To answer your questions about whether I should like you to come over here by <u>air</u> – I think that air travel is much safer and more ordinary than it used to be, in fact, people are flying all over the place every day. I <u>can't</u> advise you any more than I could about coming over here in the beginning of the war. I think you were right to stay – I believe you would have been miserable and frustrated had you come, and I should never have forgiven myself if I had over-persuaded you – If <u>you</u> are willing to take the risk of coming with Jennifer and anybody else by air, then I shall <u>have</u> to be <u>fairly</u> calm about it!! But just now my one and only thought is the imminent "event" – We can worry about the other later. Put your name down for an air passage. You can always change your mind. Someone will always take it if you don't. Huntly has been asking about sea passage for you, also. We will meet sometime in 1946 – if not before, provided all is well with us. I am trying to cultivate a little <u>faith</u>, a thing in which I have been woefully lacking all my life –

Stuart wept a little when he received your news. He is always emotionné under certain circumstances – The only thing that upset me, aside from the anxiety, was the sudden thought that I might not be able to see you as soon as I had hoped, but that was a <u>selfish</u> thought. It is better, if you wished another child, to have it now than to wait another year. That would mean nearly two years – and Jennifer would be 7 – It <u>has</u> been sad that I couldn't see her in her babyhood, but I was so pleased that you and Gerald and Jennifer came through this war alive, that I couldn't find it in my heart to complain. I have *had some bad moments, of course, but I have been very lucky, and am immensely grateful.*

I am glad that Gerald is getting some sailing. I think Vera Bromley must be crazy to wish to deprive <u>any</u> man who has been through this war, of a little fun —[1] *Why? — Maybe Rupert exaggerated or perhaps it was the straw in a long series of differences. I can't imagine any woman being so selfish otherwise. The women who consider matrimony as a jail sentence are very irritating. Of all the things I have to complain of in the matter, I should say the opposite of that was* AI *— in my estimation — lack of initiative to do things, to make plans, to go away — Both Stuart and Huntly, the two men who come closest to my every day life, seem <u>rooted to the spot</u>. Even my brother was like that. They might as well be vegetables growing in a row. Huntly is always complaining of being <u>bored</u> and does <u>nothing</u> to alleviate his boredom — Stuart seems only bored on Sundays. It's amusing — I am seldom bored at all, but I will say, I have been almost as <u>confined</u> as a German General in a concentration camp.*

1. Bougie's reference to Vera Bromley née Selby, b. 1910, is a response to a letter from Ginnie written on 17 June 1945 reporting Vera's reluctance to let her husband go sailing.

29th July 1945   Black Potts

I was so *stunned* over the election, that I thought the "shock" might have some effect! but no — Isn't it ghastly?[1] I just cannot take in the fact that the great Churchill is no longer our Prime Minister. Everyone is stunned and amazed. *Can* you imagine what our foreign policy will be like now — and who is there to stand up to old Jo Stalin? I am *sure* that there are thousands of 1/2 wits in this country who voted Labour, not realizing that they were voting against Churchill. Rosemary, in helping Sir George in the election, said they had to explain this fact to the yokels time and time again. Even dear old Nannie who insisted on voting Conservative, couldn't understand my depression on Thurs. evening and said, "But Churchill will surely continue to be our Prime Minister, won't he?" I *ASK* you — What in God's name is going to happen now?

1. The Labour Party, led by Clement Attlee, won the election by a majority of 146 seats.

5th August 1945   *Richmond*

Friday was "My Day" just as it was yours – I had the big news at 5.45 Friday.
That was fast work. I cannot tell you how relieved I was to know that it was
over – Gerald's message said "All very well" – That was so wonderful to hear
– I had got it firmly fixed in my mind that you were going to have a boy, and
I feel certain that Gerald must have wished it that way, but save for him, it
doesn't matter – certainly not to us – and I can think of dozens of reasons why
a girl is preferable – I have been reading a scientific article on the subject of
the determination of the sexes – It is just accidental –

I can scarcely wait to have the details and what the baby looks like. If she
is like you or Gerald or Jennifer etc. Good Lord, what I wouldn't give to be
there – I sent a cable off to you at once, and a telegram to Huntly, but I gather
he is at Chat, because I've had no answer –

My third excitement on Friday, was that someone came up to me, waving
a Saturday Review of Literature and congratulating me on my "verse" which
had appeared in the magazine. It is the best of the American Literary pub-
lications, and I was very pleased that they published it. One Melville Cane,
to whom I had sent it, asked my permission to submit it to the Review! I had
no idea they would publish it, but there it is! I don't dare tell Florie!! I will
explain the whole story and send you a copy – but, now, I can only think of
you and the new member. I have done some very good praying in the last six
years, but my knees are giving way under the strain.

Now for my 4th excitement. I have been asked by the Montreal Gazette if
they can publish a letter I wrote about Emily Dickinson. I don't know if that
can be done, because it contained Mr. Cane's poem about Emily and that is
copyrighted, and it is possible that my "poem" (?) may be copyright also.

8th August 1945   *Richmond*

I sent you a letter on Sunday, and as it is so easy to communicate now, with
restrictions etc "Gone with the Wind", it is really fun to write once more – I
always felt during the war either that I shouldn't clog the mails or that my
letters really were going down in friend "Davy Jones' locker" –

Since I last wrote the horrible news of the new atomic bomb has come out
– the thought of future possibilities – Fontaine Armistead has been working
on the project for nearly 2 years – and today, the announcement that Russia

has declared war on Japan! – Also, I am reading Vansittart's book about what
to do about Germany! However, the big news in my life, is you and the new
baby and Jennifer's pictures – Jennifer grows on you. She seems prettier than
when I first took a look. I do it at intervals, and she always improves. That is
a good sign. It's like the test in buying a painting, as Huntly would say.

15th August 1945   Black Potts

I have been longing to write to you for 10 days, and now I feel I just can't let
Peace in the World go by without sending you at least a few lines. Well, well,
well! Happy V-J [Victory in Japan] darlings!! Of course I am wondering
what you are doing to-day, and do hope you have recovered from flu, Boogie
dear in time to celebrate. I was thrilled to get your cable and your 2 air-mail
letters of Aug 5th and Aug. 8th but rather worried about your flu – and am
praying you are better – and do so hope you'll be able to get to Canada in
the next few days – This heat can't be doing you any good, I will be *so*
relieved when I know you have arrived.

I was *so* enormous before and the baby was so tiny that a friend has
nicknamed her "the Mighty Atom" – she weighed 6 1/2 lbs. She is *quite*
adorable – very *bright* brown eyes, hair brown fluff, and a lovely pinky skin
– she is beautifully made, very rounded with small bones – Wouldn't it be
wonderful if she was a little Boogie?? and isn't it fun to have one blond,
blue-eyed daughter with white skin – and a little Boogie with sparkling
brown eyes –

I felt really so much better by Tuesday that I made plans to see several
people – then VJ came along! As Sister says "Japan has stolen all our thunder" –

Thursday morning – VJ + 1

Wasn't able to finish this last night – I am afraid I am quite unable to
take in the events of the past 10 days, Russia declaring war [on Japan], the
atomic bomb, and now Japan's surrender –

Postwar Letters

27th August 1945   Black Potts

Soon we will start talking about the "good old days" when we were at war! First, we have the Labour Government, then cuts in our rations, soap, clothes – and now *more* cuts – and the bottom surely has been reached when black-out material is to be 2 coupons per yd! Our next 24 coupons usable beginning Sept. 1st must last until May – (for instance 1 coat and skirt – 18, and 2 prs. stockings 6) I don't think they *could* cut the lard which is 1 oz. per week, (could they?) unless they just cancelled it out – and we are going to have Black-out next winter to save fuel – What a mess England is in, with no peace-time factories going, and all this de-mobbing. I don't know if the squirrels are gathering their nuts early this year, but it certainly looks like a hard winter – [1]

1. The end of war did not mean the end of rationing, which continued until 1954.

13th September 1945   Black Potts

Monday [Pothier] took me to lunch at the Old House, then went up to London to dinner – Gerald came back that evening, feeling rather discouraged that the latest job-venture has fallen through, but he is still full of hope. He is trying to 'start something' in the West Country, but I can't say more about it at present, and the idea being that we try and find a house in Devonshire or Cornwall. We are going down to Plymouth for four days the end of this month, and have a look around. I am not sure if *I* like the idea of living in Devon, but of course if Gerald's job is there, we will have to live there. I do wish this job would materialize, as it would make it so much easier to know what sort of a house to look for and *where*. If we bought a house that needed repairs, they could be done while I was in America — that is, if we can *get* any repairs done in these days —

I think what I would rather have than almost anything in the world is concentrated orange juice — I was able to get 2 bottles a month for Jennifer until she was five, and 2 bottles for myself on my 'maternity book' — now the only one in the house entitled to it is Cookie.[1] First, I had to get her registered, then collect her identity card (!), with that I got a ration book, thinking we could then collect her orange juice — quite forgetting it was lease-lend and ça n'existe plus — so to my joy rec'd your letter the next day that you might be able to send some —

I have been discussing jobs, houses etc. with Gerald, arranging for Jennifer to start lessons next week; sorting out Gerald's clothes as he was demobbed last Friday (the house is covered in machine guns, map cases, tail-coats and everything you can think of); making appointments for myself at the dentist, the chiropodist, the hairdresser's; the dressmaker; trying to persuade the Fuel Overseer to let us have some more coke as our ration has run out and am told we aren't supposed to have any until November; trying to get rooms at an hotel when we leave here in December; and so on ad nauseam.

Cookie is named "Angela" for the time being but we can always change it before the christening. Then Heaven knows when *that* will be. Gerald has asked Bill Kingsmill to be godfather, but I haven't decided on *females* yet.[2] Do you think Margie [Hart] or Elsie D. [Duffield] would like to be one?[3] Bill A. [Anson] was to be 2nd godfather if it was a *boy* — You couldn't be more right about "la dénouement" — O Boy — WAS it a dénouement? but all too long to tell you about now.[4] Anne came down from London last Friday to see me — she is living there now with her Mother, having just returned from a holiday in Scotland, and Bill is living in Chelsea Barracks!

1. Cookie: nickname for Angela Potter.

2. Lieutenant-Colonel William (Bill) Kingsmill, 1905–71, a Grenadier Guards officer and the Conservative member of Parliament for Yeovil from 1945 to 1951.

3. Elsie Duffield née Wallis, b. 1909, a Canadian from Montreal.

4. "La dénouement" refers to Ginnie's meeting with Anne Anson over her affair with Gerald. Ginnie and Anne's friendship came to an abrupt end at this point. See also Ginnie's letter of 23 October 1947.

22nd September 1945   Black Potts

Gerald was "de-mobbed" last Friday and had a busy week in London having to, of all things, help organize "thanksgiving week" in London! a dreary job, to end his military career –

We ran out of coke, and were told we couldn't have any more until November – but I have managed to get a permit from the Fuel Overseer to have a bit more – thank Goodness – as really not very easy to go without hot water with a household of seven, when one is a tiny baby – Thank Heaven they sent some to-day as we literally had not one bit left.

Gerald, Jennifer and I had a "family outing" in London – Gerald had helped to organize a parade for thanksgiving week, and took Jennifer and me to see it. It was his last day in uniform, which thrilled *him* enormously – I couldn't help regretting that I would never see him in uniform again, as I am just like a housemaid over uniforms – We drove up in "Annabelle" and went to Finsbury Barracks in the City where we saw the whole parade (4,000 men) assemble, from a balcony – then drove to Ludgate Circus to see it all go by again – *seven* bands – and Jennifer was thrilled – I hadn't been in the "City" for years, the damage is worse than I had imagined – and it is incredible the way St. Paul's stands out, completely surrounded by devastation – (the night of the Big Fire in the city we could see it from here – the whole sky in the direction of London was a red glow) – We then went to the 500 Club for lunch, I was relieved to see a few other children there – Jennifer behaved very well until the end, when she suddenly put her head on the divan and her feet on the table – so I extricated her, and dragged her to the ladies' –

I had my hair done on Thursday, and after lunch Gerald took Rosemary to the train – wearing his new demobilization clothes, grey flannel trousers, a gaudy tweed coat, and the most god-awful green hat which we *think* is made of card-board – [1] Thank Goodness I insisted on his getting a good suit made at John and Pegg last Autumn! He is of course, *thrilled* to be out of the Army – and walked into "London District H.Q." the day after the parade, wearing the London suit, a soft black hat and neatly rolled umbrella!

We went up to London on Friday on a shopping tour – Gerald went to Fortnum's and *five* other big shops, not one could produce a *handkerchief*! Fortnum's tried to get him to buy a dressing-gown, as it was the only thing they had! He eventually found some socks and *one* pair of pants – I went to SEVEN shops trying to find a pair of shoes for Jennifer, but never got any – so my *priority request* is for a pair of shoes for her, size 12 1/2, in a *wide* fitting – as she has very fat feet. There are no gym shoes, and no dancing slippers made – so she will have to do gym and dancing barefoot – but don't know what she'll wear *walking*. I went to John Bell and Croyden as I had a credit there of £4, bought a tiny sponge for the baby, a powder-puff for myself, and a bottle of milk of magnesia – and *owed them* six and five pence! I then met Gerald who had sold a lot of military clothes for £1 – and we had lunch which cost nearly £2.

After lunch Gerald took me on a tour through Battersea, where he had the Street Fighting School – the whole area is completely devastated, except for a tiny pub called the "Dewdrop Inn", and he took me in to meet the proprietor and his wife –

1. For those leaving the military, the government provided basic men's clothing of a suit, a raincoat, a shirt with two collars, a hat, a tie, shoes, and two pairs of socks.

24th September 1945   Black Potts
You can get utility brassières, they only fit where they touch (?). If you want a proper brassière I am told you have to get a medical certificate that your *bust is deformed* – I thought [Dr.] Maxwell would die laughing when I asked him to give me a prescription for a bust-bodice!!

12th October 1945   Black Potts

I [was] a little disappointed in Devon and Cornwall, not that the country and the sea aren't simply beautiful, but the *houses* are disappointing – the towns like Truro are *hideous*, and so built up – all around Torquay and Paignton is dreadful – but *Helford* is too adorable – Exeter has been badly bombed – and the middle of Plymouth is *absolutely flat* – I have seen nothing like it except in Battersea and around St. Paul's. The shopping centre and heart of Plymouth just doesn't exist any more – *What* a battering they must have had –

We drove back here on Thursday and [Gerald] rang up and made an offer (subject to survey) for the Brixham Trawler "Peel Castle" (!) that he had seen at Penzance – idea being that he and John Orme buy her together, and launch out into the Fishing Business![1] There is plenty of scope in Brixham as the business is pretty dead, and apparently plenty of men who are anxious to sign on as crew. There is a terrible scarcity of boats, and Gerald was lucky to find one –

On Sunday morning he rec'd the news that the survey had been very successful, there were shouts of joy as you can imagine when they told him she was a grand little boat, with a good engine and that he was very lucky to get her at a reasonable price, so now Gerald and John Orme own the "Peel Castle" – Gerald to run the "fishing end" and John the finance side and work at the London end –

Gerald left for Brixham yesterday and plans to stay at the Lupton Hotel for a fortnight. He intends bringing her around from Penzance to Brixham this week-end, and starting to get her fitted out for fishing as quickly as possible – and hope to be fishing in less than a month. He has signed on a skipper and will collect a crew of 2 or 3, and intends going to sea himself as a hand – and is going to learn the business from the bottom up! When they have sold enough fish to pay back for the boat, they hope to buy another boat etc. The important thing is to muscle in *now* when good prices are being paid for fish, and to get there first before anyone else has the idea. In time they hope to have refrigerated vans to collect the fish the moment it arrives in harbour, take it straight to London to cut out the "Middle man", also take it to outlying districts where it is difficult to get owing to bad distribution and lack of refrigeration. Funnily enough there was a long article in the Times about "Fish" only last week, I have sent it on to Huntly and asked him to send it to you. It says exactly what Gerald and John have been discussing these past few weeks – Their original idea was to buy boats from the Admiralty that could be converted, but there are none available as yet, besides they have since discovered that the engines wouldn't be suitable, so they may have to build in the end – but anyway for the present they have got the 'Peel Castle' – The only other trawlers G. found had no engines, and it's impossible to get Diesel engines at present. We shall wait a few weeks to see how Gerald gets on, before deciding to take up a permanent abode in Devonshire –

All this happened so quickly that it has taken my breath away – I am such a conservative old tortoise that I can see no further than having to leave this house, and getting to America.

So now I am a fishwife!! In a few years time I may be seen walking through the street of Brixham wearing clogs with a basket of fish on my head and yelling the Devon equivalent of "Sardinis [Bichi?]" – Do you suppose I'll have to mend the nets? Perhaps *Jennifer* could be taught to do this – she is quicker at grasping things than I am!

1. Captain John A. Orme, a Grenadier Guards officer and stockbroker.

22nd October 1945   Black Potts

I am going up to London to-morrow to see about my passage and hope there's a chance of my getting to you in January – I have had a letter from the European Manager of the CPR who had just heard from Mr. Coleman. Have just rec'd a letter from Huntly suggesting I bring the children and leave Nannie behind, and get another Nannie out there – I had just written to Huntly the day before asking if I could bring her and the 2 children and if I can't get a passage for Nannie I will come alone w. Jennifer – as I am sure you will understand from Nannie's letter you have just rec'd, how much the baby means to her – and from my point of view, I certainly would not want to lose her – Apart from this, she has been a *wonderful* friend to me – Angela is her 12th baby (that she has brought up from the month) and she is very proud of her "dozen". I hope Nannie will live with us until she retires

— and have intimated to her that it is her 'home' for as long as she wants it to be. When and if we are ever settled in Devonshire I shall insist on Nannie doing less work, but if she did only half of what she does now, it would be as much as most *young* Nannies do — Of course (as you probably realize) she is *practically* illiterate — can really, just manage to read and write. Any word of more than 2 syllables has her stymied, and one has to guess at what she means. But if she has the baby to look after she won't worry about anything else. Whether she is in Montreal, Richmond or Timbuctoo won't make any difference to her (I don't *think*) as long as the baby is all-right. I don't think she is very keen on the idea of going to America, but I know she longs to *show* you the baby and *Jennifer* — She has led such a sheltered life, I pray she won't be flustered by the boat, and travelling etc.

21st December 1945   Black Potts

I have asked the C.P.R. to give me passage any time after Jan. 15th — then I get back to Portsmouth from Devon, collect Nannie and Angela and deposit them at Hermione's and somehow get Jennifer and myself to Liverpool — then 9 days in a freighter with "the dynamo" and then Canada — hip hip hooray![1] The thought of *that* just keeps me plodding on — May these next few weeks fly by — I need not tell you how emotionné I feel at the thought of seeing you all again —

1. Hermione Ellison, d. 1956, was Angela's godmother and lived near Farnham in Surrey.

4th January 1946   Lupton Hotel
                                                     Churston Ferrers
                                                     Nr. Brixham, S. Devon

We had a grand Xmas dinner — roast goose with apple sauce and stuffing, mince pies and Christmas pudding! and collapsed onto the sofa — three different kinds of cakes for tea, our eyes were glazed by dinner-time and we couldn't eat any more — As we were leaving the house there was no object in saving food, and Bella cooked everything in sight, and we enjoyed the last few days in a sort of 'for tomorrow we die' outlook.

I can't tell you how dismal I felt at having to leave my beloved Black Potts. It was awful!! It *was* a small consolation that the river was rising considerably, it was very cold and foggy, and the boiler was leaking! A good time of year to leave it. I can't imagine what I would have done if I had had to leave on a beautiful day with the chestnut trees in bloom! –

7th February 1946   Lupton Hotel

Many thanks for your Jan. 28th letter. I *still* have no news, and expect to go stark staring mad and start sticking straws in my hair any day now. I rang the C.P.R. yesterday and *implored* them to get a move on. They *assured* me they would do everything possible to get me a passage, but had *no* news of anything definite. I *must* try and get to you soon or I'll burst.

The news is dreadful – strikes everywhere, cuts in rations etc. Let's hope I get to you before we go to war with Russia!!

Gerald has been to sea every day this week, and comes home absolutely whacked after banging about for hours on end in cold, wind, rain, snow, sleet etc.

Pothier ! arrived in England on leave on Sunday and is coming down here for 2 days to pay us a visit. I am just off to meet him on the 3.40 from Paddington and will post this letter on way – Am looking forward to seeing him, and hear all his news and his plans – I gather he may be off to Canada next week, and am so jealous I could die. Wouldn't it be marvellous if he could take Jennifer and me in his trunk? I wonder if it's any good my trying to get on board as a stowaway?

18th July 1946[1]   Montreal

We got back from Ivry last Sunday in time for dinner – Then Peter M. rang up and I went out with him – (!) Monday night I went dancing at the Normandie Roof with Tommy Molson – (he said he was delighted I was here in the "open season"). Tuesday Gerna came to tea, and I dined with Elsie [Duffield] and Duff. Wed. took J. and La Anderson to the Berkeley

to lunch, had hair done while darling Huntly took them to Belmont Park!!
That evening had dinner with Huntly and *let my hair down* about LIFE
with G. – didn't say *too* much – and praised him etc. – think you would
have approved of what I said! Huntly was *divine* and seemed to already
have the situation in a nutshell. Fell into bed – after 4 hectic evenings (all
so different) as had curse, and headache –

O Boogie darling I love you so much and it seems so utterly ridiculous
that I shouldn't be with you – I feel pretty confused and don't know *what* I
should do about going to Richmond – If you weren't an incredibly unselfish
person I would be there with you now. Please for God's sake *take care* of
yourself my dearest BOOGIE B. (I shall start counting the days until you
come to Devon.)

With much love to Daddy – I *do* so hope he's getting on all right and not
in pain. What a consolation that he doesn't know how ill he is.[2]

1. Ginnie had spent four months in the United States and Canada visiting family and
friends. Her relationship with Gerald had not been going well, and it was during this period
that she had her affair with Pothier Doucet in Montreal.

2. Stuart spent some months in the hospital following an operation whose nature is not
revealed in the letters.

21st July 1946   *Richmond*

I do not know what to say to you. I am trying so hard not to feel sorry for
myself – Perhaps it was better that I tell you goodbye, abruptly like that.
I might not have been able to face an ordinary goodbye. I must *realize that*
I had you for four months, and that was marvellous. Although we had all
sorts of handicaps, we have had a few wonderful times – Just to be able to
look at you and talk to you was worth everything – It was great fun to make
Jennifer's acquaintance and I have become very fond of her, and have missed
her cheery face, and happy laugh more than I can say –

I wish I could keep you darling. You know that I always want to do that –
I have no idea what is going to happen, or how everything is to be arranged
– I may hear from you tomorrow –

There are very few people in town, and all the restaurants are closing for two weeks, including the Chesterfield. We shall have to live on raw tomatoes and peaches. I am completely devastated at losing so much time with you, and of course, absolutely miserable that you are going. However, I know that you must see Angela — Darling, don't forget what you mean to me — and how much I love you. I will write again, anyhow, to the boat — Be sure to take some fruit and maybe biscuits on the boat —

24th July 1946   *Richmond*

I was thinking about my reactions yesterday, and trying to reconstruct in my mind what had happened to me since the war began — I was in agony about you — then the inbetween years were better, but I certainly got a definite nervous reaction about the end of November last. I began to lose sleep and to be very nervous and apprehensive — I am sure you must have noticed that I was nervous but I hope it didn't make you unhappy — My only wish is that you should be happy, and that I would take steps to overturn the Universe if necessary, on your behalf — Being with you for so long as four months was wonderful for me — and I am really much better, and don't lose sleep the way I did last winter. I am all right, and am going to begin to look forward to seeing you again before very long — If I can get to you, I shall. If I cannot, we must find a way for you to come back — However, it is impossible to tell now what may happen, and it is useless to dwell on anything definite at the moment — No one gets through this life without pain and drama, and sometimes tragedy — The thing is to be able somehow, some way to meet it. I always remember reading somewhere "Life is like a nettle. If you grasp it firmly, it doesn't sting you" — Of course it sometimes stings you no matter <u>what</u> you do, but in the main, it is wise advice —

Enough of all the aphorisms — I loved having you and Jennifer, and in spite of all our handicaps, it was wonderful — You are just as sweet and lovely as ever, and you are more attractive. I grew very fond of Jennifer and miss her terribly. She has great personality, which makes itself felt when she is away — In other words, you don't forget her — that is more than you can say for most people —

I will write you to the boat, and hope you will get it — God knows, I pray that all goes well —

9th August 1946   Canadian Pacific
                                                   Beaverburn

I am afraid I haven't done any writing while on board as looking after Jennifer on an overcrowded cargo boat seems to be a full time job – but will now try and give you a short description of our journey while Jennifer wrestles with one of the passengers in a corner of the lounge – We were told to be on board the Beaverburn by 10 a.m. on Friday August 2nd but as the boat wasn't even in Halifax by then, this was of course out of the question! We arose about 8, had breakfast, dressed and packed, and were ready to leave the hotel by 9.30 – then milled about and waited – and went back to our room, and watched her coming in, and went aboard about 11.30 – had lunch at 12 – and we finally set sail in a howling gale about 4 p.m. The Beaverburn was originally built to accommodate 12 passengers, and we number *36* – so it certainly doesn't *accommodate* 36 as we are jammed in like sardines. It has the same sized rooms, i.e. a small lounge, and a small dining saloon, and the same number of cabins as the 'Corrales'!! Jennifer and I are in a cabin (originally a small single cabin) with a Miss Ruby Mickie who is returning to her home in Ireland – she has been living in Toronto with her sister, and is a cousin of Mrs. James Cantlie's – (Stuart's mother) – I think she nearly passed away when she saw she had to share a tiny cabin with a child!! but after taking a look at the other passengers, she consoled herself somewhat. I thought "how awful to share a cabin with an elderly spinster who is probably very fussy" but soon realized how lucky I was – as she is by far the nicest person on board, is very sweet to Jennifer, and has a sense of humour. There is a pretty ghastly crowd of people on board, one a horrible leery old boy whom we refer to as Charles Laughton.[1] There is an English family – mama, papa, and 2 daughters aged 14 and 18. These 4 are referred to as "the mummies" or "the living dead" – they stand in a little group huddled together looking disdainfully and disapprovingly at *everyone*, and never never smile, and practically never speak – Whenever we are playing and laughing, or I am having a scene with Jennifer, they are *always* there. It is very disconcerting – they remind me of some dreadful Greek tragedy – the "shades of death" or something always there to make you feel that you shouldn't allow yourself to feel happy or gay and that you'll be dead soon anyway! They give me the creeps –

There's a family named Donovan with 2 little girls aged 6 and 4 — so fun for Jennifer to play with, though they are of course only half her size! I play racing-demon in the evening with a red-faced sturdy Scot named Mr. Bennett and a little mouse named Miss Macpherson who is very sweet.

Nearly everyone was seasick almost as soon as we left Halifax, the wind was dead ahead — and it was fairly rough. Thank goodness I didn't feel sick though Jennifer complained of a headache — We have to get up at 7 a.m. as breakfast is at 8 and one is expected to arrive as the gong sounds — There is only 1 stewardess and 1 steward so one daren't stay in bed — We unfortunately have the 1st sitting (with all the other children) lunch at 12 — and dinner at 6 — Jennifer and I have a bath at 5 and it's a scramble to dress, struggling around poor Miss Mickie and be ready for 6 o'clock dinner.

The gale 'abated' by Sat. night, and Sunday morning was calm and a thick fog. We were moving along *very* very slowly and the old foghorn was blowing off at intervals. I was standing out on deck about 10 a.m. Sunday when a most exciting thing happened — Suddenly a ship loomed up *immediately* in front of us — We held our breath, heard the 3 sharp blasts — signal for "full speed astern" — the other ship turned slightly on our starboard side, and missed us by about *three feet*! (This is *NOT* my imagination) We all rushed to the BAR as soon as it was open —

Later the fog lifted and we had one of those rare days in the Atlantic when the sky and sea are bright blue — We all sat in deck-chairs in the sun — The next day there was no wind, but a terrific swell, we had racks on the tables for 2 or 3 days.

We felt we had really had quite an adventure in the fog when we learned afterwards that *grain explodes* if it gets wet — so we thought if we had been hit, we would have had to go on board the Fort Ste. Croix and return to Halifax while the grain and all our luggage went to the bottom —

We passed Bishop's rock this morning, and are supposed to dock in London to-morrow.

Our only other excitements have been a school of porpoises and a flight of wild geese (!?) God knows where *they* were going. We have just passed a few fishing trawlers but I didn't recognize Gerald's among them!

I have a slight sinking feeling in my stomach, it is strange to be going back to England to no home — and I keep wondering what news I'll have of Daddy — We are passing the Devonshire coast, it is needless to say, raining, which makes me think of cold and seagulls, and more rain – and boiled turbot with photographic paste sauce, and then I try and switch my mind back to Canada, to that glorious sunshine, Nellie's cooking, martinis at the Ritz, filet mignon at Café Martin, the hot baths!, the loons and the bullfrogs at Ivry, the silver birches, Huntly's trees – and all the glorious times I have had on my *wonderful* holiday – It was far, far more wonderful even than I had expected, because I expected a lot!

1. Charles Laughton, 1899–1962, British stage and film actor.

2nd September 1946   Lupton Hotel

I will try and remember some of our "goings-on" to relate to you. We arrived on Monday the 12th – had a hectic time unpacking – We have 3 rooms next each other. G. & I have a large double room overlooking the garden. Jennifer has a tiny room next door, and Nannie and Angela are in the 3rd with cot; buffer chair; store of linen in one corner; washstand covered in odds and ends; a spirit stove and saucepan in the grate; chairs covered in clothes and hot water bottles; and nappies hanging on lines at the window. As Gerald is no longer fishing he had to leave "the Dungeon" so all our possessions are bunged into this one room.[1] Luckily we have 2 desks, 2 wardrobes, 2 beds, a washstand, a dressing table, several chairs. We also have all our clothes, papers, a wireless, 3 prs. rubber boots, a primus stove, oilskins, a typewriter, all our trunks, tins of stores lying on the floor, and a *rubber dinghy*. Just *why* we have the rubber dinghy I haven't quite made out yet, and haven't "gotten around" to asking Gerald for an explanation.

Gerald rec'd a message from Harold Coyde, his skipper, that the starboard engine on "Peel Castle" had seized up and was beyond repair. This awful news was almost too much for poor G, and as he rushed into the hall, the heavy brocade curtains and gilded pelmet went with him. It is really too depressing as the new trawlers won't be ready before Xmas, so now there will be no money coming in. G. has gone on the beer-wagon to save money – Peel Castle's engines overhauled would take 3 months and cost £700, so is not worth it. Gerald is either going to sell her, or convert her into a motor-yacht and live on her – probably the former – as it would be too expensive to convert.

In the meantime he is going dotty if he has to go on living here – and we *must* try and get some sort of a house. We looked at one yesterday that we *might* be able to get. It is *perfectly hideous* – a red and stucco villa in Brixham overlooking the bay (lovely view) faces *North*; the sun practically never reaches it, it has no garden, but it *has* got a "cat's lavatory" or small grass plot in front about 2 ft. X 2 ft. where we could put the pram on warm (?!) days – no telephone, but it has electricity and gas. 3 recep, 3 bed and 1 (antique) bath first floor up, and same on 2nd floor up. It is perfectly bloody but rent is £150 a year and I could manage to run it on my own –

I have been writing for *hours* and really must stop. (Finished on Sept. 3rd 1946, just 7 years after the beginning of the war – doesn't it seem incredible?)

1. At this stage Gerald was concentrating on running the fishing company rather than going out on trawlers himself.

13th September 1946   *Richmond*

What I would do without the good Huntly, God knows – He has been wonderful to me, and so sweet about you – I think the time you were there with him alone made a great difference in his feeling about you – He has mentioned it to me several times – So it was just as well that I went away – Human relationships are so terribly important, and sometimes so very delicate, and depend on such strange and unexpected and unheard of things, that Life at best is a gamble –

I am sorry that the sweet Mrs. E[llison]. is having a marital disillusionment, but, if it doesn't go, it just doesn't – and there's no use in hanging on beyond a certain time. I do think that the alternative is, sometimes, as bad as what you have, but that is for everyone to decide for himself – Especially men, are so often just the victim of glands – If they recover from that, they might be all right as husbands – I am beginning to be almost a man hater – They seem so utterly stupid to me, and they have made such a mess of this world, which could be quite enchanting if they had any sense – However, they have proved they haven't, so that's that.

Lilian Warren wants to send you a parcel or two so I gave her your address and suggested some Brunswick Stew, raisins etc. The shipping is tied up in strikes, but let us hope it will be moving soon. Poor old Truman is a complete weakling, and can't do anything but give in. We will have inflation, if he keeps at it, and I shall have to keep my wits about me not to get caught in another one like 1929 – "Fresh crack in Wall St." – Do you remember? – We have had one small sized crash already – Most of my things are good and should be safe, but I am going to keep my eyes open just the same –

19th September 1946   Lupton Hotel

Yesterday G. and I started out (in the driving rain) to try and get a few things done about the house. It is practically an *impossibility* to get *anything* done – and very discouraging. The electrician says that *if* he can get some plugs he *might* be able to put in 2 power points – but the Brixham electric plant is on its last legs anyway – and one shouldn't use the fires much in the *really* cold weather because of the heavy load etc. etc. The electricity is on D.C. so we can't use our wireless, and can't buy a new or an old one, the refrigerator can't be made D.C. Anyway the electricity costs *10D a unit*!! We *might* be able to get gas points but we cannot get gas fires for hire or buy – and so on and so on! The only 2nd hand carpet we can buy costs £50 so we have given that up! This morning I went to see the Fuel Overseer, and filled in forms, in order to get our ration of coal and anthracite. Then to the Food Office where I got Angela's months ration of orange juice (2 bottles) and *dropped one in the street* – then to three different drapers to try and get gingham for the smock Jennifer must have at school – but no one had any gingham. Then went on a tour in search of cigarettes, got 1 package – The chemist told me where I could get a box of matches, then stood in queue and got our month's chocolate ration; by that time it was 12.30 and no time left to do any scrubbing.

Gerald has started a class of Looe Redwings at Torbay – small racing dinghies – He has ordered one – they cost about £130 and may be delivered by Xmas so he hopes to have some winter's sailing!

28th September 1946   *Richmond*

Martha McN. has given me an embroidered head band and belt for Jennifer. I shall send it in the next parcel. I address all of them to Lupton Hotel, not knowing what else to do, so you had better make enquiries about them. 8 go from Montreal — 4 from Denmark and 3 or 4 from here each month. I have some Ness Café [sic] to send contributed by Lewis Warren. All you have to do is put a teaspoonful in a cup, and pour boiling, or very hot, water, over it! I had some, and found it quite good.

    Darling, of course you must know that I am perfectly miserable about your being there. You are almost the only thing that matters to me. I have spent the best part of my life trying to make your life happy, and when I realize what you have to endure, I feel I am going quite mad — I do not <u>think</u> you <u>can</u> go on like that. Of course, you don't tell me what <u>you</u> say, and I can't make out what stand you are taking. I think Rosemary is right — There is a complete note of instability there, I think — I always like to be fair, in any case, but fair, or not fair, you must have a chance to be happy — Don't let anyone tell you that you aren't an adorable person, because all sane people think so — Yes, I knew about what H.R.D. [Huntly] did — wasn't it just like him? My impulse would be for you to see a good "lawyer" when you go to London. Let him advise you <u>how</u> to proceed, because you <u>must</u> be in the right, and the other one on the wrong side, if anything should happen — I wish <u>so much</u> that I was there — You must tell me everything you wish to tell me — You know I love you more than anyone in the world — These things happen to many people and no one can judge others —[1]

1. This paragraph refers to Ginnie's current dissatisfaction with her marriage, and her consideration of beginning divorce proceedings. Gerald was no doubt having difficulty adjusting to civilian life and was drinking heavily at the time. However, the couple stayed together and remained married until Gerald's death in 1981.

7th October 1946   Lupton Hotel

Bathed, dressed at Cr[anmer] Court and joined Gerald and Robin and Vera Sinclair at the Mirabelle at 8 o'clock where we had quite a good dinner!!?[1] Ran into Sammy McLean who I had last seen at Chez Martin in Montreal with the Duffields in July – We then went on to the 400 – Gerald and Robin were in dinner-jackets, Vera in a dinner dress, and I wore my dressy black afternoon dress (as I hadn't taken any evening clothes to London). *Believe it or not* they refused to let us in, as I was not properly dressed – Can you imagine the *pomposity* of a dirty little night club in these days of shortages of clothes, of coupons, and of *everything* – Two jews with bleached blondes pushed past us, and sailed in – Gerald remarked that if you haven't got a jewish nose and a Rolls Royce there is no point going to London nowadays and I believe he is right.

Next week I must start in and scrub the house with a vengeance as the P.C. furniture arrives on the 21st and Barker's on the 24th – There are still no gas points in the house, no cooker – and the boiler, gutters and windows still to be cleaned – and the *entire* house – We have practically no carpets or curtains, but are just going to do without. With luck we may be more or less installed by beginning of Nov. The very un-aristocratic address is as follows:

> Highfield
> Berry Head Road
> Brixham

Thank God it at least is not called Aqua Vista, the Nest or Veryan. Edward suggests "Potter's Squat" – I will cable you when we move in, otherwise please continue to send letters to Lupton.

1. Cranmer Court is an apartment block in Chelsea, London, where both Bougie and Ginnie lived in the final years of their respective lives and where these letters were found after Ginnie's death. At this point Ginnie would have been staying in one of the guest rooms.

20th October 1946   *Richmond*
We have abolished controls over most foods – It doesn't mean we get much more – Meat has soared to such heights that people who aren't well off can't buy it. Naturally, everything is in a mess – but these conditions will straighten themselves out eventually.

There was a beautiful concert on Friday, given by a woman named <u>Jonas</u> — She is a Pole, and now in this country — She refugeed to South America, after seeing her entire family shot by the Germans. She is said to have walked 1000 miles in order to find a <u>boat</u> to take her out of Europe — She plays divinely on the piano.

I have just given Nana's <u>harp music</u> to the Public Library — as it was <u>Civil War</u> music — and they are interested. We may give them Nana's harp. It will be taken care of.

29th October 1946   *Richmond*

Stuart and I went to the Country Club today for lunch — there were hundreds of people and I only saw three I knew — It is very hoi polloi now, in fact all the public places here have deteriorated since the war —

The lectures, plays and concerts have started in full force. I get very tired of lectures, and last night I was made quite ill by hearing one Mr. Markham, who has lived for years in the Balkans, talk most pessimistically about our slim chance of avoiding war with Russia! All I have to say is, that I think we might as well commit hari-kari and let the Tartars have the world, as go in for another war —

22nd November 1946   Lupton Hotel

We have been to the house again all day to-day and the rest of us plan to move on Tuesday — giving me Monday to shop, get the ration cards sorted out, register at the local shops etc. I took Gerald's ration card to the local Food Office, asked if anything was needed before I registered him for milk, was told *no* but that I *had* to register him at Drew's — the nearest dairy. At Drew's they told me they couldn't register him without registration card; went back to the Food Office where they said they couldn't give me his registration card without his identity card; went back to the dairy to explain couldn't get it to-day as G. had gone to Exeter for the day (with identity card) — All this for *2 pints a week* — Asked about tuberculin tested milk for Angela — Drew's didn't keep it and said I should go to Jane's.[1] Jane's said they *might* supply it but I would have to call for it every day — Jennifer is rated as an adult and gets the same ration of "un-tested" as us —

1. Milk certified free of the tuberculosis bacillus was available in the UK from 1923, but compulsory slaughter of infected cows did not begin until 1959. For further information, see P. Atkins and P. Brassley, "Mad Cows and Englishmen," *History Today* 46 (September 1996): 14–17.

25th November 1946   *Richmond*

I have collected a few more things and will send them off before the <u>coal</u> strike grows worse. If we can't down John L. Lewis this time we are lost.

30th November 1946   *Richmond*

I was amused to hear about Jennifer's fights in school, but she is certainly very pugnacious — Everyone who undertakes to look out for her will have to make an effort to put a little of "the fear of God" into her — However, her determination and independence will be good in this new and difficult world we are having to live in, and, if she can put those qualities into the right channel, she may become a real person — The fact that she isn't jealous is a good sign for her character. Have you ever thought of having her take some religious instruction? Is there a Sunday school to which she can go? It is rather necessary for her to live in "the tradition", and to know something about spiritual values — Of course, one has to be careful about <u>what kind</u> of instruction she has — She is too intelligent to just swallow anything. In this terribly animal world, which I personally abhor, I believe it is necessary for these young children to learn something about the roots of <u>English civilization,</u> which after all, is inherited from Greece and the Jews! — We live by it, without realizing it, and you can only make a character by the day by day instruction — All children, or most of them, are born savages — Angela seems to be different — However, you can't tell at her age — A mother has a big job — and when I see all these pathetic looking morons rushing into matrimony and motherhood, it makes me shudder — As for husbands, the less said the better. I haven't much opinion of them —

8th December 1946   *Richmond*

I have been thinking constantly this past week of you, wondering how you were getting along − I wish I didn't worry so much about you. It would be better if I could stop it. This d——n coal strike is over, thank God. I began to have nightmares about how all the people would be fed, and get their fuel − All shipments were cancelled, but I think the parcels I sent you got off. I hope so −

Florie had a tea-party Thursday afternoon − and that evening I went to "Arms and the Man" given by the Abingdon Barter Theatre group, run by Bob Porterfield − They got some money from the State, and Bob made a speech before the curtain, saying it was the first State theatre in the U.S.[1] They did the dear old Shaw play very well −

1. The Barter Theatre, Abingdon, was founded during the Depression in 1933 by the actor Robert Porterfield. Audience members brought produce to barter in exchange for a ticket.

11th December 1946   Highfield
                                                    Berry Head Road
                                                  Brixham S. Devon

Not having kept house for nearly a year, I found I was terribly 'out of touch' with rationing, and until now haven't had to cope with B.U.'s (Bread units) and *still* don't understand it! − The weekly rations are the same as they have been for *years* i.e. 2 ounces butter, 1 ounce lard, 4 slices bacon etc. but the *points* are all different and seem to be *more*, i.e. things take more points. We have 32 a month now instead of 20 but a tin of tongue for instance, is *60* points. *What* I would have done without your parcels from home, I simply *can't imagine*!! The meat is still 1/2-worth per week and 7D for children. Vegetables are very expensive − and the egg ration still one per month − so you can imagine how thrilled I am when your parcels roll in − We miss all the wonderful fresh vegetables and the eggs we had at B. Potts but we do get plenty of *fish*.

As I explained before this hideous semi detached villa we live in is built of tiles, stucco, brick and stone − all thrown together into a veritable nightmare – We face North, looking out over Torbay and back onto a cliff so the sun never reaches us, but as there is practically none anyway this doesn't matter.

Brixham is a most picturesque little place – a very narrow main street where dogs, prams, old men, old women, shoppers etc. are continually milling about, and it is like an obstacle race to try and drive through it. 9 times out of 10 there is a 'blockage' when 2 lorries try to pass each other and then all the residents join in, shouting, giving advice and instructions. It is quite amusing if you are not in a hurry – I am beginning to understand the Devonshire language a bit better. It is completely lacking in grammar, has no h's and the r's are verrry rrrolled – This morning shopping I would have said, "Good morning, how are you. Isn't it cold?" I heard an old man say " 'alloa – 'ow goes it? Sharrrp, ain't it?" Nearly everyone in Devonshire appears to be lame, and certainly *everyone* is hideous – I have never seen so many different kinds of ugly faces. I walk along in my old coat, a bandana over my head and a shopping bag full of cabbages and leeks and wonder how many years it will be before I look like old Mrs. Smarrrdon, or if I already resemble her a little.

31st January 1947   Highfield

"Come to glorious Devon for a restful holiday, and bask in the sun amid the tropical palms . . . the warmest spot in England" – etcetera, etcetera, or so it is supposed to be – Our milk was brought to us this morning *on a sledge* – We have been literally snowed in for several days – the only other person who delivered anything was the postman. He trudged up the hill and brought us a few soggy bills, and the "Highway Code" – the latter not much use at present as Violet the Van is lying on the hard completely snowed up – and no cars are on the streets.[1] Apparently England has had a record blizzard, and no one in Brixham has seen anything like it within living memory. It is an extraordinary sight to walk along Brixham's main street – most of the populace are throwing snowballs, and all work has virtually ceased – The various costumes range from bits of sacking tied around the feet, to old girls in borrowed Wellingtons with fishermen's stockings pulled over them, giving the effect of piano legs; some people have mufflers tied around their heads so only their eyes are showing — Gerald looks very 'picturesque' in fishermens trousers, Wellingtons and stockings, an enormous leather jerkin, bright yellow driving gloves, and the inevitable Guards' beret and pipe! The whole scene in Fore St. is like a Brueghel paint-ing — A few intrepid trawlers go out to sea. We watched one when it came in to-day and heard one of the fishermen say "We 'ad a proper dusting we did, sometimes it was so thick we didn't know where we was to" (Brixham for where we were). It was all very interesting "pour la statistique" like the floods at Windsor, but after a few days begins to pall, especially as there are now no vegetables left in the shops, and we are told the milk won't be delivered to-morrow. The milk was delivered to our dairy yesterday on a tractor from Fish Farm, and when they got to Berry Head Road, a small boy ran in front and shovelled the show —

My days are more or less the same: — get up at 7.30, leave house by 8.20 and take Jennifer and Wendy to school, fetch baby's milk, shop, get back by 9.30 or 10, make beds, prepare lunch, do as much housework as possible before cooking lunch — lunch at 1, wash up, clean kitchen etc. and stop at 3 in order to rush in to Paignton to collect Jennifer, drop Wendy at Fish Farm and collect "buckshee" milk, back at 4 or 4.15 — have a rest, get tea, wash up; put Jennifer to bed; get dinner, wash up; prepare breakfast tray etc., finish about 11 — and have a hot bath and fall into bed — [2]

Gerald has been in his element since the blizzard, shovelled snow, etc and brought our food up from the grocer on his back — He certainly can get things done, as no one else can get a telephone or a cooker —

1. The Highway Code is a UK Government publication setting out the laws of the road.
2. Wendy McCarthy, b. 1941, from 1963 Colley, later became a lawyer.

10th February 1947   *Richmond*

I know I am going completely crazy if this cold spell in England doesn't end, and if the radios and newspapers don't stop the harrowing stories. I go about wringing my hands in a frenzy of anxiety, and just pray that you will be all right. If it gets any worse, I think all of you had better take the first boat for the U.S.A. Of course it has been dreadfully cold here but it is easier to keep warm in the house – It has snowed in Florida, lately, and the orange crop is ruined.

Today, to the Club to hear Erica Mann, daughter of the (former German) novelist, speak about Germany.[1] *They are American citizens now, and she has been in Germany as a correspondent for a newspaper since the War – She says the Germans are as arrogant as ever and completely ungrateful for the millions we send to help them live through this awful period –*

1. Thomas Mann, 1875–1955, a German-born novelist and Nobel Prize winner in 1929.

11th February 1947   Highfield

You seem to be so worried about us, Boogie B., that I think I'll send a cable to you to-morrow to reassure – we are all-right so please don't worry about us – Thanks to you we have plenty of food and warm clothes – and we are very lucky *so far* that we haven't had our electricity cut off like most of England – though I hear it shall be shortly. Luckily we cook on gas and have gas fires in the nursery, dining-room (where we sit) and my bedroom. The pressure is pretty low but it *is* still going. The drawing room has a coal fire but too cold to sit in there at the moment so we have shut the room up. So far no burst pipes, and we've got our ration of anthracite, so we have hot water – As long as I can have a hot bath at night to thaw out before going to bed, I can stand almost anything! Hot water is surely the greatest luxury – also the greatest *necessity* – in this world.

We have . . . had Florie's Xmas parcel to the children, and I'll write to her to-morrow. In the last few days we have also rec'd 4 January parcels from Ye Olde Cheese (list is in other letter) and 1 parcel for Nannie from Denmark – the first Denmark parcels for some time, but I expect the others will turn up shortly. I can *honestly say that I don't know what we would do* without your parcels. They really make all the difference in our lives, as everything you send is on 'points' here, though most of the things are unobtainable anyway – The Cdn. Cheddar in last "Olde Cheese" boxes is *delicious.* I do not see how anyone can exist on the present rations in this country without extras – especially in this cold weather – the cheese and bacon are still 2 ounces a week, and as for the "points" there is so little choice these days – 32 points a month each, but for instance, a tin of syrup is 20, a tin of peaches 16. An ox tongue is something like 64! A comedian on the wireless the other night said he had just proposed to a girl – "She's not at all pretty but she has some friends in the States who send her parcels" –

21st February 1947   Highfield

It has been snowing steadily since 8 o'clock last night, not just a gentle snowfall but a sho'nuff blizzard – and the *usual* Easterly gale. Great waves are breaking over the breakwater, and the lighthouse at the end is blotted out by snow and spray – The only thing we can see is the road in front of the house (covered in snow); about a dozen or so trawlers and yachts anchored in the outer harbour, facing the wind; and the dim outline of the breakwater with the grey angry sea beyond. I am getting sick of seeing those same boats facing the same direction! It has been blowing an Easterly gale for weeks on end and I am *not* exaggerating when I say that we haven't *seen* the sun (not even for 5 mins) since the middle of January – I think this last fall of snow has made it a bit warmer, after the *bitter* cold of the last few days. I don't think I have ever been so cold, in fact I know I haven't.

As you probably saw in the papers, the South West has had electricity cuts as well as the rest of England – the power is off between 9–12 and 2–4. This doesn't affect us much except when we need a light in the dark kitchen – and we have electric fires in the study, night nursery, and G's dressing-room, but they aren't needed at that time of day – We still have enough coal for a fire in the drawing-room – now that the new mantelpiece is in, and there's felt on the floor, the room is less like a barn – We haven't any more anthracite for the boiler, but G. was able to get a little coke so we still have hot water. The gas pressure has been appalling, but at least it's still going, and we *can* cook (*just*) though it takes about 20 minutes to boil a kettle – Thank Goodness the gas is better to-day – the gas fire in the nursery gave out hardly any heat yesterday – We keep Angie warm by wrapping her up and putting her in her pram in the dining room with a hot water bottle. All this glorious snow seems such a *waste* here. I would like to be somewhere in the hills with a pr. of skis and needless to say, a steam-heated house!

Most of the papers and magazines that are still able to be printed are *lambasting* Shinwell and Attlee and the Labour Govt. in general.[1] It is incredible that they have been able to make *such* a bloody mess in *such* a short time. I gather the "Daily Worker" and such papers, however, say the fuel crisis is due to "Tory mismanagement in the past" – (They even hint that *Jack Frost* is a Tory! and has sent us this weather.)

Wednesday February 26th

The weather has definitely improved, the house is much warmer – the glass has been put back outside the kitchen, and the new drawing-room fire is a great success, so now I can write with more ease – my chillblains [*sic*] are fast going, I can even get my ring on my finger, in fact the thermometer in the hall is up as high as 50° and it is wonderful not to be aching with the cold any more.

On Sunday the *SUN was shining* for the first time in something like 35 days – I took Jennifer down on the quay in the morning and we *stood in* the sun. That afternoon Gerald and I and Jennifer went for a long walk along Berry Head. It was really beautiful, the sun was glorious, and the snow was sparkling and scrunchy – the sea a bright blue and the distant hills covered in snow. I thought all the exercise might tire out the 'little darling', but she was as fresh as a daisy and as cheeky as ever – She is certainly a difficult creature. Monday night she had a spanking which had little or no effect, last night she was put to bed immediately after tea – and just said it was "great fun" –

Mrs. Bartlett comes in most days to cook lunch – a great help! so I only have to get the dinner.[2] I am still a perfect fool at cooking but in a way I am glad I *have* to do it now, so I may learn something! Thank God for the 'made up dishes' you have sent me – the "Kraft Dinner" is delicious –

1. Emanuel (Manny) Shinwell, 1884–1994, from 1970 Baron Shinwell, was a British Labour politician first elected as a member of Parliament in 1922. He was minister for Fuel and Power 1945–47 and chairman of the Labour Party 1964–67.

2. Mrs. Bartlett (Barty) was the cook to the Potter family from 1947 to 1953.

28th February 1947   *Montreal*

I went to see Henry V. . . . I should love to see it again, and be able to take in all the fine points of the production. It was a good thing to see what can be done with Shakespeare in the movies — The longer I live the more I love "Will" — It is certainly a wonderful and charming movie —

We had a very comfortable journey up here — not a very long wait in Washington. They let us have two bedrooms — usually they connect but this time some official of the Railway was sandwiched in between. Some man got on at N.Y. and joined said official and I heard him say, "My God, here I am on this bone shaker again". I remembered it in the night when at New Haven, Springfield and Bellow Falls, I was thrown almost out of bed by the bumps. I think every train in New England adds something to the Montrealer in the night — Huntly met us with François and we came up to the house for our second breakfast! —

I forgot to tell you that I lost my underclothes on the train — As we were nearing the St. Lawrence and a wild wind was blowing the snow about, I didn't relish the idea of getting off, minus my <u>drawers</u> — I searched frantically, and finally rang for the porter and called Stuart — The porter was larger than Stuart and you can visualize the three of us in the small space, throwing bed clothes about in the search. The porter said, "Madam, no one would want your underclothes" and I agreed with him, but almost added, "You do not realize that my corset is a French antique". In the end, I discovered that in a fit of absent mindedness, I had packed them in the bottom of my dressing bag — so the day was saved — I must now go and try to buy something to wear on my <u>head</u> on the train —

7th May 1947   Highfield

I must go and have a bath before the water gets cold — Thank God it's *fairly* warm at the moment, as we are *not allowed* by the *Gov't* to have a gas or electric fire until next October!!! Children under 3 and people over 70 are exempted — so we have one in the nursery in the mornings, but the *damned* nursery fire doesn't work very well. They have promised us a new one, but Angela will probably be *over 3* before we get it.

? June 1947   Highfield
From *Ye Olde English Cheese*

May parcel to *Jennifer* rec'd June 14th

1 tin of *burst* maple syrup	2 tins spiced ham
1 pkt. Batamix	1 tin chicken
2 pkts. noodle soup	1 tin pears
2 pkts. hot chocolate	1 tin steak & onions
1 fruit cake	1 tin olive oil
1 Canabec cheese	1 tin sausages

May parcel to *Nannie* rec'd June 14th

1/2 lb. tea	1 tin pears
1 fruit cake	1 tin chicken
1 Canabec cheese	1 tin maple syrup
1 pkt. dates	1 tin pears
2 pkts. noodle soup	

May parcel to *me* rec'd June 25th

2 bars chocolate	2 tins steak & mushrooms
8 pkts. noodle soup	4 tins steak and kidney
2 pkts. dates	

There is also the *April* parcel to me which I don't think I have acknowledged – rec'd May –

1 fruit cake	1 box nuts
1 pkt. dried apricots	1 box dates
1 tin corn syrup	1 box stuffed dates
1 tin chili con carne	1 tin peaches
1 tin chicken	1 tin steak & onions
1/2 lb. tea	

I am sure I rec'd *at least* 2 more parcels of this 'type' as I have 4 tins of corn syrup, several tins of chili con carne (very good), stuffed dates, nuts, etc. but though I thought I kept a very careful check, I *cannot* find the other 'April' lists, and don't believe I have ever acknowledged them.

Am enclosing list of lovely parcel from Christian's [see below] with the *delicious* little Vienna sausages and corned beef loaf.

The *Smithfield ham* also arrived and has been duly cooked according to instructions and eaten with much relish – a god-send these warm evenings to give Gerald with salad on his return (late) from racing etc. A *thousand* thanks.

Have also rec'd a parcel from Huntly – the handwriting looks like Nellie [Clark]'s.

A few days ago rec'd a parcel for Jennifer from Huntly in *your* hand-writing, containing a wool scarf, a scrap-book and 2 adorable *knitted turtles* holding large luxurious bars of soap.

and last week the *DIVINE* parcel containing:

Kleenex (O joy)

3 bars of my favourite soap

a perfectly beautiful pale blue cardigan for Nannie

a jar of 30-day cream

and 2 prs. of Nylons –

What a parcel – and a *million* thanks my dearest Boogie B. God knows what I would do without all this *wonderful* food, but it worries me to think how much money you are spending on us.

Enclosed with letters:

USA Customs Declaration dated 22.4.47 for food parcel from R.L. Christian Co. Inc., 206 N. 5th St., Richmond, Va. as follows:

		$
2 cans spaggetti [*sic*]	2 lb.	.30
1 cake cheese	5 1/2 lb.	4.00
2 can peaches	3 5/8 lb.	.80
2 pkt. dates	1 lb.	.54
2 lb. evap. peaches	2 lb.	.80
2 can corn beef	1 1/2 lb.	.98
6 tin sausage	1 1/2 lb.	1.20
		8.62

10th July 1947   Highfield

We were all (i.e. Mrs. Bartlett, Nannie and I!) intrigued to hear of Princess
Elizabeth's engagement to Philip of Greece – and spent a good part of the
day looking at newspapers etc., also listening to the broadcast of the King
unveiling the memorial window in Westminster Abbey – very moving.

12th August 1947   *Richmond*

*Naturally I am very worried about the state of things in the world, and es-
pecially England, because of the people, and because England is enormously
important to us, as well. I am trying to understand the world, and to find my
own philosophy to meet it – I have read Toynbee's Study of History and the
new Philosophy, known as Existentialism which came out of France when the
Germans left –*[1] *It is primarily a <u>German</u> philosophy and stems from Hegel
and others. It is purely materialistic and my "reason" rejects it – and I think
that it makes Life seem quite impossible. I <u>need</u> something more – About
England – I have great confidence in the English people, and I think England will work out of the trouble. It will be hard, but she has been in trouble
before, and had very terrible periods all through her history. I do not think
she will ever be like France – The French always try to live by "reason" and
it doesn't work. Englishmen are always more profound than they <u>seem</u>, and
they aren't a bit logical, but somehow, they manage better than the French –
My guess is that they will recover – We <u>must</u> help, because we <u>need</u> them –
not for any sentimental reasons – If we are <u>patient</u> it is because it is for <u>our</u>
best interests – We talk about the Russians over here all the time – No one
knows what they are up to, but most of the intelligent people I know think that
they wish to keep Europe in a turmoil because they want to plant Communism
everywhere – Then, as 1/3 of the country is completely devastated and they
have practically none of the comforts of life, the Party in Moscow is afraid for
the <u>people</u> to know how much better off we are, and so, the "iron curtain" –
There is a <u>remote</u> possibility that they might use the Atomic bomb against us,
but they know that we are going ahead with everything in the way of weapons
– <u>Our</u> business is to keep the American people from going to sleep!*

Everything is <u>very</u> expensive here – We are in an inflation period – Food

is exhorbitant [sic], but that can't go on forever — and the demands of Labour will have to come to a stop some time — We made a big mistake when we let the "controls" go — I was certain of that — one gets very <u>tired</u> of controls, but after a <u>world</u> war, everything is completely upset — and now our meat is so expensive that almost no one can eat it — I am weary of all these things, and have come to the conclusion that the small simple things are the only ones worth anything — such as seeing Angela play with Biddy, or Jennifer having a swimming lesson, or going on a picnic!! Alas, my mind works overtime, and I read all these abstruse books, and fall to sleep, exhausted with an hour of Taoism, or the Fourfold Root of the Principle of Sufficient reason —

Ian Reid's book has just come from Jo — Stuart took it at once and read it.[2] He found it most interesting. I haven't had a chance to look at it —

1. Arnold Toynbee, *A Study of History*, abridged by D. C. Somervell (London: Oxford University Press, 1946).

2. Ian Reid, *Prisoner at Large* (see the letter of 27 May 1945).

8th September 1947   *Richmond*

It is my experience that <u>most</u> men are selfish. As you say, G. is very intense — and I am afraid that J. is like him. You will have to find a way to teach her to be <u>unselfish</u> — It has its points, of course, and its drawbacks — If you are to do anything well, you have to be concentrated on it, but if it is something trivial, the game doesn't seem worth the candle — There is no doubt about G. being very selfish — He is full of élan and can get things done, if he <u>wishes</u> to do them — The fact that he has his friends all the time, and doesn't accept yours, is very stupid, of course — I am afraid that the Englishman considers himself "lord of all he surveys" — It is a hangover from the past. They have been brought up that way, and think that anything else is beneath them.

However, matrimony is difficult under almost any circumstances — God knows I have never had much to say in its favour — You have to think of the alternative — What would that be? I have a very independent spirit, and things irk me more than most — There have been many times when I have felt I couldn't "make the grade" — I have gone along all this time with a 100% <u>negation</u> — To me, that is maddening — You have the opposite to contend *with. There would always be something to contend with, in any matrimonial arrangement, so one has to decide whether it is worth it or not, with the alternative in view — I am afraid that you are too sweet about everything, but we will discuss all this when I see you —*

Stuart seems fairly well — He can't do anything, and I don't see how he stands it, as he has very few resources and isn't interested in many things or many people, but outside of occasional sarcasm in my direction, and others as well, he is usually in a good temper — He has never thanked me for anything I have ever done for him, but I am used to that, so I can laugh. The situation is absurd, of course — However, I am not any worse off than 9/10 of women. You can see that I am a feminist.

18th September 1947   Highfield

I shopped with Jennifer all Tuesday afternoon and managed to buy her 2 nightgowns, 2 prs. socks and 3 pr. pants. This came to £5 and *20 coupons*. I noted this with some depression, as our next lot of coupons (20) must last from October 1st to March!! It is *ridiculous* that we should be expected to clothe children on this amount! The basic petrol ration comes off shortly, everyone is furious at this latest cut, and fats, meat, etc. are to be cut. It is really *pitiful* after 2 whole years of so-called peace. Gerald missed all the news of the cuts as he was in Spain [on an ocean race to Santander] when it was announced, so you can imagine how he felt when the news *sank in* on his return —

13th October 1947   Highfield

Everyone [in London] was very full of the latest political shuffle — i.e. a polish jew and conscientious objector being made *Minister of War*!![1] Someone said that if he was as good at his new job as he was as Minister of Fuel, we wouldn't have any war either! Really this government seems to have gone completely 'crackers'.

1. Emanuel Shinwell.

15th October 1947   *Richmond*

I heard from Canadian-Pacific in England. They will deliver to you the letter I wrote guaranteeing your support. Remind them. I have to decide what to do about meeting you in Halifax – Stuart can't do it. It means 3,000 miles on a train for me – going and coming back here – I feel that I want very much to do it, but I don't want to overdo anything because I must be well, while you are here – I don't think, either, that I can expect Huntly to do it. He is wonderful, but can't do as much as he once did – and has been quite down and out with a terrible cold and cough, lately. I should never forgive myself if I was the cause of doing anything to handicap him. He is looking forward with great pleasure to your visit – We will have to think it out. I think you and the others will need a two or three day rest before coming on to Richmond, and should stop in Montreal for that time – My idea is to be here Christmas, where we can do as we please, and let the children have a good time and the run of the apartment, where we can have a tree, and toys – etc. I can get Anderson, after the holidays I think, to coach Jennifer in the late afternoon, so she won't fall behind.

21st October 47   *Richmond*

I wish I could tell you exactly what to do about the vaccinations – It was New York which had the small-pox scare and demanded that everyone should be done – You are not going to New York. As I found I could get the apartment here for Christmas, and feeling that it might be better to have that here, where the children could have the run of the place – and not be in someone else's house, I had the idea that it would be better to come here first. You can take a two day's rest in Montreal and then come down on that comfortable train to Washington – Of course I don't know what "the ropes" are about entering this country, except what you went through the last time. It is, perhaps, better to meet all the possible demands over there – and I agree with Jennifer that it is better to have it over with before you leave –

(There are no further letters from Virginia Dickinson Reynolds [Bougie] until 1951.)

23rd October 1947   Highfield

I was sorry not to get to London this week, as the wedding might have been fun, but I couldn't go for various reasons, and then I heard from Rosemary that "Mipsie" would be there, and very much to the fore – as her Elizabeth was one of the child bridesmaids – [1] Well, I just didn't feel up to facing 'Mipsie', I haven't seen her since the débâcle and don't particularly want to – Anyway I had the curse, and my new hat wasn't ready! When I saw May Graham the other day she said that "A. sent me her love (!?) and was *very hurt* that I had dropped her" – Can you imagine the nerve? I told May that I was sorry I couldn't discuss the 'drop' with her, but that I did not wish to see A. May said "There must be some misunderstanding"! and added that "I don't know what the trouble is, but you know *all* men fall for Anne, they can't help it and neither can she" so I told her that I wouldn't be such a fool as to be stuffy about *that* sort of situation! and assured her that was *not* my reason. (Well it's not, it's the lying and hypocrisy)

I am feeling much better – and Angie is all-right again, having had a high temp. when she cut her last tooth – G is busy skinning dogfish to-day and smells to High Heaven! We have just had a letter from a pompous local asking us to *tea* – G says he won't go unless he can wear his boots and fish-y overalls –

1. A press cutting is enclosed with this letter covering the marriage of Captain the Honourable David Bethell and Ursula James. The guests included Princess Elizabeth and Princess Margaret. "Mipsie" is a nickname for Anne Anson.

19th November 1947   Highfield

We are all agog over the Royal Wedding to-morrow and intend to spend most of the day listening to the wireless! I shall *scream* if I leave here [for the States] before the film is out, and if I just miss it in US! as I would like to pop in every day and just see the "news"![1] The wedding pictures aren't being shown in Brixham until *Dec. 11th* so hope and pray they will be shown in Paignton before that –

I hope you will not be too shocked by my appearance! Have no new clothes, and look a little haggard in face and barrel-shaped round middle.

Jennifer is rapidly becoming like a small elephant, the *top* half is all right, but what are we going to do about her *rump*?

1. The wedding of Princess Elizabeth and Prince Philip, Duke of Edinburgh.

19th April 1948[1]   Highfield

Well at last! I have the time to get at my desk, find some ink, and a pen and try and get off a letter to you — It seems such a *long* time since I said good-bye to you in Montreal, Daddy and to you at St John Boogie — am glad I got off a letter at Halifax to let you know that all was well, and hope you rec'd my cable sent on arrival in London — The weather at Halifax was foul — cold and windy and *pouring* and the first few days at sea were cold and sea rough — but there was an enormous cargo on board so the old girl rode the waves well — and the 'movement' was entirely different from going out, in fact she was incredibly steady — and none of us were seasick! thank goodness, and didn't miss a meal. There was a pretty dull crowd on board, but at least the boat wasn't overcrowded and full of immigrants so it seemed much more 'pre-war' than my other post-war crossings — All the stewards, etc. were very nice — I *never* saw the captain, so our 'royal welcome' at St John didn't impress him! I thought at *least* he would ask me to tea once, didn't you? . . . Went to several films — Jennifer opened her cards etc on her birthday and was thrilled with her camera and her 'view-master' — she had a cake with candles at tea-time, 2 other children and paper hats.

We didn't arrive in Liverpool until the Thursday after all, sent Gerald a marconigram to get us rooms at the Berkeley, and had one from him that he couldn't meet us in London as his manager was ill —

After finding our 17 pieces of luggage, we awaited the customs officer, and chatted with a *charming* policeman who said, "It's worse than ever in England now, you can't even get 'anged" (the death penalty has just been abolished). I took a good look at the customs officer when he arrived, smiled sweetly and began my tactics I used last time, but I soon saw that he was the young, green, variety who was anxious to assert himself, and was going to make it difficult for me — he had *no* sense of humour, and was not in the least helpful — he made out an *enormous* list of things I had to pay on, and took me over to the office, luckily presided over by a very nice man, who scratched off everything he possibly *could* and said, "I don't like this job, madam. Please don't be mad with *me* but with Cripps" −[2] In the end I had to pay £20 duty − it's hard to bear! but at least I have never had to pay before − and *last* time didn't pay a penny − so try to look at it as £10 each time to make it seem less bad! −

1. From December 1947 to April 1948, Ginnie took her two children and their nanny to the United States and Canada.

2. Stafford Cripps, 1889–1952, a British Labour politician who was chancellor of the Exchequer 1947–50.

6th May 1948   Highfield

Sat. morning took Jennifer to her riding lesson and sat in the Churston Railway station and wrote letters while waiting for her − That afternoon G. had to go over to Hallsands to collect some barrels etc. so took me with him, a *divine* drive, and I am longing to shew it to you − the country at its best, and bluebells and primroses everywhere. The villages the other side of Dartmouth are quite unspoilt, a relief after all the victorian horrors in this part. All that *divine* part was used as a training-ground in the war, and in places the trees have been shelled etc. and 1 or 2 villages razed to the ground.[1] I saw the village where 'Barty' lived, which missed the 'shelling' and is *most* attractive − We had dinner at Ella Trout's hotel at Hallsands. Ella is a famous character, she has crab boats and lobster-pots and beats all the men at it, also runs the hotel and a farm − and won the O.B.E. in the *last war* for rescuing a stark naked nigger, the only survivor from a ship that was torpedoed and sunk in a *gale* off Hallsands!! They have a sentry-box where people take turns watching for shoals of fish, then they rush out dropping nets and pull the fish in to the beach − We had *fresh salmon* for dinner!! −

1. The U.S. Army training area where exercises for Normandy landings were carried out was centered around Slapton. For details see Grace Bradbeer, *The Land Changed Its Face: The Evacuation of the South Hams* (Newton Abbot: David and Charles, 1973).

28th July 1948   Highfield

Spent Fri cooking and cleaning up the house (Mrs. Moore is *also* on holiday) and went to meet the London train, as Nannie's sister Evelyn arrived to spend a week with us − [1] Nannie hasn't seen her for ten years, and Evelyn is on holiday from Alexandria (Egypt, not Va!). She is Nannie to some rich Greeks who are relations or friends of the Greek Royal Family. She showed me photographs of "this is me with Princess Tania and Princess Sophie" − [2] Of course they have an enormous staff and Evelyn never has to lift a finger − I think she was a bit shattered at our "establishment" and all that Nannie has to do − She looks *exactly* like N. *but is 20 yrs.* younger −

1. Mrs. Moore was a maid to the Potter family from 1948 to 1954.

2. Queen Sofia of Spain, b. 1938, married Prince, later King, Juan Carlos in 1963.

4th August 1948   Highfield

The Olympic Games are on in full swing, and all next week as well − [1] To-morrow we have a full house, before the race on Friday; and Sat. is Carnival Day in Brixham! The Brixham Regatta is on 19th, 20th and 21st culminat-ing in the fireworks etc. on the 21st − but the Dartmouth regatta is the following week, and we might see something of that! − and we are *thrilled* that you will be here for 3 or 4 weeks, and are busy making the house look nice for your arrival −

If you leave M[ontreal]. on the 14th I expect you will arrive in Liverpool on the 22nd and I could go to London that day − D.V. Do hope I'll be able to! Am *thrilled* to *death* at the thought of seeing you − *Of course* we want you to stay HERE − there is no question of your going to a 'pub', darling. We are just *thrilled* to have you.

1. The Olympic sailing dinghy trials were being held in Torbay.

30th September 1948   Highfield

Thank you so much for your cable which I received this morning. I was delighted to know that you had arrived safely [in U.S.] and that you were all well — I am of course longing to hear how you got on, and whether it was amusing at all — or was it ghastly? Did you meet Mrs. Law? I saw the enclosed in the paper on my way down in the train last Thursday — [1]

1. A press cutting enclosed with this letter reports on Richard Law, member of Parliament (son of Bonar Law, a British conservative politician and prime minister), who was traveling to Canada on the *Empress of France*, as was Bougie.

20th November 1948   Highfield

I was amused at your voting for Thurmond, but agree about Truman and Dewey! [1]

I was just about to say that I had 'no news' but then realized it would be "or what killed the dog" as since last writing to you we have acquired the following: —

1 2 month old puppy

1 large blue lorry

1 Rover car (ordered 3 1/2 years ago)

and have sold: —

1 yacht (Zadig)

1 van (Violet)

I am left pretty breathless over all this, as it all happened so suddenly — Gerald decided to *build* a new boat, and told them 'he wouldn't consider building before they sold Zadig' and presto! they did — Now he feels it's a silly time to build, so at the moment nothing is happening. At this point the car we ordered 3 1/2 yrs. ago arrived, and the lorry ordered 1 month ago arrived — so the van was sold yesterday! He carts his own fish-boxes to the station, saving 6 pence (6D) on each box. I feel very sentimental about dear old Violet, and we won't have much petrol for the new car — The new owner of 'Violet' allows him to go on landing the fish with it! so *I* am the only one that is inconvenienced — but I *may* be able to shop in the new car once a week —

Nannie has been with us 8 years (on Nov. 14th) so I gave her a little present — and then the Royal Prince was born, to mark the anniversary! [2]

1. Strom Thurmond, 1902–2003, a lawyer and politician, was governor of South Carolina 1947–51 and a U.S. senator 1954–2003. He stood as a states' rights candidate in the 1948 presidential election and supported segregation.

2. Prince Charles, heir to the British throne.

11th December 1948   Highfield

I went up to London on the early train Monday – . . . . Stayed at the Berkeley [Hotel], and at 10.20 Tuesday morning met Jennifer at Victoria Station. She was looking very well and in good form – on arrival at the Berkeley I discovered *all* her clothes had been sent in the trunk to Devonshire, rang up Hayford's and luckily her new dress was ready so we dashed around and she put it on, then for a fitting for new jodhpurs and riding coat – and then to lunch with Grannie Potter at the 500 Club where we had an excellent lunch, and a very nice time, and Mum was looking *so* well, and told her all about G's job etc.

On arriving home at tea time heard that Mum had died at 1 p.m.!!! while I was in the train, and Gerald was motoring to Southampton on business. Poor Nannie couldn't get hold of either of us – You can imagine the shock to hear this news when I had lunched with Mum yesterday!! She felt ill about 8 a.m. and they got a doctor and she died of cerebral haemorrhage at 1 p.m. What a wonderful way for her to go but a terrible shock to her family –

I feel Mum had a wonderful death, so cannot feel sad for her – as she was far from well and another thing, she saw *all of us* recently and must have been pleased to think all her children and grandchildren were well and happy (I told her I was!!). I am so sorry for Joanie; of course she won't be able to go to the funeral, as she is "expecting" in a few months.

15th March 1949 (1)   Highfield

As I may get disturbed before I finish a long letter, perhaps I had better give you a brief summary of the headlines, and try and write details later: In Brief:

a) Jennifer has recovered from the measles

b) After many vicissitudes Pygmalion is at sea again

c) We have bought a house!!! (the house Ballymagowan) as we have made an offer for it and Dr. Brownlow Smith accepted it. We had turned it down as being too expensive, and then lo and behold he accepted it, to our surprise – he is getting out in June, and we plan to move in about Sept. or October – as G. will be away most of August –

I then went out to canvas subscriptions for the Conservative Party! and felt in no mood for it.

15th March 1949 (2)   Highfield

Gerald and I have agreed to have the house in *both our names* and to each pay half – As he already owes me nearly £2000 for Zadig, this means I will have to cough up £3000 more – luckily his mother's money has just come through so he is paying for the house out-right, and I am to pay him back when I can – so I have plenty of time to look over my "capital" and see what is the best thing for me to sell – I hope you think this "share" plan a good one – and we can leave the 'other half' to each other – so if G dies first the house is mine and vice versa –

19th April 1949   Highfield

A small private letter to tell you how absolutely *thrilled* I am at the thought of your arrival. You know that I would *much* rather see you than go to Cowes Week, but I'm afraid G. would be awfully disappointed if I didn't go as he reserved the room months ago – and am sure he wants me to see the start of the Fastnet.[1] Of course *I* want to see it very much too! but if I have to *choose*, I would far rather meet you –

1. Gerald planned to participate in the ocean race from Cowes, Isle of Wight, to the Fastnet Rock off the south coast of Ireland, returning to Plymouth.

12th July 1949   Highfield

The launching of Fandango is to be on Tues. 26th – Jennifer's school now breaks up on Mon 25th and I shall arrange for Miss Waldron to meet her in London and bring her back here that day. I go to S'ton on Sunday 24th with Gerald, and drive the car back here on aft. of 26th. The boat, though *launched*, will *not* be ready for Cowes or the Fastnet so all that is off – disappointing for me, and *VERY* for Gerald – but it just can't be helped – He will sail her around here beginning of Aug. if she is ready and he *still hopes* to go in the Plymouth–La Rochelle [race] about Aug 14th, to be away a fortnight (so that would just fit in beautifully with *us* – you and me – if it comes off, as you would see G. but we would have a nice time to ourselves for a bit!!)

As for bringing things over, the only thing I *really* need is – as usual – *stockings* – preferably the rosy-beige variety for summer dresses if you can get them in length!! I only have one pair of light ones left. The only other thing I can think of is a corset – and this is too complicated for you in the hot weather – unless it is cool in Montreal and you are to be there several days, do not give it another thought. I believe I got the last pr. of Flexees size 29 waist at Simpson's but corsets are easier here now I hear, and I can have one made at Marian Jacks in the autumn. The only *other* thing I can think of is some *steak*!! They could put it in the refrigerator until you get to Liverpool – but then, it might not keep until we get to Devon, so perhaps it's best forgotten also. Remember to buy yourself 200 cigarettes on the boat as they are still scarce here and *very* expensive.

13th September 1949   Highfield

I miss you simply dreadfully but it was *wonderful* having you so must try and be 'Pollyanna' about it. Thank you so very much for being so sweet to all of us, and for all your kind help and assistance –

11th November 1949   Greenmarch[1]

                                           Churston Ferrers

                                           South Devon

On Tuesday there was a *sou'westerly* gale blowing and the furniture van from S'ton arrived at 7.30 a.m. when it was barely light. The van couldn't get in the drive so everything had to be carried from the road – in the rain of course. In case you don't know it the *front door* faces sou'west, and the carpenter chose that day to *take the door away to be repaired* — so the rain came in like this ===== Just as he was walking off with the door the vanmen walked up with 2 pairs of skis, an ice-cream freezer and the insides to the grandfather clock — and said brightly "Where shall we put these?" I said vaguely "I had *planned* to put the skis in the garage" — "Certainly madam" — I said "But it isn't built yet!" It was so much like a surrealist nightmare, that I burst out laughing —

The next day we had our first meal in the dining-room and to celebrate we opened the bottle of champagne that the Moggridges had given us — . . . and we shared it with the Bartys and Barty made a charming little speech —

The next day Rockhey's came to lay the dark red carpet in G's study — all the furniture had to be moved out and then in again and Gerald had a wonderful time putting all his books away; Mr. Crabbe came to hang the mirrors and some pictures — I had produced the portrait of the Rev. Joseph Winter (1770) as being the most respectable ancestor for hanging in the front hall. Gerald was much against having "a d—— parson in the front hall". I told this to Crabbe who later said "I have been thinking about that portrait, ma'am. The *gay* friends of Major Potter's will be amused; *some* people might be impressed; and the vicar, when he pays his call, will be delighted — so I think 'we'll' hang it" — Wasn't it sweet? So I agreed to his decision.

1. This is the house referred to as Ballymagowan in Ginnie's letter of 15 March 1949. Bougie chose the name which denoted that the land marched with the green of the local golf course. It remained the Potter family home until 1984.

17th February 1950   Greenmarch

[Monday] evening Gerald brought Gordon Somersby in for a drink. He was here on a short visit from Lundy Island where he and his wife Jane, and Geoff Douglas have been catching lobsters for the past few months — they have done *very* well, but I gather Jane is a bit fed up living in a tin hut! Jane's brother goes to America next week to lecture at *40* U.S. universities

— His name is Dylan Thomas and he is apparently a well-known poet — have you ever heard of him?[1] (I haven't) His wife is a daughter of Augustus John —[2] I wonder if Thomas will go to Richmond? "Can't understand why people rave about his poetry", said Gordon, "I can't understand a word of it" —

We are in the agonizing throes of the General Election. I will be so glad when it is all over — I have *no* hope of the Socialists getting out — Churchill's speech last night was most depressing, the only bad speech I have ever heard him make — He sounded old and tired — and it was most uninspiring. Most of the speeches of *all* parties have been dreadful — the "peuple" hasn't enough *sense* to vote Conservative — I am promised to keep my car on the road all election day (7 a.m. to 9 p.m.) as only one car allowed per party and I thought mine would *hold* more people — so please pray for *me* as well as the Conservative party on Feb. 23rd.

1. Dylan Thomas, 1914–53, Welsh poet.
2. Augustus John, 1878–1961, British portrait and landscape painter.

2nd March 1950   Greenmarch

I meant to write to you the minute the Election was over, but felt "physically and emotionally exhausted" after all the excitement! — Well, *personally*, I was pleased with the result, as never thought the Conservatives would get in — and now the Labour Party only has a majority of 7!![1] They will be tied hand and foot, and not able to get on with their horrible nationalization — and if things go wrong, the "Tories" won't get the blame so perhaps it's "a good thing" for the time being!

1. The majority was actually by five.

10th November 1950   Greenmarch

On the Tuesday afternoon I had to go to the Town Hall at Torquay where various organisations including E.S.U. were giving a reception to the United Nations Del. who as you may know are having a 'do' in Torquay at the moment.[1] I had been asked to be an official, and act as *usher* which meant greeting the delegates as they arrived, pinning a label on them to say to what country they belonged, introducing them to the reception Committee, and endeavouring to fight my way through the crowd to get them some tea – My first "victim" was coal black – from *Liberia*! I also had Ceylon, the Netherlands, France, and a few Americans – Later on someone rushed up to me, looked at my label and murmured "I am so sorry but I am afraid my geography is rather weak – *Where* is USHER?" I thought of my comeback too late, I *should* have said "Behind the Iron Curtain, near RUSSHER". Anyway I had fun telling everyone of the wonderful question.

1. This was the Torquay round of international trade talks under the auspices of the General Agreement on Tariffs and Trade (GATT). See Timothy E. Josling, Stefan Tangermann, and T. K. Warley, *Agriculture in the GATT* (Basingstoke and London: Macmillan, 1996), 25.

22nd January 1951   Greenmarch

How sweet of you Boogie to say you'll meet me in N.Y. and if I don't hear, I'll go straight to the Weylin Hotel, E. 54th St. but in the last few days the English laws have been relaxed and we are now allowed to take £35 if visiting a relation, so I *can* get myself to Richmond now, if you can't meet me – So please don't go to all that added bother and expense – as I'll just take the first train to R'd on arrival! – and prefer to go to New Haven on way to Montreal if that is all right.

21st February 1952   Greenmarch

We heard the awful news about the King, and wandered around in a daze – gloom descended on everyone, the Brixham streets were nearly empty and the shops shutting-up early when I got there.[1]

That evening we listened to the 9 o'clock news, and felt very emotionné about the King.

Bill Anson was originally coming that w/end but of course it was cancelled and he is coming this next one (to-morrow) – He has just rung to say he is slowly recovering from having walked the *entire way* in the [funeral] procession, London and Windsor – and was on guard at Westminster Hall from 6 to 12 the night before.[2]

1. George VI died on 6 February.

2. Lord Anson was one of the marshals in charge of the parade. According to his son, Patrick Lichfield, in his autobiography, he "waved so frantically at [his] father that he was forced to wave his baton in reply, thereby inadvertently signalling his troops to quick march the next two hundred yards"; see Lichfield, *Not the Whole Truth* (London: Constable, 1986), 47.

26th February 1952   Greenmarch

I was . . . in the [Hyde Park] hotel by 6 and had promised to have drinks with the Sawyers at 6.30, having given up all hope of trying to go to the lying-in-state at Westminster Hall, as had been told the queues were 4 miles long and it took about 5 hours to get through – and also the cold was intense – it had been snowing and sleeting in the morning.[1] I happened to ring Rosie Cathcart, and she asked me if I had been.[2] When I said no and why, she just said "Be here at 7". I could hardly believe my ears – When I got to their flat Alan had just returned, exhausted, from Windsor where he had been all day working on the funeral procession plans –[3] (He is the reg. adjutant of the Scots Guards and works under Julian Gascoigne –[4] Julian, as G.O.C. London District was in charge of the entire procession) – In spite of being all in, Alan insisted on taking me, and 3 others to Westminster Hall – We parked his car and we walked to an entrance in the House of Commons, or Lords, don't know which! and then walked through endless rooms and corridors and came out into Westminster Hall down the steps immediately opposite to the queue coming in from the street – Our queue filed down the right, the others on the left. I need hardly add that it was a very awe-inspiring sight – hundreds of people slowly filing through that enormous and dimly-lit hall, and *no sound* except a quiet shuffling of feet. It was very beautiful and impressive – the soldiers with bowed heads looked more like statues – I noticed they were Grenadiers, but did not of course realize who they were until afterwards – Just as we were opposite the catafalque,

Alan squeezed my arm — I turned my head slightly and saw a slim figure dressed in black standing motionless under an arch by the middle door — It was the Queen — and an enormous lump came up in my throat. She was standing with the Duke of Edinburgh, and Princess Margaret beside her — unnoticed by the crowd as they were all looking towards the catafalque, and occasionally women would stoop down and drop little bunches of snow-drops and other white flowers — We walked out into the street where the thousands of people were standing, completely silent, in the cold night air. I shall *never* forget seeing those silent crowds — I murmured something to Alan about 'how can they stand the cold?' — he just said "It's a pilgrimage" and we walked quietly back to the car — We had been there when the guard changed over at 7.40 p.m. They had 20 minutes on, and 40 minutes off for 6 or 7 hours — I watched them *very* carefully, but in spite of that, somehow one *couldn't tell* when they changed over — one had the illusion that the same ones were still standing there! I was back in my hotel by 8.30 where I met Babs [Lockwood] who had also been there at about 7 p.m. Leonard Ropner, an M.P. took her —[5] Wasn't it adorable of Alan to take me. I was needless to say enormously grateful to him —

On the Friday morning I went into Hyde Park to try my luck, picked up a heavy iron chair, which I dragged across the park and stood on it for an hour or so before the procession went by — I had a pretty good view of it as a whole, but I wasn't near enough to see anyone's face — I made friends with a New Zealand girl, and took her back to the hotel afterwards to give her some hot coffee as we were both frozen through — Later Sheila Child came in to have lunch with me, and at 2 p.m. we went to the window to stand for the 2 minutes silence — and saw the cars in Hyde Park stop — Then slowly the noise of the cars and the hubbub of the restaurant started up again —

Bill Anson came to stay for the w/end. He arrived in time for late dinner, and we were delighted to see the old boy again, as hadn't seen him for 7 years — he is just the same! Asked us if we ever saw "Her Highness" and added "I understand everyone has to *bow* to her now"!![6] I didn't realize that Bill is now military secretary to Julian Gascoigne; he had to walk in the entire procession both in London and Windsor and was on guard from 6 p.m. to 1 a.m. at Westminster the night before — so *he* was one of the 4 I saw when I went. He had to look after 42 officials mostly foreigners in the procession, and was very funny about it and various incidents including having a waiter trip over *his* sword in the royal train and overturned a pot of tea on some visiting royalty — Bill is *absurd* — It was interesting to hear about some of the things that happened behind the scenes, and of one Gren. officer who wore a motheaten bearskin that was brushed *up* instead of down, and on the platform at Paddington "General Julian had told him he was a disgrace to *any* army" — the 'poor chap' had never worn a bearskin having joined the Reg. during the war — I wish I had known that I could have had a seat in Bill's office in Whitehall — However he has promised to give me 2 seats for the Trooping of the Colour if it takes place which is doubtful, as the Queen when Princess Elizabeth was Colonel of the Reg. —

1. Derek (Tom) Sawyer, manager of the Hyde Park Hotel, London.

2. The sixth Countess Cathcart née Rosemary (Rosie) Smyth-Osbourne, 1921–80.

3. Alan Cathcart, 1919–99, was the sixth Earl Cathcart, a Scots Guards officer, and a regimental adjutant 1951–53. Between 1970 and 1973 he served as the general officer commanding and British commandant in Berlin.

4. Major General Sir Julian Gascoigne, 1903–90, was a Grenadier Guards officer and general officer commanding the London District. From 1955 to 1959 he was governor of Bermuda.

5. Colonel Sir Leonard Ropner, 1895–1977, was the first baronet from 1952. He was a shipowner and company director and served as a Conservative member of Parliament for Sedgewick, Durham, 1923–29, and Barkston Ash, West Yorkshire, 1931–64.

6. Bill's ex-wife, Anne Anson, had married Prince Georg of Denmark in 1950.

31st March 1952   *Richmond*

Tuesday I had an old friend Charlotte Beveridge from Redding, Conn. to lunch and asked Virginia Clarke Taylor and Mrs. Warren Vaughan to join us. Then I repaired to the Woman's Club to the reading class where once more I was asked to read the story of "Ste. Pelagic — the harlot" — It is a classic — and sets such a high standard that I can't find much to equal it — I have re-read a stream-lined Sophocles' "Antigone" — translation for next time — People shy away from the classic Greeks, but they read so much better and easier than the modern vague and encumbered psychological trash, that I wonder why they are considered so "High-brow" —

25th April 1952   Greenmarch

We went to bed very early, having packed, as we had to get up at 6 on Monday morning to be on time for the Queen's Birthday Parade at Windsor Castle —

Somehow managed to don black dress and coat and purple velvet hat in the time allotted, and we tore off towards Windsor, and 'made it' with 5 minutes to spare — I was thrilled to go as went to the Birthday Parade ten yrs. ago when Princess Elizabeth aged 16 became Colonel of the Grenadiers — and this parade was on her retirement as, on becoming the Sovereign, the Queen is now Col-in-Chief of the Household Brigade, and the new Col. is General Sir George Jeffreys — He looked magnificent with flowing white moustache and bearskin! The Queen appeared, dressed in black, and in the pouring rain, inspected the troops, then stood on a raised platform for the march past, gave an address — and Geordie Gordon-Lennox (the Lt. Col.) replied — [1] It was *most* unfortunate that the rain never left off as the Grenadiers all wore grey capes over their scarlet tunics — We were standing near the 'Sovereign's Entrance' and in the window above saw the Queen Mother with Prince Charles and Princess Anne — When the Queen left the Quadrangle followed by the Duke of Edinburgh, Sir George, Geordie etc. Princess Anne leant out of the window, and said "Hello, papa" —

We then went to Victoria Barracks where there was a huge marquee set up on the lawn — complete with buffet luncheon and a champagne bar and about 30 or 40 people I hadn't seen for 7 or 8 years — I had one cocktail on top of my extremely empty tummy and felt if I didn't have a sausage roll *quickly* I would be feeling no pain at all — There were hundreds of people there and a very fine party —

1. Lieutenant General Sir George Gordon Lennox, 1908–88, was a Grenadier Guards officer from 1928 to 1952. He was commandant of the Royal Military Academy Sandhurst between 1960 and 1963.

18th July 1952   Greenmarch

The White Fish man said that 40% of the trawler-owners of the Inshore Fishing in England are losing money — [1] The grant promised by the Government is *not* forthcoming, and he said never will be "as no one is interested in the small trawler-owner" – so that's that. It would seem that no matter what Gov't is in power, they are never interested in the 'little man' and the fact that Brixham 'the mother of fishing ports' is dying as a port, doesn't worry them – I told Gerald he should turn J Elliott & Son into an ice-cream bar and sell nasty 'candy floss' etc. but he says 'never' – [2]

1. The White Fish Authority was established in 1951 to act as a government inspection agency and to administer grants for improvements and acquisition of trawlers.

2. J. Elliott and Son: Gerald's fishing company in Brixham, 1945–56.

26th September 1952   Greenmarch

We went to the Cathcarts to a small cocktail party on the Sat. night. Agatha Christie was there and slipped on the slippery stone floor on her way out and came down with a crash – [1] As she has a figure like Elsie Beer's and legs like pianos it was quite a thump. [2]

1. Agatha Christie née Miller, 1890–1976, a British detective novelist, lived two miles from the Potters' house.

2. Elsie Beer, Ginnie's next-door neighbor.

10th December 1952   *Richmond*

[Saturday] evening, I went to a party at the Reynolds and after Auden the English (now American) poet read his practically unintelligible verse, an enormous supper was served – I <u>overate</u>.[1] *It was a reaction from the indigestible poetry. Florie was there in an electric blue lace dress! – She had on a fur cape and put a knitted scarf over her knees! She wanted to know how I liked her dress? – and I had to admit I couldn't see it – Will say the old girl has spirit, to say the least, but since she has someone to wait on her every moment, she is so spoiled that I shall have to make a stand!*

1. W. H. Auden, 1907–73, an English poet, moved to the United States in 1939 and became a citizen in 1946.

19th January 1953   *Richmond*
[Tuesday] I went out to Westhampton to hear and meet Sacheverell Sitwell — [1]
He read some of the most awful poetry it has ever been my displeasure to
hear, and also said that <u>*Dylan Thomas*</u> *was a* <u>*great poet.*</u> *He is younger and*
better looking than Osbert and Edith, and has quite an attractive personality
— but I can't say which of the three possesses the most mountainous conceit —
He was engaged to speak about Art and calmly read poems instead, thereby
infuriating the Heads of the University — They paid him a goodly sum —
Well he will never speak there again much to the despair of Florie who "fell
in love with him" and has talked of nothing else since —

I [went] to hear Horowitz play in the Mosque — the Schubert Sonata put
Stuart to sleep, and I had to nudge him several times. It didn't add much to my
enjoyment although his excuse was amusing. He said, "What's the matter? I
only went to sleep <u>*once*</u>*" — Yes, but he snored in the subdued passages! —*

1. Sir Sacheverell Sitwell, 1897–1988, was brother of Edith and Osbert, a poet, a biographer, and an author of art, history, and travel books.

27th January 1953   *Richmond*
Believe it or not, yesterday I met Cecil Beaton — [1] *He had given a perfectly*
brilliant lecture in the Club, terribly amusing and witty — He said it was
his first try at lecturing and had only been at it for 10 days. I told him it was
certainly as much of a success as his photography and asked about his sister
Baba whose photographs I remembered. He said her husband was killed in the
war, and she was living in London — He made all sorts of fun of himself, in
the most delightful way — and "acted" in a very original manner. The Ladies
were pleased with him!

1. Cecil Beaton, 1904–80, English fashion and portrait photographer, set designer, il-
lustrator, and diarist.

4th February 1953   Greenmarch

As a large part of England (and a lot of poor little Holland) appear to be under water I thought perhaps I had better write to let you know that *here* we are all safe and dry! It is sometimes hell living on top of a hill and getting the wind from the N.E., the S.W., and N.N.W. and *all* the others, but it is certainly better than being on low ground as this last week-end has proved — Isn't it *terrible?* God what a w/end of disasters, the missing of the Transatlantic plane and the sinking of the Princess Victoria were pushed right off the front page by the floods in England and Holland — and the *cold,* my God what it must have been like in that terrible wind —[1]

1. *Princess Victoria,* a car ferry that sank near Belfast.

7th March 1953   Greenmarch

I am wondering how the news of Stalin's death was rec'd in U.S.? I still can't take it in — the first thing I knew about it was Nannie came rushing in on the morning of the 5th to tell me Stal'in was dying, and I said sleepily "Whose stallion?" — Well anyway I shall always be able to remember the *date* of the death of "Mr. Stal'lin" — March 5th. Nannie tells me "the new man is going to be even worse as the paper says he 'ates the West" so I am not allowed the consoling fact that there's one less communist in the world.

Who should turn up but Peter Lacy —[1] We haven't seen him for a year or so — he drove down here with a friend, for the w/end to pay a visit to this part of the world and see a few old friends — didn't arrive in Torquay until 6 p.m. on Saturday, then went straight to the Brixham Yacht Club to see old Sam, had dinner, and on the way back to hotel in Torquay was hauled in by the police — the poor old boy was a bit shattered, needless to say — it was rotten luck — the friend with him was a most *peculiar* looking individual named Francis Bacon — he is apparently quite a well-known artist and is having a show in New York in the autumn —[2]

1. Peter Lacy, d. 1962, friend of Francis Bacon, 1909–92, British artist whose abstract style developed into distorted expressionism. According to Wieland Schmied, Lacy was a "fighter pilot turned bar pianist whose romantically tinged brand of sadism was exactly

attuned to Bacon's masochistic leanings"; see Schmied, *Francis Bacon* (Munich and New York: Prestel-Verlag, 1996), 15.

2. Sam Jourdain, d. 1962, worked for J. Elliott and Son, Gerald's fishing company.

8th April 1953   Greenmarch

I . . . went off to London on Tuesday morning (the 24th) and had two (2) days in London to myself which was great fun and did me a *power* of good − Had a fitting for my new suit soon after I arrived − and had dinner with Rosemary Jeffreys − About 11.15 we heard a rumour about Queen Mary so took a taxi to St James' St. and walked over to Marlborough House where quite a large crowd had collected and the bulletin had just been put up −[1] We hung around until past midnight − it was cold and a very dark night and a bit foggy and it seemed more like a strange dream − The clock on St James' Palace struck, and we saw the guard change − and several cars left Marl. House − Yes, wasn't it pathetic that Queen Mary couldn't have lived to see her grand-daughter crowned − What a moment that would have been for her −

On Wednesday morning I was out early to have a round of the shops − They were busy taking down Easter window displays and draping everything in purple or black and white −

1. Queen Mary née Princess Victoria Mary of Teck, 1867–1953, widow of George V.

10th April 1953   Greenmarch

Sunday afternoon we all looked at Television, to see the funeral procession going from Marlborough House to Westminster Hall for the lying-in-state. Julian Gascoigne was in charge of the procession, and looked magnificent in a white-plumed 'titfer'.

12th June 1953   Greenmarch

Monday was *hectic* trying to get everything ready and getting all the cooking done − Doris had C[oronation] Day off as she wanted to help with the children's teas and old age pensioners' teas on the Common —[1] 'Auntie' went off to her sister at Stokenham —[2] I took the children swimming at Babbacombe Pool in the morning and spent the rest of the day cooking and arranging the table in the dining-room and so on. We had a large white cloth with red, white and blue streamers, a big bowl of ditto flowers in the centre — The piece de resistance was a *whole* dressed salmon with the Union Jack stuck in its mouth and 'Honi Soit qui mal y pense' on its tail. I made a marvellous tomato aspic (a recipe that Mary Gordon's mother gave me that I had never used!?) and stuck an american flag in that. Then we had a dozen lobsters — a big bowl of mayonnaise, plates of potato salad, and green salad — Then blackcurrant fool, coffee soufflée, pineapple jelly and lots of Devonshire cream, cheese and coffee — and of course plenty of champagne —

Besides the 4 of us and Nannie we had old Sam [Jourdain], Anthony and Dorothy Rainey, Drina and Langwell Plum, and Alfred and Ann Plews —[3] Gerald got up at 6 on Coronation morning and kept listening to the weather forecasts, I thought he was going to go *mad* as each one was worse than the one before — it was really pathetic especially as the weather *here* was fairly good — we sat at the T.V. from 10.15 until 1.15! and I must say I thought it was *simply marvellous* — We saw the whole thing inside the Abbey — the music was wonderful, and the Queen seemed to me to have so much humility and yet majesty — After our terrific lunch, we watched the procession leaving the Abbey — Churchill and the Queen of the Tonga Islands stole the show![4]

We had tea at 5 and our guests departed — then I drove the children up to the common to see the carnival procession — We listened to Churchill's and the Queen's speech at 9 — At 10 I took them to the enormous bonfire at Windy Corner — we could see bonfires way up on the moor, several across the bay in Dorset — about 12 in all from where we were — but it must have been a wonderful sight up on the moor — The Raineys went to Buckland Beacon (the famous one of the Armada). Then we watched the fireworks from the house (we could see Torquay and Paignton and a bit of Brixham) and then the London ones on T.V. — and at 11.30 or so we crawled into bed.

I wouldn't have missed being in the country as it was a new experience for me to see all the funny little local do's and all the excitement — every child received a *mug* and a packet of sweets. On Wed. Gerald said with relief "Now we don't have to worry about *that* any more — I feel I would like sausages and cabbage for my lunch" —

1. Doris Gagg, the cook to the Potter family from 1953 to ca. 1980.

2. Bertha Stone ("Auntie"), 1889–ca. 1970, the housekeeper to the Potter family from 1951 to ca. 1962.

3. Anthony Wakefield Rainey, 1917–86, was an officer in the Special Branch of the Royal Marines and a partner in J. Elliott and Son. Dorothy Eileen Rainey, formerly Monck-Mason, b. 1920, was an Auxiliary Territorial Service officer from 1939 to 1945. Drina Plum née Tabrum, 1925–57, died from polio. George Langwell Plum, 1913–2004, was a lawyer, a yachtsman, and an all-around sportsman who later became Gerald's sailing partner. Alfred Plews, 1915–85, was a lawyer. Ann Plews née Clayton, b. 1933, was from 1978 called Martin and from 1992 Clayton Martin.

4. Queen Salote Tubou, 1900–1965, the queen of Tonga from 1918, was instantly recognizable due to her large girth.

17th June 1953   Greenmarch

We got a taxi, had plenty of time to spare as it is only a short distance to Whitehall, and 'our' entrance to the 'do' [Trooping the Colour] was via Treasury Passage in Downing St. The crowds were so thick in Parliament Square that in the end we had to get out and walk — but were in our seats by 10.30 — the required time — About 1/4 to 11 an open carriage arrived with Prince Charles and Princess Anne, also the Queen Mother and Pri. Margaret — then you could hear the Procession coming up the mall, and as the clock struck eleven *precisely* the Queen entered Horse G[uar]ds. Parade on "Winston" — It was a marvellous sight, and I was thrilled that Jennifer was able to see it all — The colour being trooped that day was the 1st Bn. Grenadiers (Gerald's old Bn — and I was sorry that he hadn't been able to see it, as he really wanted to go very much, but Anthony had planned to leave for Spithead in Rulewater on Thursday afternoon, and there just wasn't time for G to get back here) — The rain held off until just at the end, so luckily we didn't get wet. Saw several old friends, and it was all the greatest fun —

We arrived at Hythe pier [in Southampton] about 2, where Rulewater was anchored – Gerald, Ant [Anthony Rainey], Derek [Sanderson] and Langwell Plum having arrived in her the night before, from Brixham – We had a quick lunch and sailed off, spent the whole afternoon sailing through the Fleet, and saw all the destroyers aircraft-carriers, submarines etc. anchored at Spithead – also the *Russian* destroyer, and the beautiful Italian training ship the Amerigo Vespucci – also the American, Canadian, French, Dutch, Spanish destroyers – and of course thousands of yachts, including Creole, and lots of old friends, and several yachts from Torquay and Brixham – [1] We anchored off Lee-on-Solent for the night after that marvellous sail, and after late dinner sat in the saloon and sang to Anthony's "squeeze box" –

Up at 7 on the day in order to dress ship overall at exactly 8 a.m. when the Navy did – a large breakfast and then all our chores and scrubbing and washing up – and by 12.30 we were all dressed up fit to kill in white skirts and navy blue jackets – the men in creams, and navy blazers and yachting caps with white cap-covers – Phyl and Brian Gore came on board for a drink – they were with Dickie and Sandra, moored alongside us in "Serithe".[2] Then we had our Naval Review lunch of cold chicken, salad, new potatoes – and strawberries and Devonshire cream, and plenty of champagne – about three we saw the Queen go by to review the fleet – Ant of course climbed to the top of the mast to get a better view, then Gerald followed – Later we saw the Fly past –

Up again the next morning early to 'dress ship' and after breakfast we 'weighed anchor', got up all the sails, and sailed up the Solent to Southampton Water – just as we were crossing towards S'ton Water the *entire fleet* started to move, and we had to cross it all – We passed destroyers literally within *inches* but I was not worried as old Gerald was at the tiller, and Ant was finishing off his breakfast with a most unconcerned air. We had a *glorious* sail up to Hythe Pier, where they dropped the four "Ball and Chains" and we had lunch on the end of Hythe Pier and watched them sail off.

1. The occasion was the Spithead Review, at which Queen Elizabeth II reviewed the naval fleet as part of the coronation celebrations.

2. Phyllis (Phyl) Gore née Von der Porten, 1910–90, was previously Brooke-Hitching,

then from 1961 Lady Gore, then from ca. 1965 Parshall. Lieutenant Colonel Ralph St. George Brian Gore, 1908–73, was a farmer, a wartime army officer, and from 1961 the eleventh Baronet. Richard (Dickie) Yarde-Buller, 1910–91, was from 1930 the fourth Baron Churston and was a lieutenant commander in the Royal Navy Volunteer Reserve. Lady Sandra Churston née Storme, d. 1979, was an actress and formerly Mrs. Jack Dunfee.

29th November 1953   *Richmond*

Last Sunday, I went to Jamestown with Janie Lamb and we spent the night in Yeardley House, and mostly hanging around all afternoon waiting for King Paul and Queen Fredericke of Greece to appear – [1] *They didn't turn up on Sunday, and, on Monday, Janie and I packed up to come home after breakfast. I had on my old blue wool dress, having been dressed up all Sunday to no avail. At 11 o'clock we received word they were on the way! No time to change, so we threw on our coats and walked through mud, as it had rained all night, to reach the Church – They arrived with a party of about 12 people in four cars, and we received them at the Church Gate, feeling a little bedraggled to say the least. She is tiny, with large blue eyes and a very retroussé nose. He, about 6 ft. 4 and very good looking – I believe he is Danish – Anyhow he looks it. They were very gracious, and nice – their schedule was a heavy one and they only remained about a half hour. After shaking hands all round they departed, and so did we soon afterwards – I had a very good looking Greek Aide beside me who, actually, at one point put his arm around me, having patted me several times during the short tour! They are sailing on Dec 3rd, I think, quite exhausted –*

Wednesday, I did some work up at St. James [Church] *for which I had volunteered, and that evening, accompanied by Helen Adams, went to the theatre to see and hear dear old Charles Laughton, who is the most wonderful reader I ever heard. He comes slumping on the stage with an armful of books, into which he scarcely ever looks, and recites from memory for nearly three hours. I was entranced with it.*

1. King Paul I of Greece, 1901–64, reigned 1947–64. His wife was Queen Frederika of Greece née Princess of Braunschweig-Lüneberg, 1917–75.

18th April 1954   *Richmond*
Turner Arrington took Corbin Old and me out to a meeting of the Edgar Allen
Poe Foundation Board — . . . We are sending all the original manuscripts to
the State Library to be taken care of as they were gathering mold in the Old
Stone house —

25th April 1954   Greenmarch
I took J & A to church this morning — we sat behind Agatha Christie but I
didn't recognize her until she *stood* as her legs are *unmistakable —*

13th May 1954   *Richmond*
Since I wrote you last, I have been to Yeardley House at Jamestown for two
days where we had the usual Annual Celebration in the old church. We enter-
tained the visiting clergy and their wives at lunch before the service — It was
my bit to carve the Smithfield ham, which was the hardest ham ever created
from a peanut eating pig. I almost had to put my foot on it to hold it down,
but I shaved it as thin as paper and it took over an hour to cut enough to go
around. I feel I should be decorated for it, because my arms ached for two days
afterwards — The weather was foul but we had a full church — As I passed
by the clergy changing their clothes in a 50 mile wind, one of them called out
to me — "This is an ecclesiastical striptease"

The Electrolux is running and Sadie is dusting the walls above my head —
I missed Eisenhower's visit but I hear it was a great success. They, meaning the
President and "Mamie", attended a service at St. Paul's and were given lunch
in Virginia House — The police were given a tip that someone had offered a
certain person $500.00 to <u>shoot</u> him, so the whole place was swarming with
F.B.I. agents and police. Perhaps it was just a grim joke, as nothing happened
and they said they would like to come back and bring Mamie's mother.

I hear now that the Queen Mother is going to be in Wmsburg — and the
whole Inn has been engaged. Perhaps, if she goes to Jamestown I may see her
— Shall I remind her that you kept pigs with the Ansons?!!

27th June 1954   Greenmarch

[Aunt Jo Potter] then took us to friends, the Hearnes, for tea. He is Richard Hearne the comedian, known as "Mr. Pastry" and for some extraordinary reason has been offered a 6 weeks contract at that fabulous place Las Vegas and is off to U.S. end of this month —[1] We got back to London about 7 and I wanted to put J to bed, but she refused — so we went off to see Danny Kaye in "Knock on Wood".[2]

    1. Richard Hearne (Mr. Pastry), 1908–79, actor and comedian in children's television programs.

    2. Danny Kaye, born Kaminsky, 1913–87, American dancer, singer, entertainer, and film actor.

5th July 1954   Greenmarch

Sunday was "Independence Day" — also the *end of rationing* of England — after *14 years* — in other words, since before Jennifer was born!

21st August 1954   *Montreal*

I want to tell you about my maiden voyage in the air. I waved in the direction in which I thought you were, swallowed the lump in my throat and settled down in my seat and tried to relax and look casual!

I was alone there for some time but eventually was joined by a rosy faced man from the Midlands who was not glamourous as Gerna suggested, but proved to be better than glamorous, because he was connected with B.O.A.C. and knew everything about it, and was coming out here on business connected with it.[1] After some conversation he invited me to go below to the lounge for a drink with him. I am afraid I disappointed him there, but at least he knew I was one of B.O.A.C.'s cheapest passengers, as everyone else imbibed with great abandon. It was announced that we would land at Shannon for dinner (in the restaurant) complete with champagne, which I did drink, to the extent of two glasses. We were off at about 11 and came non stop from there to Montreal — Mr. Young went to the lounge to sleep and sent the steward to remove the partition between the seats so I could stretch out my legs. I covered myself with

*a blanket, and went to sleep, without benefit of Dr. Inman's pills. At about 4
a.m. I awoke having had a really good rest. At five I was brought a breakfast of
tomato juice, orange, cereal, bacon, egg, sausage, rolls, coffee and marmalade.
I ate all but the egg with relish.*

*As the weather was bad in the North, we took the most southerly route,
avoiding Iceland and Labrador, and the first "land fall" was over Newfound-
land and New Brunswick — We passed over the top hump of Maine, and
I never saw the St. Lawrence until we were almost over Montreal. Mount
Katahdin in the White Mountains looked beautiful in the early morning light.
We were only cruising at about 12,000 ft — not so very high —*

*I must confess that I had no feeling of nervousness, once we got off — and
Gerald was right. I do think there is some vibration but that doesn't bother
me. Stuart and Petersen met me at Dorval.[2] They had been there since 6:30
— We landed at 8.15 — Why Petersen suggested going so early I have yet to
know, but Stuart says he got information that the plane would be in at 7.15
— Gerald is also right about the stupid slow way the Canadians handle the
so-called foreigners — The woman practically went to sleep between calling
out the names — and I was one of the last. I ate another breakfast at 9.50 here!
I have just rung Billy Gilmour. He only arrived after lunch today so I am
feeling very enthusiastic about air travel!*

*Before I finished the first pages of this log, I had your call — that was quite
wonderful. Because of that, and my quick passage, I have no feeling of reality
about being here instead of in England. It is incredible.*

1. B.O.A.C.: British Overseas Airways Corporation.
2. Peter Petersen, Huntly Drummond's chauffeur.

27th September 1954   *Richmond*
*Yesterday, Stuart and I went to the John Marshall House at 12.30 to a recep-
tion given by the Richmond Bar Association for Chief Justice Warren — and
afterwards to an enormous lunch in honour of said Chief Justice and Lord
Goddard, the Lord Chief Justice of England.[1] It was really very well done.
Several hundred guests, all seated with place names — As we are not "in the
law" so to speak, I was astonished to find Stuart placed practically opposite*

the two guests of honour — I was not exactly below the salt, but found myself close to our representative in Congress, and next to the Dean of the Law School of William & Mary College. Lord Goddard made a short speech, as well as Warren, and also a Mr. Goodhart from Oxford — He was very amusing, because he had made a talk the day before in Williamsburg entirely in <u>Latin</u> — He told us someone had said he understood 13 words of the Latin speech but couldn't understand a word Lord Goddard said in English, at which everyone laughed heartily, including Lord G. — Mrs. E. I. du Pont was seated on the right of Warren, as she had received a degree on Saturday. She has sent and paid for about 100 students to William & Mary, and certainly deserves to be given a degree — I was asked to the <u>do</u> at William & Mary, but declined —

1. Earl Warren, 1891–1974, was the chief justice of the U.S. Supreme Court 1954–74. Baron (life peer) Rayner Goddard, 1877–1971, was lord chief justice of England 1946–58.

6th October 1954   *Richmond*
Monday I took Florence Golsan to lunch and we went to Arthur Rank's "Man with a Million", Mark Twain's old story — very amusing, and well produced, and both the Club and Loew's were <u>air cooled</u>, so we had a very good time — I also saw Ralph Richardson in a screenplay called "The Holly and the Ivy" —[1] I never took my eyes off him, and was rewarded by the best possible piece of acting. I have decided he is the best English speaking actor living — a <u>real</u> actor, not just Richardson. I remember what Stanislavsky wrote — "You absorb the character and then imitate what you have absorbed" — He never made a false move — It is a joy to see that sort of performance.

1. Sir Ralph David Richardson, 1902–83, British stage actor who had been knighted in 1947.

2nd November 1954   *Richmond*
The other excitement is caused by Miss Ellen Glasgow's autobiography having come out, and she has told some <u>raw</u> things, about the Cabells and Henry Anderson — Col. Anderson is dead, but James Branch Cabell isn't —[1] It is not

making a very good impression – and most people are disgusted by it – I never did like her while she was living, and she seems more poisonous dead, than alive – I shall never forget how horrid she was to Anne and Tut at the time of their marriage.[2]

1. Ellen Glasgow, *The Woman Within* (London: Eyre and Spottiswoode, 1955). In her autobiography, Glasgow lambasts Richmond society, maintaining that "social charm prevailed over intelligence" (139) and that "in the South . . . conversation, not literature, is the serious pursuit of all classes" (152). Colonel Henry Anderson, Glasgow's one-time fiancé, was a lawyer, Republican gubernatorial candidate in 1921, and Virginia delegate to the Republican National Conventions of 1924, 1928, and 1932. James Branch Cabell, 1879–1958, was a prolific author of fiction, essays, and poetry. Both Cabell and Glasgow were brought up in Richmond and were long-standing friends and rivals. In her autobiography, Glasgow raised the issues of Cabell's alleged homosexuality and involvement in a murder case in 1901.

2. Colonel Carrington Cabell Tutwiler Jr. (Tut), d. 2001, was a lecturer at Virginia Military Institute. Glasgow's sister Rebe was his mother. Presumably Glasgow did not approve of Tut's wife, Anne Porter, who was a close friend of Ginnie.

8th November 1954   *Richmond*

I am now considering going to Jamestown Thursday for the day, to greet H.M. the Queen Mother, as the Embassy seems to have relented about keeping our Executive Committee away – There may be five people, instead of two – Your old school mate (Alice Davis) Lady Makins, is having a Field Day with the Queen – as her husband is the British Ambassador – If I go to Jamestown, I shall have to return via train or bus as I cannot spend the night away, at the moment –

Tell [Jennifer] I am reading a profound book about art appreciation by Bernard Berenson, so profound that I don't understand it, I fear – I am persevering though because I refuse to accept defeat. So far, I understand that a work of art must have "tactile value" or in other words, substance, to which you can relate <u>yourself</u> and it must have <u>movement</u> – According to Berenson, <u>she is right</u> – The still life is practically nothing, and he puts out all abstract subjects, such as cubes and non-objective painting – I think he has a contempt for the so called moderns, and as he is acknowledged to be the world's best *(living) critic, I accept his judgments. I haven't finished his book yet which is called "Aesthetics and History" —*[1]

1. Bernard Berenson, *Aesthetics and History* (Garden City, N.Y.: Doubleday, 1954).

16th November 1954   *Richmond*

I sent you some clippings about the Queen Mother's visit to Virginia and let you know that I had gone to Jamestown — She arrived in Richmond Wednesday at 12.30 and drove by the Chesterfield. Mrs. Willie had put out an American flag and a British one and I contributed two of my British flags — Bob Barton said the Chesterfield looked like the British Embassy — We all stood out in the street and the students in R.P.I. were given a recess, so we had quite a crowd.[1] *The latter made so much noise and cheered so loudly that the Queen turned toward that side as she passed and I am afraid she did not see our display of flags —*

I had been asked some time ago to go to Jamestown and then had been <u>un</u>asked, because the Committee at Williamsburg and the British Embassy in Washington had expressed the wish that there be no one down there except the Chairman and the President. However, on Tuesday, Ellen Bagby rang me up to say they had consented to have her ask the Executive officers and the Jamestown Committee — Irma stayed on an extra day with Stuart, and I drove down with Mrs. Granville Valentine, Janie Lamb and Mrs. Drewry — I was a bit on the spot because some of the other members of the Board were <u>furious</u> they weren't asked so I remained incog. until I could find out what had happened — as I was a bit in the dark when I went down there — There were about seven of us, and five of us remained in the Church, while Ellen and Janie and one of our legislators walked through the grounds, also accompanied by the Bishop of Southern Virginia following the Queen — As she entered the Church Ellen presented her to all of us, calling our names and the Queen shook hands with all those assembled — The Bishop read the collect for the Day, and explained a little about the history of the Church of England in Virginia. Then we all went out in the Churchyard where old Sam, the coloured sexton gave his now famous speech about the old graves. I saw the Queen was dying to laugh as she kept looking back at us, with puzzled *expression so at an appropriate place I gave a rather audible guffaw, joined by some of the party from Williamsburg and she felt free to join in. It really was very nice – very simple and all very informal and natural – When she left she said, "This place has moved me very much – I have a lump in my throat" –*

There was a dinner that evening in Williamsburg, given by Winthrop Rockefeller, and Janie reports that it was a beautiful one, and that the Queen was quite magnificent –[2] In a way, it was an historic occasion, because that is the exact spot where the English established their first permanent civilization on this Continent, and this was the first time a British Sovereign has ever set foot on it. When you think what this country has arrived at in numbers and material power, the <u>thought</u> is rather exciting – I came home (immediately after the Queen left) with Janie Saunders and Mrs. Chamberlayne in Mrs. Saunder's car – There are a lot of funny things in connection with it, but I don't want to bore you –

As long as we are speaking of celebrities, Huntly had dinner with Mendes-France last night in Montreal.[3] I shall be interested to hear what impression he made on Huntly –

1. R.P.I.: Richmond Professional Institute.

2. Winthrop Rockefeller, 1912–73, governor of Arkansas 1967–71.

3. Pierre Mendes-France, 1907–82, was a member of the French National Assembly 1945–58 and 1967–73. He was appointed minister for National Economy by Charles de Gaulle in 1945 and served as prime minister from June 1954 to February 1955.

27th February 1955   *Richmond*

Friday evening I went to hear Victoria de Los Angeles sing in the Mosque.[1] Born in Barcelona, de los Angeles is now a star at the Metropolitan Opera – She sang some fascinating Spanish things and has a golden voice – Coming home, Mrs. John Pinder (<u>not</u> Dinky) but Mrs. <u>Ned Rennold's</u> mother said to Mrs. Robins – "Isn't it interesting that she is a Californian?" Mrs. Robins replied that she was Spanish, whereupon Mrs. Pinder produced her program and said "It's on this – it says <u>de los</u> Angeles" –

1. Victoria de los Angeles, 1923–2005, Spanish soprano.

1st May 1955   *Richmond*

I haven't told you that I saw <u>Cinerama</u> Sunday night for the first time, and
feel that I have actually <u>been</u> to Venice, Spain, Vienna, and even Edinburgh
since last week — I don't know if London has Cinerama, but I consider it
quite marvellous — We <u>were in the gondola</u>! The illusion is almost perfect —
too perfect on the rollercoaster which caused screams from the audience. I just
closed my eyes during that bit —

5th May 1955   *Richmond*

I am still confined to this apartment, coughing uproariously — I shouldn't pay
any attention to it if I were not running a little temperature every afternoon.
Frank Blanton has bet me I won't have it today![1] *I don't feel ill, just a lit-*
tle <u>weak</u> and naturally quite bored. However I have been reading Stendhal's
"The Red and the Black" a most exciting novel which I had never read before
— I get a little weary of the heavy emphasis the French put on sex, but besides
that, they are so satiric and witty, at their best, that I can't put the thing down —
The penuriousness of the French provincial and the worldliness of the Jesuits
are the main characteristics of this one —

1. Dr. Frank McFaden Blanton, b. 1920, Bougie's doctor in Richmond.

22nd August 1955   *Ivry*

You will observe where we are! It was Life's darkest moment when I was told
I must leave relatives and friends in the London airport, and when I saw
you and Gerald waving to me, I knew I must become <u>wooden</u> so I would not
cry —
We did not go to Gander because of adverse weather reports, but landed
at Goose Bay, Labrador instead — We disembarked there and breathed some
delicious crisp air in a temperature of about 45° — There was a weird assem-
blage of people on board — One man opposite me had to have oxygen, and
another old boy over 80 fell in the passage, going the wrong way to the toilet,
and was hauled back into his seat by the Steward, most effectively assisted by
the giantess seated beside me — I was glad I didn't have to do it, because I
had taken quite a dislike to him from the first — We came in one and a half

hours late and after all the unnecessary fuss in the Dorval airport, it was noon
before Stuart, Huntly, Petersen and I reached Montreal, and I was in a bad
mood –

11th September 1955   Imperial Hotel Tramontano
                                                      Sorrento

We planned to go to Positano (on the road to Amalfi) to-day and have a
swim and have lunch there – yesterday we planned to go up Vesuvius – we
haven't even *seen* Vesuvius except for a few minutes when the clouds lifted
since we have been here – Anyway the one thing we *have* accomplished is
G's "pilgrimage" to the Salerno beaches, and to all the places around here
which he knew in the war –

On the way here, he pointed out Monte Camino to me (where Ralph
[Howard] was wounded) and the mountain which he (G) had assaulted![1]
It was much higher than I had expected, and looking at it and realizing
the conditions and heat and no water etc. and the frightful undergrowth –
I was not really surprised that he should have been decorated for it.

1. The range of mountains that includes Monte Camino is near Teano, roughly thirty
miles north of Naples.

27th September 1955   Greenmarch

Glad you rec'd my cable, and the letters from Italy – What a trip, we went
3600 miles in "Second Childhood" – Gerald kept talking about the "Grand
Tour" – ("tour de force" *I* thought.) anyway the result of that tour, is I now
have a very good idea of Italy as a whole. It was like a geography lesson,
and I could tell you where the Apennines are, and the Dolomites – and the
colour of towns like Siena – It was like a sort of "summing up" after a
series of lectures – to give one a good idea of the whole – The thing I liked
the most in the Sorrento part of the world was the abundance of plumbago
and bougainvillea draped over every wall – After the heat, and traffic, and
noise of the journey down there, we had hoped for a quiet place – of course
it was beautiful looking over the Bay of Naples from our balcony, but even

there you could hear the "toot-de-de-toot-toot" of the autobusses – I am afraid Gerald had no idea how trippery that part of the world would be – *thousands* of horrible Germans, in their busses or their 'Folkswagens' or occasionally a Mercedes – the place was *lousy* with 'Krauts' which I found very depressing. Lots of horrible Italians, English, Americans, even Spanish and S. Americans! also –

The shops in Sorrento are fascinating as you know – beautiful hand-made blouses and lovely wooden boxes – If you walk through the tiny dark narrow streets early in the morning or late in the evening, you see little men making little boxes in every doorway – but if you *do* go early in the morning it is best to take an umbrella as they empty their pots de chambres out of the windows –

I told you about going to the beaches of Salerno, and to Battapaglia and Gerald's old haunts in a previous letter, and on the way back we took a so-called "short cut" which turned out to be a narrow road, full of pot-holes, and clouds of fine white dust. We were frightened the low-slung car would have a bad knock in those awful ruts and had to go slowly – horrible children ran out into the road and tried to grab my arm, one man on a mule tried to flick Gerald's beret off his head with his whip. We were glad to get off *that* road in one piece. Except for 'that road' and the miles of slums in Naples, the children all seemed very healthy and good-looking and full of smiles.

We left Sorrento before 8 on Monday morning the 12th – got 1/2 way to Naples and Gerald remembered he had left his cinecamera behind so we had to go all the way back for it – grr! We went through Capua – and Gerald shewed me where they had stayed for several days, during the war – and the Germans were on the other side of the narrow river – with high banks on either side. They had been ordered to go down the bank on ladders, cross the river and climb the other bank – (as easy for the Huns to pick them off, as sitting birds) I remembered Gerald telling me the story, of how he took Julian G. [Gascoigne] for a walk along there, one night, and then it was quite obvious to G that the place was full of 'Krauts' t'other side, and when I saw the place, was glad the order had been cancelled! We drove on past Monte Maggiore (Gerald's "hill") and Monte Camino (Ralph Howard's 'hill') – through lovely country to Monte Cassino, a *most* impressive place –

2nd October 1956   Greenmarch

Poor Gerald has reluctantly decided to sell the business — It is very hard after the eleven years of hard work he has put in, but there is nothing else for it — Anthony has lost all interest — and Sam does practically nothing but *grumble* — and draw out £10 each week — His and George Maddock's wages are far far more than the business makes nowadays — at least they made a lot of money at one time — Thank God for the "market garden" to keep G. occupied. I have a feeling G. will probably find something else as well, so am not *too* despondent about it. No good waiting until the thing falls about our ears — so *hope* it'll sell.

23rd October 1956   Greenmarch

I *will* be glad when the U.S. elections are over, we get nothing about it much in the papers, so I don't know what's going on — The English and Americans seem to understand each other now as little as they did *before* this last war, it is a great pity — the English Speaking Union's puny efforts are like banging against a stone wall of prejudice and misunderstanding on BOTH sides —

7th November 1956   Greenmarch

It seems *awful* that I have not written to you since before your birthday — and so much has happened since then! (an understatement!). I am so glad you rec'd the letters and etc. on the 29th and thank you very much for your cable — I have been longing to hear from you to know *your* views on the international situation — though perhaps you felt as perplexed as I do! I kept tearing out clippings to send you — and then either lost them or 1/2 a day later the situation had changed so much that they were 'stale' — Last week was gloomy indeed, and very difficult not to feel completely miserable about everything — anyway thank goodness the US elections are over! I expect you were glad that Eisenhower was re-elected — Everyone here seemed completely *divided* in their opinion of whether England and France were right to walk into Egypt.[1] Many people felt that England had disgraced herself by doing such a thing — Of course the Socialists jumped at it and hoped to overthrow the Government — At the present moment of writing it would appear (to me) that [Anthony] Eden did the courageous and sensible thing, as he must have known all about the Russians pouring ammunition into Egypt and taking the opportunity when U.S. had her eyes only on their forthcoming election — What a world! Well, let's hope that the U.N. in Egypt will do some good — and let's also hope that Mr. Dulles is replaced by someone else — If only he could have been *firm* at the time when it was needed — I expect the U.S. was shocked (as 1/2 England was) at the English and French walk-in — Now France is furious with us for not continuing; the U.S. more anti-British than ever; and a majority of British angry with US for not standing up with them. Let's hope the Big 3 can get together again. As for Hungary, it's too dreadful —² Well, I can't go on like this as am running short of *paper*!

1. Ginnie is referring to the Suez crisis.

2. In November 1956 Warsaw Pact troops invaded Hungary and overthrew the moderate government led by Imre Nagy.

10th November 1956   *Richmond*

The shouting and the tumult of the Elections are over and we have Eisenhower and Nixon again — If the former gives out, it will be embarrassing to have someone who <u>looks</u> like Nixon as President — As Dulles is ill, we won't have him for some time — I had a letter from Lesley who suggested they had operated on the wrong end of Dulles — I am so unhappy over the Mid East situation that I have stopped reading about it —

17th November 1956   *Richmond*

I was awfully glad to have your letter which arrived yesterday — of course I cannot help but be a bit worried about the state this world finds itself in, at the moment — It is all such a mess that I am bewildered like everyone else, and, as there are so many angles and so much to worry about, that I go on as if nothing were happening, and am reminded of an old friend, Kitty Fontaine, who used to say, "I have so much to do, that I think I will make a pincushion". As for my ideas on the subject of what England and France did in the Suez crisis, I have, so far, believed that it was perhaps the expedient thing to do, so you might say that I have inclined to the Bun Curling attitude – instead of the Cedric Braby one –[1] *I can understand that the world was somewhat shocked by the fact that the U.S. was not notified, but, under the circumstances, perhaps those two nations could not go on just talking forever – and doing nothing – I have volubly defended the incident, whenever I have heard any criticism – The fact is, I haven't heard over much criticism of it, at all – Everyone is confused and dazed by the constant changes and all the thrusts and counterthrusts. Naturally, Russia is at the bottom of all of it, and wishes us to be confused, and it is important that we remain as calm and confident as we possibly can be – I might say, though that the U.S. is as divided on the subject as England seems to be.*

I have not been very enthusiastic about Eisenhower's administration lately – and although I chose the lesser of two evils, when I voted for him, I really wanted to vote for the man who came out for States' Rights, but was afraid I might be helping to elect Stevenson –[2] *Our two major parties are now exactly alike, and both are socialistic. The Republicans, in effect, bought the negro vote, and for that I have a supreme contempt! I consider that going down the drain with socialism, which is now a universal trend is complete assininity* [sic], *and the result of superficial values and fuzzy thinking. It may look all right on paper, but it doesn't work – If the Communists in other European countries, other than Russia, and Communists on this continent, are not disillusioned and disgusted by Russia's brutality in Hungary, then they are hopeless criminals and beyond hope –*

Aside from the Middle East tinder box, I am so incensed by what the power drunk politicians are doing to this country that I am afraid I will put my blood pressure up to boiling. I can't go into all this, as like you, I shall run out of paper –

I had the chance to have a long talk with Judge Lindsay Almond whom people say may be our next Governor, Wednesday evening, at an after theatre party at Agecroft, and he said it was dangerous and iniquitous (the high handed performances in Washington).[3] *When we parted his eyes were flashing and his face was red with fury – and he said he must see me again! His wife was with us, so it was all right! I think he was interested to have met a* *female who had political convictions, innocent of <u>sentimentality</u> – that is the curse of the American public –*

Tuesday, to a St. James' Church meeting of Woman's Auxiliary and to He-len's and my reading in the Woman's Club – We chose four "Essays" of Max Beerbohm's – two very amusing ones and two rather poetic and serious ones – I read the funny ones because Helen laughs so much, she spoils the effect. One was called "Hosts and Guests" and the other, "On seeing people off" which is a scream – [4]

Wednesday I had to go to the Church Bazaar – I bought some <u>pickle</u> and presented Helen with one of the jars, because she asked me to get her some – She has just called me to say she sampled it, and it is the most <u>awful pickle</u> she ever tasted – Well, at least we had a laugh over that one – From the Bazaar I trailed down to the Womans Club to lunch with Janie Lamb, and to my astonishment had an "<u>excellent</u> dejeuner" and heard a man named <u>Fishwick</u> lecture on the "Virginia Gentleman" – It sounded awful, but ac-tually turned out to be quite interesting – He said a <u>few</u> of those who came to Virginia <u>were</u> "gentlemen" and wished to preserve their forebears' way of life, and that those who were not gentlemen wanted to become gentlemen, and it was compounded of that nostalgic desire, and European romanticism – and it actually did create a different point of view from the rest of the New World immigrants, and persists to this day – He added it was our besetting sin – really quite funny, and I suppose there is a bit of truth in it. Even if it is an illusion, it is preferable to some other Americana I can think of.

1. David (Bun) Curling, 1923–93, was director of the J. Walter Thompson advertising company. Cedric Braby was Gerald and Ginnie's lawyer.

2. Bougie is possibly referring to the South Carolinians for Independent Electors Party, which nominated Harry Flood Byrd from Virginia as a presidential candidate, but more likely to the States Rights Party, which nominated Thomas Coleman Andrews. The con-vention for the latter was held in Richmond on 15 October.

3. James Lindsay Almond Jr., 1896–1986, was a Virginia state attorney general from 1948 to 1957 and governor of Virginia between 1958 and 1962. Agecroft Hall was a fifteenth-century English manor relocated to Richmond from Manchester.

4. For "Hosts and Guests," see Max Beerbohm, *And Even Now* (London: William Heinemann, 1920), 125–26; for "Seeing People Off," see Max Beerbohm, *Yet Again* (Lon-don: William Heinemann, 1951), 17–26.

17th February 1957   Richmond

*Tuesday I went to Mrs. Greenhow Maury's house to a political meeting and
heard Coleman Andrews talk about what was going on in Washington. When
he said "The Jackasses" did this or that, I was more than delighted! We asked
questions and he told us some very interesting but disturbing things. He thinks
Eisenhower has very bad advisers and says he is in the hands of a powerful
group of which his brother Milton is a member – they are socialistic – Soon,
the wheels will begin to turn, and a new political party is to be launched – It
will be conservative but here, it cannot be called that, and it may be named
the "Constitutional Party" – As there are states where it is forbidden to use
two names such as "States Rights", one name it must be – All 48 States are
organizing now, so as to be ready for the next election – I hope it comes off
– Mr. Andrews said it was something of a headache to have to deal with all
the crackpots, who are springing up with wild ideas – like tares in the wheat
– Dulles is under constant fire, but the President hangs on to him??*

*Things are rather tense in the South, as we are resisting the so called "Civil
Rights" bill which the socialists are trying to put through Congress – We shall
have the Gestapo if it passes – so let us hope it won't.*

10th March 1957   Richmond

*Friday I shopped a little, went to the Bank, sent more flowers to wheezy old
ladies, and landed up, in the pouring rain, at the Valentine Museum at 8 p.m.
to see pictures of some restorations of what <u>we call</u>, old houses – and to hear
Mr. Howland explain. This seems to be "restoration year" – That speaker is
head of the National Trust here, which is a fairly new thing in the U.S. I used
to correspond with Ulysses S. Grant III about it when it was being launched
as he was its first President.*

*Saturday, I went to C.O. Alley's agency and made a deposit on my passage
via Empress of Britain – I can change if I <u>have</u> to, but it is a good comfortable
accommodation in a cabin by myself, and I thought I had better take it.*

25th March 1957 (No.1)   Greenmarch

Gerald was asked to race Griffin the R.O.R.C. yacht in 1 or 2 races and *refused* (much to my annoyance) as he said "younger men should have the opportunity" —[1] Since then he has had a letter to say that Owen Aisher and Sir Giles Guthrie have *given* the lovely yacht Ex-Yeoman (which won the Fastnet a few years ago) to the R.O.R.C. — and they want *Gerald* to race her in the Fastnet and if he does there are several people who are anxious to sign on with him![2] I was *thrilled* that he was asked, after all his natter about being a has-been! and I think he was too — and think he's going to accept. It also suits *my* plans very well!! — as will be more *free* with you and the children.

1. R.O.R.C.: Royal Ocean Racing Club.

2. Owen Aisher, 1900–1993, was chair of Marley Tile Companies and was elected yachtsman of the year in 1958. Sir Giles Guthrie, 1916–79, was the second baronet from 1945, a lieutenant commander in the Fleet Air Arm 1939–46, and chair of BOAC 1964–68.

25th March 1957 (No.2)   Greenmarch

The news was so terrible last week that we really felt we were going to have a general strike — as they had in 1926 (before my time) — Gerald had more or less arranged to drive a train! if the G. strike occurred. Well, apparently there *isn't* going to be a railway strike anyway — and in Bermuda Eisenhower, Dulles, Macmillan, and Selwyn-Lloyd are singing "Auld Lang Syne" —[1]

Gerald and I went to see "Anastasia" with Ingrid Bergman and Yul Brunner — It is a *must* for you if you haven't already seen it! as it takes place in Paris in 1928 — terribly nostalgic-making and yet *so* romantic and glamourous, and also so well acted that I came out walking on air!!

1. A four-day summit was held in Bermuda to patch up quarrels over Suez, endorse support for the European Common Market, and agree on an arms policy. Harold Macmillan, 1894–1986, the first Earl of Stockton, was British prime minister 1957–63. Selwyn Brooke Lloyd, 1904–78, for 1976 Baron Selwyn-Lloyd, was secretary of state for foreign affairs 1955–60.

4th May 1957   *Richmond*

I was supposed to be at Jamestown Monday for the dedication of the Cross we put up in memory of those poor first settlers, who died of starvation and a few other unpleasant things, but I couldn't do that and go to the English Speaking dinner for Lord De la Warr as well, so I chose the latter festivity because I wanted to see him because of his ancestor, Thomas West, the Lord De la Warr who was our first Colonial Governor in Virginia —[1] *The younger brother left descendants in Virginia and it is from that one, we are descended. Naturally I did not bore him with those details, but I was just rather curious to see what he was like. Both he and his wife are perfectly charming, and Bessie Morton told me today that they were wonderfully easy guests. As he had been Postmaster General in England, I told him I thought he had the best postal service I knew of — ours has been a joke of late —*

Thursday I went to Anne Johns to a meeting of the National Cathedral Association, and, then, to the Page House to be there for the rehanging of the portraits which I have had refurbished a bit —[2] *Had the glass taken off and the frames touched up, etc. I was rather frantic about that as I have changed things around and was afraid I might have the wrath of the Board rain on my head. I made the President join me, as well as one or two others — I was determined not to assume complete responsibility — I think I have done a good job, and hope they will like it — I have been working on it for two months with very little help, but the walls are beautifully decorated and I have new curtains, lamp shades etc. I removed the awful paintings, which offended me, and when I have completed it, I shall present it to the Board with my compliments and possibly resign as Chairman —*

1. Herbrand Edward Brassey Sackville, 1900–1976, from 1915 the ninth Earl De La Warr, was a British politician who was postmaster general from 1951 to 1955. Thomas West, the third Baron De La Warr, 1577–1618, was the first governor of Virginia, after whom the state of Delaware was named. The link between Bougie and her ancestor is not known.

2. The Page House, Richmond, was bequeathed to the Association for the Preservation of Virginia Antiquities by Gabriele Page and used as APVA headquarters until 1984. It is now called Pusey House.

25th August 1957   Greenmarch

[Monday] evening Sandra and Dick Churston very kindly asked me to dinner to meet Agatha Christie – Her husband, Professor Mallowan, the Egyptologist also there – and her daughter, with husband, as well.[1] Daughter is a "plum bum" and impossible to talk to. Agatha is a very nice old girl, but every now and then she would be very inattentive and one felt she was thinking up a fresh plot. Dickie was in his best form so it was amusing if faintly "sticky" at times. Dickie has asked me to race in the Torquay regatta, very sweet of him, but I don't know if I'll go.

1. Max Mallowan, 1904–78, British archaeologist.

9th September 1957   Greenmarch

Angie returned from Cornwall on Saturday evening, having had a wonderful time and thoroughly enjoyed herself surfing – I was glad to see her home again and looking well – as every time I thought of her living in a caravan and going to a communal lavatory I got sweaty hands! I suppose one is stupid to worry – but difficult not to – I am definitely not letting them go to public places at the moment. As you probably know, there is not enough [polio] vaccine in England to go around – and so far only the under tens have had it.[1] I am seriously considering if it would be a good thing to try and have some Salk vaccine sent from U.S. – the english says *theirs* is safer; the US have agreed to send Salk, but do *not* wish to make the english kind there – what a muddle – It would be a bit tricky to have Salk sent over, as I gather it has to be refrigerated. I am going to find out what Phyl [Gore] is going to do about Maxine – I thought if I *could* get it, it would be best to have it done in the Xmas holidays – as believe 'they' don't approve of having it done in the summer months –[2]

1. Polio vaccinations were not taken up by many in Britain until 1959, when a major footballer (soccer player) died from the disease. By the early 1960s the amount of cases had fallen due to mass immunization; see Tony Gould, *A Summer Plague: Polio and Its Survivors* (New Haven, Conn.: Yale University Press, 1995), 173–74.

2. Maxine Gore, b. 1947, from 1968 Eugster.

27th September 1957   *Richmond*

We are having a rather tragic time, <u>here</u>, about the Negroes — although Richmond is quite calm. I am sure all the foreign newsheets are having a field day. The Southerners simply loathe Eisenhower, Brownell, the Yankee Atty. General, and the nine "old men" of the Supreme Court, and would secede from the U.S. if they could —[1] It is unspeakable for the President to send Paratroopers to Little Rock <u>before</u> he knew what <u>might</u> occur — Even the Wall St. Journal has censured him for that — The disappointment in Eisenhower is profound, and everyone I know thinks Dulles is very stupid. How awful that this great country has such inadequate leadership — Well, at least it will be interesting to know what Virginia will do when the N.A.A.C.P. and the "Pinks" in Washington begin to attack <u>us</u>. I am sure the Governor will <u>close the schools</u> — What fun that will be for the would be scholars! It is coming, and I hope we give the Federal Government in Washington as much trouble as possible without all of us being put in prison. There aren't enough prisons, so maybe you will hear of me being in a concentration camp!!

Personally, I like all the negroes who work for me — and 9/10ths of the poor things don't know what it is all about, and don't <u>want</u> to go to school with the white children. The <u>real</u> issue is much deeper than that. It is the States Rights to manage their own affairs — We are conservative, and the Yankees are growing pinker every day — We find the whole business loathesome, and are angry —

---

1. Herbert Brownell Jr., 1904–96, U.S. attorney general 1953–57.

30th September 1957   Greenmarch

I have been reading all about Little Rock Arkansas with great interest. How humiliating for the 101st airborne troops to have to go there — what a mess it is. 9 coloured children insisting on going to a white school of nearly 1000 — Isn't it ridiculous? and the press makes me sick — all my Southern blood comes to the fore on these occasions. Was glad Joy (who is a Yankee) agreed with me! Gerald says he can imagine how you are feeling about it!

22nd October 1957   Greenmarch

I do so hope you were able to get to Jamestown and am anxiously awaiting your letter. The Queen seems to have been a great success in Canada and the U.S. − (I hope she really was) but I shall be glad when she gets home this afternoon − imagine having the train journey to N.Y. then 14 hours 'on view'; and then flying the Atlantic − whew −

16th December 1957   *Richmond*

I sent you a cable so that you would know I had been to Montreal and had returned in safety, and this letter will just be a log of that Hegira. I was able to get a bedroom on the Montrealer at the last minute and left here Wednesday at 11.50 a.m. I was quite comfortable and got a good night's sleep which was fortunate because of the hard and distressing day ahead of me, as Huntly was to have his service at 2 o'clock on Thursday −[1]

I sat so close to the coffin all covered with pink roses, during the service, that I was afraid I was going to make a spectacle of myself − but managed not to. The Bishop and the Dean conducted the service which was very impressive although Nellie, a Presbyterian, thought it <u>cold</u>. I like it <u>impersonal</u> − and don't want any personal references − In spite of the blizzard, the whole centre of the cathedral was filled, which was a tribute as so many of Huntly's friends are older people − I went with the rest of the family to a chapel for a 5 minutes service on top of Mount Royal. It was very weird as we got out of the car − like a sort of Valhalla with a howling West wind, covering everyone with snow, including, as well, the coffin and the pink roses which covered darling Huntly. I was glad of that − He loved the snow! All this was because he is to be cremated and the others are up there now.

I am <u>very</u> glad I went − They were all so appreciative and were perfectly sweet to me − Before I left Guy [Drummond] said "We all know how much you meant to Huntly and realize how faithful you have been" which I answered by telling him that no one could possibly know what he had meant to you and me nor how much he had done for us through the years. They all wished for you, but of course knew that it was impossible for you to get there. I shall never forget their kindness −

Florence is certainly nearing her end and that will be a blessing. She has been very sweet and is so pathetic that I feel sometimes I can't take it —

1. Huntly Drummond died in December 1957.

7th March 1958   Greenmarch

I waved to you [from the aeroplane] as I left, and saw you and Gerna [Gilmour] waving — then I got *behind* the "Montreal Star" and cried buckets . . . I had a wonderful seat, by the window, and very very comfortable — Sat next to an english businessman who was I think, Jewish, and a bit 'ow, ow' but he was *very* nice, rather a gentle soul and a nice sense of humour. I had a drink or 2 and we had an excellent dinner, with champagne about 7. Around 10 o'clock they turned out the lights and everyone settled down, but me, to sleep. It was a glorious night — crystal clear! — a full moon, and below us I could see ice-floes, in spite of the fact we were so high up. The steward confirmed they were ice floes and not clouds — so it wasn't my imagination! Later on I looked out of the window, and saw the beginnings of Northern Lights, and dared not stop looking in case they got better — The ordinary white lights gradually changed to *deep rose* and green. I have never seen anything so beautiful — I watched *fascinated* and felt so elated, and superior to the creatures who were snoring and unaware of the beauty they were missing. I wanted to wake them all up but felt I wouldn't be very popular! — The lights faded out just before midnight and I fell asleep. Just after 1 a.m. the stewardess rushed in, turned on all the lights said "Good morning everybody we will be having breakfast shortly"!!! I paid no attention of course — until I was handed some scrambled eggs and ate them lackadaisically — we landed at 2.30 a.m. Montreal time! *7.30* G.M.T. I felt I had hardly left the ground. Just over NINE hours direct to London — *incredible.*

29th September 1958   *Richmond*

I was dreading that awful "crack of doom" feeling at the airport when they call out that visitors must part from the <u>departing</u> ones, and remembered that play "Outward Bound" —

The plane was the most luxurious one I have ever been in and the service on Boac is "par excellence". I found myself seated beside one Mr. <u>Lincus,</u> if that is the proper spelling, a jew who lives in London but has a strong and strange accent — I couldn't place it — He told me immediately that he had taken a berth and I could have <u>both</u> seats which was marvellous. I was wrapped in 3 blankets after dinner, and really got some sleep — Lincus drank quite a lot of champagne before dinner, as well as white and red wine during the meal — Even I indulged a bit. We had a little conversation and he told me he lived in Belgrave Square and asked me if I knew where that was! Anyway I was grateful to Lincus for giving me extra room — I should have been happier if Capt. Gray hadn't come on the scene and informed us that we were taking a rather northerly route to <u>try</u> to escape a "depression" with high winds — It was quite bumpy at times and there was a beastly disagreeable sound as of hail blown against the portholes —

Arriving near New York a thick fog prevented our landing, so we circled about for over a half hour and the pilot informed us there was too much traffic on the runways, as well, but the plane was handled wonderfully — You felt <u>nothing</u> when we touched ground, and the shaking from "going into reverse" to slow up, was negligible —

16th November 1958   *Richmond*

Tuesday to the Auxiliary meeting in the Church, where one Page Williams spinster, and psychiatrist discussed <u>sex before</u> and after marriage. As with few exceptions, all the people present were over 65 years old, I think it was a waste of time. One question pondered was as follows — Do women give into men more often than men do to women? I answered that one! and said, "Since the Amazons disappeared from the scene women have given in to men, for that is the only way they can get a chance but make no mistake about their secret weapons. They usually know what they are doing, even if the men don't" — A hush fell on the audience! I only stay in that group in order to debunk some of the things in the Book they are studying. The only sensible things are what one was taught at mothers knee —

14th July 1959   Greenmarch

I had a comfortable journey back [from London], in an empty compartment save for one american man who was coming to see Sean O'Casey to celebrate his 75th birthday − (didn't know O'Casey lived in Torquay − and sorry to say I can't remember anything he wrote either!)[1]

1. Sean O'Casey, 1884–1964, an Irish playwright whose plays include *Juno and the Paycock* and *The Plough and the Stars.*

8th November 1959   *Richmond*

Last night − to a party at Louise Reynolds' where the English poet Stephen Spender read his poems −[1] *I intended to resign from the Poetry Society, but was urged to stay on − I really do not enjoy it, and only hung on because of Florie − Spender is one of the best contemporary poets, and is leonine looking, but he mumbles, and most of his audience didn't hear very well. I* <u>heard</u> *but the new poetry bores me −*

1. Stephen Spender, 1909–95, an English poet and critic.

18th December 1959   *Richmond*

Last night I met the Hesbys downstairs wandering about at midnight, and found out they had been giving the waitresses and cooks a party in the large dining room.[1] *The Hesbys cooked steaks and various things and waited on the maids − Martha, in my dining room, told us tonight that they had purposely complained of the service and cooking "just as we did", and she seemed to think that part of it was most enjoyable! Certainly the negroes have a sense of humour.*

1. Mr. and Mrs. Hesby managed the Chesterfield Apartment block.

19th September 1960   *Richmond*

I have seen Miss Lowry and heard her troubles, talked to Janie about A.P.V.A.
and the damage at Jamestown which actually isn't too bad.[1] *Since "Donna"*
visited us we have been threatened with "Ethel" and "Florence" (not Night-
ingale) but they seemed to have petered out – Instead, we have Castro in New
York, worse than any hurricane –

I had a letter from Parke Rouse of the Jamestown Foundation, asking for
your address – I think you are going to get an invitation to the unveiling
or something of the statue of John Smith in London, and they hope to have
the Queen Mother and the Lord Mayor of London. Parke wanted to know if
there were other Virginians in England who would be eligible – I sent Helen
Norman's name, and rang her up to ask if she knew of any – There is the
obvious flock of Lady Astor's relatives and she named Joyce Grenfell –[2] *I*
thought she was over here with Caroline – are there two of them?

1. A.P.V.A.: Association for the Preservation of Virginia Antiquities.

2. Joyce Grenfell née Phipps, 1910–79, was a humorous writer and a stage, radio, and television performer. She was Nancy Astor's niece.

16th October 1960   *Richmond*

We are relieved that the table banging Mr. K. [Khrushchev] has left –[1] *There*
were pictures of his shoe which he removed in order to bang more effectively
– We (meaning Emma Gray, et al) are reading a history of Russia and have
got as far as the entrance on the scene of the first Romanoff, who was the great
nephew of Anastasia, wife of Ivan the Terrible. She was actually a Roman
Princess and that is I presume why the family were Romanoffs – Dear old
Ivan adored her, and only became terrible after her death, although he mar-
ried five or six other females! It is really quite intriguing, and of course the
Russians have not changed much since the Tartar Invasion, which brought
barbarous rule to the old Russ for about 700 years – They seemed fairly
innocuous before that and there was a lot of Viking blood – a nice clean in-
heritance in comparison with Tartars (I may not be spelling that properly)

Now, we are being bored out of sanity, by this truly ridiculous campaign for President — I have ceased to read about it and won't look at their foolish antics on television —

The prospective Democratic Vice President, Lyndon Johnson is a "you-all" type of Texan and has injected the only comic element into the speech making — [2] *Henry Cabot Lodge his opposite number has alienated some Southerners by promising to put a black man in the Cabinet if the Republicans get in —* [3] *In spite of that, I shall <u>have</u> to vote <u>against</u> Kennedy, as I have no one to vote <u>for</u> — a sad state of affairs in a "Time of Troubles" — I shall be glad when it is over — It is so disillusioning. Tomorrow, I am going to a Ladies* ["Republican" crossed out] *Repugnant luncheon in the Commonwealth! pour le statistique — will report on it — I may be lured to make a few remarks, and may be ejected.*

1. Nikita Khruschev, the leader of the USSR 1958–64, demonstrated his anger at accusations of imperialism at a UN General Assembly by removing one of his shoes and banging it on his desk in protest.

2. Lyndon Baines Johnson, 1908–73, U.S. president 1963–69.

3. Henry Cabot Lodge Jr., 1902–85, was a Massachusetts senator 1937–44 and 1947–53 and a Republican vice presidential candidate in 1960. He was ambassador to Vietnam 1963–67 and Germany 1968–69.

22nd October 1960   *Richmond*

I went to a party at Gen'l. Vincent Meyer's Sunday, a quite large dinner where we sat at small tables — We talked about our terrible and boring political campaign for President and nice Mr. Arthur Collins agreed with me in toto, so of course <u>I</u> had a good time — We are all terrified that Kennedy will be elected — It had never occurred to some of us that an Irish Mick would arouse such interest — I am thinking of where I can go to <u>live</u> if those radicals take charge. Mr. Gallup is so uncertain that he won't risk taking the usual poll — a bad sign —

On Thursday it rained so hard that I wondered how I should ever get out of the house through the soaked ground to the car, but the rain kindly stopped for us at one o'clock and we were taken to Festival Park [Jamestown] *to have lunch with several officials and Mr. and Mrs. <u>Walt Disney</u>! He was rather*

quiet and non committal, middle aged, and I think, very weary as he had been
sightseeing for three days, and at Yorktown, had been pursued by about 2000
teenagers asking for his signature – Mrs. Disney is quite nice and, also, quiet.
After lunch we were all taken on a tour of the Island and our pictures were
snapped with the creator of Mickey Mouse, but I don't think it has been in
any of the Richmond papers – I was going to send it to you just for a joke – I
shall now have to be content with having been "taken" with Alpha the black
servant, and the King & Queen of Greece! That was possibly Omega, as well,
for me –

30th October 1960   *Richmond*
You will see from the enclosures that I started this last week by an encounter
with Malcolm Muggeridge, who really was most amusing as a speaker, in
a kind of Oscar Wildeish way although, of course, not exactly in the same
category.[1] I had a little talk with him afterwards, as the chairman for the
lecture insisted that I speak to him – I also saw him in "I'm All Right Jack"
which is extremely funny –[2] Helen insisted on my going so we had an early
sandwich in the Clover Leaf and dashed off to the Westhampton Cinema for
the 7.15 performance – As soon as it was well started, I realized I had seen
it in England, before – Well, it was quite well worth a second viewing, so I
never confessed that I had already seen it.

We had our first reading performance in the Woman's Club on Tuesday –
subject: "The Anatomy of Snobbish-ery" – by a Hungarian named Koestler
now living in England –[3] It is really priceless, and convicts almost everyone.
I could certainly read myself in it – and everyone said they enjoyed hear-
ing it.

Did I tell you in my last letter that I heard that Reynolds Metals had con-
tributed $250,000 to help elect <u>*Kennedy,*</u> *and there is a rumour that if K. wins*
the election, Richard Reynolds, Jr. is slated to be Ambassador to England![4]
Imagine the water plug coming out of that colossal thing the U.S. has put up
in Grosvenor Square –

In the meantime Castro has seized a 3 million dollar plant of theirs in Cuba.
The fight for the next President proceeds unabated, and you can see that even
Mary Belle Meade has written to the paper –

1. No enclosures were contained in the letter. Malcolm Muggeridge, 1903–90, was a British writer and journalist.

2. *I'm All Right Jack* (1959), directed by John and Roy Boulting.

3. Arthur Koestler, 1905–83, a Hungarian writer who escaped imprisonment by the Nazis and fled to England in 1940.

4. Reynolds did not become U.S. ambassador to England. David K. E. Bruce filled the role 1961–69.

15th November 1960   Greenmarch
Gerald woke me on Wed. morning to say "*Your* new President is Roman Catholic; it's raining again; I had a lot of bills this morning; and I think the lettuce crop is ruined" – I said "thanks very much, I will now see what bad news Nannie and Auntie have for me". Luckily there was *nothing further* – and your nice letter lying on my breakfast tray –

31st March 1961   *Richmond*
I thought, as long as it is pouring torrents and too wet to go out, it would be better to begin this communication on Good Friday than April Fool's Day. I may not be able to finish it, but I have just dispatched a cable to you to thank you for the lovely <u>purple</u> hydrangea which was much admired down in the lobby – When I gave the message to the operator in Western Union, she asked me what "Bougie" meant, because she had a friend who called her husband by that name! I said it was a long story, but stood for "sparking plug", at which she was a little taken aback, so after making sure of the word in Cassell's Dictionary I rang her again and told her it also meant candle. She said "that is better" and thanked me profusely for taking the trouble, so I have made a friend in W.U.

    We are having a rather beastly time with the "blacks" – Poor old Alex Fleet was badly beaten first outside his residence on Plum Street as well as two women living near – We think that one of them may not live – The negro has confessed, but hasn't yet been convicted – Carrie (Reynolds) Smith was sitting at her desk that same evening when she looked up to find a black man in her drawing room – Carrie <u>never</u> locks her front door! says its a nuisance – Well, she managed to get him out, but when she saw his picture in the paper *she realized he was the same man who had beaten the three people – She says she has sent for a locksmith – because her family has demanded it – but still doesn't want to lock the door! She was at Bessie's luncheon on Tuesday and had to leave early as the police were waiting to take her testimony – There have been several other crimes committed, but I won't go into them – This especial neighbourhood is very brilliantly lighted at night and there is a permanent guard employed by R.P.I. so we are better off for protection here I am glad to say –*

4th June 1961   *177 Cranmer Court*
London SW3

Yesterday, I took Barbara to "Dazzling Prospect" with Margaret Rutherford, who was the whole show, as the play was all about a horse race in Ireland, directed by John Gielgud but nothing of a play – We had a bit of dinner at the Causerie in Claridges – She came back with me to collect my hatbox, to go for the night to Nancy Perkins <u>Field</u>-Lancaster, who has a house near Oxford. I am going with her aunt Nancy Astor! to the House of Commons on Wednesday to a tea for Lady D. MacMillan!![1]

1. Viscountess Astor née Nancy Witcher Langhorne, 1879–1964, who was born in Virginia, was the first woman to take a seat in the British House of Commons in 1919. Dorothy Macmillan née Lady Cavendish, d. 1966, was the wife of Harold Macmillan.

1st July 1961   *London S.W.3.*

On Thursday, I went to the Houses of Parliament, met Cassandra and Mr. Wise at 12.30 –[1] *He took me to the House of Lords, first, and then we had lunch with lots of members and their wives – Mr. Butler was at the next table with wife #2, and a pathetic looking boy – I don't know <u>whose</u>.*[2] *Megan Lloyd-George was just behind me – I couldn't turn round but could hear her giggling.*[3] *Cassandra and I then went in the Gallery and listened to the Members until 4 oclock – after which Roy Wise took me into the Crypt to see the 14th Century Chapel, which is quite wonderful – and I dropped Cassandra*

in Eaton Square and came here, rather exhausted, but I thoroughly enjoyed
the whole thing —

    1. Bougie was visiting with Cassandra Noel Wise née Coke. Roy Wise, 1901–74, was a
British Conservative member of Parliament 1931–45 and 1959–66.
    2. Richard Austin Butler (RAB), 1902–82, was the British home secretary 1957–62 and
foreign minister 1963–64. His second wife was Mollie Courtauld née Montgomerie.
    3. Lady Megan Lloyd George, 1902–66, was the Labour member of Parliament for Car-
marthen 1957–66. She was the daughter of David Lloyd George, the Liberal prime minister
of Britain 1916–22.

26th September 1961   *Richmond*
There was a concert that night, by the New York Philharmonic Orchestra
with that arch showman Leonard Bernstein conducting, and Mr. Moody had
mailed tickets to me on faith which was very kind, as the place was sold out.[1]
They played Beethoven's 5th Symphony, and finished off with a rousing ren-
dering of Dixie which brought the audience of 5000 to its feet accompanied
by quite a few rebel yells! — quite barbaric and exciting —

I have just come from an Executive Board meeting of the A.P.V.A. which lasted
three hours, where the nine women all talked at once, and tomorrow I have
an appointment with Mr. Kelley, Trust officer, when I shall settle my business
affairs, left with them for five months — After that, I can draw breath —

    1. Leonard Bernstein, 1918–90, the American conductor, composer and pianist.

8th January 1962   *Richmond*
I have been trying to clean this apartment, and get rid of Christmas cards,
etc. I did have yours, for which many thanks — It came in after Christmas,
but so did a good many others — I had some very pretty ones this year and
have saved a few including yours — The others I give to the Church as they
seem to have some use for them — I spent the morning cutting the names and
personal messages off — Old Blanche was here cleaning brass for me, and
said her husband had been Santa Claus for a Bank! As William is quite black,

I presume it was a negro Bank — She said there were a lot of children at the Bank party, among them William's niece, who, after sitting on his knee and telling him what she wanted for Christmas, came to her and said, "There's something very funny about Santa Claus — He looks like Uncle William — I am going to ask him about it" — "Oh no", said Blanche, "He's going back to the North Pole right away" — whereupon the small niece looked fixedly at her and said "You mean to 1018 Idlewild Avenue"!

This place is a bit of a mad house now, and the only real pleasure I get from the people, I have from contact with the blacks — They have a sense of humour and are amusing anyhow — I had a young boy here Saturday working for me, and I started him dusting books — He goes to the Negro University here — I left the room, and when I came back into "de tea room", he had put the dust cloth down and was just reading the titles on the books — and he said "You have quite a collection of nice books. What <u>college</u> did you attend?" — I felt I had to save my reputation with the budding scholar, and answered that my family was "very literary"! but that when I was his age, women in Virginia didn't go to college!! I am certain I lost cast.

24th February 1962   Greenmarch
We were thrilled *of course* about Colonel Glenn's terrific success in the 'capsule', and the excitement in U.S. must have been *terrific*, though the interview with "Mamma and Papa" Glenn was painful, the one we saw last night when they interviewed Col. Glenn himself was *most* impressive.[1] He shewed such charming *modesty* that it was very awe-inspiring —

1. The astronaut John Glenn, b. 1921, was the first American to orbit the earth. He was a Democrat and served as a U.S. senator for Ohio 1975–99.

10th [?] *March 1962*   *Richmond*
To go back to New York — we had a very interesting and satisfactory four days. Saw the visiting Old Vic do Macbeth, Paul Schofield [sic] *in A Man for All Seasons, Wendy Hiller and Maurice Evans in The Aspern Papers, and heard the Turandot of Puccini — undoubtedly one of the most magnificently*

staged performances I have ever seen – also lovely music with Birgit Nillson
[sic] in the title role – quite wonderful –[1]

   Besides all this, I went to the Museum to see the Rembrandt recently ac-
quired at the highest price ever paid for a picture! I bought two hats at Sax 5th
Ave, and was on the corner when Col. Glenn came riding up 5th Ave – They
turned at 50th Street – I could almost have touched the car, but the crowd
was so great that I couldn't see him – but that didn't matter, because I was so
intrigued with the ticker tape demonstration – my first experience, and really
fantastic –

1. Paul Scofield, 1922–, was a British actor and director. The play *A Man for All Seasons*
is by Robert Bolt (London: Heinemann, 1960). Wendy Hiller, 1912–2003, dame from 1975,
was a British stage, film, and television actor. Maurice Evans, 1901–89, was a British stage
actor. Michael Redgrave's *The Aspern Papers* was adapted for the theater from a story by
Henry James (London: Samuel French, 1966). Birgit Nilsson, 1918–2006, was a Swedish
soprano.

17th March 1962   *Richmond*
Speaking of "unfinished business"! I seem to have a great deal of it – I went
down to the Trust Co yesterday to interview my friend Mr. Floyd Kelly about
making my will, at their suggestion, because they keep changing the laws
here – Now, I have to have a <u>number</u>, even though I haven't any interest in
"Social Security" – When everyone has to answer to a number we might as
well join up with the U.S.S.R. It infuriates me – As there are about 10 of the
Irish Catholic Kennedys running this Govt. now, I am fearful of our never
getting out of their grip – It shows signs of becoming a <u>dynasty</u> – I should
like to penalize all the ignorant asses who voted for John K.

   The weather here has been beastly for two months – That dreadful storm
has devastated the Va coast – Almost all of the lovely sand beach at Va Beach
has disappeared and we are asking for 10 million dollars for the poor people
who have lost all their possessions – We are lucky in Richmond, the damage
to the trees is bad and, especially, the magnolias – but that is nothing –

23rd October 1962   Greenmarch

WELL! I have got everything organized – have arranged for Nannie to go into a nursing-home, written her family, organized the house, paid all my bills, written all my business letters, done washing and ironing, ordered food for the house, bought a dress and a hat etc etc etc. Rushed out with letters at 7 pm last night, put dinner in stove, and finally sat down to enjoy (?) television after dinner – and just *happened* to hear the news!! Can't imagine what is going on and don't understand any of it except that it looks pretty grim – [1] Expect it seems worse over here? Anyway there it is. *I* am all set, and D.V. and wind and weather and Mr Kennedy permitting, I am off on Sunday –

1. Ginnie is referring to coverage of the Cuban missile crisis.

1st February 1963   *Richmond*

This has been the most trying winter everywhere in the western world, except <u>*Alaska*</u> *where it has been unusually warm – That is ridiculous, and so is almost everything else at the moment – There was an amusing old negro story in the paper this morning – Eve got tired of not having anyone to talk to – so she, as Adam was always fishing, persuaded Adam to ask "de Lord" to make some people, which he consented to do, but* [as] *night was coming on and he hadn't put their* <u>*brains*</u> *in, he promised to return in the morning to finish – But, when he got back the creatures had walked away, and "they is been multiplying all over the world ever since"! –*

As for de Gaulle, I am enclosing a few newspaper articles – Everyone is furious with him, and some think he cannot, cannot "get away with it" – He seems to be sidling up to Russia! – and he wants Spain to refuse us the privilege of maintaining bases – I think the Americans now realize that he wants more than anything to keep <u>*America*</u> *out of Europe – and that some of his desire to veto England's entry has to do with that – One cannot see what he is up to, exactly at the moment – but it may become clearer later on – Of course we know that the French people are completely lacking in gratitude, are selfish, self centered and grasping –*

I have been "brought up", so to speak, on the idea and ideal of the At-
lantic System, the Monroe Doctrine which for a long time was implemented
by England before we had a real Navy, and then the main thing was to pre-
vent Germany from getting too much of a foothold anywhere in the Atlantic
− Also Russia has always been trying to push her influence out into both the
Mediterranean (on the way to the Atlantic) and the Pacific − It is a game of
chess and I am not clever enough to know where De Gaulle thinks he is going
to end up. Maybe someone will lie in wait for him on those trips between Paris
and Colombey les deux Eglises!! He is very much detested at the moment over
here − but that, of course, is not the point −

I hope that all is going well and that the worst is over as to weather! Un-
doubtedly, this has been a beastly winter, from almost every angle − Tomor-
row is groundhog day! He can crawl in his hole and stick his tongue out at the
poor "critters" on the outside −

31st March 1963   Greenmarch

Having been hibernating all winter like a tortoise, I have come to and actually read a few papers, and see to my horror that whilst I was asleep not only
has Beeching taken away most of the Railways including *dear* Churston −
Boo! Hoo! but MacMillan has thrown away the only remaining bits left of
the British Empire.[1] Welensky says he is "worse than Lord North".[2] Very
depressing. But the sun is shining and I cannot spend my life worrying over
the stupidity of man − and like Voltaire will just "cultiver mon jardin" −
c'est-a-dire, as soon as my lumbar regions allow it!!

1. Lord Richard Beeching, 1913–85, chair of the British Railways Board 1963–65 and
author of the Beeching Report, which recommended closure of many branch line routes.

2. Roy Welensky, 1907–91, was the prime minister of Rhodesia (now Zimbabwe) 1956–
63. Lord North, 1732–92, prime minister 1770–82, was blamed for Britain's defeat in the
War of Independence and thus the loss of America.

19th September 1963   Greenmarch

Buffie Rothwell has just telephoned from Manchester to ask if I could do
something for her. Her son-in-law Sir John Barbirolli wants ALL Agatha

Christie's books, and wants *me* to find out name of her sec'y and get her to send a complete list.[1] I said 'Funnily enough Agatha's husband was here this afternoon' — Loveday blew in saying she couldn't come to tea after all as she and Professor Mallowan were off to visit a mutual elderly friend in Exeter![2] — *So* I'll ring Loveday to find out name of sec'y for me. I feel like an *agent* or something getting Agatha to write to Barbirolli!

1. Sir John Barbirolli, 1899–1970, English conductor and cellist, conductor of the Hallé Orchestra 1943–70.

2. Loveday Llewellyn née Bolitho, b. 1923.

11th October 1963   Greenmarch

On Tuesday I went to first E.S.U. luncheon of the season, and took Angie. I think it amused her "pour les statistiques" — anyway she looked very nice and several people said nice things about her which pleased me. The young Page scholar had just returned from U.S. and spoke on U.S. education — seemed to think it better than the english variety but perhaps he was being polite. He had visited V.M.I. and Washington and Lee and said the Southerners usually complained of the 'language difficulty' and that Bing Crosby and Alastair Cook spoke with such english accents they were difficult to understand — I was fascinated. Then I met an exchange teacher from Texas whose tie instead of being in usual 'tie-silk' was made of lapis-lazuli and bits of string. I longed to pull it and see if it would go up and down like a Venetian blind.

We are very sad to think poor Mr MacMillan had to have an 'op' and has resigned — shudder to think what will happen to us now.

19th October 1963   Greenmarch

Just heard Lord Home's speech and are *thrilled* he is going to be the P.M.[1] It tickles me to think that an aristocrat has actually been chosen in this age of the common man. He appears to have more intelligence AND guts than most of the common men! Also I believe he is very popular and well thought-of in the U.S. which is certainly a GOOD THING.

1. Alec Douglas-Home, 1903–95, was the British foreign secretary 1960–63 and 1970–74 and Conservative prime minister 1963–64. He renounced his title of the fourteenth Earl of Home in order to sit in the House of Commons.

27th November 1963   Greenmarch
Just a line to say how horrified we were at the dreadful news about [the assassination of] President Kennedy –

Am longing to receive your reaction about the news in U.S. – an Irish American Roman Catholic, shot by a pro Castro Communist married to a Russian, shot by a jewish night club owner! What next? You *wouldn't believe* how upset people seem to be over here –

28th November 1963   Greenmarch
Last night I listened to the NEW President, and thought he spoke very well – am *longing* to receive your reactions to the whole thing. Everyone I have spoken to seems to feel that Kennedy's death is a tragedy for the world – (somehow I don't feel you would agree with this) Even the hard-hearted Mrs Fisher (who works in the market – the one you don't like) was in *tears*!!

24th September 1964   Cabrach, Scotland
Last night we listened to that smooth customer Harold Wilson answer questions on the T.V. – I wonder if there is *any hope* of the Conservatives being elected.[1] I see 4 prisoners have escaped from Dartmoor Prison, and hope they are not living at Greenmarch!

1. Harold Wilson, 1916–95, British Labour prime minister 1964–70 and 1974–76.

4th October 1964   Greenmarch
I went out [shooting] all day on the Friday and *thoroughly* enjoyed it – one of the "guns" was introduced to Gerald as "Dandy" Wallis – (later Gerald said 'Dandy' my foot, he was known as "Inky" Wallis when we were at

Eton together and was the terror of the school with his catapults and his ink bombs!)[1] Difficult to imagine the large, pompous-looking man as 'Inky'. He was very nice, and it was ridiculous that he and G. recognized each other after 40 years. Mrs Wallis was very nice, rather a hearty woman who asked me if I "worked a dog". I wanted to say 'If I HAD a dog I wouldn't know how to WORK it" but it was a pleasant change after the 'hot-house flowers' Pamela [Cayzer] and Margaret. Dandy or Inky arrived with three guns to shoot, not only had I never seen anyone shooting with 3 guns, I have never even *heard* of it! He is apparently quite a well-known shot. Quite a retinue it was, Dandy with one wife, 2 loaders, 3 guns, and 4 dogs! We went off cross-country in the jeeps and Land Rovers, over streams, across heather, even the drive there was adventurous – Then a terrific hill to climb, Gerald was the top butt, I nearly *burst* trying to get up there and lay down *panting* on my arrival. Mrs Wallis and I dished out the lunch, hot soup and delicious salmon fishcakes in a big thermos – etc. etc. I didn't dare have a drink or a cigarette as we had to climb yet another hill after lunch – so took 2 tomatoes in my pocket to assuage my thirst – and of course they were completely *squashed* by the time I got to the top! It was very hot and sunny – then about 5 it started to pour, so we never had the last stand – We left Cabrach after a huge breakfast, about 10 on Saturday morning – in our little 'hired car'. We didn't have to be in Aberdeen until 7 that night, so went for a very pleasant 'tour' and looked at all the little fishing villages along the coast – and went to a *thriving* fishing port named Buckie, hundreds of well-kept trawlers and it was interesting to see them – then on to Banff for lunch – usual dreary Scottish town, not much like Banff on the Bow River! It was a glorious day but my God that coast must be dour and dreary in the winter – We stood on a high point of land looking out to sea – and Gerald said "there is nothing between us and the North Pole" – Brrr. Glad the North Wind wasn't blowing that day! A little further on we saw a huge edifice on a hill, the queerest looking thing like 4 enormous plates standing on their ends – It was of course the 'early warning' contraption. It looked so eerie and horrible, I thought O Heavens lets get out of this dreary isolated place – Imagine having to live near that thing – ugh! We went to Fraserburgh on the tip end of Aberdeenshire – then on to Aberdeen, I drove most of the day as Gerald's lumbago and bad ankles still bothering him. We arrived in Aberdeen soon after 5, a wedding in full swing at the hotel. We had a welcome cup of tea – and went to the train about 6.30 – had a very good dinner! in the train, I insisted on staying up to see the new Forth Bridge – then fell into my bed and slept like a log –

1. Gerald and Ginnie spent several winter weekends every year shooting with friends in Lincolnshire and Scotland. On this occasion they were staying in Cabrach, northwest of Aberdeen, with Sir Stanley and Lady Pamela Cayzer.

11th October 1964   Greenmarch

Gerald never returned until nearly 8 on Monday evening.[1] I was beginning to get worried as thick fog and *pouring* – he turned up exhausted, they had a terrible time as from the time they left here 7.30 am Sunday until arrival 2.30 p.m. on Monday aft. they never saw *a thing* – which speaks well of Gerald's navigation!! They tried to keep inshore out of the shipping lanes, and he said the only *thing they saw* were the ripple of waves signifying they were near the land!! – ugh – horrible, glad I wasn't there – I must say I was terribly impressed with G's navigation, they 'hit' the Calshot Spit lightship dead on the nose at the entrance to S'ton Water – and eased their way up to Camper & Nicholson's yard up a *small river* at Southampton –

My God, the Election next Thursday – I feel sure Labour will win, also Johnson in U.S. as am certain the English & American electorate too stupid 'en masse' to do otherwise – However we shall see!

1. Gerald had been sailing his yacht from Brixham to a shipyard in Southampton in order to sell it.

18th October 1964   Greenmarch

What a week! an atomic bomb in China, Kruschev retired (or sacked), the Queen insulted by the French Canadians in Quebec; and Harold Wilson as Prime Minister. It has really given one a head-ache. I nearly went *mad* when the Election Results started coming in – It hardly seems possible, the only consolation being that the Labour Party only have a majority of four — What a mad world! Now I await the news of L. Johnson elected President —

Gerald left for Lincolnshire on Friday morning. I remained glued to the T.V. and got *terribly excited* when at one point it was nearly neck-and-neck. I must say Richard Dimbleby was brilliant, the whole thing very well done — if only it had been a *game* and not the future policy for England.[1]

1. Richard Dimbleby, 1913–65, was a British journalist and commentator who was the anchorman for election broadcasts.

25th October 64   *Richmond*

You were right to say "What a week" — As the world seems to have gone mad, the only thing we can do is try to keep our heads. As far as the French Canadians go, they have always wanted to separate, I think — The French hate everyone but <u>themselves,</u> and St. Laurent was prophetic when he stated, the French Canadians are anti-British, anti-American, anti-<u>France</u> and anti-Canadian — but it was beastly of them to put the country in such an embarrassing position —

I am rather worried about the Russian crisis — About the Election in England, it is hopeful that the margin is so close, and it is to be hoped that the Conservatives can force another election in maybe another year before the Socialists do too much harm —

Our trouble is different because when a man is elected President, he is there for 4 years, at the least, unless he is impeached, which is a very difficult thing to do — This campaign has been nothing short of <u>filthy</u> and really shameful — Mr. Johnson has been connected with three scandals, which are not being properly investigated — Those in power seem to have the ability of holding everything up until after Nov. 3rd. He has been definitely connected with Billie Sol Estes (what a name) who is in prison, with Baker, whose affairs were proven to be crooked to say the least and now his best — and most intimate friend, Jenkins has been arrested twice for sex perversion in the YMCA!![1]

An Episcopal Church "convention" has produced numerous assinine [sic] and dangerous situations, and many of the laity are threatening to withhold financial assistance, and last but not least, there has been a negro in the

Chesterfield dining room twice lately having dinner! If Mr. Hesby refuses to take him in, he can be sued by the Government! That is what we have come to – It is very sad that this country, which offered so much, has become so rotten so soon in its history –

I was infuriated by a very <u>poisonous</u> article written by Arthur Schlesinger, Jr. entitled "The Case against Goldwater", which was published in the Oct 21st Daily Telegraph, I am shocked that they published it –[2] *He is a pseudo-intellectual left winger, an intimate of Kennedy's – Why would the English conservative press do that? and why should they give ground at Runnymede for a statue to Kennedy – I give up!*

I am sorry that Angela disappointed you – The young these days seem to be a bit too careless and independent for words, and I think it would be a good idea for you to say so –

1. In the presidential campaign of 1964, the Republican candidate, Barry Goldwater, accused Lyndon Baines Johnson of building his wealth on shady deals with dubious characters, although this was never proven. Billy Sol Estes, according to Irwin and Debi Unger, was a Texan entrepreneur who had "illegally parlayed the federal agricultural price support programs into a fortune." The link between Johnson and Estes was tenuous, although the latter had donated campaign funds to LBJ in 1954. Bobby Gene Baker and Walter Jenkins were both close aides. Baker took advantage of his political connections to further his investments, and Jenkins was arrested in October 1964 for homosexual activities. See Irwin Unger and Debi Unger, *LBJ: A Life* (New York: John Wiley, 1999), 330–31.

2. Arthur Meier Schlesinger Jr., b. 1917, historian, author, and social critic.

13th November 1964   Greenmarch

Well the election may have taken longer in U.S. and been more 'dirty' but I only hope they are not going to make quite such a MESS of things in U.S. as they are trying to do in England – My God, it is absolutely *deplorable* – Of course Wilson is hoping for a snap election in the Spring – and assuming all the pensioners and widows who will now get more money, will vote for him, then God help us – one wouldn't mind paying more I/Tax if it would help the country to get on its feet, but it will only cause inflation. I think the most frightening thing is that we have two *Hungarians* as economists behind Wilson and Callaghan –[1] Expect they are Communists!?

1. Thomas Balogh, 1905–85, life peer, was an economic adviser to the government 1964–67 and minister of state in the Department of Energy 1974–75. Nicholas Kaldor, 1908–86, life peer, was a special adviser to the chancellor of the Exchequer 1964–68 and 1974–76.

22nd November 1964   *Richmond*
"It is cold here" now, as it was that day when I spoke to you over the telephone just after the war had ended, and your reply was "It is warm here" — I am only spending 15 cents on this information today — I remember it cost $25.00 "just after the war", but I can hope that it is warm there this time as well —

11th December 1964   Greenmarch
On Sunday I drove with Gerald to Plymouth to go over every detail of "Oberon" with the new owner.[1] It is sad but all good things come to an end and he and George always planned to sell after 3 years — Some say that ocean racing can only be described as "standing fully-dressed under a cold shower tearing up £5 notes" and I think Gerald has begun to take this view. But am sure they will have a *little* boat, possibly a new catamaran — The new owner of Oberon is a surgeon named *Waterfall* and he operates mostly on Waterworks — I feel he should live, not on the Yealm but at Piddle Hinton on the Piddle, in Dorset.

1. *Oberon* was the yacht Gerald and George Plum had owned jointly since 1962.

24th January 1965   *Richmond*
The day on which that towering personality and unique genius, Winston Churchill died, is bound to be a sorrowful day — The whole world will be in mourning for him — But no one could wish him to linger in a half world — and it was a happy thing that he had that 90th birthday tribute — I feel that the world cannot be the same again without him, but at least it has the memory of his superb example and his unequalled challenge —

How the memory of him dwarfs those holding the so called "reins of Government" now – almost anyway –

There is nothing adequate to say about the tragedy of such a loss –

27th January 1965   Greenmarch

Not much Greenmarch news to impart but what we have been doing seems so trivial *anyway* compared to the events of this week. Thank you for your letter about Sir Winston – One was glad for him and his family that he is 'at peace' but overwhelmed by the memory of all he did for the free world – Surely the greatest man of the century and possibly the greatest englishman of all time.

Just after the war one was too close to past events to really take it all in, but *now* when those days are recalled, one wants to *sob* at the dramatic realization that ONE man held us together, and by *his* courage and the courage he gave us, won the war – Every time I think of his speech in June 1940, in those dark days, I feel 'overcome'. I can remember where I was sitting when I heard his broadcast, and he made me feel quite different as I am sure he did *everyone* else –

We have just seen the lying-in-state at Westminster Hall on the Television – thousands of people shuffling past in that *bitter* weather, having queued for hours, to pay homage – I think it was *thrilling* that the flags were at 1/2 mast in both France and U.S.

30th January 1965   *Richmond*

Your letter of 27th just received – This is a day of remembrance and magnificence, and all of the Western world, our world, is in a sense static – I have not seen anything of the funeral but I may see a bit of it, redone, this afternoon in a way, which I don't pretend to comprehend. It is snowing again – and the temperature stands at about 18° – Everyone I see seems to be moved by the drama of the Hero, and the reaction to his life and death –

Wednesday, to the opticians to see if I needed any change in the lenses of my glasses – only a slight difference in the right eye. When the optician looked at my age on his record his mouth dropped open and he said, "You are quite

wonderful" — I giggled and said, "Don't tell anybody about my age". Professional secret he replied, but I admitted that I sent up to High Heaven a daily thanks that I have good hearing and quite good eyesight for one who remembers the first telephones!

Yesterday afternoon I went down to Katherine Tilghman's apartment to try to see something of Sir Winston's funeral — It was very complicated to bring over here, according to the papers, but it was quite good, and I should have hated to miss it — The world, somehow, can never seem the same without him — such clear sight, enormous courage and puckish humour — There was a memorial service in St. Mark's Church, but I think most people were glued to their T.V.s and preferred to see the service in St. Paul's — I was very sorry to read that the Gloucesters had a bad accident on the road going home?

These ballpoint pens are defeating me.

15th October 1965   *Richmond*

Tuesday to a Church meeting. . . . It was a shambles of a meeting as half the circle members were discussing certain metaphysical aspects of Christianity, and the other half talking about watermelon pickle, and the sale of pecans. I wanted to make a pun about being in a pickle about our religion, but refrained —

Thalhimers is having a terrific English display and there is a red London double decker bus, running up and down the streets, and window displays with Lion etc. and "Brave Brittania" placards — The Richmond Symphony's coming concert is to be all English music —

12th June 1966   *Richmond*

At Emma Gray's we were herded in a bedroom which was air conditioned, and read about Diderot — Helen took a violent dislike to poor old Diderot and got what I thought was an unfair impression of one who seemed to me to be a great genius, so when I came home I translated an appreciation of him from my history of French literature, in which your name was written in the fly leaf, and read it to her the next day — She was so impressed by my having translated it, that she stopped protesting about him —

3rd August 1966   *The Martha Washington Inn*
                                                       Abingdon Virginia

This is a very nice Inn, and everyone, quite cooperative — It is furnished largely with old furniture — 18th and early 19th century pieces — Abingdon is a pretty village with some charming old houses — The Barter Theatre is just across the street from the Hotel — convenient, especially in the event of <u>rain</u> — It is much cooler now, which is a Godsend —

    When we appeared downstairs, Bob Porterfield rushed over and kissed me! He, as you possibly know, "invented" the Barter Theatre, and has run it ever since the depression in '29 — Now he is also the Chairman of the Committee which runs this Inn — He is witty and loveable [sic] and tactful with all and sundry, and is the "power behind the throne" so to speak, in this <u>old</u> Virginia town, one of the unchanged villages, now so rare — The servants and waitresses are local <u>whites</u>. There are only a few negroes, but white or negro, they all shake your hand when you arrive and say how glad they are that you have come! In fact, the whole thing is quite unique and "olde worlde" — not imitation, but real, and I like it so far, very much —

26th August 1966   Greenmarch

Many thanks for your Aug 23rd letter received this morning — hope you will receive my letter (written at HPH [Hyde Park Hotel] yesterday morning) by to-morrow, or at least by Monday — to say all well and awaiting your arrival at Room No 722. I go up on Wed 31st — and am meeting you at London Airport D.V. on Thursday morning — note flight is Pan Am 106 —

    I am looking forward to Thursday Sept 1st!!

∿

Virginia Dickinson Reynolds (Bougie) died on 3 September 1966 after suffering a stroke at the Hyde Park Hotel, London, on 1 September, the day she arrived in England for a visit.

APPENDIX 1

THE CHANGING VALUE OF MONEY, 1930–65

The Changing Purchasing Power of the U.S. Dollar

The table below shows the number of dollars in 2002 that had the same purchasing power as one dollar in the following years:

1930	10.76
1935	13.12
1940	12.81
1945	10.01
1950	7.47
1955	6.72
1960	6.08
1965	5.71

Source: J. J. McCusker, "Comparing the Purchasing Power of Money in the United States (or Colonies) from 1665 to Any Other Year Including the Present," Economic History Services, 2004, http://www. eh.net/hmit/ppowerusd.

The Changing Purchasing Power of the British Pound Sterling

The table below shows the number of pounds in 2002 that had the same purchasing power as one pound in the following years:

1930	48.63
1935	53.97

1940	39.37
1945	27.16
1950	19.65
1955	15.57
1960	13.91
1965	11.88

Source: J. J. McCusker, "Comparing the Purchasing Power of Money in Great Britain from 1264 to Any Other Year Including the Present," Economic History Services, 2001, http://www.eh.net/hmit/ppowerbp.

The Exchange Rate between the U.S. Dollar and the British Pound Sterling

The table below shows the number of dollars required to buy one pound in the following years:

1930	4.86
1935	4.90
1940	3.83
1945	4.03
1950	2.80
1955	2.79
1960	2.81
1965	2.80

Source: Lawrence H. Officer, "Exchange Rate between the United States Dollar and the British Pound, 1791–2000," Economic History Services, 2001, http://www.eh.net/hmit/exchangerates/pound.php.

It should be noted that prior to 1971, the pound sterling was divided into twenty shillings, each of which contained twelve pence. Pence were often denoted by a "D." Shillings and pence were written using a slash; for example, 10/6 equaled ten shillings and six pence.

APPENDIX 2

GENEALOGICAL CHARTS

THE DICKINSON FAMILY

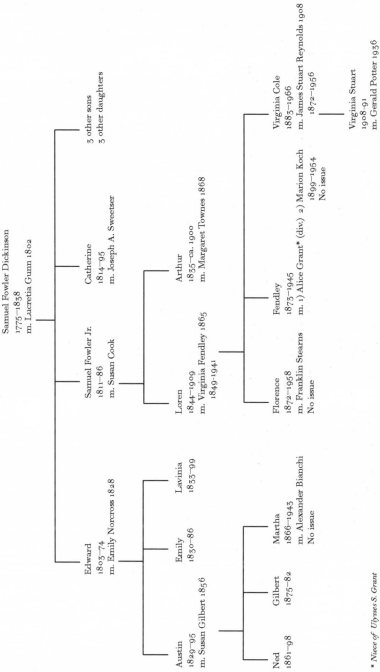

Samuel Fowler Dickinson
1775–1838
m. Lucretia Gunn 1802

Edward
1803–74
m. Emily Norcross 1828

Samuel Fowler Jr.
1811–86
m. Susan Cook

Catherine
1814–95
m. Joseph A. Sweetser

3 other sons
3 other daughters

Austin
1829–95
m. Susan Gilbert 1856

Emily
1830–86

Lavinia
1833–99

Loren
1844–1909
m. Virginia Fendley 1865
1849–1941

Arthur
1855–ca. 1900
m. Margaret Townes 1868

Ned
1861–98

Gilbert
1875–82

Martha
1866–1943
m. Alexander Bianchi
No issue

Florence
1872–1958
m. Franklin Stearns
No issue

Fendley
1875–1945
m. 1) Alice Grant* (div.) 2) Marion Koch
1899–1954
No issue

Virginia Cole
1883–1966
m. James Stuart Reynolds 1908
1872–1956

Virginia Stuart
1908–91
m. Gerald Potter 1936

Niece of Ulysses S. Grant

THE DRUMMOND FAMILY

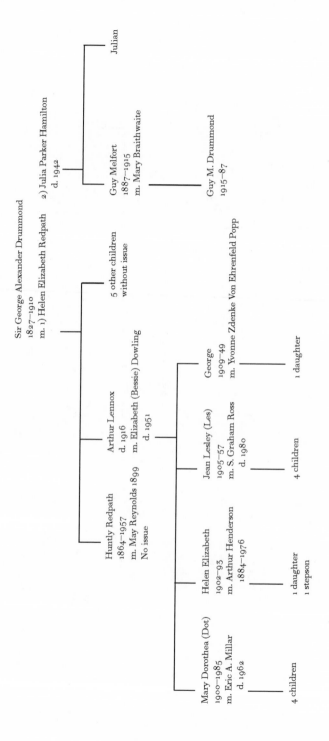

Sir George Alexander Drummond
1827–1910
m. 1) Helen Elizabeth Redpath   2) Julia Parker Hamilton
                                        d. 1942

Huntly Redpath
1864–1957
m. May Reynolds 1899
No issue

Arthur Lennox
d. 1916
m. Elizabeth (Bessie) Dowling
d. 1951

5 other children
without issue

Guy Melfort
1887–1915
m. Mary Braithwaite

Julian

Guy M. Drummond
1915–87

Mary Dorothea (Dot)
1900–1985
m. Eric A. Millar
d. 1962

Helen Elizabeth
1902–93
m. Arthur Henderson
1884–1976

Jean Lesley (Les)
1905–57
m. S. Graham Ross
d. 1980

George
1909–49
m. Yvonne Zdenke Von Ehrenfeld Popp

4 children

1 daughter
1 stepson

4 children

1 daughter

THE POTTER FAMILY

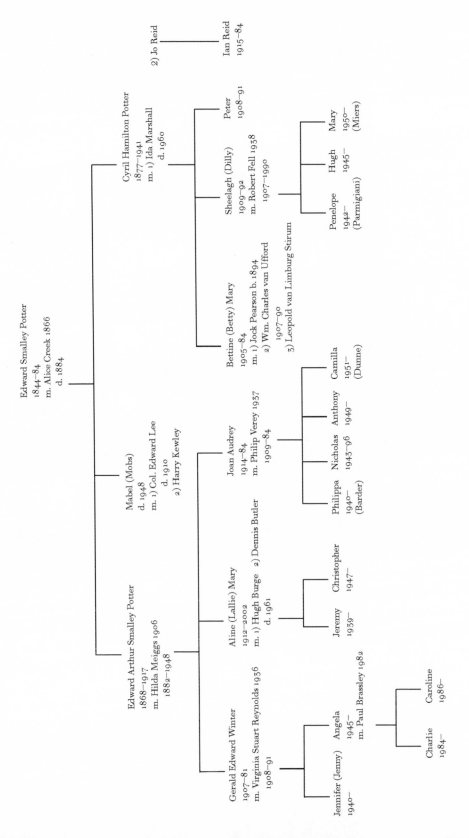

Edward Smalley Potter
1844–84
m. Alice Creek 1866
d. 1884

Edward Arthur Smalley Potter
1868–1917
m. Hilda Meiggs 1906
1882–1948

Mabel (Mobs)
d. 1948
m. 1) Col. Edward Lee
d. 1910
2) Harry Kewley

Cyril Hamilton Potter
1877–1941
m. 1) Ida Marshall
d. 1960

2) Jo Reid

Ian Reid
1915–84

Peter
1908–91

Sheelagh (Dilly)
1909–92
m. Robert Fell 1938
1907–1990

Penelope
1942–
(Parmigiani)

Hugh
1945–

Mary
1950–
(Miers)

Bettine (Betty) Mary
1905–84
m. 1) Jock Pearson b. 1894
2) Wm. Charles van Ufford
1907–90
3) Leopold van Limburg Stirum

Gerald Edward Winter
1907–81
m. Virginia Stuart Reynolds 1936
1908–91

Aline (Lallie) Mary
1912–2002
m. 1) Hugh Burge   2) Dennis Butler
d. 1961

Joan Audrey
1914–84
m. Philip Verey 1937
1909–84

Jeremy
1939–

Christopher
1947–

Philippa
1940–
(Barder)

Nicholas
1943–96

Anthony
1949–

Camilla
1951–
(Dunne)

Jennifer (Jenny)
1940–

Angela
1945–
m. Paul Brassley 1982

Charlie
1984–

Caroline
1986–

THE REYNOLDS FAMILY

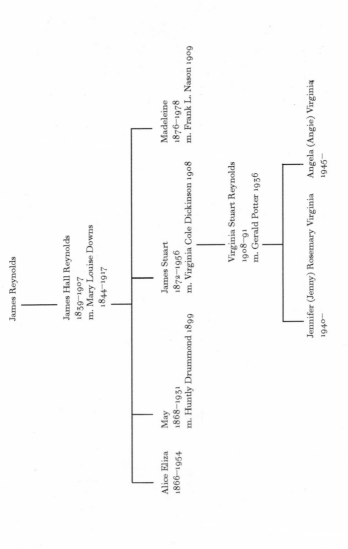

James Reynolds

James Hall Reynolds
1839–1907
m. Mary Louise Downs
1844–1917

Alice Eliza
1866–1954

May
1868–1931
m. Huntly Drummond 1899

James Stuart
1872–1956
m. Virginia Cole Dickinson 1908

Madeleine
1876–1978
m. Frank L. Nason 1909

Virginia Stuart Reynolds
1908–91
m. Gerald Potter 1936

Jennifer (Jenny) Rosemary Virginia
1940–

Angela (Angie) Virginia
1945–

INDEX

The Publications of the Southern Texts Society

BOOKS PUBLISHED BY THE UNIVERSITY OF GEORGIA PRESS

A DuBose Heyward Reader
Edited and with an introduction by James M. Hutchisson

To Find My Own Peace: Grace King in Her Journals, 1886–1910
Edited by Melissa Walker Heidari

The Correspondence of Sarah Morgan and Francis Warrington Dawson,
with Selected Editorials Written by Sarah Morgan for the Charleston
News and Courier
Edited by Giselle Roberts

Shared Histories: Transatlantic Letters between Virginia Dickinson
Reynolds and Her Daughter, Virginia Potter, 1929–1966
Edited by Angela Potter